FROM SETTLEMENT TO CITY

ACKNOWLEDGEMENTS

The co-operation of many people has been sought and willingly given in the preparation and compilation of this district history. My grateful thanks are accorded to those, both inside and outside of the district, who have contributed time, research, information and photographic material.

My greatest thanks must go to Beth Brittle, formerly of Houghton but now of Norwood, who not only translated the whole of my not very legible manuscript into immaculate typescript, but for the past two years, has acted as reader, adviser and sometimes as stern overseer of almost every word I have written. My thanks, too, to Mrs. Brittle for her help with information and with identification of photographic material.

Particular thanks must also be given to Len and Rita Cocks of Hope Valley whose enthusiasm for and knowledge of the history of Hope Valley have been so readily shared with me; to W.J. *(Bill)* Bustelli, Chief Librarian of the City of Tea Tree Gully Public Library, for nudging me into undertaking this district history and for his interest in its progress; to Mayor John Tilley, and Councillors Don Stuart, Gordon Sinclair, Tom Milton, Ted Basnec and George Hislop, who as members of the Book Committee smoothed the way to publication with their goodwill; to Don Allnutt, President of the Tea Tree Gully Branch of the National Trust for his friendly help; and to the many 'old-timers' of the district with whom I have spent so many pleasant hours 'digging up the past'.

A more complete list of those who have contributed in some way or other to the making of this history appears at the end of the book.

I owe a special debt of gratitude to the State Library of South Australia; to Mr. Len Marquis and his ever-helpful staff of the Newspaper Room; to Mr. R. Commane, Mr. Denis Marfleet and Miss J.M. Ide of the Photographic Section; to Mr. John Love and the staff of the State Archives and to the staff of the South Australian Collection; and to Mrs. D. Leaney and the staff of the Sales Office for their never-failing help.

I must also record my debt to the late Tom Mudge who spent so many hours in the Newspaper Room at the tedious task of compiling for me a list of District Councillors *(vide Appendices I - IV)*.

I am most grateful for the courteous and practical help I have always received from various members of the staff of the Corporation and of the Public Library of the City of Tea Tree Gully.

Last but by no means the least of my thanks go to my wife, Eva, who best understands the pangs of authorship and has always willingly shared them with me.

PREFACE

Aware of a growing need for a district history, the Corporation of the City of Tea Tree Gully in 1974 commissioned the preparation of a manuscript for publication.

One of Council's concerns was that with the increasing imbalance of residential and rural areas, the boundaries of the district itself could change. This has indeed happened in this year of publication (1976) with the Hills Ward being transferred to the District of Gumeracha and with it, the old villages of Houghton and Inglewood and the historic precincts of Paracombe, Glen Ewin and Hermitage.

This present history of the District of Tea Tree Gully therefore serves to mark the end of an era.

There can be no doubt that the generalised feeling of a need for a district history has been given some urgency by the dramatic transformation of the local landscape during the past decade. Almost week by week more farmlands, vineyards, orchards and market gardens are being submerged in the tide of suburban subdivision. Familiar landmarks are disappearing and old families are moving out. The outlines of the townships of Hope Valley, Modbury and Tea Tree Gully have already been blurred by residential expansion.

There is not only a need to record a way of life which is fast disappearing and to perpetuate the memory of the district's early settlers. There is also a need to provide some guide to the past for a whole new community of 'settlers' who have made their homes in the district.

It should not be expected however that this present volume can provide a complete history of a local government area which until this year covered an area of nearly 50 square miles and had its beginning nearly 140 years ago when the colony of South Australia was founded.

The book has grown, with the agreement and encouragement of Council, to a considerably greater size than was originally intended. Much material, however, still remains unused and this will eventually be made available to the City of Tea Tree Gully Library.

It has not been possible to include the history of every pioneer family and of every organisation in the district. The limitations are not only those of space available but also those of available information. The district has never had a newspaper of its own and few written records of families or organisations have survived.

The most valuable sources of reference have been official documents and the reports of local correspondents which found publication in contemporary Adelaide newspapers or journals. From such sources I have attempted to reconstruct, with the generous help and local knowledge of the descendants of pioneer families of the district, the emergence of the district as a separate entity, the establishment of its villages and the pattern of its economic and social life in the century following settlement.

Ian Auhl
MODBURY
June 1976

LIST OF MAPS

CONTENTS

NOMENCLATURE

The manner of writing and even of spelling the placename, Tea Tree Gully, or its toponyms, has varied over the years according to its use or the personal predelictions of its user.

It has appeared as Teatree Gully, Tea-tree Gully, Tea-Tree Gully, Tea Tree Gully or even occasionally, as Ti-tree Gully if its user believed its derivation to be Aboriginal.

Throughout the text of this book I have used the form Teatree Gully to indicate the original gully to which the name was applied; and the form Tea Tree Gully to indicate the township, district, council, city and electoral district on which the name was later conferred. This use conforms the most closely with its general usage, past and present.

The Author

DECIMAL CURRENCY AND METRIC MEASUREMENT

The changeover to the decimal and metric systems has created difficulties for historians and their readers. In the present work I have retained the currency and measures of the particular period under consideration.

It is perhaps only necessary, for the sake of a younger generation, to set down the following equivalents, *viz.*

one pound (£1) = $2.00
one shilling (1/-) = 10 cents

To say, however, that the modern two dollars is the equivalent of the old-time one pound is to deceive nobody.

PROLOGUE

'A Week in the Bush'

In the spring of the year 1842, less than six years after the foundation of the colony, two young men decided to spend a few days together in the country. Their destination was a recently purchased section of land 'lying about thirty miles to the north-east of Adelaide and hitherto quite unknown except to a few casual explorers'.

The journey, made in a dray pulled by one horse, took the two friends along a route through Walkerville, across Gilles Plains, past Dry Creek, up through Teatree Gully to Houghton and on to Chain of Ponds and beyond.

Two years later one of the young men, Charles Wilson, published an account of the journey in *The South Australian Oddfellows' Magazine*. Charles Wilson had arrived in South Australia from London with his parents in 1838. He was then a young man of twenty. Wilson was a keen and observant naturalist and South Australia's first entomologist. He later became Chief Clerk of the Supreme Court.

Wilson's article, entitled a *Week in the Bush*, is the earliest recorded description we have of a journey along the bush track which later became, for the greater part, the Main North East Road.

We shall travel along the bush track with Charles Wilson and his friend as far as Chain of Ponds.

In the spring of the year 1842, I was invited by a friend to spend a few days with him in the bush. Though I had begun to consider myself an old colonist, having been then four years in the province, my rambles had hitherto been confined almost exclusively to the park lands round the town, and the adjacent villages, varied by an occasional stroll among the hills and dales of the Mount Lofty Range, or a walk to the Port or Glenelg. True, I had been to Gawler Town when it contained but a few scattered houses; I therefore felt much desire at least 'once and away' to 'bush it' in the true primitive style, where nature more than art supplies the comforts of life.

Our destination was a section of land which my friend had lately taken for farming lying about thirty miles to the north-east of Adelaide, and hitherto quite unknown, except to a few casual explorers.

We first directed our course east of Adelaide, to the Chain of Ponds, through which we intended to pass our way, as my friend had there some land and crops. Our road first led through the prettily wooded but un-romantically-named village of Walkerville. For two or three miles we drove briskly onward, over one of the smooth roads of the country, lined on either side by the Eucalypt of all sizes, showing here and there open vistas and glades, with the sun shining through the light and airy foliage, of every shade of green.

The grasses and shrubs were at this season in their fullest luxuriance, the ground beneath the surface being everywhere well supplied with mois-ture from the rains of the preceding months, which gradually recede during the prevalence of our long and dry summer.

Here and there stood a cottage, with its enclosure for poultry and its garden of flowers, terminating the long four-railed fences, through which might be seen the waving corn, now arrived at half its growth. These signs of cultivation became scarcer as we advanced and we soon issued on the plains.* The country was now entirely open, with a distant view of the mountains on the one side and low wooded lands on the other.

These open prairies in the summer season wear an air of calmness and solitude, for scarcely a bush is visible on the sides of the road for several miles; but, under the refreshing influence of Spring the scene harmonized with our thoughts and feelings. We felt none of that longing for refreshing shade which travellers experience at most other seasons of the year, when traversing the open plains so frequently met with in the interior.

As the sun rose high in the heavens, we did not fail to pay proper atten-tion to the refreshments. At intervals I looked out for some large or un-known bird and had laid my gun loaded in the back of the vehicle, but nothing of consequence as yet appeared.

By mid-morning Charles Wilson and his friend were on a bush track following Dry Creek through present-day Modbury.

Thus we proceeded, and passing the Dry Creek [which name it does not rightly bear at this time of the year], we entered once more the wooded lands, which now extended to the lower range of hills. Here a short check was put to our journey by the snapping of some part of the harness, in ascending the higher grounds!

The scene now changed as they began to ascend the hills through the gully known, even then, as Teatree Gully.

We again set forward and began to ascend the hills: here a few low cot-tages † ran along the precipitous side of the road. From the good-natured

* Gilles Plains, then a sheep station, held by the Colonial Treasurer, Osmond Gilles.

† One of the cottages in the gully would have been that of the Cornishman, John Tre-geagle, who, in 1840, had helped to cut a track up through the gully.

'lassie' of one of these, we borrowed a tin pannakin, to be returned when next we passed, for neither of us had arrived at the bushman's feat of being able to drink comfortably out of a bottle.

The features of the country gradually became more romantic and we left all signs of human habitations behind. Less striking in the bold projections of its rocky and overhanging steeps than the road over the Mt. Lofty Range, the winding path yet bore much resemblance to those lovely mountain passes, the character of the highlands of South Australia being strongly marked in the unrestrained and sportive twists and turns of the gum-trees and in the exuberant growth and tangled nature of the underwood.

Here, too, the trunks of the large Eucalypti — the lords of the forest — are unscathed by the axe or saw of the woodman, and their evergreen foliage rests untouched by the aborigines, who form their woorlies in the plains below. Ever and anon our ears were saluted by the singular thrilling note of the great kingfisher [Laughing Jackass so-called] and the answering call of its mate!

Early in the afternoon the friends reached their first village since leaving Walkerville — the little Village of Houghton — and descended to their destination at the northern extremity of the Chain of Ponds.

We passed through the village of Haughton [sic], situated in one of the narrow valleys of this hilly region. This village which is about fifteen miles from Adelaide, contained about half-a-dozen houses; it has since [Wilson meant by 1844] increased in size and importance.

Having descended the hills, our way lay over several small creeks on our approach to the Chain of Ponds. The harness again occasionally required attention — proof that it was not colonial — but we had conquered the greater part of our journey. The Chain of Ponds* extends about five miles, with many turnings and windings in its course. It consists of small pools, which, during the present season are many of them very deep but at no part is there any stream or flow of water.

At the northern extremity of this chain stood the section of my companion, half of which [forty acres] was cultivated and enclosed. As we here intended to rest for awhile, we alighted, put the horse into a small stable, and littered him down. After refreshing ourselves also, we repaired to the cultivated grounds. As my friend lived in town, there was no house on the land, but adjoining the fences stood a barn containing some of the unthrashed corn of the previous year. Scattered among the surrounding sections, a few farmers cottages were visible. The owner of one of these now advanced and gave him an account of 'how things had been doing since his last visit'.

*   The chain of water-holes known as the 'Chain of Ponds' vanished under the waters of the Millbrook Reservoir in 1918.

Wilson and his friend stayed overnight in the cottage of a farmer and his family.

The building was formed of large logs placed perpendicularly in the ground: these, through the shrinking of the wood, had already parted company, but the days were sufficiently warm to render this of small importance. In the evenings however, the wind, finding an easy passage between them, and likewise occasionally coming through the open doorway was kept out by various banners, unadorned with armorial bearings.

There were three rooms — on one side, the dairy, with its array of pans and pots for milk and butter; on the other, a bed-room, occupied by the farmer and his family; the middle room, which is about the size of the two former, was used as a sitting-room, but, at night, by ourselves and friends, as a sleeping apartment. It was furnished with a long and easy sofa, a table, chairs and forms, a box or two for additional seats, and above all, a most spacious fire-place, in which were constantly piled many blazing logs. Mid-way between the ground and roof was stretched a beam, a useful addition, on which to hang the bacon, hams, onions etc. and other productions of the farmyard and garden.

SECTION I
OCCUPATION AND SETTLEMENT

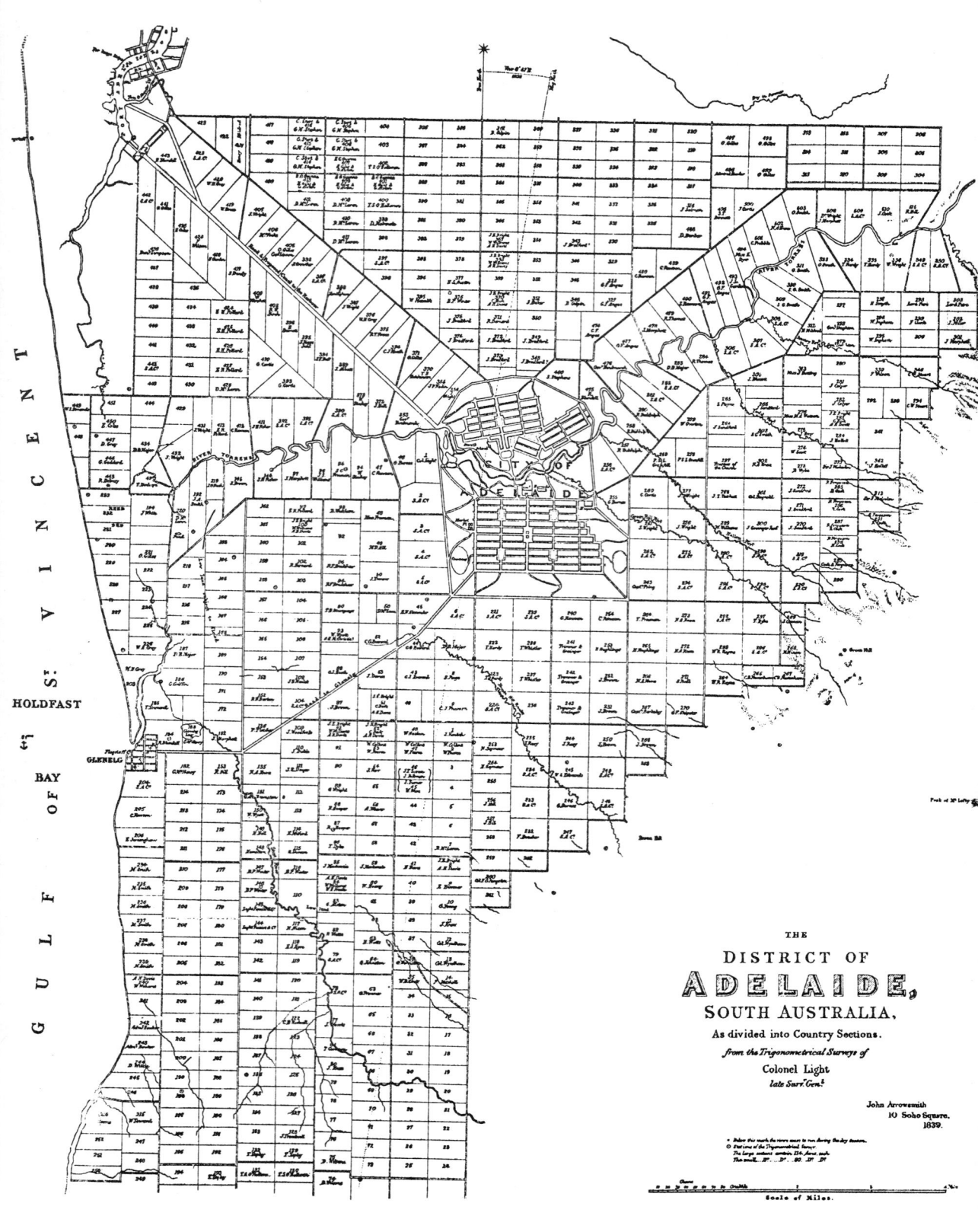

THE
DISTRICT OF
ADELAIDE,
SOUTH AUSTRALIA,
As divided into Country Sections.

from the Trigonometrical Surveys of
Colonel Light
late Surv.r Gen.l

John Arrowsmith
10 Soho Square.
1839.

Scale of Miles.

I

OCCUPATION 1836—1838

'We shall . . . take possession of it as a sheep-run'

Settlement of the district known to us as the local government area of Tea Tree Gully and which includes the old villages of Houghton, Steventon (Tea Tree Gully), Hope Valley, Modbury, Inglewood, Highbury and Golden Grove, did not begin until early in 1839.

This was more than two years after Captain John Hindmarsh came ashore from the *Buffalo* at Holdfast Bay (Glenelg) at 2 p.m. on December 28, 1836 to proclaim the new colony of South Australia.

During that two-year interval before settlement of the district began there was some 'squatting' along the River Torrens and its tributaries, by shepherds in charge of flocks of sheep and by 'overlanders' watering and fattening cattle before sale.

George Anstey, whose name is perpetuated in Anstey's Hill, arrived from Van Diemen's Land (Tasmania) early in 1838 with sheep to sell to a meat-hungry colony. Anstey later wrote in a letter to his friend Thomas Giles, 'Within five weeks of that day he [Charles Bonney, who had just overlanded cattle from New South Wales] accompanied me to look for a sheep station on the Little Para for my one flock of sheep then depasturing on the Fifth Creek at the foot of the hills'.

Bonney's own cattle were depastured along the banks of the Torrens near the foothills. 'Adelaide was then a collection', he wrote, 'of rude huts with a few more substantial buildings in course of erection. Up to this time they [the people of Adelaide] had been living almost exclusively on Kangaroo flesh'.

Osmond Gilles, South Australia's first Colonial Treasurer, also had a sheep station adjoining the Torrens in the district which became known as Gilles Plains.*

This station, a few miles from Adelaide, was then, in early 1838, the

* The O.G. (Osmond Gilles) Road also preserves his name.

Map 1.   Colonel William Light's Survey of 1838 showing the 'country' sections around Adelaide. Dry Creek is shown just north of the survey.

farthest out sheep station in the colony. John Barton Hack relates in his diary of May 5, 1839 how an old man, a shepherd in the employ of Osmond Gilles on his sheep-walk, was attacked and killed by Aborigines when he unwisely refused their demands for one of his sheep.

The Little Para River, which has its headwaters at Paracombe and runs through Inglewood and Lower Hermitage, was known to the 'overlander' Charles Bonney and to George Anstey in 1838.

Even earlier, in 1837, we have a record of 'squatting' on the Little Para in letters written by John Barton Hack to his friend Henry Watson in England.

'April 20, 1837 — I have been riding with S ..... [Hack's brother, Stephen] to see a fine country he had discovered about ten miles off, and have been delighted with the beauty of the valleys, which are filled with the richest black mould I have yet seen anywhere, and springs of water in all directions, which we know to be always flowing, as the tea-tree which will never flourish without water constantly round its roots, is growing abundantly. We shall send two men tomorrow to build a sheep-fold and take possession of it as a sheep-run'.

There is other evidence that the springs and waters of the Torrens, the Little Para River and Dry Creek and their tributaries were well-known before selection and settlement.

But while there was considerable 'squatting' by stockholders on these streams in the district there was no permanent settlement unti 1839 despite the proximity of the area to Adelaide and its popularity with the 'squatters'.

The reason for this delay must be sought in the history of the early surveys of the colony.

Although 'squatting' was not illegal, there could be no permanent settlement without survey.

It must be remembered that when the first settlers arrived in the colony the site for the future capital had still to be agreed upon. Colonel William Light, with orders to fix a site, had arrived in South Australia in August 1836, four months before the arrival of the Governor, Captain John Hindmarsh, but the site chosen for Adelaide had to await the Governor's approval. This was given on December 31, 1836.

Light wasted no time. By March 23, 1837 he had surveyed the site of the capital and had pegged out the sections — enough anyway for migrants holding preliminary land orders to leave their tents and 'rude huts' at Holdfast Bay and on the banks of the Torrens and to begin building cottages on their own city allotments.*

But then the surveys bogged down. The 437 holders of preliminary land orders were entitled not only to their one acre in the city for each preliminary land order held but to a 'country' section of 134 acres for each acre held in Adelaide. Those already in the colony insisted upon their legal right to

* The main streets of the new capital were named in a special ceremony in May 1837.

have their sections surveyed anywhere outside of the capital — an almost impossible task for Light.

A compromise had to be made. Eight districts — six on the mainland and two on Kangaroo Island *(See Map 2)* were proclaimed and selection of land was confined to these districts. They were all coastal districts south of Adelaide — districts favoured for various reasons by the early settlers.

As can be seen by the map of Light's districts, Districe 'A' did include some of the future Hope Valley area, but Light's surveys did not go north of present-day Grand Junction Road or east beyond the present Reservoir and Reids Road at Hope Valley.

The result was that only fifteen of the sections in the present district were surveyed by the end of 1838 — sections 509, 510 and 515 and sections 304 to 315, a matter of a few hundred acres. *(See Map 1)*

Areas outside of these defined districts had to await survey before they could be settled.

This then is the explanation of why there was no settlement in the present district until 1839 and why the only occupation was by 'squatters' who leased sheep-walks — as they were called — for a few pounds a year and hired shepherds to tend their flocks of sheep.

Early in 1839 however the position changed suddenly and dramatically.

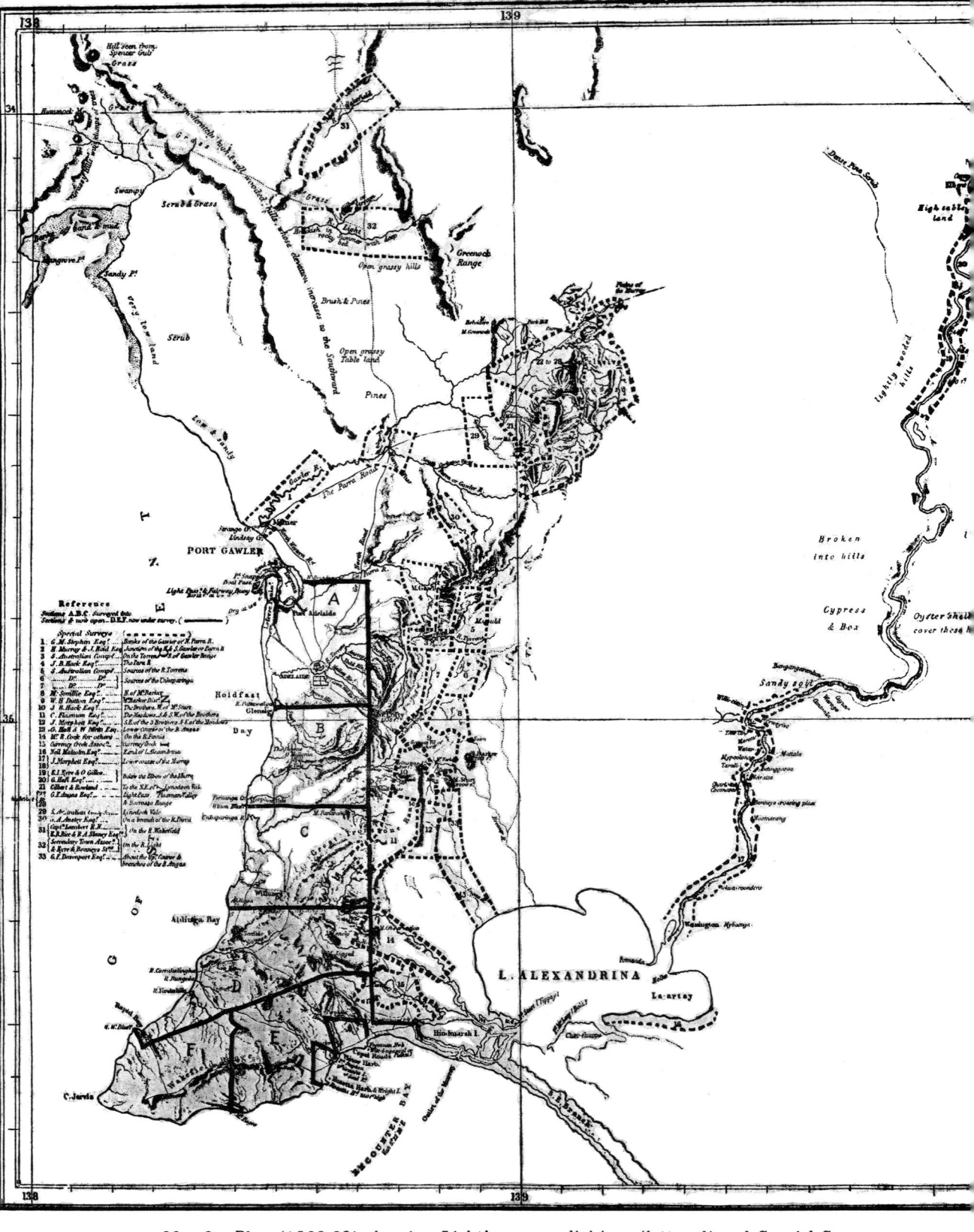

Map 2. Plan (1838-39) showing Light's survey divisions (lettered) and Special Surveys (numbered). Special Survey No.4 included the areas of Hermitage, Paracombe, Inglewood and the Little Para River.

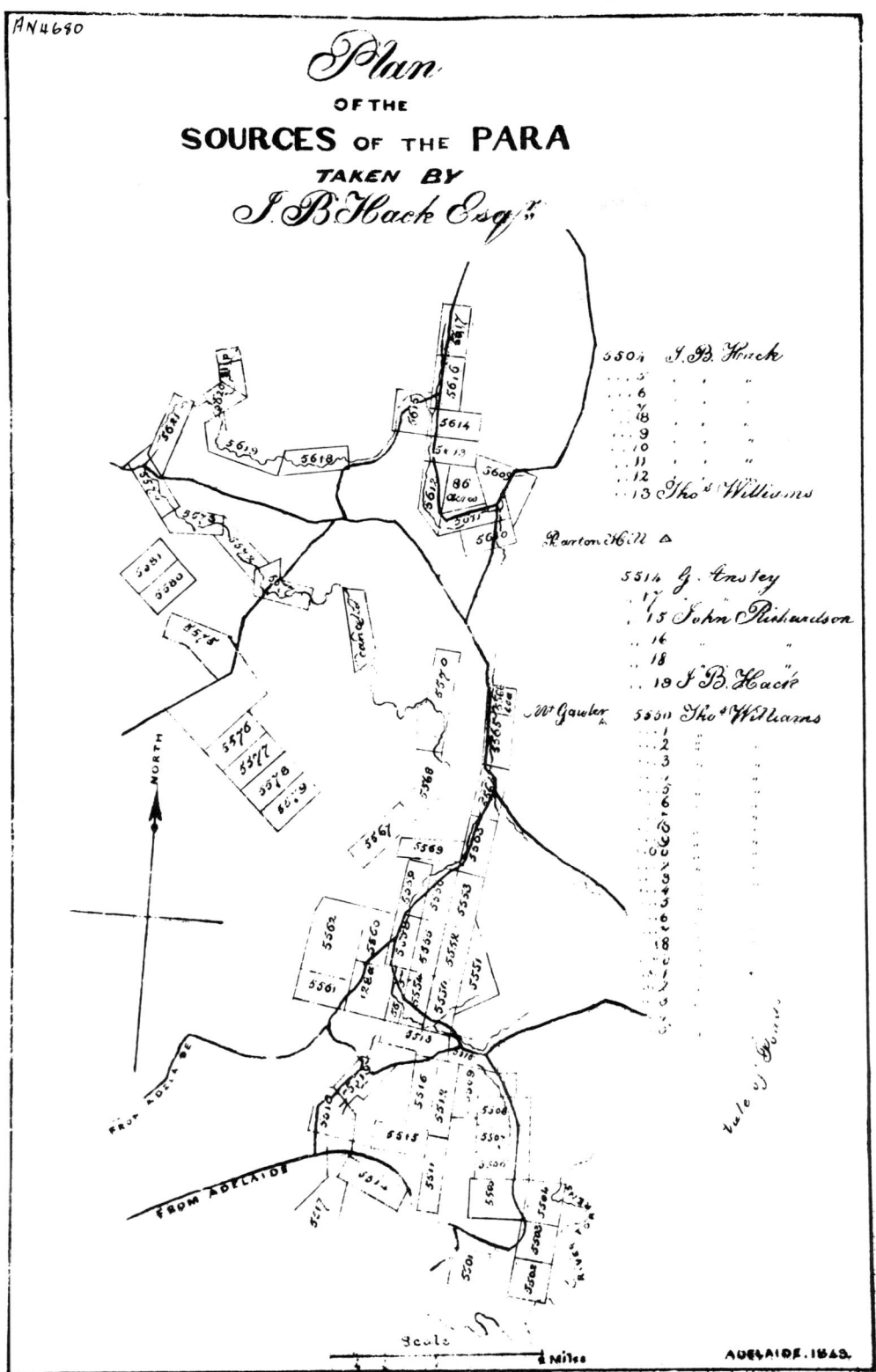

Map 3. Detailed plan showing sections of Special Survey (No.4) taken on the Sources of the Little Para River at Paracombe and Hermitage by J.B. Hack in 1839. The 1843 plan shows a pattern of roads and also the owners of sections of the survey. (S.A.A.)

2

SPECIAL SURVEY—1839

'picking the eyes out of the country'

With the exception of the few 80-acre sections *(See Map 1)* of Light's early surveys, the first land in the district to be surveyed for settlement was a large tract of 4000 acres.

Its location was described as 'between the Torrens and the Parry [Para] * near the sources of the latter stream'. For want of any other name at the time, the surveyed area was referred to initially as the 'Sources of the Para River' or 'The Little Para Special Survey'.

Superimposed upon a present day map, this survey is shown to include the later sites of Houghton and Inglewood with Golden Grove just outside the western boundary.

The survey, known later as the Third Special Survey *(but numbered 4 in Map 2)*, was taken up by John Barton Hack on January 16, 1839.

The system of Special Surveys permitted the applicant to select 15,000 acres of land in any area outside of Light's eight defined districts and to apply to have it surveyed. The applicant upon depositing the sum of £4,000 with the Colonial Treasurer was then entitled to choose a 'compact area' of 4,000 acres from the 15,000 acre survey — a rich prize for those few in the colony who possessed capital.

It was a system which Governor Grey later condemned with good reason as 'picking the eyes out of the country'. Charles Sturt, the explorer and Colonial Secretary at the time, was even stronger in his condemnation. 'The Special Surveys have secured all that is valuable in the way of water to a few individuals ... The idea of chequering ... [the country] as it suits the fancy of the applicant is preposterous and the consequences will be severely felt as the population increases'.

Such a condemnation certainly applied to the Special Survey on the sources of the Little Para taken by Hack.

* The name 'Para' was unfortunately conferred on three streams — the North and South Para which unite at Gawler, and the Little Para, much of which forms the eastern and northern boundaries of our own district.

Settlers, in 1839, suddenly discovered that they could now take advantage of the land regulation made in London in 1835 which permitted application for special surveys in the proposed new colony — that is if they had the necessary £4,000.

The beginning of 1839 saw English gentlemen or their agents hurrying around the countryside on horseback in all directions looking for suitable areas of 15,000 acres. By the end of 1840, South Australia was chequered with 37 Special Surveys, ranging from Port Lincoln to the River Murray.

The first Special Survey displaced John Barton Hack from the cattle 'squatting station' he was then leasing near Mt. Barker. Hack then on January 12, 1839 deposited £4,000 with the Colonial Treasurer and demanded a Special Survey on the sources of the Little Para — an area which he and his brother Stephen, as we have seen, already knew.

On January 28 he accompanied the surveyor, George Ormsby, to the area to mark out the approximate boundaries of the 15,000 acres.

'A few weeks after the survey', Hack wrote later in his reminiscences, 'Mrs. Hack was desirous of seeing the new country we had taken out and after we had removed our Adelaide dairy to the Little Para Survey, I drove her out in a phaeton I had purchased, up the Teatree Gully and over the survey ... I had a man on horseback with tandem traces to help up the hills'.

Hack, however, had not taken the survey for himself only. In his reminiscences he stated, 'I joined with Mr. Thomas Williams and Colonel Gawler in an application for a survey on the Little Para, 14 miles from Adelaide. Mr. Williams took 2,000 acres and 1,000 acres each fell to the Colonel and myself. On the choice allotted to me I put up a dairy and began sending butter to Adelaide'.

By April 1839 the area taken had been surveyed by a private surveyor into 64 sections, each of 80 acres 'a little more or less'. Forty-five of these sections (approximately 4,000 acres) were then selected by Hack, Williams and Lieutenant George Hall, private secretary to Governor Gawler. It seems likely that Lieutenant Hall, who was a personal friend of Gawler's, acted on his employer's behalf. A glance at the sections as shown on the plan (See Map 3) will reveal that the sections, far from being in one 'compact area' as prescribed by regulation, were scattered widely over the district — in fact they were disconnected chains of sections placed astride almost the entire course of the sources of the Little Para where it winds from its headwaters at Paracombe down through Hermitage, and astride Gould's Creek, the northern tributary of the Little Para. Thus was secured, as Sturt said, 'all that is valuable in the way of water to a few individuals'.

Sixteen further sections of the Special Survey were advertised for general selection in April 1840.

Governor Gawler made little use of his twelve sections on Gould's Creek. He returned to England in May 1841. His 1,000 acre share of the survey was disposed of in 1845 — half to Andrew Shillabeer and the remainder to Joseph Gould of Chain of Ponds. The tributary of the Little Para running through these sections is still known as Gould's Creek. A hill nearby was named Mt. Gawler.

Hack, also, did not retain his sections for long. He placed a young English migrant, Joseph Barritt, in charge as manager of his new cattle and sheep station. It was Barritt who built the dairy and took the butter to Adelaide for sale. Hack provided Barritt with thirty cows and Barritt agreed to pay his employer a percentage upon the butter made.

Hack, in 1839, took up another Special Survey, 'a singularly beautiful tract' of 4,000 acres south of Mt. Barker. In May 1840 it was advertised that 'Messrs. J.B. and S. Hack intend leasing their portion of the Special Survey at the Sources of the Little Para in small farms at £4 per acre for purchase or twelve shillings per acre yearly rental'.

It was clear that both Hack and Governor Gawler had acquired their share of the Third Special Survey for speculation rather than for genuine settlement. Only Thomas Williams remained to settle on his share of the survey which he named *The Hermitage*.

Such land speculation was rife throughout the colony in the time of Governor George Gawler and the mania brought the young colony of South Australia almost to the point of bankruptcy in 1841. It also led to individual insolvency and the debtors' prison, even for such men as John Barton Hack himself, who became insolvent in mid-1843 and found himself in the debtors' cells of the Adelaide Gaol.

Hack's sections lay astride the headwaters of the Little Para River where it runs down the shallow valley (in 1840 known as Strangways Valley) through Paracombe to Inglewood. The present road through Paracombe now divides the original sections and separates the districts of Gumeracha and Tea Tree Gully.

Towards the end of 1840 Hack sold his sheep and cattle station — 400 acres to Jacob Hagen and 600 acres to John Richardson — for £3 an acre, three times as much as he had paid for it one year earlier.

The story of Hack's subsequent life can be followed in the publication *Pastoral Pioneers of South Australia*, and in his own reminiscences. It is the story of a great-hearted, if unsuccessful, pioneer.

3

PARACOMBE

'£1 per week and their grub'

Although both Jacob Hagen and John Richardson developed the properties which they had acquired from Hack on the Little Para at Strang-ways Valley and built cottages for the workmen they employed, they left the oversight of their flocks and herds to managers — two enterprising young men, Joseph Barritt previously working for Hack, and Walter Duffield.

The stories of Duffield and Barritt are two South Australian pioneering success stories. It was the sort of success which Edward Gibbon Wakefield envisaged for settlers in the new colony he had planned on the shores of southern Australia. For Duffield and Barritt South Australia was indeed a land of opportunity. It was an opportunity however which required a lot of hard work.

Listen to Joseph Barritt as he made his way to take up his first job, a few days after his arrival in the colony, as manager of Hack's property on the Little Para in 1839:

'I took a supply of provisions, a cask of pork, flour, potatoes, tea and sugar, and, in the company of an old man, who was living there, proceeded to the place. But before getting ten miles on the road, going down a steep gully, the fore-horse began to kick, broke away from the cart and ran off and has not been heard of since. Night coming we were obliged to bush it. It proved to be a very wet night, so that we could not keep a fire but my mackintosh kept me quite dry'.

Barritt arrived at Little Para the next day where, he wrote, 'I found two very good huts, a man and wife and two sons and a daughter, whom I hired and then proceeded to build a dairy which we completed in a fortnight'.

It was a few days after Barritt's arrival that Hack with his wife and three children came up to see him in their phaeton, with Samuel Brady act-ing as postillion. 'So you see', wrote Barritt home to his parents in England, underlining the words, 'some of our nobs can come it pretty stiff'. As he [Hack] left he said to me, 'Joseph, if at any time thee want anything, send me a note and thee shall have it'.

Hack was as good as his word — when Barritt saved up enough to purchase his first dray for £25, Hack generously provided the horses.

When Hack divided and sold the property in the following year, young Joseph did not have to leave his cottage and dairy; instead he undertook the management of the 600 acres acquired by John Richardson, a Rundle Street sharebroker and agent.

Barritt now found he had a neighbour — another young man, Walter Duffield, from his own county of Essex.

'It is very comfortable', wrote Barritt to his parents in 1840, 'to have a neighbour from the same part of the country as myself, who is Walter Duffield; we are as intimate as brothers'.

Duffield, who had arrived in the colony in 1839, had started life in his adopted country by carting wood from the Mt. Lofty Ranges to Adelaide with a bullock team. In 1840 Hagen appointed Duffield, then twenty-three years of age, manager of his 400 acres on the Little Para.

Both young men later became landowners and successful pastoral pioneers. Duffield held a seat in the South Australian Parliament for 18 years. The two men remained friends and sometimes partners in pastoral enterprises throughout life.

Hagen, Duffield's employer, was a wealthy Quaker who had arrived in the colony in 1839 in the *William Barrass*. Hack and Hagen had been schoolmates in Essex. It was Jacob Hagen who gave the name Paracombe to the 400 acres he acquired from his friend Hack. There is a Parracombe in Devonshire, England, which Hagen may have had in mind as both he and Hack originated from County Devon. However, as the name of Hagen's property was always spelt Paracombe, with one 'r', it is just as likely that the name refers to the Little Para itself which ran through the property. Indeed in early directories the name Paracombe frequently occurs as two words — Para Combe — which seems to suggest a hybrid derivation from the Aboriginal word Para, meaning creek or river, and the English word combe — a narrow valley.

Hagen did not live at Paracombe for long: he purchased a beautiful estate at Echunga where 'his house and garden in this picturesque spot were among the finest in the colony'. Hagen retired to England in 1854, leasing his property at Paracombe, some of it to Joshua Crouch. Only the Hagen Arms Hotel at Echunga today commemorates his name.

Joseph Barritt had arrived in the colony in September 1839, on the migrant ship *Anna Robertson* with a letter of introduction to Hack. When Hack sold out to his friend Jacob Hagen, Barritt, as we have noted, remained in his cottage at Little Para to manage for John Richardson.

Richardson seems to have been a generous landlord. His payment of £100 per year to Joseph Barritt, plus the use of a horse, appeared generous to the young overseer.

'What a set of fools', wrote Barritt in a letter home, 'the labouring

John Barton Hack who in 1839 took
out the first survey in the district.

Jacob Hagen who named Paracombe and
began to develop it as a sheep and cattle
station.

Migrant ships at anchor at Port Adelaide in the 1840s. On the right is the *Emerald Isle* mentioned
in Hack's Diary.

class of England must be if they refuse the chance of migrating to this country.

'It strikes me some of the young working farmers would do much better here than clod-hopping about at home all their young days; for here, if they cannot command sufficient capital to do anything for themselves, they can earn £1 per week and their grub ... I only wish I had come to this part of the world as soon as I left school'.

Barritt, in November 1840, decided to lease an 80-acre section from Jacob Hagen. He began to build a home for himself close to the springs in front of Duffield's cottage on section 5506.* His diary of January 11, 1841 states:

'Carted today one load of broad palings for building my house. I carted them eight miles from some stringy-bark ranges. Some of the hills are so steep that we are obliged to chain the wheel of the dray, which throws an immense weight on the bullock's neck; likewise we cut what we call a drag, which is a middle-sized tree to draw behind the dray to keep her back ... Fancy to yourself that you can see me coming down a steep narrow ridge with six bullocks, just wide enough for the dray, with a heavy load, where both sides are so steep, almost frightful to look down, so much so that if the bullocks were not under command and we were to get off the track, that they and the dray would be precipitated down and smashed.

'My heart has been in my mouth when driving down such places, but practice makes perfect: I don't fear them so much as I did at first'.

Joseph named his new home of stringy-bark slabs *Hazeleigh*, after his old home near Maldon in Essex.

In 1841 he wrote to his fiancée in England, Mary Ann Harrisson, and asked her to join him at *Hazeleigh*. On March 7, 1843 they were married at the Friends' Meeting House, North Adelaide 'at a public assembly of the people called Quakers'. The Quaker Meeting House, a wooden pre-fabricated building brought out in sections in 1840, can still be seen in Pennington Terrace, North Adelaide. The land on which it stands was given by John Barton Hack, Barritt's first employer, and himself a Quaker.

The young couple's first child was born at *Hazeleigh*, Para Combe, and here, five years later, Mary Barritt died in premature childbirth.

Agricultural records of 1840 show that when Richardson took over from Hack 120 acres were fenced in 'partly with posts and four rails, partly with bank and ditch, and 2½ acres with posts, rails and palings'.

On the property, besides sheep and cattle, there had been sown 8 acres of wheat, 8 of oats, 4½ of maize, 4½ of potatoes, and 2½ of vegetable garden and orchard. 'Unfortunately', the report goes on to say, 'the crops were nearly all destroyed by cattle, in consequence of the fencing not having been completed in time'.

* Now part of the Paracombe Blocks.

By 1844, Barritt had 120 acres of wheat under cultivation* for Richardson at Paracombe.

After his wife's death in 1848, Barritt made up his mind to build himself a new home in the country. He acquired a land grant of three 80-acre sections in Lyndoch Valley.

Some months after shifting to his new home in Lyndoch Valley, his first-born child, Joseph Earn Barritt, then aged 5 years, was accidentally drowned when father and son were crossing the South Para River.

Joseph Barritt died at *Riverside*, his property near Lyndoch in 1881. The property is still in possession of the Barritt family.

A year after Barritt's death his life-long friend from his pioneering days at Paracombe, Walter Duffield died at his home *Para Para*, a two-storey mansion at Gawler, which still survives.

* In February of 1844 Benjamin Boyce, a young man who had been working for Joseph Barritt at Paracombe, wrote a letter to his people in Lincolnshire.

Boyce had jumped ship when the migrant vessel *Moffatt*, of which he was a crew member, arrived at Pt. Adelaide in 1839. He remained in hiding for a month, then worked in Adelaide for a time. At the time of writing the letter Boyce had been working for some time for George Anstey and then for Barritt at Paracombe. He had by then married Louisa, a girl he had met on board ship.

Boyce's difficulties with spelling and punctuation add a piquant flavour to his description of his life in the new colony.

'My sun was born on the 22 of March 1843 and whe was murred on the 15 of September and ar living very comfortable together i think she will make me a very gud wife too days after whe was murred i went out in the bush sheep shering mee and my brothers in laws wifes brother toock a thousand to sheer at seventeen shilings per hundred and rachings our rachings ar of ten pounds of meet 12 pounds of flour 2½ pounds of tea 2 pounds of shugar that is the rachings each man is alowd per weeke

when we had dun them whe went to sheer for a gentleman callad mister ansty hee ad got about 14 shousands to sheer whe toock them to sheer at 15 shilings per hundred and rachings thear was 12 of hus for to sheer them

whe arvist [harvested] on the plains from the latter end of ocktober till about crismas time and then whe go in the hills about crismas to reeping i live withe a gentleman named Jospeh Barrot in the bush i whent thear to arvest last year and after whe ad dun harvesting i engaged to be with him at twelve shillings per weak and rachings to plow and drive bulocks whe do all the work with bullocks on a count of it been so hille and i stopt with him till i left to be married and to go a shering and to go arvesting on the plain and then to go back to him and whent back to him on the. wedensday after crismas to reaping a ten shilings a nacor [an acre] whe finished reping on the 14 of January thrashing for mister barrot at sixpence a bushel whe thrch all with the frail [flail] on a count thear is no thrachings machins with hus

Mister Barrot as got a farm of a bout oun hundred acors ... i ham a going to in gage to be a hoverseer for him so i shall take my wife hup thear with me it is a bout thirtenn miles from adelaid the owner of the ground is a cuming england his name his Jacob Hagon and mister barrot is going to sing too hundred bshels of weeat to london ich i am bisse thraching now and so the ship is to sail on the sixth of february'

4

HERMITAGE 1839 - 1853

'the first gentleman to make his home in the country'

On board the *Platina* which arrived at Port Adelaide on February 9, 1839 were three men who were to be closely connected with the early development of the district. Travelling steerage was a young man of 22, Robert Symons Kelly, who later gave Modbury its name. Among the cabin passengers were Arthur Hardy from Yorkshire and Thomas and Mrs. Catherine Williams and their family of two sons and four daughters from Northamptonshire. Arthur Hardy settled on the Torrens at Paradise on a section of land where the Paradise Bridge crosses the river. Thomas Williams, a few months after arrival, took up a share of John Barton Hack's Special Survey on the Little Para River. *(See Map 3)*

Williams named his new home *The Hermitage*. Loyau, in his biographical work, *Representative Men*, states that Thomas Williams was 'the first gentleman to make a home in the country, form the first garden and vineyard and one of the first sheep and dairy stations'.

This may well be so, as Williams was settled with his family at *The Hermitage* before 1840 and we must remember that in 1839 anything beyond a few miles from Adelaide was the country.

The agricultural returns for 1840 show that Williams and his two sons had wasted no time in clearing and fencing and had the largest area (31 acres) under cultivation in the Northern District which then extended no further than the embryo village of Gawler.

The 2,000 acres of the Special Survey which Williams had taken up lay along the course of the Little Para River, much of it where it runs through Lower Hermitage today, with another chain of sections on a tributary and a third chain of 5 sections along the river west of the present Snake Gully Bridge.

By 1840, on the Hermitage sections, Williams had 47 acres of land cleared and enclosed, 'partly with posts and three or four rails, partly with bank and ditch, partly with log-fence'. Williams proudly added, in his return, that one half-mile was enclosed 'with an iron-wire fence' — a great rarity at that time.

In the enclosed area, the 18 acres of wheat he and his sons and labourers had sown by hand in June of 1840 had yielded 270 bushels 'one quarter of which was smutted'. Barley had produced at the rate of 36 bushels per acre. Oats had been cut for hay. The potato field had produced 'about two tons to the acre'.

Around *The Hermitage* a small English-style manor-village was developing — 'one large dwelling house, two Manning cottages [portable, wooden houses imported in sections from England], four stone cottages for labourers, dairy, stock-yard, with 12 milking-bales and barn, built of sawn timber'. It was an impressive establishment and one which Thomas Williams meant to be impressive and befitting his status.

In 1841, John Barton Hack rode out to visit his friend, Thomas Williams, at his new residence. Neither of them would have considered it possible on that day that within two years both would be declared insolvent and find themselves in debtors' cells at the Adelaide Gaol.

Williams was a friend of Governor Gawler. It was Williams, Hack and Gawler who had originally shared the Special Survey of 4,000 acres on the Little Para.

There is an account of a visit paid by Governor Gawler to *The Hermitage* in August 1842. 'Early on Tuesday morning his Excellency, accompanied by William Giles, Esquire, of the South Australian Company, left town on horseback upon a visit to the splendid property secured by the company upon the River Torrens, its sources and tributaries.

'En route, H.E. and Mr. Giles called at *The Hermitage*, the residence of T. Williams, Esqu., with whom they breakfasted and who accompanied them to the company's station at Gummaraka where fresh horses were in readiness for H.E. and party'.

Squire Williams, as he was known to his labourers at Hermitage, had been a banker before leaving for South Australia and had held the position of High Sheriff for Northamptonshire. He had, we are told, assisted Edward Gibbon Wakefield and George Fife Angas in obtaining the grant of the new colony for settlement. He was a shareholder in the South Australian Company, whose preliminary purchases of land in the proposed colony largely helped to finance it.

While at *The Hermitage*, Thomas Williams took an active interest in the life of the young colony and in the organised development of agriculture.

At the first agricultural and horticultural exhibition held at Fordham's Hotel in Adelaide in March 1841, Williams judged the horticultural exhibits and himself won a prize of three guineas for the best sample of barley. A professional maltster who judged the barley section stated that the barley grown at Hermitage was 'very much superior in malting qualities to that generally used in England'.

In January of 1842, in the Legislative Council Room, 'Thomas Wil-

31

liams, Esquire, of the Para, moved the establishment of the society to be called *The South Australian Agricultural and Horticultural Society'* — the Society whose Annual Show has been a feature of South Australian life ever since. It is interesting to note that of the eight committee members of the Society appointed in 1842, three members, Williams, Jacob Hagen and Angus MacLaine of Ardtornish (Modbury) were all pioneers of the present district.

It was Squire Williams who, together with the South Australian Company, made the first cut through Teatree Gully in February of 1840 with the help of his own men.

Thomas Williams had land: he had social standing: he had ideas and energy. There was only one thing he lacked and that was ready money. Most of his land on the Little Para was held under mortgage to a London financier. Douglas Pike in his great history of early South Australia, *Paradise of Dissent*, says that Williams was something of a Micawber, always waiting for something to turn up.

In June 1843, the new governor, George Grey, nominated Thomas Williams, as a leading land-holder to be one of the four members of South Australia's first Legislative Council.

On August 10, Williams resigned and a few days later declared his insolvency. What followed next reads like a mid-Victorian melodrama.

Squire Williams now found himself confined in the debtors' section of the Adelaide Gaol. There also at the time was John Barton Hack, who related, in later years, how at his residence at Echunga 'he was awakened at 2 a.m. by two sheriff's officers under a warrant of attorney' and conducted to the Adelaide Gaol. One of the reasons for the hasty erection of the Gaol in 1840 was the number of insolvent debtors created by the land speculation so rife in the colony in the time of Governor Gawler.

Squire Williams managed, however, to save his Hermitage estate, if not himself. He made over the 2,000 acres on the Little Para to his daughter, Elizabeth, as a dowry on the understanding of a marriage being 'intended to be solemnized' with a Mr. Peter Peachey, and said Peter Peachey agreeing to discharge a debt of some £2,100, being the amount owing to the Bank of South Australia.

Peachey lived at Glen Osmond where he owned the Wheal Watkins silver-lead mine.

The marriage of Peter Peachey, aged 43, and Elizabeth Williams, aged 22, duly took place on May 30, 1844 'at the residence of Mrs. Williams, *The Hermitage'*. As Mrs. Williams signed as a witness to the marriage, it is safe to assume that Squire Williams himself was at that moment still languishing in gaol. The sum of £2,100 duly changed hands and Elizabeth and her husband acquired the land, although they went to live at Glen Osmond.

Williams himself was eventually declared insolvent and was only able to pay 'two shillings in the £' to the rest of his creditors. His wife and sons

Left: Mrs. Frank Warner, pioneer of Hermitage. Below: Pioneer home of Mr. and Mrs. John Warner at Hermitage, built in the 1850s. This photo c.1880, shows Mr. John Warner and his wife (nee Anne Neale) and their children (L.to R.) William, Frank and Maria with Miss Johnson, teacher-in-charge of the Hermitage School.

Thomas and Hannah Roberts of *Greenwith Farm*, pioneers of Golden Grove. Roberts, his wife and five children arrived in South Australia in the ship, *Sir Charles Forbes* in June 1839.

continued to run the Hermitage property.

Thomas Williams and his wife returned to England in 1849 and resided at Queen's Square, Bloomsbury, now part of London, where Williams died in 1881.

A few months after Squire Williams and his wife returned to England, Elizabeth Peachey's husband died at Glen Osmond of 'brain fever' at the age of 48.

Mrs. Peachey returned soon after to *The Hermitage*, in possession now of most of her father's original estate.

In January of 1853 she arrived home with her two children from a two-day visit to Adelaide to find the residence 'entirely destroyed by fire'. The house was a large wooden frame house brought by her father from England in sections. 'No part of the house was saved nor any of the furniture or clothes'.

In 1853 Mrs. Peachey still held nearly 1,000 acres of the original survey, but the estate was gradually sold off and other families moved into the Lower Hermitage.

One of her neighbours was John Lithgow who had moved into the district in 1850 when he acquired 30 acres from John McGilton, close to the Little Para. In 1871 Mrs. Peachey, at the age of 49, married John Lithgow, a widower of 57, 'in the house of Mrs. Peachey'.

Gretna Green, the original home of John Lithgow, built in 1850, later became the home of George Johnson who, not fancying the marital implications of the name, changed it to *Linlithgow*.

In the 1890s Mrs. Elizabeth Lithgow and her husband retired to Adelaide to live. John Lithgow died at Stepney in 1897 at the age of 83 and Elizabeth Lithgow (Peachey, nee Williams) in 1899.

Others had moved into the sections of the Special Survey by 1853, when Hermitage* became part of the first District Council area — families with surnames still familiar in the district today.

One of the earliest of these families was that of John McGilton who took up sections of the original survey in 1846. Mr. Murray McGilton still owns part of the original sections. The original McGilton home, *Lowood*, built of a pug made of mud and cow manure, has recently been demolished. The second home, of wattle and straw daub and stone, itself more than a century old is now being restored. Some of the saw-pits where the red-gum beams and uprights were sawn and adzed are visible nearby.

In 1855 William Verrall of Houghton moved into the Hermitage area when he acquired a part of Section 5567 from Mrs. Peachey. Mr. and Mrs. T.C. Verrall still own sections in the valley, including the original homestead section of Thomas Williams.

There were other families living along the Little Para at Lower Hermi-

---

*The name Hermitage, by 1853, applied generally to the area. Today the terms Lower Hermitage and Upper Hermitage are in use.

tage in the 1850s whose surnames are still familiar in the district today — Joseph Stringer, William Neale, John Warner, George Johnson, Mark Coleman, John Byers and George Millar.

Despite Squire Williams' setbacks, largely undeserved, he can be remembered as a great agricultural pioneer, both in the district and in the colony. The story of the subsequent life of his sons in South Australia is told in *Pastoral Pioneers of South Australia*.

5

VOYAGE OUT

'commit this sister to the deep'

There is a tendency to picture our pioneers from studio portraits in the family album — as bearded and venerable old men, and serene, if rather careworn old ladies. It is a misleading image.

Most of the migrant families who made the long voyage to the new colony in the south of Australia were young. The promise of a free passage induced many young couples to marry and migrate. Preparations for departure generally took some months. One result of this was that upon arrival 'the ladies were either a little above or a little below or just at par'. The long voyage had the unexpected result, wrote Douglas Pike in his *Paradise of Dissent* of turning many of the vessels into floating maternity wards.

Free passages to South Australia were granted only to those who, married or single, were under thirty years of age. Although the rule was often relaxed, it was enough to ensure that the majority of our pioneering forefathers were young people. Older families had to pay their own passage out — a matter of £15 - £20 for those travelling steerage and of £60 - £100 for cabin passengers.

Such regulations reflected an attempt by the colonisation commissioners in London to ensure a suitable balance between capital and labour in the new colony. 'Emigrants must chiefly be agricultural labourers, shepherds and female and domestic servants. All the adults must be capable of labour and going out with the intention of settling in the colony. Persons intending to buy land in the colony or to invest a small capital in trade there are not eligible for a free passage nor any of their families'.

Shipboard conditions were vastly different for those with capital who usually occupied the few cabins on board, and for those with free passages who were crowded together in the steerage between decks. In many migrant ships the only privacy, apart from sheets draped across sections of the steerage, 'was to be found in the single closet placed at one end of the steerage accommodation'.

In stormy weather the steerage passengers might be battened down for days at a time below deck. In the heat of the equatorial crossing, no breath of fresh air might find its way below for days to drive out the fetid air. Some of the migrant ships became death ships, with dysentery, diarrhoea, infectious diseases and plain sea-sickness taking great toll. Children were the greatest sufferers while many mothers died in childbirth. One migrant ship, the *Douglas* lost 21 of its 125 passengers. In another, only the father of a family of six survived a particularly long voyage of 6 months.

Other voyages were more serene. Edward George Day, an early headmaster of the Hope Valley School, whose shipboard diary* written in 1850 during his voyage on the *Countess of Yarborough* has been published, tells of a pleasant voyage without tragic incident.

John Barton Hack, who took up the Special Survey on the Little Para, began to keep a diary before he and his family left Portsmouth on June 18, 1836. The final entry in the diary is dated May 11, 1839 — a few months after Hack took up his land at Paracombe. The diary, leather-bound, with a brass clasp, is now in possession of the South Australian Archives.

Oddly enough John Hack and his family were not setting off for South Australia when he began his diary. The family were to board the *Emerald Isle* at Plymouth for a holiday in Madeira. Hack later mentioned in his reminiscences that he emigrated 'because my health had become feeble and it was necessary for me that the next winter be spent in a warm climate'. As John Barton Hack lived to the age of 79 we can only suppose the medical advice was sound.

The second entry in Hack's diary records that on boarding the *Emerald Isle* at Portsmouth, the 'steam packet' was anchored for some hours alongside the *Buffalo* then loading goods 'belonging to South Australian emigrants from London'. As Hack recorded, a short talk with Captain Lipson of the *Buffalo*, on the opportunities offering in the new colony was enough to persuade Hack to change his destination — and with it his destiny. He returned to his home at Greyling Wells near Portsmouth to dispose of his leather business.

August 31 saw him and his wife and their six children ('our six olive branches') and Hack's brother Stephen, on board the *Isabella* bound for Launceston and South Australia. The ship did not weigh anchor at Spithead until September 3 and after a week's 'beating about' and much seasickness the ship finally cleared the English Channel.

It was not until five months later — February 11, 1837 — that the passengers of the *Isabella* found themselves close to Kangaroo Island, sailing along Backstairs Passage with a fine breeze. 'We ran on', wrote Hack in his diary, 'till dark, and having performed the requisite distance, anchored and fired a gun. Not very long after, the master of a vessel came on board and told us there were lying in the bay [Holdfast Bay] the *Coromandel*, *Buffalo*,

* Now in the South Australian Archives.

38

Rapid, John Renwick and *Cygnet* and in the river [Port River] 15 miles further the *Tam-0-Shanter* which is stranded, the *Africaine* and *Wm. Hutt*'.

Seasickness claimed its victims in the first few days at sea. Hack recorded in his diary on the second day out:

'Had a stormy night. Our cot swung so much against the locker at our head and the bulwarks at our feet that we could get no rest and poor Bbe [Hack's name for his wife, Bridget] was thrown out. I called up Stephen and after unhooking the cot we laid out our packages and boxes underneath but when the ship tacked we slid with such a shock to the lee side that I was obliged to lash the cot to the side of the cabin and hold on as well as we could. ... We are all as sick as can be. Poor Bbe can scarcely hold up her head. I am not much better.

We cannot make way at all and were driven back during the night to Portland Bill and are now off Alderney with a S.W. gale blowing'.

It was a fortunate ship which had no shipboard deaths to report upon arrival at anchorage — although, by way of compensation there were often shipboard births to register.

Joseph Barritt, who arrived in the colony as a lad of 20, some six months after Hack and rented land from him on the Little Para *(v.Chapter 3)* — mentioned in a letter to his brother and sister in Essex 'the death of the wife of Mr. Morton, a cuddy passenger, whose remains were put in a coffin and in a few days confined to the mighty deep. The Revd. B. Quafe performed the service, and when he came to the words 'commit this sister to the deep' the sailors gently raised the coffin over the ship's side and it sank instantaneously, which was a solemn warning to all: the poor husband was distracted.

A few days after, the cuddy cook was likewise committed to the deep, with the exception only of being served up in his hammock; he died of dysentery of which many are taken off here'.

Another passenger recorded that the main enemies to be feared were not the occasional pirates of the high seas but measles and whooping cough.

'These diseases attacked the juveniles with great and fatal effect and we lost twenty-four in all; as many as three in each family.

The great heat near the 'Line' proved too much for many of the little ones and one after another they succumbed. Three in one day had to be committed to the deep, the last of them in the evening, the funeral service being read by the light of a lantern.

A burial at sea under ordinary circumstances is a sad sight but doubly impressive when the mourners are gathered around the gangway at dark and the darkness made more visible by the feeble light of the candle'.

In the long months at sea, the pioneer passengers in their little sailing ships of a few hundred tons, usually experienced their first and worst storms in the region of the roaring forties. There, as far as 41° South, as young Joseph Barritt wrote home 'the winds blew very cold from the South Pole'.

'We had now a week of tremendous heavy weather, so that the hatchways were battened down, and water came down a great deal in our cabins, so that we got wet beds for some time.

We shipped a great many seas, particularly one evening when I was on deck which caught me with several others and drove us with considerable force against the bulwarks, but not much hurt besides giving us a good ducking; the waves truly rolled mountains high. They looked awfully grand and I enjoyed the sight of them by day, but rather dismal at night; but the worst is often a storm with little wind. When the sea is subsiding she then rolls tremendously, almost on her beam ends, so that there is no such thing as keeping in bed without holding on tight, but it is a most laughable thing to see and hear the cooking utensils rolling about.

From the Isle of St. Paul's we had a fine run to Adelaide and anchored in Holdfast Bay by the 21st of 9 month, 1939. On the next day some of the passengers landed, of whom I was one, and very glad to set foot upon the sandy beach'.

After his four-month journey on the *Anna Robertson*, young Joseph Barritt was eager to make a beginning in his adopted country. On the day he landed, anxious to see Colonel Light's capital on the Torrens, he joined a party in a walk up to Adelaide. Joseph found the town 'in a forwarder state than I expected'. He also found John Barton Hack and handed him the letter of introduction which obtained for him his first job as manager of Hack's survey on the Little Para at Paracombe.

The party returned from Adelaide to Holdfast Bay too late to go aboard so had to 'bush it'. 'We made up a fire', wrote Barritt in his diary, 'and got a little hay to lie upon: had a very restless night of it, and got aboard in the morning, and a day or two after all of us landed at the port, where I and my companions pitched our tent for nine or ten days, till we got our things ashore. We then hired a house in Adelaide and a bullock team conveyed our things there'.

Within a few days Joseph Barritt set off to take up his new job on the Little Para — a pioneer of 21 years of age determined that his adopted country would indeed be a Land of Promise, at least for himself.

6

HOUGHTON

'the most picturesque of towns'

The Village of Houghton was one of the earliest settlements in the Adelaide Hills. It was certainly the first community to develop in the present district. Houghton was laid out as a village in 1841 by John Richardson.

John Richardson arrived in South Australia with his wife in April 1838 as cabin passengers on the *Lord Goderich*, and set up in business in Adelaide as a house, land and commission agent. By June 1840 Richardson had acquired, as we have seen, 600 acres of the Little Para Survey at Paracombe from John Barton Hack, and had placed young Joseph Barritt in charge as manager of the property.

John Richardson named his new property *Houghton Lodge*. The statistical report of 1840, already quoted, informs us that the buildings at *Houghton Lodge* consisted of 'one stone dwelling-house, seven cottages for labourers, stock-yard, with calf-pens and milking bales, etc.' The stone dwelling-house was probably the house originally built by Hack and occupied by Joseph Barritt as manager for Richardson.

It is difficult to establish the precise location of *Houghton Lodge*, but at least it is possible to establish that it was on Section 5510, on the Little Para River where it runs through Inglewood. *Houghton Lodge* was not part of Houghton itself and preceded the establishment of the Village of Houghton.

Richardson had come to South Australia, not as an agriculturist, but as a sharebroker, land agent and surveyor. He was essentially a land 'developer' to borrow a modern term. The 600 acres he had acquired on the Little Para was held under mortgage to John Morphett who had put up much of the £2,027 purchase money. Morphett, an English solicitor, had been a welcome convert to Wakefield's principles of systematic colonisation in South Australia. In 1835 he had written, 'The purchase of land in new colonies, experience has shown to be one of the most profitable modes of employing capital which commercial enterprise or speculation has ever discovered'.

Morphett arrived in the colony before its proclamation. He was soon

Township of Houghton.

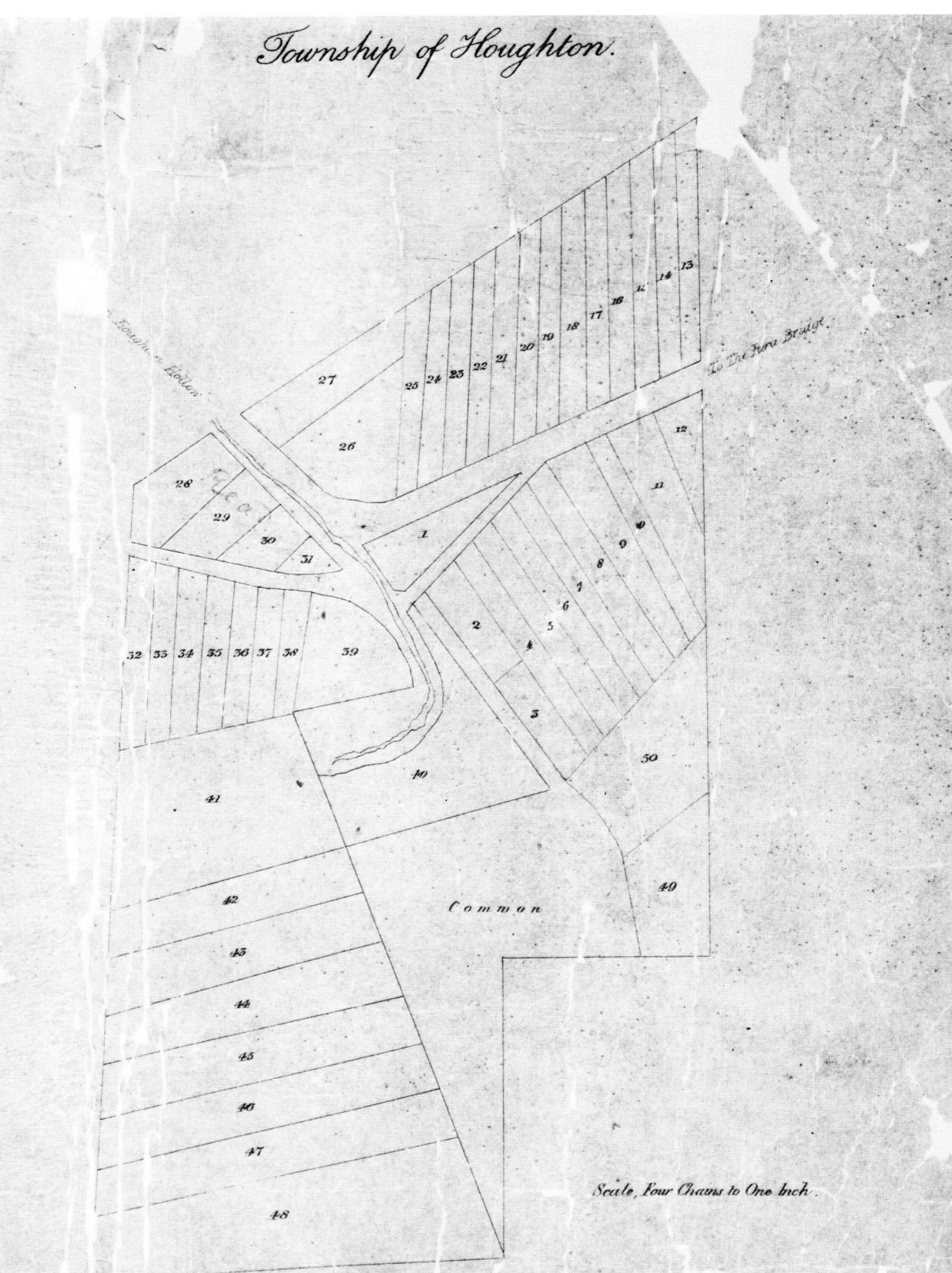

Map 4. Village of Houghton (section 5519) as laid out by John Richardson in 1841. The original plan shows the Village Common. In 1841 there was only one road of entry into Houghton. Department of Lands, South Australia.

busy putting his 'profitable modes of employing capital' into practise in South Australia, either with his own money or on behalf of English capitalists. The capital of John Morphett and his brother, George, played a great part in the early development of the district of Tea Tree Gully. John Morphett was the original grantee of the 134 acres of the gully (Section 1559) to which was given the name, perhaps by Morphett himself, of Teatree Gully. According to the publication *Pastoral Pioneers*, John Morphett often worked on the principle of one-third of any profits to the owner of the land. Joseph Barritt, Richardson's overseer at *Houghton Lodge*, mentioned in a letter to his brother in England in 1840, 'This is the place to invest capital — £15 per cent on mortgage on good security'. Little wonder the debtors' prison in the Adelaide Gaol was kept full.

One of the sections which Richardson had acquired in 1840 was a hilly section, separate from his other sections on the Little Para, and of little use for agriculture. This was section 5519.

In 1841 Richardson decided to subdivide the whole of section 5519 of 80 acres into allotments and to lay it out as a village — the Village of Houghton.

A plan of the village, deposited now in the Lands Titles Office in Adelaide, is entitled 'A correct Plan of section 5519 on the Little Para Survey laid out as a village called Houghton'. *(See Map 4)* Subsequent conveyances of allotments generally contained the words 'as has been laid out as a Section Township by John Richardson'. The conveyances often indicated that the money, however, was to be paid to John or George Morphett by direction of John Richardson.

Houghton, then, came into being as a result of the private — and profitable — enterprise of John Richardson.

We can safely assume that Richardson gave the village its name of Houghton. He had already given by 1840 the name *Houghton Lodge* to his property on the Little Para. We can also assume that John Richardson and his wife had some close connection with a Houghton somewhere in England as they named their son, born in Adelaide in 1842, Charles Houghton Richardson. Rodney Cockburn, in his book *The Nomenclature of South Australia*, suggests that Houghton was named after the village of Houghton-le-Spring, near Durham.* The rest of Cockburn's story concerning the naming of Houghton is, however, apocryphal and confused with the subsequent naming of Inglewood.

The 80-acre section of the Village of Houghton was laid out into fifty allotments with a village common of some 10 acres or so. Thirty-eight of the allotments were elongated blocks of less than an acre, each fronting a road. The other twelve allotments were steeper blocks and not so suitable for domestic tillage.

The names of the roads are shown as Houghton Hollow Road, Horn

* There were six Houghtons in England in the 1800s.

Street, Cemetery Road, King William Street, Elizabeth Street and Black Hill Road.

Elizabeth Street, now non-existent, was named after Richardson's wife; and Horn Street after William Porter Horn who took up lots 4 and 5 in 1852; King William Street was named after King William IV who had died in 1837, the year following settlement of the new colony. It is only recently that officialdom decided to change the name to plain William Street, an offence which has not been entirely forgiven in Houghton.

The plan, with its division of land into elongated strips for domestic tillage and its Common, was no doubt modelled on the lay-out of a typical English village. The village later became even more English in appearance with plantings of oaks and elms, some of which survive and now have reached majestic proportions.

One of the first allotments was sold to a 'Charles Millar of Little Para, Yeoman' who in October 1841 paid the sum of £30 for allotments 22 and 25, comprising nearly 3 acres.

When Charles Wilson made his journey to Chain of Ponds in the spring of 1842 *(v. Prologue)* he and his friend 'passed through the village of Houghton, situated in one of the narrow valleys of this hilly region. This village, which is fifteen miles from Adelaide, contained about half-a-dozen houses; it has since [1844] increased in size and importance'.

It is odd that Wilson did not mention Houghton's first public building, *The Travellers' Rest*. Perhaps by 1844 he had forgotten its existence. In April 1842, a publican's licence was granted to Thomas Neale. In the *South Australian Government Gazette* of April 1842 the name of the public house is given as the *Travellers' Rest* and its situation as Houghton Village, Hack's Survey. The *Travellers' Rest*,* standing on its own triangle of land, was a centre-piece of the village of Houghton for the next hundred years. There is nothing left today of the *Travellers' Rest* but the triangle of land, surrounded by three roads, where the hotel once stood.

By 1844 many of the allotments had been sold and the remainder (about 35 acres) were then conveyed from John Morphett to George Morphett, as mortgagor.

The sections which had been sold — allotments 11, 19, 20, 21, 22, 23, 24, 25, 28, 29, 30, 31, 40, 41, 42, 43, 45, 48, 49 and 50 were mainly sections more suitable for domestic tillage, or the larger sections for dairy cattle. The steeper sections remained unsold.

By 1844 the village had a blacksmith, George Barrass from Chain of Ponds, who had acquired lots 23, 24 and 25; a storekeeper, Thomas Battersby, on allotments 11, 19, 20, 21; and allotments 1, 40, 41, 42 and 43 had been conveyed to the Society for the Propagation of the Gospel in Foreign Parts, a missionary branch of the Church of England. The public house, yards and gardens on allotment 1 were leased to the publican, Thomas

* Pictured on Dust Jacket.

Houghton Village c.1866 with the 1842 *Travellers Rest* (shingle roof) in the foreground. Upper left is the Union Chapel with the cottage of Rev. W.R. Squibb abutting the Black Hill Road. To the right is the 1866 Methodist Church. The Congregational Church had not been built.

Post Office and General Store of Thomas H. Possingham, Houghton c.1890.

Mrs. Pat Murphy and her son Steve relax outside of their wattle-and-daub cottage at Houghton c.1908.

Travellers Rest Inn, Houghton — now demolished. The 'omnibus' dates the photo as c.1918.

Neale, for a period of five years by the Society.

A labourer, William Reeds, and Houghton's first butcher, also occupied allotments 28 and 31 and the strip of land fronting the creek along lots 28, 29, 30, 31. A few years later Reeds also acquired lots 2 and 3 in King William Street, and lots 26 and 27. In 1845 lots 8 and 9 were purchased by a widow, Anna Catarean Rehn.

In 1843 a chapel had been erected on allotment 18. The Union Chapel, as it was named, was used by the Congregational, Wesleyans and Episcopalians of Houghton who had joined forces to build it early in 1843 — 'The people themselves carting stone and sand, burning lime, sawing the timber and splitting the shingles for the roof'. In 1847 the trustees of the Chapel conveyed the use of the Chapel during the week to a schoolmaster, William Riccardo Squibb, for the sum of ten shillings per annum. Squibb had arrived in the colony in 1839 and had taught in schools in Adelaide before moving to Houghton in 1847 as its first schoolmaster. The school returns for 1847 show that 26 children — including 5 from the Teatree Gully — were attending the school in the Union Chapel. In 1850 Squibb gave up his position as schoolmaster and purchased allotment 17 alongside the Chapel, where he built a home for his family.

Houghton had its first regular postal service by 1848. Following a petition from the inhabitants of Houghton, Gumeracha, Chain of Ponds and Reedy Creek (Tungkillo) drawn up by Squibb and containing 150 signatures, postmasters were appointed at Houghton Village, Chain of Ponds and Reedy Creek Mines. Houghton's first postmaster was the storekeeper, Thomas Battersby.

One of the reasons for the establishment and early development of Houghton was that it was on the original line of road across Gilles Plains, through the Teatree Gully to the special surveys which had been taken on the sources of the Little Para at Hermitage and Paracombe and on the sources of the River Torrens at Chain of Ponds and beyond by the South Australian Company. There was no defined road beyond Walkerville — merely a bullock-track across the plains and through the uncleared scrub.

William Flavel in his recollections written in 1901, has left us a description of a journey he made along the track in 1842.

'I think it was in the year 1842 it was arranged to remove our family from the Reedbeds to the Chain of Ponds, a distance of about twenty miles north-east of Adelaide, The track was good so long as the ground was level. The sand at the foot of the Teatree Gully was heavy hauling for our four bullocks, but as soon as we got fairly into Teatree Gully it was steep and sideling for the rest of the journey, but worse in the neighbourhood of Houghton than anywhere else. At that time no sidelings had been cut nor creeks filled up at crossings. We had to find a crossing the best way we could.

'Our destination was a shepherd's hut on land belonging to the South

Australian Company. We arrived after dark and in trying to cross the Chain of Ponds to get to the hut we got bogged and had to leave everything there until the morning, when we were up early and carried the things from the dray up to the hut, yoked the bullock and pulled the dray out of the mud.

'Things then looked worse than was expected for the axle was broken and no blacksmith nearer than Adelaide; but the bullocks and dray had to go back somehow, so we chained the wheel to the side of the dray to keep it upright and started on our return journey of twenty miles with one wheel locked. We had to shift the wheel several times to prevent the tyre from getting worn through.

'A short time after this a man started to work as a blacksmith in the shell of an old hollow gumtree near the place where our axle broke and he worked there at his trade for years afterwards. That blacksmith's name was George Barris'.

William Flavel, of course, was speaking of George Barrass, Houghton's first blacksmith — and, it seems, the only one in the 1840s between Walkerville and the Chain of Ponds.

With the only blacksmith on the track, and the only inn, the little village of Houghton became a focal point for travellers and teamsters. Its school, its chapel, and its post-office made the village a focal point, too, for the settlers of the district. The community life which developed in Houghton in the 1840s resulted in the little village playing a leading part in the development of roads, services and finally of local government in the district in the 1850s.

Houghton had one advantage in the 1840s which it lost in the 1850s. Before George Anstey arrived at Highercombe in 1842, the only track through the hills to the new settlements on the Little Para and the River Torrens was via the Teatree Gully. The track then passed through section 5519, as Richardson well knew when he subdivided it as the Village of Houghton. It then passed over the Black Hill on a track still known today as the Black Hill Road to the creek crossing near the present Inglewood Inn to Richardson's farm, and on over Breakneck Hill to Chain of Ponds.

A track from Lower Hermitage joined the main track at the summit of Teatree Gully.

With the arrival of George Anstey at Highercombe another track which soon became known as Anstey's Hill led up from the river crossing at Paradise to Anstey's Highercombe Estate. An extension of this track then led down into Houghton.

By the 1850s two lines of road which roughly approximated to the present Main North-East Road and the Lower North-East Road converged on and met at Houghton, making it even more of a centre and a natural meeting place than before.

Unfortunately for Houghton's future fortunes, and development, a deviation was made in the main north-east track in 1854 in order to avoid the steep pinch over Black Hill. The traffic on the road via Teatree Gully no longer needed to pass through Houghton. The idea of a bypass road, it appears, is not such a modern idea after all.

The first immediate result of the bypass was to encourage the development in the 1850s of a second little settlement at the foot of the old track over Black Hill where it met the newer track. This settlement was named Inglewood.

Houghton, the first of the villages which developed in the present district, is the last of the villages to retain a recognisable identity, along with something of a village atmosphere. It still retains its village common. The Union Chapel, built in 1843, is still standing, now derelict and partly unroofed.

Cottages built in William Street in the 1840s and *Bristol House* in Houghton Hollow, originally the home and butcher's shop of William Reeds, and built in the same decade, are still occupied.

Houghton's earliest store has survived. Now remembered as *Longbotham's Drapers Shop*, it was originally the shoemaker's shop of Thomas Battersby and built in 1844. In 1848 it became Houghton's first post office and Thomas Battersby remained postmaster until 1851. The shop and one-eighth of an acre of land was sold, first to a bootmaker, Henry White, and then to Henry Ellis who in 1854 advertised:

> HOUGHTON VILLAGE — Store and dwelling situated on pt. Section 5519. Shop, 4 rooms, kitchen and bakehouse mostly of stone. This is a good opportunity for a quiet country business in one of the most picturesque of towns. Now in occupation of Henry Ellis.

In 1856 Josephus Longbotham acquired the house and store for £178 and began the little drapery business which continued for many years. Longbotham died in 1888 at *Roseberry*, Walkerville but was buried in the Houghton cemetery.

Perhaps, with a little help from the present Town Planning Act the Village of Houghton, 'the most picturesque of towns', may be allowed to retain its identity and survive into the next century.

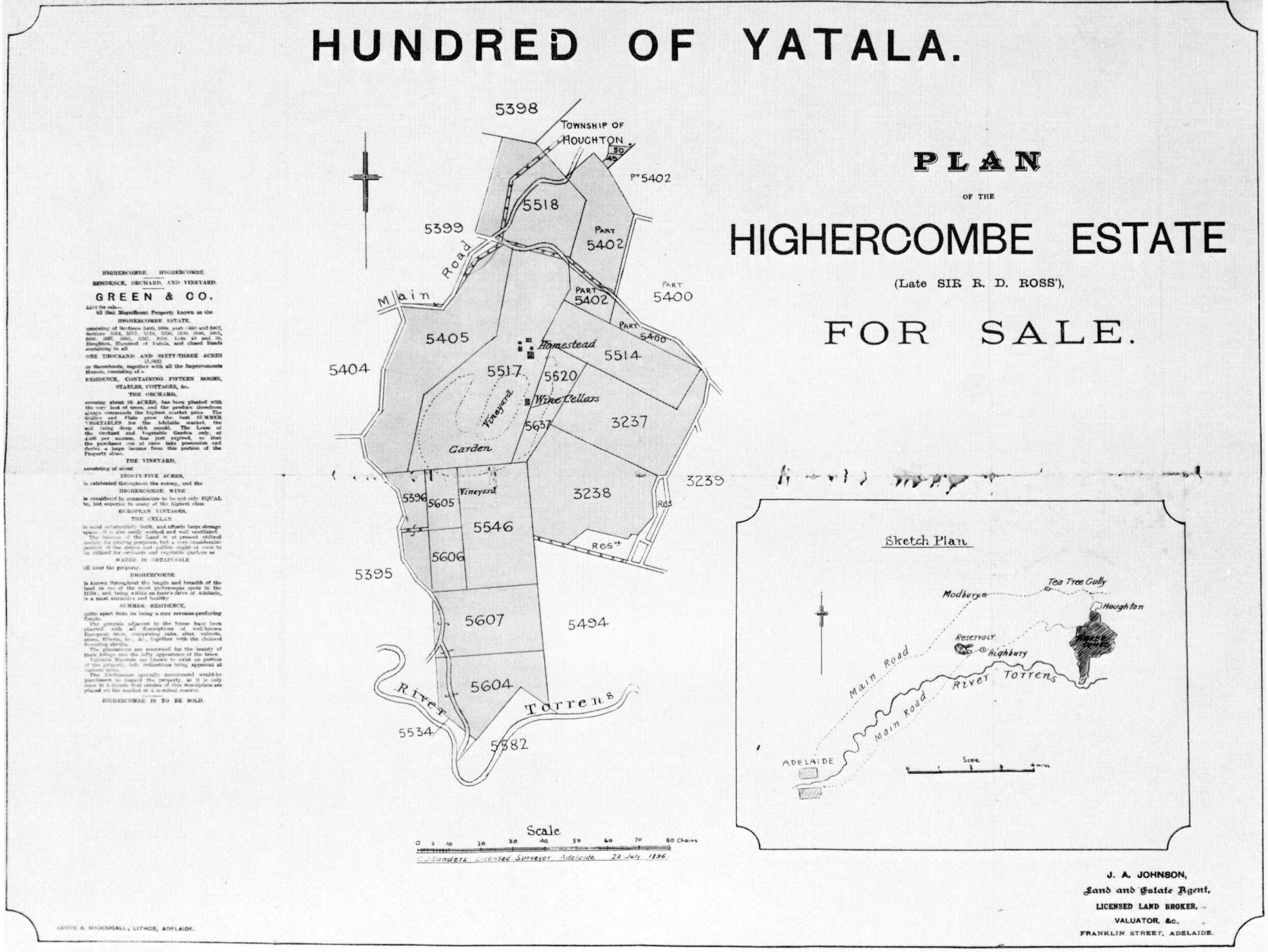

HUNDRED OF YATALA.

PLAN
OF THE
HIGHERCOMBE ESTATE
(Late SIR R. D. ROSS'),
FOR SALE.

Sketch Plan

Scale

J. A. JOHNSON,
Land and Estate Agent,
LICENSED LAND BROKER,
VALUATOR, &c.,
FRANKLIN STREET, ADELAIDE.

Map 5 Plan (1914) of Highercombe Estate, originally established by George Anstey, showing position of homestead and vineyards. Courtesy Mrs. Jean Steuart.

7

HIGHERCOMBE AND GLEN EWIN

'I advise you to go to the beautiful hills'

It was the general opinion of the first colonists that the valleys of the Adelaide Hills would prove more suitable for agriculture and horticulture than the Adelaide plains. The plains around Adelaide might be useful, it was suggested, as sheep stations. Indeed, this was their first use.

It was to be a few years before experience showed that the Adelaide plains were suitable for agriculture. Complete lack of knowledge of climate conditions in the new colony is one obvious reason for the mistaken opinion. Settlers, too, were misled by the opinions of such men as the great Captain Sturt himself. Delivering a lecture, upon his arrival in South Australia in 1838, to a group of settlers on the prospects of agriculture and horticulture in the colony, Sturt had cautioned would-be farmers 'not to attempt to break up the land on the plains or you will meet with sad disappointment'. 'You must not expect', Sturt went on, 'to get crops of grain or fruit on this side of the ranges; but I advise you to go to the beautiful hills, valleys and flats between the ranges; there you will find excellent soil and plenty of good water. If you attempt to cultivate land around Adelaide you will be grievously disappointed'.

Sturt was soon to be proved wrong as far as agriculture on the plains was concerned, but he was correct enough about the prospects for horticulture in the Adelaide hills.

One of the first successful attempts at horticulture in the district — indeed in the colony — was made by George Alexander Anstey on his estate at Highercombe. *(See Map 5)*

We remember that Anstey arrived in the colony from Van Diemen's Land early in 1838 with sheep for sale, and, with the overlander Charles Bonney, had set out to look for a sheep station on the Little Para. In 1840 Anstey arranged to purchase two sections of the Special Survey on the Little Para originally taken out by John Barton Hack. These were sections 5514 and 5517, comprising 240 acres, for which Anstey paid £240. He named his new estate *Highercombe* and after some initial experiments in agriculture, began to establish the vineyards, orchards and extensive botanical gardens which were to make *Highercombe* into a horticultural show-place.

George Alexander Anstey was 24 years of age when he arrived in South Australia. He was born in 1814 in Kentish Town, London. His father, Thomas Anstey, had been born at Highercombe, near Dulverton, Somerset, and after practising law in London had decided, in 1823, to emigrate with his wife and three children to Van Diemen's Land. He had there established *Anstey Park*, an estate of some 20,000 acres.

His eldest son, George Alexander, after helping on his father's property, married in September 1837 and, early in 1838 left to build his own career in the new colony of South Australia, no doubt provided with enough ready capital to ensure success.

In 1838, shortly after his arrival, he purchased two city acres from the Governor, Captain John Hindmarsh. In 1839 Anstey offered part of his land, 'a most eligible and valuable spot of ground on the North Terrace, for the erection of the future *Kirk* of the Established Church of Scotland'. This land is now the site of the present Scots Church. Anstey's second city acre adjoined this block at the back, facing Rundle Street.

Agricultural statistics reveal that by 1840 George Anstey had begun clearing, fencing and ploughing on his new property in the hills and had named it *Highercombe*.

Evidently Anstey began building his home at *Highercombe* late in 1841. He mentions in one of his letters that in 1841 he was on his way 'towards *Highercombe* then in the course of building, riding up on my faithful old horse, *White Surrey* from his home on North Terrace'.

By this time, Anstey's flocks of sheep had increased. He took up a sheep run on the River Gilbert in the mid-north, and by the end of 1841 was one of South Australia's largest stock-holders, running nearly 10,000 sheep and employing a considerable number of shepherds to look after his flocks.

Mrs. Jane Isabella Watts, in her reminiscences *Family Life in South Australia*, published in 1890, has left us a lively description of the housewarming party which took place at *Highercombe* in April 1842. The house was not then the mansion it became later on.

'The original proprietor of *Highercombe*', wrote Mrs. Watts, 'that kind-hearted but somewhat excitable gentleman, G.A.A. — had just completed certain improvements to his house and grounds, and a number of guests had been invited from town to be present at the house-warming. It was arranged that they should go first some miles further on to a picnic given by the owner of P. [Paracombe, Jacob Hagen] and his partner, Captain H— [John Hart] ... and at its conclusion they were to drive over to *Highercombe*, join in the festivities and sleep there.

'For some reason or other the picnic was not a success, though nothing could be more unique and delightful than the evening party which followed; nor would they have met with a more cordial, hearty reception at the hands

Right: George Alexander Anstey,
pastoral pioneer and founder of the
Highercombe Estate. **Below**:Higher-
combe House 1901. Originally the
home of George Anstey, the house
was subsequently the residence of
South Australian Premier, G.M.
Waterhouse, and then of Sir R.D.
Ross. In 1901 it became the home
of Mr. and Mrs. Lorenzo Goodwin.
L.to R.: Mr. Lorenzo Goodwin,
Mrs. Alice Isabel Goodwin and her
brother George C. Catt.

Mr. and Mrs. George McEwin, pioneers of *Glen Ewin*. McEwin and his wife Jessie arrived in South Australia in 1839 in the *Delhi*. George McEwin was then 24 years of age.

Glen Ewin c.1864. This view shows the home with its 1859 additions. The figures of Mr. and Mrs. George McEwin are visible in front of the residence.

of Mr. and Mrs. G.A.A., who vied with each other in their endeavour to make every person as comfortable as circumstances would permit'.

The description of the house and of the evening, which follows, shows us that even the wealthier pioneers still had to be prepared to rough it in the 1840s.

'Their new sitting-room, some 22 feet by 18 feet, which had been prepared for dancing was looked upon in those days [April 1842] as a hall of vast proportions and was the envy of all beholders. It was at this time their only reception room, and therefore, when the ladies arrived they were at once ushered into the two or three small bedrooms set apart for them. From these being so full of beds and luggage a delightful scramble ensued, and the difficulties they experienced in performing their toilettes were neither few nor small.

'The supper was laid in the verandah, which had been enclosed with flags and decorated with evergreens and flowers, but the crowning fun of the night was the sleeping accommodation prepared for all the gentlemen but two, Judge C— [Cooper] and Mr. A—, the seniors of the party, to whom was given the only bedroom that could be provided.

'Whilst the supper was in progress the floor of the dancing-room had been covered by servants with a thick layer of straw and here with a large fire burning in the grate and a good supply of blankets as a covering 'the heavy swell' and the careless bushmen alike reposed. Many of them had been too much accustomed to camping out on the bare ground with only their saddles for a pillow to care much where they slept; but one dapper little man, lately from London, could not make up his mind to seek for rest on so lowly a couch, and in his tightly-fitting evening dress suit and stiff cravat stood upright in one corner of the room till morning dawned, the very picture of misery.

'Another wiser in his generation than his comrades, having an inkling of the accommodation that was in store for them, artfully 'planted' a sofa cushion during the evening and succeeded in that way in securing a resting-place for his head when the hour of retirement came.

'One little episode of this pleasant visit must not be forgotten. The writer of these pages and her friend had been 'scrooged' into a tiny bed, belonging to one of the children, in the same room as Mrs. B—, their hostess and her baby.

'After talking and laughing for some time over the events of the day, Mrs. G.A.A. insisted upon it that they must be hungry, and in a trice she had her dressing-gown on and was in the verandah collecting such dainties as she thought they would approve of.

'There was something so enticing and novel in their surreptitiously partaking of a second supper — eaten in bed, too, when everyone else was supposed to be fast locked in the arms of Morpheus — that if anything, this fresh supply was more appetising than the first.

'The next morning, after an excellent breakfast, one and all bad adieu to their hospitable entertainers and took their departure for town, having enjoyed a most pleasant visit to a very lovely spot, with which, in after years, when the property of Mr. A's son-in-law and his third daughter, Lina, we became still better acquainted'.

The establishment of *Highercombe* was directly responsible for bringing another horticulturist into the district, a young man of great ability and remarkable energy, who not only played a leading part in horticultural development in the district but in the development of its local government. This was a young Scotsman, George McEwin.

McEwin, before he arrived at *Highercombe* to superintend the planting and landscaping of its gardens, had, as we shall see, already made a notable contribution to the theory and practice of horticulture and arboriculture in the new colony.

George McEwin was born in the south of Scotland in 1815. His father was then manager of the estate of the Duke of Buccleuch.

By the age of 18, young McEwin had become a botanist of considerable ability and a life member of the Arboricultural Society of Edinburgh. As a professional landscape gardener he had, before he left for South Australia, laid out gardens in Scotland and Liverpool. His father, with the rest of his family, had migrated to Melbourne in 1838, and is reputed to have been responsible for laying out the gardens at Jolimont Government House, near Melbourne.

In 1839, George McEwin and his wife, Jessie, then living in Liscard, Cheshire, had sailed for South Australia from Liverpool in the *Delhi*. They eventually settled in a cottage in Kermode Street, North Adelaide. Here McEwin had taken a position with the pioneer horticulturist, George Stevenson — himself a Scotsman.

Stevenson, the editor of South Australia's first newspaper, the *South Australian Gazette and Colonial Register*, was at that time transforming the four town acres of land he had acquired fronting Melbourne and Finniss Streets, North Adelaide, into the horticultural show-place of primitive Adelaide. A section of Stevenson's cottage in Finniss Street still remains. At great expense he had planted every variety of shrub, vine and tree procurable in Australia and from overseas in his garden. Stevenson is recognised as 'The Father of Horticulture in South Australia'. He did not agree with Sturt's poor opinion of the Adelaide plains as unsuitable for agriculture. 'I have seen', he said in 1839, 'no finer samples of wheat, barley and oats in any part of the world than were produced last season in the immediate neighbourhood of Adelaide'.

Such faith as Stevenson's in the future of the struggling young colony was sorely needed in the colony just then. What colonists needed, too, coming from a country with climate and seasons so different, was a practical guide to gardening in the new colony.

This was supplied in 1843 by George McEwin.

The book, published in London, was entitled *The South Australian Vigneron and Gardeners' Manual.* *

McEwin completed the guide while living at North Adelaide. He felt that such a guide was essential to colonists as other books on the subject were 'totally inapplicable to this Colony in their general practice and are calculated to mislead if acted upon'. The book, of course, was based on McEwin's own experience in Stevenson's gardens at North Adelaide.

In the same year as his manual was published, George McEwin and his family moved to Anstey's property at Highercombe. The change in circumstances is recorded in the diary which he began on the day he accepted the position at *Highercombe*.

> 'November 1st, 1843
>
> My engagement with G.A. Anstey, Esqu., commences this day on the following terms: Forty-five pounds per annum, a house, vegetables, and provisions for self and family, including milk, soap, candles, etc. etc. Also an interest in the nursery stock by allowing me a liberal percentage on all young trees sold which I may raise.
>
> The conditions specified in the agreement were: That I was to have sole control and management of everything connected with my department except in so far as new improvements or alterations would of course be subject to Mr. Anstey's approval, suggestion, or disapproval as the case might be, but at the same time there would be no interference in detail'.

If only 'the excitable Mr. Anstey' had kept his promise of 'no interference in detail' he might have retained the services of George McEwin. But then there might not have been a history of Glen Ewin to record.

The reception accorded to the McEwins by Mr. Anstey and his wife was cordial enough, as George McEwin recorded in his diary:

> 'December 6th, 1844
>
> Arrived at Highercombe in the evening and found things in readiness. Was kindly invited by Mr. Anstey up to the house to have tea, and he also evinced a kindly feeling towards us by personally attending us with wine and ordering the necessary improvements about the house to be completed without delay'.

The following day George McEwin recorded that he 'perambulated the

* *The South Australian Vigneron and Gardeners' Manual* - This handsome little book, advertised as 'Indispensable to every Settler', was re-printed at intervals over the years and McEwin published a revised edition of it in 1871. The book, now of historic interest, has recently been reprinted, in Facsimile Edition, by the State Library of South Australia.

grounds' in company with Mr. Anstey, who pointed out the improvements he expected McEwin to make at *Highercombe*.

Although McEwin's diary records no complaint against Anstey until the week in which he left his services, it is obvious from the diary that his employer looked upon George McEwin as a head gardener rather than as a professional landscape gardener. The diary entry for Christmas Day, 1843, records:

'Monday December 25th
Self and Joseph at same work as yesterday [i.e. grubbing a large gum tree at the lower end of the vineyard] in forenoon. Pannon and Pepper in copse cutting the last of the stakes wanted and burying a dead bullock in the compost heap. Christmas: A half holiday. Weather rather warm, but nights invariably cool'.

In the year in which McEwin served at *Highercombe* extensions were made to the vineyards. A large holding dam (still in use) was constructed and the planning of the walks, and the planting of the 'pleasure gardens' which still surround the dam at Highercombe was begun. McEwin also established a tree nursery for the botanical section of the gardens.

The diary shows that McEwin obtained seeds for his nursery from such diverse places as Mauritius, from the Sydney Botanic Garden, from the Horticultural Society of London, and the Swan River settlement in Western Australia. Fruit trees were obtained from George Stevenson's garden at North Adelaide.

In October 1844, George McEwin had decided to leave *Highercombe* and informed Mr. Anstey of his decision. He records his last three days with Anstey with some very plain speaking:

'Monday 13th [October]   Having given up my situation three weeks ago, Mr. Anstey has assumed a most offensive demeanour towards me, which today broke out in violent paroxysms of rage, and ended by agreeing that I should leave his service on the 15th ultimo. Employed all day in making out a list of fruit trees, plants, seeds, etc.

Tuesday 14th   Delivered to Mr. Anstey all the articles in my charge, with catalogue of plants, trees, etc. Went in afternoon to Mr. Williams of *Hermitage* and got liberty to occupy an empty house on his ground until I got one put up on my own land.

Wednesday 15th   Left the place early in the morning with drays and all our things and got into our fresh domicile, determined that unless necessity compelled me, never again to take another situation! And although our prospects at present are not of the brightest description, still we think we can see our way pretty clearly.

The conclusion I have come to with regard to following my profession in this colony in the capacity of a servant, is, that the advances in wealth, dignity and refinement on the part of the leading colonists, are so very low compared with the mother country, as to render them inappreciable of the talents of a practical Gardener, and dead to the elegancies of the higher branches of the science!'

George Anstey's attempts to play the part of the Squire of *Highercombe* brought him into collision, not only with men like McEwin, but, as we shall see, with the Legislative Council itself. Attempts at establishing a squirearchy in the new colony were not uncommon but they were never very successful, although Anstey and Thomas Williams at *Hermitage* were occasionally accorded the title of Squire by those in their employ.

George McEwin made no further entries in his diary after resigning from his position at *Highercombe* until July 1845 — nearly nine months later. Then he wrote:

Glen Ewin, July 1845

Tuesday, July 29th

'As there is a blank in the entries of this book I shall here enter a few of the leading events that have transpired since we settled at this place.

On 10th December finished our present residence consisting of a two-roomed house 24 feet by 12 and weather boarded, walls 8 feet 6 in. high. We removed into it on the 12th December. Finished stockyard and got home our cows [which from six have increased to 17] on 26th of Decr. Finished dairy same time 8 by 10 feet. Also fenced in a garden temporarily and planted potatoes and melons.

Discovered indications of copper and lead and silver; let the mine to N. Fletcher and S. Clare who commenced to work it on the 28th April. Found first piece of solid ore at 8 feet from the surface.

Finished garden fence in June. Sowed 1 acre of wheat on 21st July'.

Such were the modest beginnings to the *Glen Ewin* estate, born of the determination of George McEwin 'never to take another situation'.

Records of the Land Titles Office reveal that McEwin had purchased section 5561 which became *Glen Ewin* in August of 1844, two months before he left Anstey's employ. The 80 acre section for which he paid £83 consisted of steep hills and valleys astride some springs in a small creek leading into the Little Para. McEwin was forced to borrow £30 in order to purchase the section. In July of 1845 he sold thirty acres of his land to George Dunn for £30 in order to repay his debt to Benjamin Mendez DaCosta.

McEwin's first ambition was to make himself self-sufficient on his property. He developed a domestic garden and a dairy as soon as possible. He sowed his first acre of wheat and made it safe from cattle by a three-railed fence, the timber for which he felled, split and morticed himself. He commenced planting a vineyard with vine cuttings from Williams' *Hermitage* vineyard nearby. He, no doubt with his wife's help, churned butter — sometimes a full keg of 62 lbs. in one week — and carted it into Adelaide for sale. On other occasions it was wheat which was carted. 'Went to Adelaide in morning with dray and wheat to grind', he wrote in his diary; and on another occasion, 'Went to Adelaide with dray and 14 bushels of wheat to grind. Slept in town all night and went to church in forenoon. Returned home in evening'.

There were other journeys to make — 'Went to village [Houghton] this morning with the wheelbarrow to bring over goods which were brought there for me from town by the Mount Crawford dray' and 'Went to Gawler Town in search of mare and returned on Thursday unsuccessful'; 'Went to Hope Valley to the German Shoemaker's for shoes'.

The diary is a record of hard unremitting labour. Through it shines McEwin's delight in all things that the soil produced and his keen observations of the inter-relations of climate, soil and situation, both in *Glen Ewin* and on neighbouring properties. By 1854 his vineyards were producing sufficiently to enable him to begin the commercial production of wine. He recorded in April 1854, 'Our Wine cellar is rather small; intend building a larger one before the next vintage'.

By this time McEwin was well established at *Glen Ewin*. He was an active member of the South Australian Agricultural and Horticultural Society and was beginning to take a leading role in district affairs and to press for local government in the area.

As befitted a cautious Scotsman, McEwin was in no hurry to create an impression — he notes in his diary that he did not build himself and his family a new house until 1859. And it was twenty years later again before the present homestead of beautifully dressed sandstone, quarried on the property, was built on the site of the original cottage. The four stone rooms of the 1859 additions were retained and incorporated into the present structure.

George McEwin truly earned the respect increasingly accorded to him throughout the district.

At *Highercombe*, by 1853, Anstey's house had been enlarged to sixteen rooms; the oaks, elms and Norfolk Island Pines were flourishing. The steep vineyard of 2,000 vines was in full production and Anstey had built large wine cellars. The walls of this building are still standing. Anstey, like McEwin, was showing an interest in local affairs, but mainly at a political level and intended to further his own interests and ambitions. He managed to get himself nominated in 1849 as Chairman of the Road Board for the Hundred of Yatala. For a brief period in 1851 he was a nominated Member for Yatala of the Governor's Legislative Council.

In 1851 his father, Thomas Anstey, died at *Anstey Park* in Van Diemen's Land and George Alexander Anstey returned there with his wife and family, now considerably enlarged by the births, between 1838 and 1847, of five children.

Except for brief visits, the last in 1868, Anstey never returned to South Australia. In 1854 he took up permanent residence in England and died in Harley Street, London, in February 1895, in his eighty-first year.

YATALA

8

EARLY ROADS
1839—1849

'In every new colony the question of roads and road-making is a burning one.
Dwellers in old-established cities can form no conception of the wild enthusiasm, the fiery
oratory, the impassioned earnestness displayed over a question of road-making.'

Edwin Hodder's statement (above) made in his *History of South Australia* published in 1893, applies in full measure to the development of roads in the district of Tea Tree Gully — and in particular to the main lines of road through the district.

It could be said that it was the question of roads which initially brought the district together and supplied settlers with their first common interest. It could also be claimed that it was the same question of roads which eventually split the district in two in 1858.

It was the machinations of the fiery George Alexander Anstey, the Squire of *Highercombe*, which were primarily responsible for both the initial arousal of local interest in district roads — often in the form of opposition to Anstey — and for the subsequent division of the district into two factions and, later, into two council areas, even though by then Anstey had left South Australia for good.

The line that any particular road took in the new colony was determined primarily by the pattern of settlement rather than by any deliberate planning. In unsurveyed countryside, the line taken was the one which offered the least resistance to the bullock wagons which made up the colony's main traffic.

Two factors affected the main line of roads in our own district. One was the need to find the most suitable line of road up and over the Teatree Gully Range — one that would satisfy both the settlers of the district and of the districts then developing beyond at Chain of Ponds and Gumeracha. The other important factor influencing the pattern of roads in the district was the private interest of such influential settlers as George Anstey and Alexander McDonald.

Both of these men were accused, with good reason, of arranging to have a road opened which led to their own properties — Mr. Anstey 'in order to have a good road to send his fruit to market' in Adelaide, and Mr. McDonald

Map 6. Plan of Hundred of Yatala (Proclaimed 1846). The eastern section became the District of Highercombe in 1853 *(cf. Map 9)*. S.A. State Library.

'in order that he might lay out his section of land into allotments' where the road crossed the River Torrens at Paradise and 'to put up a public house'.

To understand how much private interests could influence the siting of public roads, it is necessary to look at the position in 1839 when settlers first began to move into the district.

The only survey which affected the district at that time was Colonel William Light's 1838 survey. *(See Map 1)* This had divided the districts surrounding Adelaide into 134-acre sections as far north as the Grand Junction Road and as far east as Section 306, where the continuation of the present Reservoir Road once passed through what is now the Hope Valley Reservoir and continued along Reids Road to the ford on the River Torrens and into Silkes Road.

Beyond this surveyed area, which in 1839 barely entered the district, was unsurveyed land through which settlers on horseback and in bullock drays or wagons made their way to their selections or sheep runs by the best route they could.

Within the surveyed area around Adelaide, Light had laid down a pattern of main roads which still exists today. From this surveyed area there were two possible main roads of entry from Adelaide into the present district. One was the North Eastern Road, although this halted at the present junction with Blacks Road and continued east, along the present Lyons Road, to Reservoir Road. Here, where the surveyed road ended, were the beginnings of a small settlement which, in 1842, became known as Hope Valley. A second line of road entered the district from the present Lower North East Road via a ford over the River Torrens which still connects Silkes Road with Reids Road.

These 'main roads' were little more than lines of road on a map. They were unfenced tracks through open country. Even as late as 1854, the metalled section of the main North East Road, which carried most of the traffic into the district, extended only as far as the O.G. Inn from Walkerville. Beyond that the road across the Gilles Plains was a mere track, impassable sometimes for weeks during the winter. The Grand Junction Road existed on paper only until the late 1840s.

A fascinating account of the road across Gilles Plains into the Tea Tree Gully district and of how its black soil became known as 'Bay of Biscay' soil was published in the *Adelaide Observer* in 1882.

'I often travelled over the Gilles Plains, as they were called', wrote the correspondent, 'and the neighbourhood, when a lad about forty years ago, and then it had more of the character of Biscay land than now. The stratum beneath the dark black alluvium consists of limestone rubble and the water collects in small hollows on the surface, in which the vegetation decays, forming a weak acid solution which slowly dissolves the limestone and the slight hollow above is increased by the falling in of the soil.

'In time the whole country assumes a billowed appearance and when

64

the bullock-drays of the first colonists passed over these plains the vehicle rocked and pitched and rolled so much that it reminded the travellers of their recent experience in crossing the *Bay of Biscay* — hence the name — and the effects of *mal-de-mer* were not seldom experienced by them'. The writer added that by 1882 these hollows had been levelled down by continuous ploughing for hay-growing, which by then had become the principal agricultural occupation of the Tea Tree Gully and Gilles Plains area.

We have seen that the earliest settlement in the district was in the hills area at Hermitage, Paracombe and the village of Houghton. The route to these places from the village of Walkerville was across Gilles Plains and through the Teatree Gully. Before long this was the route through to the new settlements beyond at Chain of Ponds and Gumeracha. The line of road, no more than a track, was referred to as the 'North Eastern' line of road to the River Murray.

There was indeed only one other line of road across the Adelaide Hills to the east. This was the Great Eastern line of road through Glen Osmond and Crafers to the new Special Surveys at Mt. Barker.

It was easy enough to find an entrance into the valleys of the foothills of the Teatree Gully Range. It was much more difficult to find a valley which did not end in a sharp rise, too steep to take bullock-wagons over. Only the Teatree Gully presented a gradient which could be negotiated all the way. The permanent springs in the gully encouraged teamsters to use this route, even though until side-cuttings were made, the swampy teatree gully was sometimes impassable.

The first person to effect improvements in the gully was John Tregeagle under the direction of Thomas Williams of *The Hermitage*. As an ex-Cornish miner, Tregeagle no doubt was well able to handle a pick and shovel. Tregeagle came to live in the gully in 1840 as a tenant of John Morphett, the original grantee of section 1559 which included most of the gully itself and its springs.

In giving evidence in 1865 concerning the water reserve in the Teatree Gully, the Chairman of the Committee of enquiry put the following questions to John Tregeagle:

How long have you resided at Teatree Gully?

Ever since I have been in the colony.

How long have you known the road?

It is twenty-five years last February [i.e.February 1840] since I went into the gully to live there.

You knew it before the present Main North-Eastern Road was cut?

I knew it before the Central Road Board was in existence.

Then you remember the original cut?

Yes, I was one that helped to cut it.

Under whose direction?

The South Australian Company and Squire Williams who used to live at *The Hermitage*.

Later, in 1850, Tregeagle undertook to cut through the hill at the top of the gully for a sum of £200. 'Tregeagle is a Cornish miner', wrote a supporter, 'and knows what he is doing'. The offer was rejected, perhaps fortunately, as hard stone was met with — sandstone, which proved to be good quality building stone from which many of Adelaide's finest buildings were later constructed.

Squire Williams of *Hermitage*, of course, had a personal interest in the line of road, as did the South Australian Company which had taken up Special Surveys at Chain of Ponds and 'Gumaraka', as it was then spelt.

Although the gully section was originally private land, a suitable line of road through the Teatree Gully was laid out as early as 1842, although it was not until 1854 that the line of road from Grand Junction Road through the gully to Chain of Ponds was gazetted a main line of road by the Central Road Board.

In 1842 however, as John Tregeagle had stated, there was no Central Road Board. Until 1849 when the first Central Road Board was appointed, the colony's roads, which consisted mainly of roads in and around Adelaide, were the responsibility of the Colonial Engineer.

By 1842 the only public expenditure 'on the road which is intended to be the main road to the Little Para, Gummeraka and Mt. Crawford' was on 'four very substantial bridges thrown over different creeks'. The 'substantial bridges' were logs of wood cut from the nearest red gum tree. One of these bridges was known as Gollop's Bridge. It spanned the branch of the Little Para at the foot of Black Hill Road, just beyond the present Inglewood Inn. Built in the 1840s by John Gollop of Houghton, it was eventually replaced by the present stone bridge in 1863.

By 1842 the north-eastern road had been 'cleared of trees and stumps to a distance of 7 miles from Adelaide'. Even by 1850 there were still plenty of stumps on the road. In February of that year a team of bullocks bringing a dray load of wheat to Adelaide from Chain of Ponds, descending Teatree Gully, hit a stump. 'The jerk dislodged a sack of wheat and caused it to slide over the front of the dray dislodging the driver'. The frightened bullocks took off down hill and the wheel passed over the driver. 'The deceased's head', wrote the enthusiastic reporter, 'was crushed and his brains lying on the road'.

In October of the same year a complaint was lodged against a contractor who had, it was stated, adopted a dangerous mode of removing stumps on the road near Gilles Plains by burning them out and leaving fires blazing along the road, unattended. The official instruction to contractors removing stumps was they should be cut off '6 inches beneath the surface of the ground'.

Until 1844, it appeared that the only main line of road through the district, whether it entered from Walkerville across Gilles Plains or across the Torrens at Reids Road, must converge on the Teatree Gully on its way to the Villages of Houghton and Gumeracha. The former was the route taken, as we have noted *(v. Chapter 6)* by William Flavel in his journey by bullock-team to the Chain of Ponds in 1842 and, in spring of the same year, by young Charles Wilson and his friend in their dray to the same destination *(v. Prologue)*.

The route most favoured by teamsters for the conveyance of heavy loads to Adelaide or Port Adelaide was the northerly route which led from the Teatree Gully and followed a line of road through Ardtornish *(q.v.)*, Gilles Plains and Walkerville. This was so despite the often impassable condition of the Gilles Plains during winter. This line was much preferred to the longer route through Hope Valley and across the Torrens.

The main loads which moved along this route were wheat for the South Australian Company's Mill at Hackney, built in 1843, lengths of timber for fuel or fencing, and the hay required increasingly for fodder in Adelaide and Pt. Adelaide. This northerly route, which by-passed Hope Valley, very soon acquired the name of The Hay Road. As an added advantage to teamsters it was possible to turn off at the Ardtornish Corner* and travel directly along the Grand Junction Road to Port Adelaide.

It seemed then in 1844 that from whichever branch — the southern via the Torrens or the northern via Gilles Plains — the main line of road might enter the district, the route over the hills would be up the Teatree Gully to Houghton, Chain of Ponds and Gumeracha. However there was neither enough settlers nor, as yet, any constituted body to determine or define such a trunk road.

There is no doubt that if it had not been for the initiative ('effrontery' was the word preferred by the *South Australian Register)* of the Squire of *Highercombe* there would, indeed, have been no alternative line of main road. George Anstey was however never one to wait upon authority.

In 1842, soon after he took up residence at *Highercombe*, he began the construction of his own road down to the plains. By 1844 he was petitioning the Governor, through Captain Sturt, the Colonial Secretary, for an amount of £100 to help meet the cost of construction. Construction meant little more than the removal of trees, rocks and stumps, and probably the making of a few cuttings.

This line of road was immediately dubbed 'Anstey's Hill' — its official

* Junction of Main North-East Road and Grand Junction Road.

name of Highercombe Hill was soon discarded.

As a rival to the route through Teatree Gully, Anstey's Hill became the most contentious road, not only in the district but in the colony. Anstey's determination to have his road declared the main line of road through the district soon resulted in the matter becoming a district issue and very soon a public issue. For the next ten years the relative merits of the two lines of road — the northern line through Walkerville, Gilles Plains and Tea Tree Gully to Houghton and the southern line through Paradise, Hope Valley and via Anstey's Hill to Houghton — were debated frequently and at length in the Adelaide newspapers and, after 1849, at meetings of the newly constituted Central and District Road Boards.

At the local level Anstey's private piece of enterprise resulted in a sudden and impassioned interest in the two opposing lines of roads. This spread to the settlers at Chain of Ponds and Gumeracha. Factions developed and found local leaders to speak for them. Such men as Robert Milne of Upper Dry Creek, R.S. Kelly of Modbury, William Holden of Hope Valley, and George McEwin of *Hermitage* spoke for the settlers who favoured the northern road through the district; Joseph Ind of Paradise and John Gollop of Houghton spoke for those who favoured the southern route over Anstey's Hill.

Almost unwillingly Anstey, in pursuing what was mainly self-interest, had provided an issue which first brought the district together at local meetings (frequently in opposition) and provided a stepping stone to the formation of the first District Council in 1853. It also allowed the district to discover its natural leaders.

As we shall see, commonsense came to the rescue in 1854 when both lines of road were proclaimed main roads under the Road Act. Such a solution had been first mentioned in a letter to the *Register*, signed 'Calm Observer' early in 1853. As the two lines of road to Houghton and beyond had both been in use for ten years, the argument had deteriorated by then into a mere matter of which road should receive the government road grant. In the event little money was spent on either section except on that portion leading from Hope Valley to Anstey's property at *Highercombe* — a fact which was to be remembered bitterly by electors in the Hundred of Yatala when Anstey became a contestant for a seat in South Australia's first Legislative Council in 1851.

Soon after settling in at *Highercombe* Anstey must have determined to open up his own line of road to Hope Valley. The party which had attended his house-warming in 1842 *(v. Chapter 7)* used the long route via Teatree Gully and Houghton — until then the only one.

Anstey's only authority for pegging out a more direct route for himself was based on a spoken promise made by Governor Grey in 1842 that the new line of road would have his approval. On this slim basis, Anstey had set about forming a 'Para and Chain of Ponds Road Committee', consisting of a few settlers who supported the new line of road. The committee had subscribed the sum of £50 towards the formation of the road and in October of 1844 had appointed 'two settlers, William Inns and Joseph Barritt to peg out the road down the hills through sections 5547, 5549 and 5626' to Hope Valley.

Anstey, with the road already in use, had then applied to the new Governor, Governor Robe, in September 1845, for the £100 which the clearing of the road had cost him and his committee. 'The old road through Teatree Gully', he wrote, 'is circuitous, incapable of improvement, and passes through private land without reference to its owners'. Anstey's letter received no more than a brief acknowledgement.

Nine months later Anstey wrote again, saying that the new line of road was nearly finished. This time Robe, through the Colonial Secretary, Captain Sturt, replied. To Anstey's annoyance, Robe stated that 'Governor Grey's spoken approval did not mean that Anstey had been authorised to begin the work'. He refused Anstey any subsidy. Indeed it was not until September of 1847, after many persistent and irritable letters from Anstey, that a grant of £50 was made — only half the sum claimed. Anstey seems to have accepted the amount without protest. He no doubt realised that the payment of the subsidy meant that his road was now at least officially recognised.

But Anstey had not only opened up a public road — he had opened a public controversy which was to continue until 1854.

Governor Robe's decision to meet Anstey's request for payment had resulted from an inspection of the rival lines of road in August of 1846. On horseback Thomas Burr, the Government surveyor, had ridden over and examined both roads as far as 'where they met at the Village of Houghton'. He wrote to Robe, 'From what I have said you will perceive that I am in favour of the road made by Mr. Anstey and I must say that he deserves credit for the laying of it'. The Teatree Gully road only served, in his estimation, the 'dozen or so settlers at *Hermitage*'.

With the building of the new road at Highercombe Hill, as Burr referred to it, it now appeared that this would inevitably become the main line of road through the district to the Chain of Ponds and the districts beyond. The Teatree Gully route would be relegated to a minor role as a district road.

Two important government ordinances were, however, to give the road issue the opportunity for public hearing. The first ordinance was that of October 1846, when the settled areas around Adelaide were divided into Hundreds. The population of the colony had by that time risen to 22,000 — and the new divisions into hundreds, such as the Hundred of Adelaide, the Hundred of Para Wirra, the Hundred of Yatala, although they were primarily administrative divisions, gave some cohesion to the scattered settlements within their boundaries.

The settlements at Houghton, Hope Valley, Hermitage and in the Tea-tree Gully itself, found themselves within the Hundred of Yatala. *(See Map 6)* The Hundred was bounded on the south by the River Torrens from the coast to below Paracombe, on the east by a line approximating to the course of the Little Para and on to Gould's Creek, on the north by Gould's Creek and the Little Para to the present Pt. Wakefield Road, and south along this (the Old North Road) to Grand Junction Road and so to the coast at Semaphore. It excluded Adelaide and North Adelaide. The boundaries of the Hundred of Yatala remain virtually unchanged today.

It was a large district, and one area had little in common with any other in 1846.

In 1849, however, another government ordinance gave the hundreds more of a common interest. This was the formation of a Central Road Board and the appointment of District Road Boards 'for the making or improving of roads in South Australia'.

The first District Road Board for the Hundred of Yatala was formed in December of 1849. As, oddly enough in the light of the battle to come concerning roads in the district, no meeting had been held in the hundred to recommend the five district commissioners to the board, the appointments were made by the new Governor, Sir Henry Edward Fox Young. The appointments were announced in the *Government Gazette* of 1849.

'His Excellency has been pleased to appoint the following gentlemen as District Commissioners for the Hundred of Yatala:

Messrs.   George Alexander Anstey of Highercombe
Alexander Macdonald of River Torrens
Howard Blyth of Dry Creek
John Stuckey of Dry Creek
William Spicer of River Para'

The five men were appointed to remain in office until January 1, 1851, when new elections were to be held in each district.

It is obvious that, from the beginning, the eastern sector of the hundred (our present district) was well represented. At the first meeting of the District Road Board held in the *Bremen Hotel*, Hope Valley, in May 1850, Anstey was appointed as its Chairman for the year. Macdonald was the owner of sections of land on the north bank of the Torrens at Paradise and Blyth and Stuckey both held property along the Dry Creek. The only 'outsider' was William Spicer who was a resident of Salisbury on the Little Para River.

Moreover, the first Clerk of the District Road Board was Mr. Edward Prowse of Hope Valley, whose appointment dated from February 10, 1850. Prowse was also appointed Surveyor of Roads for the Hundred of Yatala.

Edward Prowse was then schoolmaster at the newly-opened Hope Valley School. In 1853 he became first Clerk of the District Council of Highercombe.

With Anstey as Chairman of the District Road Board, and meetings at the Bremen Hotel, Hope Valley, and most of the members and the Clerk living in the same district, it was obvious that roads in this section of the hundred would get favoured treatment and that Anstey's own road might get something more than favoured treatment.

9

THE CENTRAL AND DISTRICT
ROAD BOARDS
1849—1854

'taxation without any representation'

The formation of the Central Road Board and of District Road Boards in each hundred in 1849 were steps towards the formation of District Councils after 1852.

The task of the Central Board was to define main and district roads.* The care and management of these roads when gazetted was vested in each District Board, consisting of five Commissioners and a Clerk.

We have noted that Anstey was nominated Chairman of the board of five commissioners for the District of Yatala. But even prior to his appointment, Anstey had begun a campaign for a bridge across the Torrens to connect with his own road from Houghton and Highercombe.

In October 1849, he attempted to clinch the matter of a site for a bridge. By public advertisement he convened a meeting at William Dinham's flour-mill *(v. Chapter 10)* on section 811 on the Torrens. At this 'monster meeting', claimed a subsequent correspondent, 'there were present three men, including G.A.A., Esqu., two boys and a dog'. The two other men were Dinham and Alexander Boord — Dinham's neighbour.

Anstey wrote to the Governor stating that the meeting 'having as a body' inspected the various sites, had resolved that the line pointed out by Mr. Dinham (leading past Dinham's mill) as the best site for the bridge and its approaches. He stressed that the work should be carried out that summer as cartage via the Gilles Plains line of road would by the following winter be impracticable.

Despite the special pleadings of Anstey and his friends, the first district bridge over the Torrens was not constructed until 1857. Until then traffic crossed at the Paradise Ford, close to the site finally selected for the proposed bridge.

The new District Road Board did not hold its first meeting until March

---

* Some idea of the system of district roads which had developed by 1842 may be gained from *Map 3*, although it should be remembered that any roads shown were mere tracks through unenclosed land.

of 1850. 'Nothing had been done except to appoint a salaried staff' reported the *Register*, the salaried staff consisting of Edward Prowse, of Hope Valley as Clerk and Surveyor at a salary of £92.10.0 a year.

This was, however, merely the calm before the storm already brewing.

In February of 1850 the Central Road Board announced a Dray Tax and set out the scale of duties payable:

1.	Wagons or Drays (drawn by more than two bullocks or one horse) the tire of the wheels being less than 4½ inches in width —	£ 2. 0.0
2.	Wagons or Drays (drawn by more than two bullocks or one horse) the tire of the wheels being more than 4½ inches and upwards in all —	1.10.0
3.	Carts and other vehicles (drawn by not more than one horse or two bullocks) the tire of the wheels being less than 4½ inches —	1.10.0
4.	Carts and other vehicles (drawn by not more than one horse or two bullocks) the tire of the wheels being 4½ inches and upwards —	1. 0.0
5.	Spring carriages	1. 0.0

Drays were to carry a licence-plate or number.

The ordinance tells us something about horse-power relative to bullock-power; it also indicates that the narrower wagon-tires were held mainly responsible by the authorities for cutting up the roads.

The reaction to this 'odious Dray Tax' was immediate. A meeting of ratepayers of the Hundreds of Yatala and Para Wirra was held in the main room of the *Morning Star* at Chain of Ponds in March. Nearly 100 rate-payers crowded into the hotel's assembly room. The protest meeting continued for four hours and resolved:

1. That the Dray Tax was unjust.

2. That the Government should line out and complete main lines of road and also fix and line district roads.

With the formation of the District Road Board in 1849, settlers had found themselves, for the first time, ratepayers. They evidently considered this a doubtful privilege.

It was for varied reasons that settlers of the district did not find their first taste of the democratic process of self-government very palatable.

They found their entitlement, as landholders, to vote for the five members of the District Road Board stacked in favour of large and often absentee landowners. The scale, laid down by the Road Act of 1849 was:

20	acres nor more than	80 acres	1 vote
80	acres nor more than	160 acres	2 votes
160	acres nor more than	320 acres	3 votes
320	acres nor more than	640 acres	4 votes
640	acres nor more than	1000 acres	5 votes
1000	acres and upwards		6 votes

The woodcarters and bullock drivers forced to pay the Dray Tax claimed that their position was even worse than that of the small landholder with only one vote — they had, they said, 'taxation without any representation' on the District Board.

Landholders, conversely, asserted at public meetings that the only privilege that the Road Act seemed to confer, apart from the right to vote, was the privilege of paying land tax.

On March 21, 1850 the Commissioners of the District Road Board announced that they had decided on a levy of 4½d. per acre on all purchased land in the district. They also announced that they would be present at the Bremen Hotel, Hope Valley, on Friday, April 19 at the Dry Creek Public House, North Road, on the Monday following, and at Riseley's Half-Way House Hotel, Port Road, to collect the rates personally. This would also give ratepayers in the Hundred of Yatala the opportunity to lodge any complaints concerning their assessments.

A published list of the road assessments for 1850* provides us with a useful precis of landholders in the present district, both owners or occupiers, and of their acreage. It contains names still familiar in the district. The list also reveals the presence of a group of large landholders — Anstey, Robertson, Shillabeer, Stuckey, Milne, Bagot, Boord, Crouch, Nihil, Gooch, Gollop, MacLaine, Kelly, Blyth and McDonald — many of whom were to emerge before long as men of influence in the district. Both local and state government, when they finally developed in the colony, were weighted in favour of colonists who had managed to acquire broad acres. Generally speaking it is plain, however, that the larger landholders accepted the responsibility which their land-power conferred. The personal ambitions of such men as Anstey and McDonald were more than outweighed by the general concern for the development of the district of such men as George McEwin, Robert S. Kelly, Adam Robertson, William Holden, Angus McLaine, Robert Milne and John Gollop.

Both the Dray Tax and the 4½d. per acre assessment for the Hundred of Yatala, having been condemned at public meetings, there was little inclination to pay the levies. It was stated that when the Clerk and Commissioners met to receive the assessments at the notified collecting places 'they went away with empty pockets'. The Chairman, George Anstey, retired to

* v. S.A. *Government Gazette* **March 28, 1850** p.212.

74

his den at *Highercombe* 'baffled and breathing out revenge and making occasional descents to the *Bremen Hotel* at Hope Valley whence he called on the Government and asked for power of law to make the ratepayers cash up'. At a public dinner held by the Anti-Land and Dray Tax League, held in January of 1851, Anstey was referred to as *The Highercombe Charioteer*.

The Yatala League, as it was called, with nearly 1,000 members, felt itself strong enough to threaten violence if the Dray Tax were not repealed. The Governor in July of 1851 felt obliged to review the Road Act and to abandon the obnoxious dray licence completely. In the Hundred of Yatala, the District Road Board took matters into its own hand and refunded the whole of Dray Tax to the owners of wagons and other vehicles.

There were two reasons why the ratepayers in the Hundred of Yatala should have been so militant. The rate of 4½d. per acre was the highest of any of the hundreds — it was 1½d. an acre in the district of Mt. Barker.

The second reason, however, was a discovery which aroused far greater indignation and which soon found expression at public meetings throughout the district. This was the expenditure, so it was claimed, of nearly the whole of the Government grant of £1,000 for the year 1850 to the Yatala District Road Board, upon one road — the road leading from the Torrens ford near Paradise to *Highercombe*. The £1,000 included an amount of £250 for a proposed bridge over the Torrens at Paradise.

The *Government Gazette* of May 1850, gave notification that the District Road Commissioners intended opening a New Road through sections 831, 830, 824, 825, 305, 304, 2057, 2058 and 510 to the proposed new bridge on the Torrens connecting the Hundred of Adelaide and Hundred of Yatala.

It was obvious from the inclusion of sections 831, 830 and 510 that the Board of which Anstey was Chairman intended to ignore the route through Teatree Gully and the needs of the settlers of the northern section of the district. It was also obvious that the Chairman would be accused of spending the £1,000 grant from the Central Road Board upon the repair and development of a road which led to his own property.

The first broadside in the coming battle was fired by Charles Millar of Houghton and took the form of a letter to the *Register* early in July. Millar claimed that 'three-fourths of those who knew the locality would without hesitation declare that the very best road from Houghton to Adelaide would be one carried through the Teatree Gully. But G.A. Anstey resides at *Highercombe* and Mr. McDonald on the Torrens, consequently the very best road must necessarily pass their own doors'. Anstey, claimed Millar, had engineered the grant of £1,000 for his road as Chairman of the Board, 'or rather the controller of the Board' for 'when the lion roareth who shall not fear' or, as the Chinese express it, 'When the ass brayeth who shall not bow his head'. The libel laws of 1850, it is apparent, allowed a freedom and colour of speech scarcely permissible today.

In the same week of July a public meeting was held at the *Bremen Arms Hotel*, Hope Valley, for 'the purpose of ascertaining the general opinion of the new intended line of road from Houghton to Adelaide as proposed by the Commissioners'.

The meeting was chaired by Richard Smith who held land on Dry Creek, near present day Modbury. Settlers in the northern sections and at Hope Valley had now found a spokesman. A map of the district was exhibited showing the proposed line of road.

The following resolutions were adopted 'without a single dissentant voice being roused':

1. That it is the opinion of this meeting that the Commissioners of Roads have consulted their own interests at the expense of the ratepayers at large.

2. That the making of such new roads from public funds is grossly unjust to ratepayers.

3   That the Commissioners are unworthy of the confidence of ratepayers and ought to be immediately dismissed.

4. That Mr. Holden be requested to forward all documents on the subject to Mr. Hanson, urging him not to sanction the appropriation of monies.

5. That a public meeting be called for this day week.

As the new road passed through Hope Valley from the Torrens it may seem difficult to explain the objections of residents of that small settlement. Hope Valley, however, was already on a line of road to Adelaide via Gilles Plains and Walkerville. Despite the winter difficulties of this line, it still carried most of the north eastern traffic to Adelaide. Many of the residents of Hope Valley, too, were Germans with relatives at Klemzig. Settlers of Hope Valley were thus more interested in the improvement of the line of road across Gilles Plains than the road which crossed the Torrens. They found a literate and able spokesman in William Holden, their postmaster and the one who had given the settlement its name. Holden, too, knew enough German to act as an interpreter for the many German settlers at Hope Valley.

By the time the next meeting was held — once again at the *Bremen Arms* — William Holden had received a reply to the resolutions of the meeting held the previous week. The reply was evasive. When advised to explain its contents to his German neighbours at the meeting, Holden replied that he would do so if someone would first explain the contents to him. The Commissioners merely informed the residents of Hope Valley that they were fortunate the road passed through their settlement at all. If it had crossed the Torrens at Dinham's Mill instead of at Paradise, the line of road would have by-passed Hope Valley completely. The settlers, however, refused to be grateful.

The reply of the District Road Board, read out at the meeting, did not refer to the objections of the settlers in the northern sections of the district that £1,000 was being expended on a road which served nobody in their area. Robert Milne of *Drumminer*, Upper Dry Creek, who was to become Chairman of the first District Council in 1853, was present at the meeting and claimed that Commissioner Anstey had 'no more mind than a schoolboy helping himself'. It was as if, he said, the Surveyor-General who had examined Anstey's line of road and recommended it had said —

'I like a goose when it is well cooked. I like to enjoy a walk in the garden. I like a glass of home-made wine. Mr. Anstey keeps a good table so the quicker a road gets me there the better'.

The meeting concluded with a call for 'Three Cheers for the Yatala League' and a threat, 'Commissioners of the Hundred of Yatala beware of the coming storm!'

The District Road Board met a month later in the *Bremen Arms*. The landlord, Hermann Freidrich Koch, probably benefited more from the burning question of roads than any of the settlers. We can imagine that many a dry argument found its way from the meetings in Hermann Koch's 'Assembly Room' to his front bar to be continued there.

At the August meeting of the board, Anstey 'speaking excitably' read out the list of objections to his fellow Commissioners who sat, it is reported, 'as mute as lambs'. The petition was signed by 97 ratepayers who had attended the July protest meeting. The objections were many and varied. The new Anstey's Hill line of road was too swampy near the Torrens, too sandy close to the foothills and too steep — objections which could, however, be applied equally to the route via Teatree Gully.

More relevant was the objection that a good road via Anstey's Hill would cut off the residents of Houghton from the Western part of the district and that the largest portion of the traffic from Houghton and Gumeracha was with North Adelaide, Walkerville, Bowden and Port Adelaide. It was this objection which in 1858 led to the split in the District Council of Highercombe, although by that time the residents of Houghton, having been by-passed by the line of road through Teatree Gully, were vehemently in favour of the Anstey's Hill road.

The petition re-iterated once again the slur that the new line of road was of advantage to two people only — Mr. Anstey and Mr. Macdonald. Perhaps it is not to be wondered at that the Chairman was obdurate in his reply to the petitioners and over-ruled all their objections.

There was only one further protest meeting for the year 1850 — this time at the *Bird-in-Hand Hotel* at Dry Creek, on the North Road. Mr. Anstey was doing all he could, it was stated, as Chairman of the District Road Board 'to have a good road to send his fruit to market'. William Holden of Hope Valley proposed 'That the Governor be memoralized to dismiss the

Commissioners of Roads for the Hundred of Yatala'. When the people of Dry Creek, Houghton, Gumeracha, Hope Valley and Chain of Ponds were all in favour of the main line of road via Teatree Gully, why must a smooth road lead 'to the snug little garden at the top of Anstey's Hill', 'for the conveyance of one man's melons and strawberries' to Adelaide.

But George Anstey was not to be downed by democratic clamor — not yet. He had one card left which he was about to play.

Meanwhile, during 1850, the Road Board had made little headway in the general improvement of district roads — partly because of the opposition it had met locally, but also because of general opposition throughout the settled districts of the colony to the Road Act of 1849. With the Dray Tax abolished and a refusal of ratepayers, particularly in the Hundred of Yatala to 'cash up', District Boards were in financial strait-jackets, and their problems, indeed, appeared insuperable.

One of the objections to the expenditure of £1,000 upon the Anstey's Hill line of road was the expense of fencing it. A quarter of the money voted would be needed merely for fencing complained the ratepayers. And yet there was no way for a constituted body such as the District Road Board to avoid this expense.

As early as mid-1846 'An Act to regulate the Fencing of Adjoining Lands' had been gazetted. This required settlers to fence in their sections and give public notification in the *Government Gazette* of their intentions to do so. It is obvious that the District Road Boards could not be exempted from the Act, especially where roads passed through private property. By 1849 when the District Road Boards were constituted much of the land in the Yatala Hundred had been taken up by settlers. Not only did the roads through private property have to be fenced but owners had to be recompensed for the loss of acreage or of easy access to their property.

In 1850, in its first year of operations, the District Road Board called for contractors willing to supply 'a considerable quantity of fencing required to define the course of the North-East Road'. The type of fencing required by the Board was that in most common use throughout the colony — post and rail. This consisted of strong upright posts having two, three or four horizontal rails morticed into the uprights. The material — split gum or stringy bark — was, in the districts around Adelaide, readily available and often close to hand.

Contractors were notified that applications would be received by the Road Surveyor, Mr. E. Prowse, *Bremen Hotel*, Hope Valley for the supply and erection of posts and rails per 100. Posts were to be 7 feet 6 inches long and to measure 8 inches by 4 inches at the top. Rails were to be 8 feet 6 inches long and to measure 6 inches by 2½ inches at each end. All posts and rails were to be of sound material.

Dressed stone was required for the formation of culverts and side drains and for 'making 2 fords over the Dry Creek near Ardtornish'. Broken stone was needed, too, as a basis for road construction, on the 'macadamized' roads then just coming into use. The road-metal specified was stone broken to a 2½ inch gauge, the gauge being a metal ring of 2½ inches diameter through which any of the stones deposited in heaps by the roadside should just pass. In 1850 the only supply of such metal, unless broken by the contractor himself, was from the government quarry on the Dry Creek (close to the present Yatala Gaol) or from the Adelaide Gaol where prisoners on 'hard labour' cracked stones from the Dry Creek quarry for the streets of Adelaide.

Tenders were also called for the removal of stumps on the new line of road, the stumps to be cut off 6 inches beneath the surface of the ground.

The formation of roads provided casual work for settlers in the district. Applications were called for eight laborers, 'men accustomed to out-of-doors work' to be employed on the public roads at the rate of 12 shillings per week and rations. At the same time the Board advertised for 'six bullocks and a dray with driver for two months'.

In 1850 tenders were also called for the erection of a bridge over the Torrens on the North East Road, for which the sum of £250 had been set aside by the Board. The bridge envisaged at that time was a Log Bridge. Events of 1851, however, led to the abandonment of the project. Indeed, in 1851 the only tenders called were for fencing a new section through Walkerville and for the formation of three miles of the treacherous road across Gilles Plains. In 1853 it was reported that the sum of money laid out on the Gilles Plains road had been wasted 'in consequence of the incomplete state of the attempted improvements'. The road-metal had, it seems, almost completely sunk back during the next winter into the mud of the Bay of Biscay soil.

There were two events in the year 1851 which made the work of the Road Board for the District of Yatala difficult, one of which resulted in work on the roads being almost completely suspended until 1853. The first event was the lively election of Commissioners for the ensuing year for the Yatala Hundred, held at the Bremen Arms, Hope Valley. The second event was one which affected the whole colony — the discovery of gold towards the end of the year in the eastern states and the departure of a large proportion of the population of South Australia for the goldfields of New South Wales and Victoria.

The meeting in the Assembly Room of the *Bremen Arms* for the election of District Commissioners was advertised for 9 a.m. on January 1. From the outset it was apparent that the well-attended meeting would be a lively one. Anstey, as Chairman, stated that he and the commissioners were present merely for the purpose of conducting the election and not to listen to the opinions of ratepayers. If anyone wished to make a speech, however, stated

Mr. Anstey, 'there was no objection to his standing up on a tub outside and doing so'.

The ratepayers, however, had no intention of leaving the meeting to have their say. Instead, such was the uproar that it was the Chairman himself who left the meeting and, getting into his phaeton, retired 'to his den at *Highercombe*'. The immediate cause of his umbrage was the accusation that the Chairman had attempted 'to get up a hole-in-the-corner meeting' by not publicising it widely throughout the hundred. Instead, the notice had appeared only in the *Government Gazette*, which few read, and on a single placard which Anstey had affixed outside of the *Bremen Hotel* in his own district. This had resulted in an unrepresentative meeting and the present election of commissioners, stated Mr. Watson of Salisbury, would not represent more than 15 or 20 out of 500 ratepayers in the Hundred.

Mr. Wells of Hindmarsh complained, too, about the lack of representation — 'It was not to be borne that a few men should be picked out from one portion of the hundred and do as they pleased with the money. If they wanted Commissioners let them go down to the plains and pick some honest men'.

The accusation was no doubt well justified. At the final count for the election only 161 votes had been lodged, many of them multiple votes of the large landholders. Clearly the meeting revealed the main weakness of the District Road Boards — the area it tried to serve with roads was too large and provided too many opportunities for sectional interests to gain control. It was a lesson which was remembered when local government areas were defined after 1852 with an introduction of the 'Act to establish District Councils'.

The main discussion which preceded the January 1 election itself centred as usual around the expenditure of £1,000 upon the Chairman's own road. A Mr. Robinson expressed the hope 'that when Mr. Anstey had made his own roads, he might perhaps make some for them *(Laughter)*'. A Mr. Chamberlain said that 'he did not see that because a man possessed a few sheep he was to rule over others *(Cheers)*'.

Nevertheless Anstey's hole-in-the-corner tactics had succeeded. Despite his absence from the remainder of the meeting (he returned merely to record his votes) and the general censure of the Chairman and the District Road Board, voting for the day resulted in the re-election of four of the five previous Commissioners. The exception was Mr. W. Cook of Hindmarsh.

It is interesting to note that one of the candidates at the election was John Ridley of Hindmarsh, the inventor of the first practical wheat-stripper. Ridley polled 13 votes. Anstey, backed by the large number of votes from other large landholders, topped the poll. The Commissioners had virtually succeeded by using their entitlement to multiple votes as large land owners to vote each other back into office. But it was a short-lived victory for the Commissioners.

At the first meeting of the 1851 District Board, held in what was now termed the District Board Room of the *Bremen Arms Hotel*, Anstey was again elected Chairman for the ensuing year. However, before the next monthly meeting of the Board could be held, the Governor, Sir Henry Fox Young, called for a new election for the Hundred of Yatala.

Instead of the 161 votes which had been cast at the January poll, a total of 454 votes were recorded at the March election. The result was a resounding defeat for George Anstey and a victory for the plainsmen who had accused him of winning the previous election by his hole-in-the-corner tactics.

Of the 454 votes cast, Anstey received a meagre 32. His fellow commissioner and friend, Howard Blyth, recorded 2. The final figures are a little difficult to explain — the great number of votes cast by the plainsmen which swamped the votes in the eastern 'hills' section no doubt reflected the access to local polling booths. Distance, especially over difficult roads, was a factor to be reckoned with by early settlers in the colony. The election was also a source of satisfaction to smaller landholders. John Chamberlain, a farmer of Enfield and the owner of a single 80-acre section, had topped the poll. Chamberlain was subsequently elected Chairman of both the District Road Board and of the Central Road Board. Ratepayers in the western portion of the hundred had now found their spokesman.

The election was of significance to the eastern section of the hundred as it saw the emergence of three other landholders in the district — George McEwin of Hermitage, Adam Robertson of Golden Grove and Samuel Shillabeer — as contestants, mainly in opposition to Anstey. Squire Anstey no doubt must have felt aggrieved to find that his previous employee in his *Highercombe* garden had polled more votes at the election than he had.

The ambitions of George Alexander Anstey were, however, not to be denied. Within a month of his defeat at the local level, Anstey had become a contestant for a seat in South Australia's first elective Legislative Council, as a representative for the electoral district of Yatala. However much one may dislike Anstey's personal and driving ambition, one can scarcely accuse him of want of courage. His new intrusion into government, as we shall note, had at least the same salutary effect on our district as it had previously — it aroused controversy and opinion and brought district leaders to the fore, even though largely in opposition once again to Anstey. It also brought settlers together at public meetings and consolidated district interests. After all, settlers had come to South Australia to establish a free society — and if possible a more democratic one than the society they had left. Democracy, they were finding, was not possible without opposition.

The new District Road Board had scarcely begun its term of office for the year (1851) when it was presented with the detailed report of the Colonial Engineer's examination of the two contending lines of the North-Eastern Road. Such was the public interest in the issue that the *South Aus-*

tralian Register decided to publish the report in full in its issue of Saturday, May 24, 1851. It still makes interesting reading with its detailed descriptions of the lines of road which we still, in the main, follow in our cars today on bitumen roads.

Hamilton, the Colonial Engineer, also examined the road from Gollop's Bridge (at the foot of Black Hill, where the village of Inglewood developed in 1857) to Chain of Ponds. 'The whole line after leaving the bridge', wrote Hamilton, 'is a constant alternation of steep rises and falls whereon it is difficult for a vehicle to keep its legs, even in dry weather'. He commented on Break-Neck Hill, where in 1863 an immense cutting was made, using little more than barrow, pick and shovel, which cars still pass through just beyond Inglewood. Hamilton stated, 'it well-deserved its appellation of 'Break-Neck' with its 1 foot in 3 feet descent on its eastern side'.

Hamilton saw little immediate hope in 'the treacherous bogs' of the line of road across Gilles Plains. The main road from Adelaide, he suggested, should be the southern branch from Payneham, which crossed the Torrens close to Joseph Ind's recently erected *Paradise Bridge Inn*. (Ind had anticipated somewhat the completion of the actual bridge) and led into Hope Valley. There was in 1851 no Highbury.

Hamilton was not certain whether the main line should pass north-east from Hope Valley through the settlers' sections to the entrance of the Tea-tree Gully gorge or follow Anstey's line of road to Highercombe and Houghton. The Colonial Engineer had made his tedious journey on horseback, for most of the way, and in the heat of midsummer.

The Central Road Board and the District Road Board could scarcely have had time to receive and read the report of their engineer, when the news arrived from the eastern states which brought work on South Australian roads almost to a standstill for the next two years. Gold had been discovered and the reports of rich finds — first in New South Wales and then in the newly formed state of Victoria — could not be denied.

Not only did work on the roads come to a halt but soon a good proportion of the working men of South Australia downed tools and headed off by ship or on horseback, and often on foot, to the diggings. The life of the young colony itself seemed about to falter. Before the close of 1851 it was not only workers, agricultural labourers and miners, who were leaving but shopkeepers, policemen, public servants and even farmers.

In our own Hundred of Yatala, much of the road grant for the year remained unexpended at the end of 1851. Income for the year for the District Road Board amounted to £1,063 — little enough it would seem to expend on the main roads of a complete Hundred. By the close of the year the Board still held a balance of £380. It is of interest to note that nearly half of the payments for the year 1851 — 15 years after the foundation of the colony — were for the removal of stumps on what was a main road no more than a dozen miles from the capital.

In the following year of 1852 the total expenditure on roads in the district for the third quarter was £26.7.3. The five District Road Boards in the colony found it virtually impossible to carry on works.

The vexed question of road-making was brought to a head in 1852. Because of the depopulation of the countryside caused by the exodus to Victoria, country districts became more than ever dissatisfied with central control of their local roads. The District Road Boards had outlived their usefulness. In November of 1852 'An Act to appoint District Councils' passed the Legislative Council. The various districts now had power, if they were able to form a local Council, to tax themselves for the management and making of their own particular roads, bridges and public buildings. By July of 1853 our district had its own Council — the District Council of Higher-combe, administrating virtually the same area as the present* Corporation of the City of Tea Tree Gully. The population of the district at that time was less than 1,500, men, women and children; the number of dwellings less than 300 and the number of ratepayers 248.

The main roads through the district were still the responsibility of the Central Road Board — termed after 1851 the Central Board of Main Roads. The District Road Boards went out of existence.

In the new District of Highercombe, the new Board of Main Roads was not able, nor perhaps willing, to make up its mind which of the two competing North-Eastern lines of road should be declared the main line.

The position, by the beginning of 1854, was summed up in a piece of advice given by a newspaper reporter who wrote in the *Observer*:

'Occasional travellers may not be aware of the fact that there are now four available roads between Adelaide and Houghton —

viz. 1. By way of Payneham across the Torrens near Paradise Bridge Hotel where a convenient ford and footbridge have been built and thence by Mr. Dordy's section over Anstey's Hill.
2. The same route as far as the end of the fenced road beyond the ford and from thence through Hope Valley via Anstey's Hill.
3. Through Walkerville over Gilles Plains by the Ardtornish School through Hope Valley and over Anstey's Hill.
4. The same route as far as Ardtornish School *(q.v.)* and thence through Teatree Gully.'

It was not until this same year of 1854 — eight years after Anstey had begun his rival road over the hills — that the Central Board reached its decision. In that year it gazetted both lines of road as main roads and thus appeared to put finis to an argument which had both united and disunited a whole district. The aftermath of the argument was, however, to come in 1858.

* 1975/6

Remember! It is next Tuesday!!

BALMORAL.

On Tuesday next, 17th Sept., at Noon,

NATHANIEL HAILES

Will sell by auction, on the Land,

THAT most picturesque of Townships, one worthy to become a

ROYAL RESIDENCE,

And therefore denominated BALMORAL, being portion of Section No. 510, the property of Alexander McDonald, Esq.

Some of the allotments are situated on

THE RIVER TORRENS,

And consist of extremely rich alluvial soil which admirably adapts them for the uses of a Market Gardener ; all have frontages to the permanent

NORTH EASTERN ROAD,

Now nearly completed, the necessarily great traffic whereon will render a

PUBLIC HOUSE

Indispensable to Travellers, and highly remunerative to the owners. Each allotment is fenced on two sides. A

FLOUR MILL

For which the locality is especially adapted, would be most beneficial to the neighbourhood.

The spot is one of romantic beauty, rich woodland scenery—a winding river—the Mount Lofty range of hills—extensive plains —and a glimpse of the Gulf in the background combining to produce a panoramic effect rarely equalled. To which may be added, that

BALMORAL

is the only place in the direct road between Adelaide and Houghton where running water exists.

Terms Liberal.

Plans may be inspected at the Auctioneer's office.

Refreshments on the Ground.

SALES BY AUCTION.

HOPE VALLEY.

E. SOLOMON & CO.

Have been instructed to submit to public auction,

On Tuesday, 24th September. at Twelve o'clock,

ON THE GROUND—

SECTIONS 305, 307, and 308, ON THE TORRENS,

KNOWN as HOPE VALLEY,

and being about five miles from town, embracing along the whole line of road, and in the locality itself, scenery which for beauty would defy the pencil of the artist to pourtray.

The Auctioneers beg to call the attention of newly-arrived emigrants and others to this most desirable opportunity of purchasing a property possessing every advantage, being well watered, good soil, and within a short distance of the

METROPOLIS.

The property has been divided into

Lots of from 2½ to 10 Acres,

To suit the convenience

OF ALL CLASSES OF PURCHASERS;

And plans of the same may be seen at the Auctioneers.

Several gentlemen have already become purchasers of allotments, with a view of immediately erecting dwellings thereon, as this spot is not only removed from the unpleasant dust of the town, but has the

FINEST VIEW of the GULF

And neighbouring scenery to be obtained in any

PART OF THE COLONY.

TERMS :

Twenty per cent. deposit, and three, six, nine, and twelve months for the residue.

A cart will leave the Mart at ten o'clock on the day of sale to convey intending purchasers.

Item 1A Sale of Township of Balmoral
September 17, 1850.

Item 1B Sale of Hope Valley sections
September 24, 1850.

10

THE TORRENS VALLEY

'extremely rich alluvial soil'

The River Torrens was the umbilical cord of the infant capital of South Australia, nourishing it with its water and the products of the rich soil of the flood plains along its winding course. Sections of land along the river frontage were eagerly sought by early settlers, and market gardens established on its fertile flats. Some of the market gardens, orchards and homes established more than a century ago along its course still remain, often hidden away in bends of the river, surrounded by the ancient red gums which gave the stream its original name 'Karra-wirraparri' *(karra = red gum; wirra = wood or forest; parri = forest)* — River of the Red Gum Forest.

Criticised by Governor Hindmarsh for selecting an inland site for the new capital, Colonel William Light lived just long enough to find his choice of site on rising ground close to the River Torrens fully justified. The water supply, although it had to be supplemented by well-water in the summer months, was adequate for the needs of Adelaide for its first few years. Gardens on the alluvial flats across the Torrens at North Adelaide were soon supplying citizens of Adelaide with vegetables and fruits.

The earliest of these gardens in North Adelaide and the finest was that of the pioneer horticulturist (and editor of South Australia's first newspaper), George Stevenson. His four acres of garden had frontage to Melbourne Street and to Finnis Street. It was here that George McEwin worked and lived with his family before he began to lay out Anstey's garden at *Highercombe*. Further downstream at the Torrens ford, not far from the present Adelaide City Bridge, was the garden of Joseph Ind, which supplied the thirsty citizens of Adelaide with water-melons in the first few years of settlement. 'One of the celebrities of Hindley Street in the early days was Joseph Ind, who was a large grower of water-melons. With a bullock dray load of these he took up a good position in the street and announced they could be purchased at 1d. per lb., and if the weather was hot and oppressive he found a ready sale for them ... and probably kept many from the public-house to quench their thirst'. Ind, with the money he made from his vegetables and water-melons, was able to establish a garden further up the Torrens, and soon afterwards, to build the *Paradise Bridge Inn*, and in the 1850s to commence the building of *Balmoral*, his family home. The handsome two-storey building, close to the North-East Road just beyond the present Paradise Bridge, is still occupied today by the Ind family — fifth generation descendants of Joseph Ind.

Villages, as well as gardens, developed along the Torrens. North Adelaide, Gilbert Town, Walkerville and Klemzig early became residential areas, making use of the fertile flats and the supply of water.

Some eleven miles of the course of the River Torrens, from just west of the Paradise Bridge to the junction of the Gorge Road and road from Paracombe, form the southern boundary of the present district of Tea Tree Gully.

One of the earliest recorded journeys into this area was that of a visitor to the colony, Dr. Imlay. The journey was made on horseback in June 1838, prior to any settlement in the area. 'Having a few days to spare and wishing to see a little of the country about Adelaide before leaving, I proposed to Mr. Hill to make an excursion in bush style to the banks of the Murray'.

'The weather proving favourable we started attended by a servant and a native black and the requisite bush equipment, at 4 p.m. on 3rd January, travelling along the Torrens in a N.E. direction till we reached a romantic valley where the Torrens leaves the mountains: here, hobbling our horses we made a large fire by the trunk of a fallen tree and took up our quarters for the night.

Allowing our horses to travel at the rate of 4 miles per hour, we estimated being twelve miles from town.

In the vicinity of Adelaide the soil is of reddish colour but as we proceeded the soil and verdure considerably improved.

About 3 miles from the mountains we passed through a belt of small trees, belonging to the mimosa [1] tribe, about half a mile wide, which appeared to extend a great way up the plain.

There was a quantity of gum resembling the purest Arabic which is exuded from fissures in the bark and adhered to the trunks in masses. The black boy was afraid to eat it but after I set him the example he was continually loitering behind to indulge in a few mouthfuls.

We breakfasted at daylight and commenced en route at six — the banks of the river were now steep and inaccessible with horses [2]. We proceeded up a gully and soon reached the summit of the range. We had now a fine view of the port and the gulph from the mountains where the river makes its exit to the plain'.

(1) Mimosa tribe, here = wattle.
(2) i.e. the Torrens Gorge. A public road through the gorge was not opened until the 1920s.

In the year following the report of Dr. Imlay's journey, a number of settlers took up land grants on the north and south side of the Torrens in the area of the present Paradise Bridge. There was a ford over the Torrens, shown in Colonel Light's 1838 survey, where present day Reids Road, Dernancourt, becomes Silkes Road, Paradise, the road names deriving from the names of early settlers in this area.

Sections on the steeper northern bank below present day Dernancourt and Highbury had river frontages of a quarter of a mile or more and a depth of up to half a mile.

Light's survey shows these sections as having been granted to — in order W. to E. of the district boundary — The South Australian Company (Section 509), John Cock of Tottenham, Middlesex (Section 510, the present area of the Paradise Bridge and Dernancourt), Rowland Hill, also of Tottenham, and remembered as the originator of penny postage (Section 515), John Abel Smith of London (Section 522), Charles Gooch (Sections 815 and 814), Angus McLaine (Section 813), William Williams (Section 811), William Pinkerton (Section 810), Matthew Davenport Hill of London (Section 809) and Richmond & Primrose (Section 38 — adjacent to the Torrens Gorge). Most of these sections, with the exception of those of Angus McLaine and Charles Gooch, were owned by absentee landlords and were before long acquired by genuine settlers — at a price.

The Boord brothers, who acquired section 510 from the original grantee, John Cock of Tottenham, paid £500 for the 134 acres of land which had cost Cock £134 a few years earlier. The section had fertile flats along the river frontage and permanent springs. By 1844, agricultural statistics showed that Alexander and Charles Boord had 14 acres of wheat, 8 of barley, 1 of potatoes and 2 of garden under cultivation and their livestock was 20 cattle, 5 horses and 8 pigs.

In 1849 the section of land changed hands again — this time for the incredible amount, at that time, of £1,300. The property, known as *Gaskmore Park* was acquired by Alexander McDonald, partly as a speculative venture. The new District Road Board had decided to abandon Light's original site for crossing the Torrens at Reids Road in favour of a ford a few hundred yards downstream and to open up a new main line of road through section 510. There is no doubt that McDonald knew of this. He also knew that it was intended to erect a bridge at the river crossing. As a District Commissioner for the new District Road Board, McDonald's information was first-hand.

In May of 1850 the District Road Board announced publicly that they intended opening a new road from the bottom of Anstey's Hill to section 510 'to the proposed bridge over the Torrens connecting the Hundred of Yatala and the Hundred of Adelaide'.

A few months later Alexander McDonald inserted an advertisement in the *Adelaide Times* announcing the sale of a new township to be named

Balmoral.

The plan of the Township of Balmoral shows 18 one-acre allotments along the eastern side of what is now Balmoral Road, to Lyons Road. This road was intended to be the north-eastern road to Hope Valley. Three large allotments — 19, 20 and 21 — are also shown. The *Royal Residence*, the Public House and the Flour Mill never eventuated, but two very fine residences, *Bickham Grange* and *Balmoral* still survive to remind us of Alexander McDonald's 'most picturesque of Townships'.

The story of *Balmoral*, now the residence of Mr. and Mrs. David Ind, is the story of Joseph Ind, the celebrated seller of water-melons in early Adelaide. Ind had arrived in South Australia in 1837 with his wife, Mary, and two children. Part of his cottage in Hindley Street became a greengrocer's shop supplied with vegetables from his city garden on the Torrens. In 1840 Joseph Ind acquired a fertile river flat of 33 acres near the present Darley Road and cleared the land of timber to grow his melons and his vegetables and built a small cottage close to the Lower North-East Road. At Adelaide's first Agricultural Exhibition in 1842 Ind won prizes for the best barley, the best water-melons and the best collection of culinary vegetables. At the second Exhibition in 1844 he won prizes once again for barley and for the best and greatest variety of vegetables on display.

Joseph Ind named his property on the Torrens *Little Paradise* after another Paradise near his birthplace near Tetbury in the Cotswolds of Gloucestershire and in 1850 added a room on to the front of his cottage and applied for a licence to sell wines, spirits and ales. Despite the proximity of another inn, the *Gardeners' Arms*, opened a few months earlier on Darley Road and a protest from its licensee, James Crowle, Ind was granted a licence. In anticipation of the proposed bridge over the Torrens nearby, Ind named his new hotel *The Paradise Bridge Hotel*. Fluttering over the hotel was a banner inscribed 'Come to the Paradise Inn', while inside the tiny public bar were inscribed the words 'Who'd thought it, melons bought it'. In 1853 Ind advertised that he hoped 'to render his *Little Paradise* on the Torrens a favourite place of resort for Pic-nic parties, newly-married couples and others who wish to find an agreeable retreat away from the dust and turmoil of Adelaide'. The little hotel, delicensed in 1916, was demolished in 1958. The name Paradise, however, survived and very early displaced the original name 'Shepley' or 'Shipley' given to the location by Arthur Hardy, its earliest settler. Ind was particular about the use of the name *Paradise*. '*Shepley* is — or was — the property of Arthur Hardy', he wrote in correcting a newspaper, 'but *Paradise* is the property of your humble servant, Joseph Ind'.

In the 1850s, while still licensee of the *Paradise Bridge Hotel*, Ind acquired allotments 10 to 20 of the Township of Balmoral and on allotment 19 began to build the cellars of the present *Balmoral* residence, although he never lived to see the completion of the building as it exists today. Ind was, however, able to see the completion of the Paradise Bridge and to be present at the opening ceremony in 1857.

Joseph Ind took a leading part in the formation of the first District Council of Highercombe in 1853, and was one of the district's first five councillors.

In 1856 Ind's wife died at *Balmoral House*, 'after having taken a cold draught of water from the Torrens'. His mother died at *Balmoral* later in the same year. In May 1865, at the age of 56, Ind was killed 'by the upsetting of a dray while returning homewards from town'. At the subsequent inquest held in the *Paradise Bridge Inn*, which he had built, evidence made it apparent that Joseph Ind was asleep when the cart, in the dusk, had hit a protection post on a culvert and overturned. At the time of the accident the cart was within three hundred yards of *Balmoral*.

Alexander McDonald retained the remaining 107 acres of the section west of Balmoral Road. He had, however, borrowed £300 of the £1,300 he had paid for the section but the sale of the *Balmoral* allotments did not enable him to clear his debts and within a year or so he was declared insolvent. In 1853 the beautiful estate of *Gaskmore Park* was advertised for sale by order of the official assignee.

Improvements to the section included 'a gentleman's residence of 9 rooms erected of stone and complete'. The historic residence, now the home of Mr. and Mrs. W.A. Gilbert at Kanangra Road, Dernancourt, has been restored to reveal its original appearance, although galvanised iron now covers the original roof of wooden shingles. The walls of the house are constructed of river pebble and pug mortar, probably one of the few buildings of this construction still standing and occupied. In 1853 the building stood in its own park of gum trees 'of immense proportions', with a six-acre garden 'massively fenced', and a separate gardener's brick cottage. The park had a frontage of eight acres to the river.

Gaskmore Park passed into the hands of Edward Clark in 1853. In the 1860s Clark sold out to George Rutherford and in 1877, when the residence came into the possession of Henry Short, eldest son of Augustus Short, first Bishop of Adelaide, its name was changed to *Bickham Grange*, *Bickham* being the name of the home of the Short family in the Village of Kenn near Exeter, Devon.

A mile or so upstream from *Gaskmore Park* was *Athelstone House*. Situated on rich alluvial flats in a bend of the River Torrens just below Highbury, the house is now relatively unknown to the public. Its history, however, is as interesting as that of *Balmoral* and *Gaskmore Park*. The present district of Athelstone, across the river, derives its name from *Athelstone House*. The house was built on what was originally an 80-acre section granted in 1840 to William Williams, a licensed victualler, of Adelaide. Two years later the property passed into the hands of Charles Dinham for the sum of £250 — three times the amount originally paid for it. Charles Dinham and his brother William began the building of *Athelstone House* from stone quarried from the cliff banks of the Torrens on the property.

In 1844 a considerable area of wheat was under cultivation on the higher land on both sides of the river and William Dinham decided to erect a flour mill powered by water from the Torrens, dammed upstream and led by aqueduct to an undershot water-wheel. The two-storey flour mill, with its second storey supported by substantial beams of river red gum, still stands close to *Athelstone House*. In the *South Australian Register* of Wednesday, July 16, 1845, William Dinham advertised the completion of his mill:

Athelstone Flour Mill

William Dinham begs to acquaint his friends and the public that
his Mill is now complete and he can calculate on a sufficiency of
water-power for full work.
Mr. Dinham's terms for grinding are S i x p e n c e per bushel;
or, to such of his customers as may require him to undertake carriage
to and from the Mill, E i g h t p e n c e per bushel.
The flour produced at Athelstone Mill is guaranteed to be equal to
any made in the Colony and it will be William Dinham's chief desire
to afford uninterrupted satisfaction.
Orders may be left and enquiries made at Mrs. Templar's,
Hindley Street, Adelaide.

It will be remembered that in 1849 *(v. Chapter 9)* G.A. Anstey of *Highercombe* held a 'monster meeting' at Dinham's Mill in order to petition for a river crossing for the new main line of road at this point. In anticipation of this, Charles and William advertised their mill once again early in 1850:

Athelstone Water Mill

Charles Dinham begs to inform the growers of Wheat that the above
Mill has undergone considerable improvements and is now ready to
receive grain to grind.

Inflation is no new phenomenon. By 1850 the charge of grinding a bushel of wheat had risen from sixpence to tenpence.

The Dinhams did not wait for the District Road Board to construct a ford across the Torrens. In March of 1850 they once again advertised: 'We feel much pleasure in informing colonists in general and especially the settlers who are locally interested that the road to Athelstone Mill has been thrown open to traffic. The ford is made and more costly improvements are sure to follow. The neighbourhood is delightful and the savings of nearly two miles in distance will attract not only those who have business on the road but pleasure parties too. In short it will enable colonists to become acquainted with a delightful locality which for want of a thoroughfare has hitherto been 'a sealed book of beauty'.

So certain were the local land-owners that the District and Central Road Board would establish the crossing and the bridge for the Lower North-East main road at this point that a huge sale of land to be known as the Athelstone Estate and to include a Village of Athelstone was advertised in September 1850. The central selling point of the advertisement was that the 'new road to Highercombe, Houghton, Chain of Ponds and Gumaraka' would pass through the new Village.

With the decision to place the crossing and the bridge further down-stream at its present site, the new Athelstone Estate was by-passed. Among the many fingers burnt in the land deals were those of Charles and William Dinham. In October of 1851, 'Charles Dinham, miller, of the River Torrens' was declared insolvent. Charles had borrowed £500 from his brother for improvements to the mill, now steam-driven, and the ford. As repayment of this debt, Charles was forced to relinquish his share in the property. The conditions were harsh. It was agreed 'that Mr. Charles Dinham shall have the little mare, Gypsy, and the best dray, harness and saddle'. He was to take his household furniture and 'nothing more beyond that and render up possession of everything within 24 hours'.

But William Dinham, too, was heavily in debt to John Green Coulls, blacksmith and coachbuilder of Hindley Street, Adelaide. In 1855, Coulls paid the sum of £4,600 to William Dinham for section 811 'together with the Mill, Steam-Engine, going gear, machinery, furniture and all things now standing on the section'. The large amount seems almost certainly the amount owing to Coulls on mortgage by Dinham. Dinham became a miller at Yankalilla and, later, both Charles and William took up farming at Rapid Bay where William died in 1869.

John Green Coulls, a Cornishman, gave up blacksmithing and took up market gardening. He enlarged *Athelstone House* which became almost a little village in itself by 1862.

The ford constructed by Dinham did not remain a public thoroughfare after the mill closed down. The story of *Athelstone House* and Dinham's Mill gradually faded from public memory, but the property is still in posession of the Coulls family after 120 years.

Oddly enough, although few signs remain of the old aqueduct to the flour mill, the concrete lined aqueduct from the Torrens Weir now passes through the property on its way to Hope Valley Reservoir.

Many of the market gardens along the river frontage have continued to supply vegetables and fruit to the Adelaide market for well over a century.

HOPE VALLEY AND HIGHBURY

'I felt inspired by hope'

Next in time to Houghton, which was laid out as a village in 1841, the township of Hope Valley was the earliest of the settlements in the present district of Tea Tree Gully. It was a village which grew haphazardly rather than by deliberate planning. An 1851 planned subdivision, some half-a-mile west along Grand Junction Road, named Hope Town, was not able however to displace the established village of Hope Valley.

Some semblance of a township began to emerge in 1842 with the sale of a few allotments of the 80-acre section of land (Section 824) first taken up as a land grant in 1839 by Jacob Pitman. The earliest of these allotments was acquired in 1841 by a friend of Jacob Pitman — William Holden. Both men and their families had arrived in the colony in the ship *Trusty* in May 1838 — Pitman from Wiltshire and Holden from Chichester.

Jacob Pitman was the brother of Isaac Pitman (later Sir Isaac) of Bath, the inventor of the system of phonography, which became known as shorthand. Jacob Pitman himself in 1846 was giving lessons in Adelaide 'in this useful and philosophical means of writing'. Holden, too, learnt shorthand from Pitman on the voyage out.

Unable to obtain employment in his regular job as a newspaper reporter, William Holden opened a store and butcher's shop on his allotment of land facing Grand Junction Road, near present Valley Road.

It was in the year 1842 that Hope Valley received its name. William Holden told the story himself in his reminiscences. 'I had gone to town and when I returned I found my premises [butcher's shop and store] had been reduced to ashes but I could not somehow feel despondent. On the contrary, I felt inspired by hope — hence the name'.

Another version of the naming of Hope Valley was published in the *South Australian Register* of April 4, 1873. It gives the cause of the fire which destroyed Holden's shop and home as a bushfire resulting from an unattended log fire.

There is yet a third variation of the story, handed down in the Wilkey family, involving a bushfire which swept the area.

The stories vary in detail but they all have in common the bushfire and the expression by Mr. Holden that all that was left for himself and those involved was 'hope'.

In the same year Holden sold four acres of his allotment to James Hill, butcher, of Adelaide.

Holden retained his dwelling which had been rebuilt following the fire.

A further eight acres of section 824 was acquired in January 1847, by Hermann Friedrich Koch, who hailed from the village of Klemzig. In June Hermann Koch applied for a licence to open a public house on the premises he built on his land, stating that 'the house was on the road to the Chain of Ponds and other populous places and was a road of much traffic'. The licence was granted and Koch named his hotel the *Bremen Arms* after the German seaport which had been the point of departure for himself and so many of his fellow-Germans at Klemzig.

The 'Assembly Rooms' of the *Bremen Arms*, Hope Valley, and of the *Travellers' Rest* at Houghton were used for many years for the district's earliest public meetings. They were at different times the headquarters of the District Road Board and after 1853, of the District Council. The old *Bremen Arms Inn* was incorporated in 1970 into the present building and lost much of its colonial character.

In 1849, Hope Valley became a postal town on the mail route to Mount Torrens and William Holden became the village's first postmaster. Mails were delivered at a cost of 4d. a letter twice a week by horse and dray which then continued on to Mount Torrens via Anstey's Hill, Houghton and Chain of Ponds. The journey from Adelaide to Hope Valley took two hours and the mails finally arrived at Mount Torrens at 6 p.m..

When the District Road Board in 1849 decided to construct a crossing at Paradise, we noted that the new main line of road led to the establishment of the Village of Balmoral along present Balmoral Road to Lyons Road. The road was then to continue through the sections now occupied by the Hope Valley Reservoir to the Grand Junction Road and the township of Hope Valley. Until the Hope Valley Reservoir was constructed in 1872 this road did indeed cross the Balmoral Road diagonally to Reservoir Road. The sections over which it passed — sections 304, 305, 306, 307, 308 and 309 — were the earliest sections taken up in the Hope Valley area before the township began. They were in Light's 1838 survey. By 1848 these sections had passed into the hands of the newly-formed Savings Bank of South Australia.

In anticipation of the development of this road, sections 305, 307 and 308 were put up for auction on September 24, 1850 *(v. Page 84)*. 'The Auctioneers', read the sale notice, 'beg to call the attention of newly-arrived emigrants to the most desirable opportunity of purchasing a property possessing every advantage, being well-watered good soil and within a short distance of the METROPOLIS'. 'This spot is not only removed from the unpleasant dust of the town but has the **FINEST VIEW OF THE GULF** and neighbouring scenery to be obtained in any part of the **Colony**'. The 240 acres were divided into lots of from 2½ to 10 acres. Sales, however, were slow.

Sales were quicker on section 306, where the 80 acres was divided up into 80 one-acre sections in 1851, and the subdivision given the name of Hope Town. Robert Stuckey had acquired the section for £3 an acre in 1849, and two years later was selling it for £9 an acre. One of the earliest purchasers was George Shaw, an Adelaide draper, who bought 6 allotments. William Goodenough bought 9 allotments, Walter Henry 2, Edward Prowse 5, but by 1853 only 22 of the allotments had been sold. Hope Town never got on to the map, and is now part of the reservoir reserve.

William Holden's little township of Hope Valley was growing, and a thriving and integrated community was developing. Edward Prowse, previously of Houghton, who had acquired four acres of land in the new subdivision of Hope Town, had become Clerk and Surveyor for the District Road Board in 1850, with his headquarters in the *Bremen Arms*. In February of 1851 Prowse also became second Master of the Hope Valley School and advertised 'to inform his friends and the neighbourhood that the Day School is now open from 9 o'clock to 4 ', and gave notice that an Evening School would be opened on three nights a week. The school had been completed towards the end of 1849 and its first master had been Mr. Dempster.

William Holden, himself an educated man, had formed a local committee in 1849 to establish a school for the growing number of children in the village. Enough money was raised to purchase one acre of land for £10, west of the *Bremen Arms*, facing Grand Junction Road. The land was invested in a Committee consisting of William Holden, Heinrich Klopper, Joseph Farrow and Heinrich Wohlers and was held in trust until 1874 when it was vested in the District Council of Highercombe.

The one-acre block was divided into three smaller allotments — No.3 for use as a cemetery (the present Hope Valley Cemetery), No.2 for a school and schoolhouse and No.1 'for parking for horses for the cemetery and school', and 'to permit and suffer the children who should from time to time be pupils of the school as a playground'.

Edward Prowse resigned as schoolmaster after only six months. In August 1853 he became Clerk of the first District Council of Highercombe.

William Holden left the district towards the end of 1851. Earlier in the year his wife, Sally, had been killed in a riding accident. Mrs. Holden and her son had set off on horseback to visit a friend and her new baby. Riding side-saddle, her foot had become entangled in the stirrup straps as she had fallen from her horse. The horse, frightened, had set off at a gallop, dragging and trampling her for half-a-mile before it stopped exhausted. Mrs. Holden died on the roadside soon after being released.

Village of Hope Valley, 1870. The building on the extreme left is 'Klopper's barn' at the corner of present-day Valley Road. Alongside the *Bremen Hotel* is the Public Pound, and Coad's cottage.

Bremen Hotel, 1872. Note the shingle roof of the early section of the hotel built in 1847.

Stephen George Dordoy and his wife Jane arrived in the colony in 1849 on the *Trafalgar*. The name of their farm *Highbury* was given in 1857 to the area nearby.

John Green Coulls of *Athelstone House*, River Torrens. Highbury pioneer.

Athelstone House, Highbury. This section was built by John Green Coulls. The present occupier is Mr. Leo Coulls pictured in 1910 with his parents Mr. and Mrs. Arthur L. Coulls.

Holden, in November 1851 obtained a position on the literary staff of the *Register* and retained his connection with the newspaper until eighteen months before his death in October 1897, at the age of 89 years. He was knocked down by a cab in Grenfell Street while crossing from the *Register* Office to catch a tramcar home. During his lifetime he became a prominent member and later Vice-President of the Astronomical Society of Adelaide. In his reminiscences he stated that during the gold-rush in 1852-3 he had been the only newspaper reporter left in Adelaide. His friend, Sir William Sowden, tells us in his reminiscences, *Our Pioneer Press*, that Holden gave up smoking when he was 45 and thereafter smoked only on the anniversary of that occasion each year.

The gold-rush had a great effect upon the little village of Hope Valley, as it did upon the whole of the young colony of South Australia. E.G. Day who had taken over from Holden as postmaster and from Prowse as schoolmaster, left for the Victorian diggings early in 1852. The school had then been offered to the German settlers for a day school if they could provide a suitable teacher.

Many of the first settlers in Hope Valley were Germans from Klemzig. Holden had befriended them and, knowing the language, acted as their interpreter.

On November 16, 1838 the *Prince George* had arrived in South Australia with two hundred emigrants, who had been assisted in their escape from religious persecution by George Fife Angas. Wishing to settle together in an agricultural community, they had been given permission to settle on a section of land owned by Angas on the north side of the Torrens. The German community gave the name Klemzig to their village after their native town and that of their pastor, Augustus Kavel. Each family had a plot of land on lease. 'At first they began', wrote J.T. Bennett in 1843, 'by digging their garden and carrying the produce to market either on their backs or in hand trucks. By and by a German would be seen with a cart drawn by a Timor pony or a single bullock. Thus these men who began with almost nothing have got in Klemzig alone 150 head of cattle, 40 horses and ponies and had, in 1841, under cultivation 167 acres of wheat, 56 acres of barley, 10 of oats and several of potatoes'.

It was only to be expected that some of the Klemzig Germans would take up sections nearby when these became available. As small allotments of section 824, which became Hope Valley, became available, German families from Klemzig began to move into the area. There were artisans as well as farmers among them. George McEwin recorded in his diary in 1847 that he had been to Hope Valley to the German shoemaker for shoes. Heinrich Klopper, who by 1853 owned 268 acres in the district, including an 80-acre section (823) in Hope Valley itself, became the first Councillor for Hope Valley in the new District Council.

Impatient with the District Road Board, the German farmers in 1849

97

built a bridge across the creek just below the *Bremen Arms*. When the Board 'allowed the bridge to fall into disrepair' letters appeared in the press complaining about the 'Hopeless Bridge on the Hope Valley Road'. One complainant wrote that he had just come into Adelaide and that 'had I not been permitted by several proprietors of sections to pass through their lands with my vehicle, the journey to town would have been impossible because the bridge at Hope Valley is in a state of collapse'. Once again Klopper and his neighbours re-built the bridge without waiting for the Road Board.

Although the village of Hope Valley had grown since it began in 1842, the population was small and even in 1867 the total population was listed in the *South Australian Gazeteer* as thirty persons 'mostly engaged in wood-cutting and farming'.

Agricultural statistics for the year 1844 reveal the names of some early farmers in the district and make it plain that even those like James Hill and William Holden, who had shops in the village, also found it necessary to farm. Hill, the statistics showed, had 3 acres under wheat, 3 cattle and 2 pigs and Holden 3 acres of wheat, 2 of barley, ¼ acre of potatoes, 12 cattle and 3 pigs. Others were John Hill (with 18 acres of wheat, 39 cattle and 2 pigs), Wm. Bixall, Edward Kalliske, J. Randall, Wm. Glastonbury and David Smith. Much of the local wheat found its way to Dinham's mill nearby on the Torrens.

Sandwiched on higher ground between the sections on the River Torrens and Hope Valley, was an area of some 500 acres of poorer land. It was not until ten years after the valley sections on the north and south were settled that this area was first surveyed into the usual 80-acre sections. In the 1850s the area became known as Highbury. The largest, and soon the most influential landholder, was Stephen George Dordoy, who with his wife, Jane, and their five children had arrived in the colony in early 1849 as the only cabin passengers on the immigrant ship *Trafalgar*. Dordoy acquired section 819 in June 1850, and soon afterwards section 820 and named his property *Highbury*. The neighbouring section (821), belonging to the blacksmith, James Hall, was known as Upper Combe. The Dordoy family may have had some connection with a Highbury in north London, but the name, like Upper Combe, may have merely been descriptive.

The name Highbury became attached to the area generally in 1857 when Hermann Friedrich Koch, who had built the first Hotel at Hope Valley, the *Bremen Arms* in 1847, erected another hotel on his southern adjoining section 817 and named it the *Highbury Hotel*. Koch's reason for building a second hotel almost within coo-ee of the *Bremen Arms* was understandable. It would be facing the new line of road from the Paradise Bridge. The *Highbury Hotel* opened a few months before the completion and opening of the first Paradise Bridge in August 1857. Hermann Koch, in advertising the opening, hoped 'to be honoured by the presence of his old and new friends'.

12

ARDTORNISH AND BEEFACRES

'the cattle fattened rapidly upon the rich succulent grasses'

To older residents of the district the name 'Ardtornish' is probably still a familiar one. Certainly a generation ago, few in the district would not have known Ardtornish Corner, where Grand Junction Road meets the Main North-East Road. The woolshed which stood near the north-west corner of the intersection was an early landmark, although many may not have known that from 1847 until 1875 the woolshed had been the Ardtornish School 'where wool-gathering of a different kind used to be practised'.

'Ardtornish' was the original name given to the area which became known later as Modbury. In common with many other early place names, and to the confusion of historians, different names were often used for the same area until one finally ousted the other. Ardtornish, in early official documents, was sometimes referred to as Dry Creek or even Gilles Plains, and later as Modbury.

The Ardtornish Estate was certainly the earliest in the Modbury area and for some years the largest — some 1,326 acres by 1853. The first section of the estate, 640 acres, was acquired by John Morphett in July 1839, acting on behalf of the purchaser, Gillian MacLaine of Batavia. The eight sections fronted Grand Junction Road on the south and present day Wright Road on the north, and east from Kelly Road to beyond the present Modbury Hospital. In 1841 Angus MacLaine, who arrived in the colony in the ship *Dauntless* in July 1840 took over the MacLaine Estate from his brother Gillian, and added to it section 813 fronting the Torrens (below Highbury), section 1561 (Ardtornish Corner) and section 1565 of 80 acres east of where the present Golden Grove Road begins. Other 80-acre sections at the Ardtornish Corner were added later.

The MacLaines came from Fascardale, Ardrishag, Argyleshire, Scotland. Angus MacLaine named his estate in the new colony 'Ardtornish', taken from his native Ardtornish in Argyleshire. He brought with him some young Scottish families to work for him — among them Duncan and Mary McCallum. An autobiography of Hugh McCallum, a son, written in 1919, records

99

that, as there was no jetty at the place of landing upon their arrival at Port Adelaide in 1840, 'the passengers were brought off in boats until reaching shallow water and then the women folk had to be carried ashore on the backs of sailors and the men had to walk through as best they could'.

At Ardtornish the MacLaines and their retinue at first established themselves in tents handy to springs in the Dry Creek, close to the present bridge in Kelly Road. The McCallums did not move out of their tent accommodation for more than a year and two of the boys, Dugald in 1840, and Hugh in 1841, were born 'under canvas'.

Angus MacLaine had taken the land near Dry Creek to establish a cattle station and a dairy farm. By 1843 the establishment consisted of 'two dwelling houses, stockyards, cow sheds, dairy and pigsties, built of brick' and agricultural statistics for 1844 show that MacLaine had 70 acres under wheat, 150 cattle, 4 horses and 20 pigs.

The Ardtornish homestead was built on the banks of Dry Creek, near the original tentsite.

The home, originally facing the creek, is now owned and occupied by Mr. Dawson Lokan and has an entrance off Kelly Road. The original shingle roof is now covered with iron and the house has been considerably enlarged and altered to give a northern aspect. The underground rooms of the original home built into the bank of the creek are still in existence and can be entered at ground level from the creek side. The walls of these rooms are two feet thick and the rooms must have provided a cool retreat during the summer months. In the present year (1976) the 80-acre section on which the Ardtornish home stood has been subdivided as a residential area.

In 1843 Angus MacLaine returned to Scotland for a time and the estate was managed by Miss Gregorson and her two MacLaine nephews. Miss Gregorson's father, we are told, was a friend of Sir Walter Scott and his name is mentioned in Scott's novel *Rob Roy*.

After MacLaine's return from Scotland he applied for a Government subsidy to erect a school on section 1561. The school, along with a teacher's residence, was completed in 1847. The building was used for both education and religious services and was under the superintendence of the Church of Scotland in Adelaide. In 1853 thirty scholars were in attendance, although somewhat irregularly.

MacLaine returned later to Scotland and died in Glasgow in 1877 at the age of seventy-nine. Prior to leaving for Scotland, in the mid 1860s, MacLaine invested his neighbour, Robert Symons Kelly, with Power of Attorney to manage the Ardtornish Estate for a period of seven years and to make payment to MacLaine (then living again in Argyleshire) 'after deduction of all necessary expenses and a reasonable gratification for his trouble'. In October 1878, the Ardtornish Estate became part of the 'Beefacres Estate' and passed into the hands of the Hart Brothers. The Ardtornish homestead and some 49 acres of land were acquired in 1862 by Mr. Henry James South.

A son, Robert Moncrieff South, took over the property after his father's death in 1901.* The Ardtornish School, no longer in use, was converted into a woolshed and remained a landmark at Ardtornish Corner until after 1900.

The 'Beefacres Estate' has an interesting history. The estate began with an 80-acre section on the River Torrens, east of present-day Sudholz Road, and another adjoining it on the north. The name *Beefacres* was given to the property by Edward Mead Bagot — 'bluff, big-hearted, honest 'Ned' Bagot as his friends called him' — shortly after he acquired it in 1853.

Ned Bagot had good reason to name his new estate *Beefacres*. The station on the Torrens was used in connection with his cattle station on the River Murray at Ned's Corner, in the Wentworth district in New South Wales. At *Beefacres* cattle were topped up for the Adelaide market after their long journey overland. 'The cattle fattened rapidly upon the rich, succulent and nutritious grasses that there abounded'. The first 'mob' was ready for sale 'when the first diggers were returning from the Victorian goldfields and sold so well that Mr. Bagot was able to pay for the whole of the estate from the proceeds'. Within twenty years the 'Beefacres Estate' comprised 2,211 acres from the Torrens to the Yatala Labour Prison. Hard times came for Bagot in the 1870s and the whole estate was sold to Messrs. Hart Bros. The 2,211 acres of the estate, sold in December 1876, realised the sum of £28,600.

In 1878 the 'Ardtornish Estate' of Angus MacLaine — another 1,326 acres — became part of the 'Beefacres Estate'. The property was then gradually whittled down until Elder Smith & Co. auctioned the last 338 acres in 1928.

Bagot established the firm of E.M. Bagot & Co., cattle and commission agents, which, two years after his tragic death in the Yatala Stockade quarry in 1886, was merged into the company still known as Bagot, Shakes & Lewis.

An interesting biography of the 'picturesque pastoral pioneer' Ned Bagot is to be found in *Pastoral Pioneers of South Australia*.

* *v. The Cyclopedia of South Australia p.700* for further details.

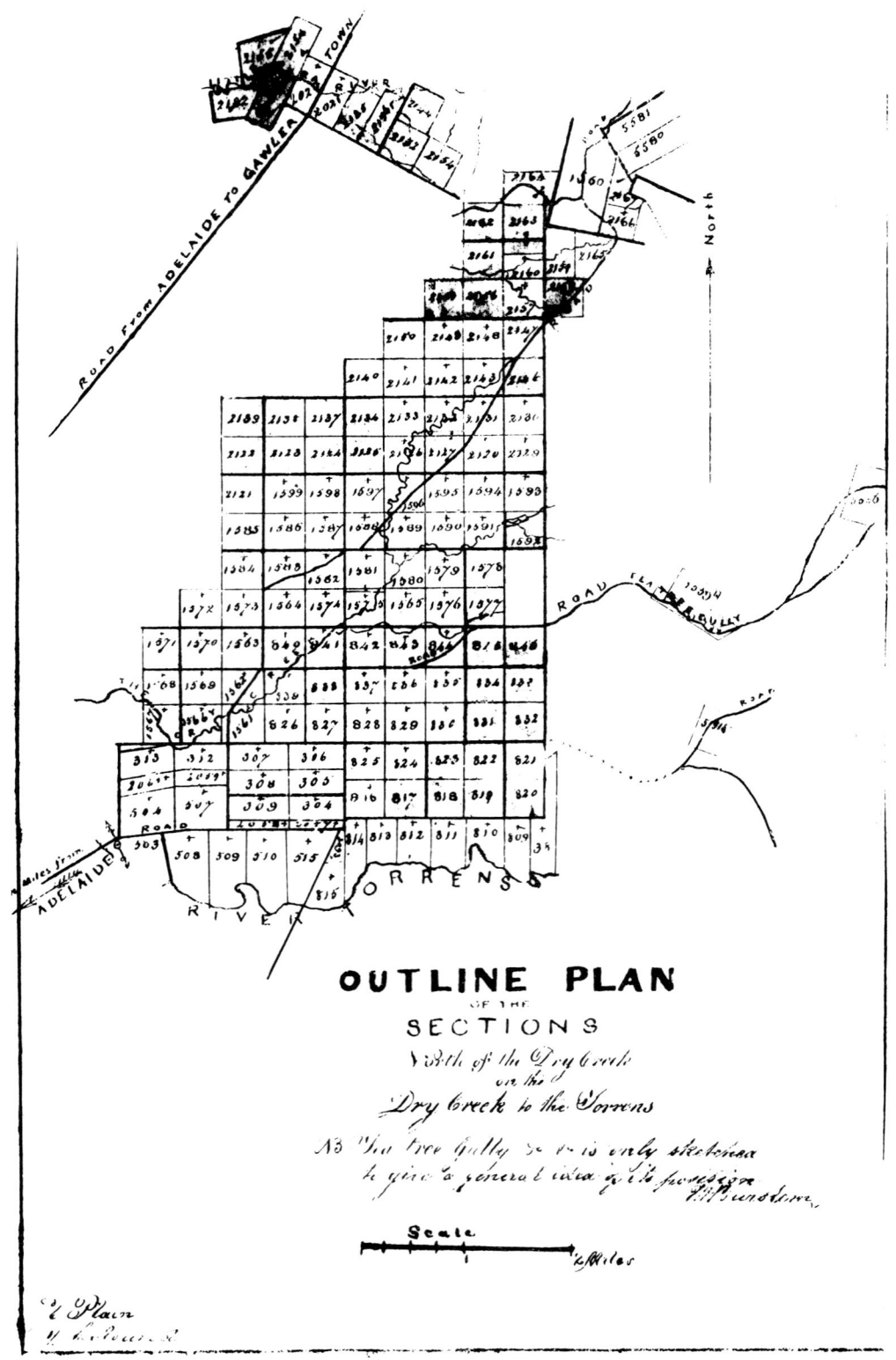

Map.7 Plan (1842) of newly surveyed sections along Dry Creek. Sections held by the S.A. Company were sections 1566-68, 1570, 1573-76, 1579-84, 1586-91, 1593-99, 2126, 2129-30, 2132-33, 2141-43, 2146, 2148, 2149, 2166. (S.A.A.)

13

UPPER DRY CREEK AND GOLDEN GROVE

'spared no expense in making himself comfortable'

The district of Tea Tree Gully is bounded on three sides almost entirely by watercourses — the River Torrens on the south, the headwaters of the Little Para on the east, and Gould's Creek, running into the Little Para, on the north. The only fully artificial boundary line is the western boundary.

Much of the rest of the district is drained by two creek systems — Dry Creek and its network of tributaries, and Cobbler's Creek at Golden Grove.

Early settlement had a tendency to follow these rivers, creeks and water-courses and the first settlers, wherever possible, selected their land astride a creek and built their homes close to springs. Along the Dry Creek and its many branches can still be found the homes of early settlers, some of them such as *Drumminor, Golden Grove House, Hillcott Farm, Greenwith* and *Eldergreen* still occupied, others such as *Ladywood Farm*, now deserted ruins.

Dry Creek first appeared on Colonel Light's 1839 survey map. Light surveyed the course of the creek and wrote 'Dry in summer' beside it on the map. This description probably accounts for the name — or misnomer — which the creek still bears. In its upper water courses, Dry Creek has many permanent springs and its banks are lined with ancient and magnificent red-gums.

This upper section of the creek which lies within the present district boundaries was often referred to as 'Upper Dry Creek', especially the section along the Golden Grove Road.

Further down the creek, where Dry Creek crossed the Main North Road, a little township began to develop in the 1840s. The settlement was officially named Montague after Sir Montague Chapman of Killan Castle, County Westmeath, Ireland, who held 4,000 acres of land in the area of Dry Creek. The name is now perpetuated by Montague Road. By 1867 the name of the little township of Montague had been replaced, except on maps, by Dry Creek.

The sections along Upper Dry Creek were first taken up in 1842 by the

South Australian Company. The sections included almost the whole of the land astride the creek and east and west of it, from Montague Road nearly to Golden Grove — an area of some 3,200 acres. Even today part of Dry Creek along the Golden Grove Road is known to older families as 'Company Creek'.

The South Australian Company was formed in London in January 1836, largely on the initiative of George Fife Angas. In effect, Angas and the Company helped in no small way to finance the establishment of South Australia by purchasing unsold land orders and by raising an amount of £200,000 with which to begin its operations in the new colony.

Among the stated objects of the Company when South Australia was reached were:

1. The erection upon their town land of wharves, warehouses, and dwelling houses and letting the same to colonists.

2. The improvement and cultivation of their country land and the leasing or sale of part of it if deemed expedient and, the object which most concerns our story.

3. The laying out of farms, the erection of suitable buildings, thereon and letting the same to industrious tenants on lease, with the right of purchase before the expiration of the lease at a price to be fixed at the time of the tenant taking possession.

The Company's ships were fitted out like Noah's Ark, carrying sheep, cattle, pigs, goats, fowls and horses, as well as a complement of passengers and a supply of tools for carpenters, brick-makers, lime-burners, blacksmiths, and boat-builders and a general cargo of everything 'from the keels of whale-ships to pins and needles'. The first three ships of the Company's fleet arrived in July 1836, five months before the arrival of the *Buffalo*. Until its arrival and the selection of a site for the capital, the Company settled their employees and livestock on Kangaroo Island, where they had made an initial purchase in London of 330 acres.

Later in the year the Company moved most of its activities to the mainland. By 1839 there were 41 tenants renting 1,273 acres from the Company. It was not until 1842 that the Company selected land along Upper Dry Creek *(See Map 7)* and along the 'Sources of the Torrens' at Gumeracha. The sections* were then allotted to shareholders of the Company who in turn could lease or sell their sections.

Most of the sections along Dry Creek were leased — many of them with the right to purchase. Unless the tenant had the right to purchase said the Adelaide *Observer* 'the tenant has no inducement to erect a superior kind of

* Sections taken up in 1842 by the S.A. Company were — 1566, 1567, 1568, 1570, 1572, 1573, 1574, 1575, 1576, 1579, 1580, 1582, 1583, 1584, 1586, 1587, 1588, 1589, 1590, 1591, 1593, 1594, 1595, 1596, 1597, 1590, 1599, 2126, 2129, 2132, 2141, 2142, 2143, 2146, 2148, 2149, 2166 *(v. Map 7 for location)*.

Left: Mrs. Adam Robertson, wife of Captain Adam Robertson of *Golden Grove Farm*, arrived in South Australia with her husband in the *Lady Lilford* in 1839. Below: *Golden Grove House*, Golden Grove. The residence, still occupied, was originally the home of the Robertson family. The village of Golden Grove took its name from the house.

Wedding of John Douglas and Margaret Clerk Robertson at *Golden Grove House*, February 1903. Mrs. Adam Robertson, seated on the ground (left) dressed in the style of Queen Victoria. Mrs. Thomas Angove is seated on her left.

Golden Grove folk c.1905. **Back Row:** Miss M. Harper, ..., Mr. Rawlings, Mrs. R. Ross, Miss G. Robertson. **Second Row:** Mr. O'Leary, Mrs. Rankine, ..., Mrs. Maidment, Mrs. Harper, A. Roberts, John Ross. **Third Row:** Mrs. F. Bowey, W. Rehn, Mrs. A. Roberts, Mr. Rankine, Mrs. Robertson, Mr. Harper, Mrs. Baldwin, A. Robertson, Miss Kennedy. **Front Row:** A. Bowey, Mr. Maxwell, F. Bowey, A. Roberts, Mr. Coleman.

homestead or to go to the expense and trouble of cultivating live fences, of planting vineyards and orchards, and of erecting farm buildings or of making other permanent improvements'. So that the land would not suffer from exhaustion of the soil through continuous cultivation, tenants were permitted to plough only one-third of their land each year.

A few of the sections along the creek were purchased outright — section 2166 by Captain Adam Robertson in 1842, Section 2156 by Thomas Roberts in 1846, section 2143 (at the intersection of present Yatala Vale and Golden Grove Roads) by James Nihill and section 1580 by Robert Milne. Milne and Robertson soon extended their holdings and established substantial homes on their estates. Both they and their families came to play a leading part in the history of the district and in its community life. Although the families have now left the district, the family homes, *Drumminor* and *Golden Grove House* have survived. *Drumminor*, the home originally built by Robert Milne, still surrounded by some of its outbuildings, has recently (1974) become a restaurant.

Robert Milne was a young man of 28 when he arrived in South Australia with his wife on the ship *Anna Robertson*. We are told that Milne was born near Aberdeen 'where he obtained a thorough knowledge of advanced Scottish farming'. For a time the Milnes lived in Gilles Street, Adelaide, and in 1843 took up land on Upper Dry Creek. The section (1580) on which the house was built and another section (1589) adjoining it on the north were bought from Henry Giles, whose father, William Giles, was the first manager of the South Australian Company.

Milne was an energetic farmer imbued with progressive ideas of agriculture. By 1862 he had 500 acres under cultivation. He was one of the very first settlers in the colony to use wire-fencing. In June of 1854 he wrote to the *Observer* advocating the general use of wire in place of post and rail and 'live' fences.

> 'Having been applied to for my opinion of wire-fencing for field enclosure I beg to say that I consider it well adapted for the purpose: that I am now using it to a considerable extent on my farm and am inclined to think that before long it will supersede the old system.
>
> I find that a 3-wire fence can be put up cheaper than a 2-rail and post fence: the cost will be 7s. per rod or £112 per mile.
>
> Under no circumstances would I recommend any party to commence the use of wire-fencing without the assistance of a person who has had some experience in such work.
>
> The wire should be painted at least every other year.
>
> I am, etc.,
> R. Milne, *Drumminer* '

Despite Milne's advocacy of the use of wire, it did not come into general use until much later, especially where timber was close at hand.

The first wire, known as 'bull wire', was thick, black, and untempered, and did not resume its shape when leant on. 'Bright wire', more tempered and more elastic, was on show at the Adelaide Exhibition of 1855, but it was expensive.

In our own district 'live' fences, in the English style, were much favoured by the first settlers. Prizes were given at district shows for the best five rods of live fence. Plants considered suitable included the common rose-bush, dog-rose, prickly acacia, boxthorn, Kaffir Apple, English furze, and olive. Remains of these 'live' fences can still be seen on many roadsides in the less closely settled parts of the district. Two men could lay down rose-cuttings round an 80-acre section in one week and 'the only expense was trimming' when the bushes grew.

Robert Milne named his property *Drumminer* after Drumminer Castle in his native Aberdeenshire. Unlike the homes of many other settlers, *Drumminer* (now *Drumminor*) was designed as a complete unit and not added to over the years. The outbuildings, too, were substantial. 'Mr. Milne', wrote a reporter in 1862, 'being living on his own freehold has spared no expense in making himself comfortable. He has a large two-storeyed house, a nice garden, a commodious cellar, large water-tank, good stone barn, stables outbuildings, etc. He considers that all machinery should be kept under cover and maintains that the first cost of putting up substantial erections is very little more than those which after a few years are worth-less'.

The title to *Drumminer* passed to a son, Spencer Alexander Milne, in 1889. A two-year-old daughter, Jeannie, in 1849, had died of burns when a kettle of boiling water had fallen in the kitchen fireplace. The open-hearth kitchen fire-place at *Drumminor* is still in existence. A second son, James Robert, had died in 1856.

Mrs. Milne died in 1908 and Spencer Milne in 1937 and the property was sold to A. and O.J. Willison of Modbury. In 1962 the home, which was in need of extensive repair, became the property of Mr. and Mrs. Gavin Sandford-Morgan. *Drumminor* was then restored and now stands very much as when it was built in the 1840s.

Robert Milne became the second Chairman of the Highercombe District Council, was a successful farmer and a member of the Agricultural Society. He died in August 1866, and was buried in the West Terrace cemetery.

The little postal village of Golden Grove derived its name from the property of Captain Adam Robertson, *Golden Grove Farm*, despite protests from the good Captain himself.

Robertson, in 1842, brought a section of land from the South Australian Company. The section he chose, section 2166, was on one of the headwaters of Cobbler's Creek, a small stream which can be seen in the gully south of the Bull and Mouth Road which leads from Golden Grove Road to Salisbury. The road received its name from the *Bull and Mouth Inn* which once existed near Salisbury. Local legend tells us that Cobbler's Creek was so named because of the cobbler who once carried on his shoemaking in a house close to the creek at Golden Grove. The legend is correct. The cobbler was Edward Barnett who carried on his business in a room of his house in the 1850s.

By 1853, Adam Robertson held nearly 1,000 acres of land south and north of the Bull and Mouth Road and had built *Golden Grove House*.

Some of this area Robertson farmed himself but in 1853 he leased 448 acres of his property to William Bennett and Edwin Hall placing the following provisos upon the lessees:

1. That they fence in unenclosed sections with gum posts and gum rails or with iron wire in lieu of rails or with iron posts and wire.

2. That in five years they would sow the seed of a plant the prickly thorn called the Kangaroo Island Thorn around the pieces of fenced land in which cereals or other grain crops are cultivated.

3. That they would not plough up any lands forming the natural outlets of water.

4. That they would remove all stones from the said lands under cultivation previous to crops being sown.

5. That they would not impound any cattle belonging to the said Adam Robertson because of insufficient fencing.

6. That they would deliver wheat to the said Adam Robertson in lieu of money for the yearly rent in the following proportion, namely: two bushels of wheat for each acre of land the wheat to be the produce of that harvest.

Captain Robertson and his wife, Elizabeth, and son and daughter came to South Australia as cabin passengers on the ship *Lady Lilford* in September 1839. For some time, as no doubt befitted an ex-sea-captain, the Captain and his family resided at Encounter Bay, before taking up land on a branch of Cobbler's Creek. His widow's obituary in the *Advertiser* in 1888 tells us that Robertson named his property *Golden Grove* 'after the ship he last commanded'.

When the people of the locality, then known vaguely as the Little Para, decided to establish a school for their children, Adam Robertson presented the subscribers with an acre of land and granted permission for the school to be named the Golden Grove School. The building was to be used 'for religious worship and sectarian education'.

There was, however, no township of Golden Grove. It was not until

1859 that the district got its first postal service. The residents, after petitioning the Postmaster-General for some years, finally invited a local correspondent of the *Register* newspaper to plead their cause. 'There is', he wrote, 'scarcely a place in the colony which has not a Post Office and at least a tri-weekly mail; but here within fourteen miles of town we are without either and must trudge three or four miles for our epistles and be dependent on the butcher or the casual traveller'. The correspondent's appeal was successful and a postal service was eventually granted.

The letter to the paper, however, offended Captain Robertson, since the correspondent had given the address as Golden Grove. '*Golden Grove*, wrote the incensed Captain, 'is the name of my farm and not of the country round about'.

The correspondent replied that apparently Mr. Robertson had forgotten that he had conferred the name on the school some years before 'and the settlers cannot be blamed for extending it to the village'.

When the local store also became the local Post Office in 1859, it was, however, designated the Golden Grove Post Office. Officialdom had set its seal on the name.

Adam Robertson died in 1864 at the age of 59. His son, John, took over the property and added vine-growing to agriculture. John Robertson was a member of the Tea Tree Gully Council, both as councillor and Chairman. He was President of the Royal Agricultural and Horticultural Society from 1893 - 1894. He left a family of three sons and six daughters.

Golden Grove house and farm was sold in 1930 to Mr. and Mrs. A.J. Strachan. Much of the estate was sold to a sand mining company in 1972. The home, a handsome freestone structure, added to an earlier structure at the back, still remains although, with valuable deposits of sands lying beneath or close to the home, its future remains in jeopardy.

14

TEATREE GULLY*

'people go miles for water there'

Teatree Gully might have remained no more than the name of one of the many gullies entering the hills face zone of the Mt. Lofty Ranges but for two deciding factors. One of these was that the gully provided a gradient negotiable to bullock wagons seeking a way over the ranges to the fertile valleys beyond.

The other factor, even more important and decisive, was that the gully contained (and still does) permanent springs. It was in the black swampy soil around and below the springs that the native tea-tree flourished which gave the gully its name.

There were other gullies entering the hills face zone in the Teatree Gully Range, some of them, such as Water Gully, containing springs but none providing easy access to the summit of the range. There was, too, the valley of the Torrens bordering the district, which cut right through the range itself to the east. Its sheer gorges and winter torrents, however, made it impassable to vehicles. It was not until the 1920s that a public road through the Torrens Gorge was finally opened up.

But for Squire Anstey's private piece of enterprise in laying out a rival line of road over Highercombe Hill (now Anstey's Hill) in 1841, the road through Teatree Gully would without doubt have been declared the main North-Eastern Road as early as 1849. As it was, the argument which raged over the two competing lines of road was not resolved until 1854.

This lack of decision by the Central Road Board inhibited the establishment of any villages and land sub-division in the northern sector of the district. It explains why the villages of Tea Tree Gully and Modbury were the last in the district to be established, with the exception of the hills settlement of Inglewood. Houghton and Hope Valley were on established lines of road and had begun to develop twelve years before. They had a well-developed communal life with shops, churches, schools and hotels by 1854

* For explanation of the two forms of the name and of its use in the text of this book (*v. Page 10*).

when the little villages of Steventon (Tea Tree Gully) and Modbury first began to make their appearance. It is reasonable to conjecture whether, indeed, there would have been any township of Tea Tree Gully at all if Anstey's Hill had been favoured as the main line of road. Teatree Gully might have perhaps remained, like many other neighbouring gullies, merely a gully, its rich soil the private domain of some market gardener.

There was little chance however that the advantages of Teatree Gully as the route of a main line of road would be overlooked by the Commissioners of the Central Road Board.

A track through the gully and over the range had been in use even prior to survey and occupation of most of the district. There is no record of who first probed the gullies looking for a way over the hills to the north-east. John Barton Hack must have used the track when he took up his part of the special survey on the source of the Little Para at Paracombe in January 1839. The track must by then have been quite passable for vehicles, as Hack wrote in 1839, 'Mrs. Hack was desirous of seeing the new country we had taken out [i.e. at Paracombe] and after we had moved our dairy to the Little Para Survey, I drove her out in a phaeton I had purchased, up the Teatree Gully and over the survey'. There was then no cutting at the top of the gully and Hack wrote, 'I had a man on horseback with tandem traces to help up the hills'.

In 1840 the track was somewhat improved, at least in its steep upper section, by cuttings. In giving evidence under oath in 1865 to a Select Committee of the House of Assembly, John Tregeagle stated that he had made the cuttings under the direction of 'The South Australian Company and Squire Williams who used to live at *The Hermitage*'.

Most of the traffic on the road through Teatree Gully was, at least after 1842, not local. Increasingly it was traffic from the agricultural sections opening up around Chain of Ponds and from the new district of Gumeracha. Indeed, until Anstey opened up his road down Highercombe Hill, all traffic from the north-east passed through Houghton and down Teatree Gully to the plains and Adelaide.

The other advantage of the route via Teatree Gully — the permanent springs in the gully — was one well-known to every bullock driver on the road. In 1865, every witness examined by the Select Parliamentary Committee concerning the Teatree Gully Water Reserve, testified to the value of the springs to travellers.

When asked by the Commissioners if the springs were of value to people travelling from a distance, Robert Symons Kelly of Modbury replied, 'Yes, it is the only water available from Gumeracha Bridge to town'. Similarly, when asked if the water was of considerable value to the local inhabitants, Kelly replied, 'Yes, people go miles for water there'. These were answers which all the witnesses were subsequently to give.

There can be little doubt that it was the presence of natural springs in

Tea Tree Gully Steam Flour Mill, built in 1853, was the first building to be erected in the Village of Steventon (Tea Tree Gully). Part of the building still remains at the entrance to the gully.

Tea Tree Gully Hotel, built 1854. The driver of the coach is *Billy* Kelton and the ostler at the horses' heads is probably Walter Beames c.1886.

Woodcutter's yard, Teatree Gully Hill, with William Watts, Rosa Sparks Watts, and baby c.1885.

Woodcutters' bush-hut in the Teatree Gully Range, in 1900. The young man is Edward Thomas.

the gully which first brought people into it — probably before any track passed through it.

The first settler in the Teatree Gully itself was the Cornishman, John Tregeagle and his wife, Ann, with their five children — Elisbeth, William, Mary, Jane, Richard and a baby born on the immigrant ship, *Java*. The *Java* arrived at Port Adelaide early in February 1840 and, according to John Tregeagle's sworn testament in 1865, he and his family came to live in the gully in the same month of 1840. As this date precedes by two years the survey and sale of any land in the gully, it can only be presumed that John Tregeagle was 'squatting' on the land, perhaps for Squire Williams or for John Morphett, who in 1842 became the first owner of the section.

Tregeagle was a Cornishman from Tregony and had taken passage as an assisted immigrant willing to undertake work as an agricultural labourer. His real occupation, however, was that of a miner but until 1841 when minerals were first discovered in the new colony, miners were not required. Tregeagle's mining experience, however, most likely found him his first job — that of cutting the track through the gully for Squire Williams of *The Hermitage*.

Tregeagle was thirty years of age when he first came to live in the gully and built his home. It is more than likely that the 'good-natured lassie' who lent young Charles Wilson the tin pannikin *(v. Prologue)* when he and his companion were making their journey through the gully in 1842, was one of John and Ann Tregeagle's children. Wilson also mentioned other low cottages which 'ran along the precipitous side of the road'. One of these must have been the cottage of John McGilton. McGilton and his wife, Ellen, and two children had arrived in the colony in 1839, sailing in the *Alice Brooks*, a tiny immigrant ship of little more than 200 tons.

In June 1842, John McGilton and his family came to live in Teatree Gully, renting a small but fertile area of one and three-quarter acres from the owner of the section, John Morphett.

This was the month when the section was first surveyed and taken up as a land grant by Morphett. The section — number 1559 of the Hundred of Yatala — was a large one of 134 acres of irregular shape. It included, as it was specifically designed to do, almost the whole of the gully *(See Map 8)* and included the springs and almost all of the rich, arable soil of the gully. As Morphett was well aware, it was a most valuable section of land — probably the most desirable single section of land in the district.

However it was not Morphett who profited most from the natural attributes of the fertile section. He managed to double the amount of £134 paid for the section in 1842 when he sold it in 1851 to the Adelaide architect, William Weir. But Weir only four years later disposed of the section for £1,000 — a truly enormous sum by 1855 standards and probably a record in the colony at that time for a single country section of land.

One explanation for the inflated price was undoubtedly the gazettal twelve months earlier of the road through the gully as the main north-east line of road. This, coupled with the possession of the springs (a possession to be strongly disputed by 1865 as we shall note) and the undoubted fertility of the black soil is probably quite sufficient to explain the high price paid in 1855 by its new owner, George Dickerson, for the section.

There was, however, an even simpler explanation of the price — the appearance in 1854 at the entrance to the gully of the beginnings of the little village* of Steventon, later to be known as the township of Tea Tree Gully. The first building in what was soon to become an important village was a flour mill. The erection of the stone mill on the north-west corner of section 5630 at the gully's entrance was not completed until 1854. Part of the mill can still be seen abutting the main road on the southern side on entering the gully. There must have been great activity in the neighbourhood throughout the year of 1854. The end of the year saw the new village with three shops, numerous houses and two hotels. In the following year the first District Council Chambers were built near the entrance to the gully.

As all this activity took place after the formation of the first District Council, the story of the development of the village of Steventon — and of the villages of Modbury and Inglewood — will have to find its place in the next section of this book. It is time to return to Teatree Gully itself and to discuss two final matters — the use made of the rich soil in the gully and the origin of its name.

The fertile section of land in Teatree Gully remained, until 1850, an isolated one. The sections surrounding it — most of them steep and cut by gullies or of poor soil — were among the last in the district to be taken up.

The gully itself, however, held a little community of farmers from 1842 onwards and through the gully passed an increasing procession of traffic. The first occupants were small farmers, renting pocket-handerchief flats of land along the gully bottom. A statistical survey of the agricultural districts of South Australia published in 1844 shows that in the 'Little Para' district five families held small areas of land in the gully.

Oddly enough to us today, the main crop grown in the gully was wheat. The hills were still looked upon in 1844 as more suitable for the growing of cereals than the plains. The principle of 'dry farming' in the lower rainfall area of the Adelaide plains had still to be learnt. The other main crop in the gully was that essential staple of farm diet — potatoes.

The statistics state that John Ellis had two acres planted with wheat and one with garden. A Mr. Hill had three acres under wheat and kept two cows and a pig. John Lee had another 3½ acres planted with wheat, half an acre with potatoes and possessed three cattle. John Tregeagle, the first

* The use of the word 'village' in this section of the book is deliberate. In the period under survey it was the term most commonly used, migrating to Australia with the first English settlers. Only later did the words 'village' and 'township' become interchangeable. 'Villages' gradually disappeared from view and 'townships' took their place.

116

settler in the gully, had an area of 2½ acres planted with wheat, half an acre with potatoes and had two cows.

The fifth farmer in the gully was John McGilton who, according to the 1844 statistics, had 1½ acres wheat and half an acre of garden under cultivation and was the possessor of sixteen cattle and one pig.

Looking at the gully today it is difficult to see where the twelve acres of wheat could have been grown by the five families. Perhaps the easier slopes of the gully may have been planted. The area planted by each of the tenants was small but the sowing and reaping of the crop was still a manual task in 1844.

The little farms in the gully were not self-supporting, and the men and boys sought seasonal work on larger holdings in the neighbourhood, mainly, in the 1840s, with Squire Williams of *Hermitage*. Williams employed eight men and two boys and in 1844, one hundred and twenty acres of wheat were cropped at *Hermitage*, yielding twenty-five bushels per acre. When asked, 'What wages do you give your reapers?', Williams had stated, '17s.6d. per acre, without rations, for cutting and binding'. The men also found casual work erecting three-rail fencing around new sections at 4/- per chain.

The wheat grown was either ground into wholemeal in the home by hand machines or, if the quantity was sufficient, taken to Dinham's mill on the Torrens at Highbury, or after 1854 to the mill erected by S. Camper & Co. at the entrance to Teatree Gully.

Another family moved into the gully in 1847. George Dickerson and his wife, Phoebe, and two children had arrived in the colony on the ship *China* on December 15, 1847. The family took over, as tenants of John Morphett, the part of the gully previously held by John McGilton and the cottage which McGilton had built. In 1846 the McGiltons took up the sections of land at Hermitage which have remained in the family ever since. The pioneer home which John McGilton built on his new section, probably in 1847, of pug and wattle is still standing alongside the Lower Hermitage Road.

George Dickerson in 1852 acquired section 5640, adjoining Tea Tree Gully on the north, a section which later became the site of a valuable sandstone quarry. In 1855 Dickerson took over the whole of the original Teatree Gully section of one hundred and thirty-four acres from William Weir, paying Weir as we have seen, £1,000 for the land and houses, £500 of which remained on mortgage to Weir. Dickerson, by 1857, had acquitted the mortgage and so secured the property to himself, living on it with his family almost until the time of his death in 1889, leasing or selling portions of it from time to time.

The name Teatree Gully first applied merely to the gully itself; later to the township at its eastern entrance and to the surrounding range of hills; in 1858 the name was given to the district generally and to its District Council;

after 1935, when the District Councils of Tea Tree Gully and of Higher-combe amalgamated, the name was applied to the whole of the combined local government district. In 1968 the name was given to the new city which had emerged, the City of Tea Tree Gully.

But the name itself has wider Australian connotations, as well as its own local story.

The word 'tea-tree', a popular name which has been applied to many specimens of the Melaleuca and Leptospermum family of trees, was first used in 1769 by the crew of Captain Cook's ship, the *Endeavour*. On his first journey to New Zealand, Cook recorded in his Journal that his surgeon had gathered leaves of the Leptospermum bush which grew in swampy coastal areas and 'brewed a tea which he pronounced to have an agreeable flavour'. The crew apparently conferred the popular name 'tea-tree' on the bush.

At Dusky Bay, in New Zealand, the ship's surgeon had also used the leaves of the same coastal tree (named by the ship's botanist, Joseph Banks, Leptospermum scoparium) mixed with spruce to manufacture a beer to help combat scurvy among the crew.

Later, in New South Wales, bushmen and settlers, short of imported tea, made a satisfactory brew from the dried leaves of different species of tea-tree.

In 1862, Ebenezer Ward, then a journalist, later a member of the South Australian parliament, visited *Highercombe* estate, established by Anstey but in 1862 the property of the Premier of South Australia, the Hon. G.M. Waterhouse.

Ward wrote in his published account, 'There are three detached gardens upon the estate. Two of these are situated in the tea-tree swamps'. Ward also recorded the use made of the leaves of the shrub for tea-making — 'We understand that tea made from the tree that grows wild in these swamps, and from which they take their name, was formerly used by labourers in the vicinity and, although not equal to Souchong, it was pronounced extremely palatable'.

Botanically speaking, the Swamp or Silky Tea Tree belongs to the Myrtaceae or myrtle family of plants. Still botanically speaking, the swamp species which grew so thickly in the gullies of the Adelaide Hills was of the species Leptospermum lanigerum. Recently, to further confuse the layman, the specific name has been changed to Leptospermum pubescens. The trees at their best grow to a height of 6 metres and flower in summer, each flower having five white petals.

We are told by an early settler, Pastor Finlayson, that when the first colonists arrived the River Torrens was covered in the bed of the stream 'with a thick, close and beautiful growth of tea-tree with a great variety of aromatic flowers and shrubs which delighted us who had been so long at sea'.

The tea-tree did not long survive the coming of settlement. Settlers

118

soon discovered that the tough wood of the shrub had an inbuilt resistance to water. The damp gullies where it grew were ideal for market gardening and the tea-tree was cleared. Because the wood did not readily rot the thicker stems of the tea-tree were used to fence in swampy areas. The saplings were used as 'wattles' in the weaving of fences for enclosures.

In Teatree Gully, the native tea-tree once grew in thickets around the springs. Even by 1865 it had not all been cleared. In that year George McEwin of *Glen Ewin*, in giving evidence to the Water Reserve Commission said, 'At that place I can state that a few specimens of the tea-tree plant were left as a memento of what was growing there and it is growing there now'.

Today, none of the tea-tree which gave the gully, and later the City, their common name, remains in the gully itself. Specimens of leptospermum still grow however in the Torrens Gorge along the district boundary section.

On its becoming a city, the Corporation adopted the five-petalled flower of the tea-tree as its emblem and, as its motto, the words:

'In leptospermo spes futuri'

A literal translation of the Latin phrase is, 'In the tea-tree is the hope of the future'. Less literally, the phrase seems to imply, perhaps, that our hope for the future depends on what we have made or are making of our past. Like all good mottoes, the phrase may be paraphrased as the individual so decides.

15

ABORIGINAL CONTACTS

'waste and unoccupied lands'

Few records survive of contact between the early settlers in the district and the original Australians — the Aborigines. The Adelaide Plains were occupied by a local group, the Kaurna (pronounced cow-r-na), when the first settlers arrived. The 'Adelaide Tribe' probably numbered, however, less than 300 men, women and children, divided into nomadic family groups or clans in possession of a hunting territory which extended from Cape Jervis in the south to Crystal Brook in the north and included the Mt. Lofty Ranges.

There is good evidence to suggest that the Aborigines of different tribes at first regarded the invasion of their territories by an alien people as a temporary situation. 'Don't I remember', wrote a migrant on the *Buffalo*, 'how shortly after our arrival the blacks wished to drive us back into the sea. They started fires in the hills, hoping the wind would carry it to the plain and burn us out. We would then be compelled to take ship and go away. Looking towards the hills in the evening we beheld a most magnificent sight. They were one great blaze of light'.

One of the earliest recorded contacts with the Kaurna people was made by James Cronk, then a young man of 25, who settled in Modbury in 1842 and died at his home in Wright Road in 1904 at the age of 93.

Before he arrived in South Australia in 1836 young James had been 'apprenticed to the sea' and had made voyages to the Cape of Good Hope and to Van Diemen's Land.

He returned to London and in 1836 sailed for South Australia on the *Africaine*, a barque of 316 tons, and the first ship to bring paying migrants to the colony. Cronk came as a steerage passenger, engaged as an 'agriculturist' to John Brown, an Emigration agent and a cabin passenger on the *Africaine*.

The ship arrived in Nepean Bay, Kangaroo Island on November 2, 1836 and finally anchored in Holdfast Bay (Glenelg) on November 10. James Cronk was present at the Proclamation of the colony a few weeks later.

Cronk was a Cockney, born in Tottenham. In November 1837 he wrote a letter to his mother, sisters and brothers living at Globe Road, Mile End, Stepney. Cronk's letter tells of his interest in the native inhabitants and of how he began 'to talk their language very fair considering the short time I have been here'. Indeed, a few months after writing this letter, Cronk was appointed official interpreter by the Governor.

In his letter home James Cronk described his meeting with the natives — for them their first meeting with a European. 'I was the first person', wrote Cronk, 'as ventured over the hills in search of them. I fell in with them about eighteen miles from town: there were thirty-five in number. The women and children was very frightened when they saw me, as I was the first person they have ever seen. They gave a shriek; the men took to their spears but did not offer to throw them at me.

The men were quite naked, as that is their usual way here in the woods, for they could not climb the trees with clothes. They use a stick in getting up; they chip a piece of bark out to place their foot in every step until they come to the limbs of the trees ...

The sun was just going down when I fell in with them: I slept but little that night: one of the natives kept singing and beating two sticks until day-break, which I thought was to keep watch.

The next morning I went out a hunting with them: the women and children was so frightened of my gun that they would not go with us; they all seemed astonished at it sending a bullet three inches in a tree at a distance of about 200 yards. I shot a quantity of birds and they got several opossums, so we had a sumptious feast.

The next morning I persuaded them to come down to our tents, the women objected to this at first. I then made motions to them that I would give them plenty of sugar and biscuit, then they consented to come; but when the women saw the ships in the bay they stared with astonishment to look at them.

They stopped close to my tent that night; the next day they went away: they came down again in about a fortnight afterwards and had several corrobories: but now they stop about town and fetch wood and water for the people for some bread'.

Cronk was appointed native interpreter in March of 1838. The letter of William Wyatt, Protector of Aborigines, recommending the appointment of Cronk stated, 'I have twice communicated with a person called James Cronk and find he is willing to accept the vacant position provided that he can obtain thirty shillings a week and rations.

The high character borne by Cronk and the confidence placed in him by the Aborigines render him extremely eligible to fill the situation. He is now getting 25 shillings per week as a survey labourer.

I may also add that he is the only man in the colony whose knowledge of the Aboriginal dialects is sufficiently extensive to be made immediately available'.

Joseph Barritt, one of the earliest settlers at Paracombe, also enjoyed friendly contacts with the local Aborigines. In a letter to his parents in England in 1840, from Paracombe, Joseph wrote:

'We have but little to fear from the natives and wild beasts; the former are harmless people, with the exception of two instances before I came of killing three whites whom, I believe, were more in fault than the blacks.

I have had as many as twenty come to the house at once begging for victuals but it is no use to encourage them, as otherwise you never get rid of them. Their usual phrase is, 'Give me bicketty. Me very hungry'. I tell them they can get plenty opossum, Kangaroo. They will say, 'Possomy no good — kangaroo long way off — white man plenty bread — plenty bullocky — plenty sugar, plenty rice ...

I have come from Adelaide at all times of the night and never seen the least to fear from them'.

Such friendly relations as Cronk and Barritt experienced were short-lived. The newcomers showed no signs of leaving and the Kaurna soon realised that they were being dispossessed of their hunting-grounds, animals and water-holes. Their fate had indeed been decided in London in 1834, when in the Act to establish a new colony in Southern Australia, South Australia was declared to consist 'of waste and unoccupied lands', thus failing to recognise the existence of land rights of Aborigines.

One of the stated objectives of South Australia's first governor, Captain John Hindmarsh, in his capacity as Protector of Aborigines was 'to protect them in the undisturbed enjoyment of their proprietary rights to such land as may be occupied by them in any special manner' — an objective nullified by the mere act of remaining in occupation of their tribal lands.

Conflict between the native population and the settlers was inevitable. 'The colonization of the Adelaide Plains and adjacent lands had a profound impact upon the Aborigines and brought their way of life to an abrupt end', but it was an end which was not without bloodshed and recriminations.

'They [the Aborigines] have at Adelaide and its vicinity killed many sheep', wrote W.H. Leigh in 1839, 'alleging in excuse —

'White man kill black man kangaroo. Black man kill white man kangaroo'.

Killing of each others animals occasionally resulted in the killing of each other.

The earliest — and perhaps only — incident in our district involving a murder and the subsequent hanging of a native occurred in April 1839.

The tragic incident took place close to the River Torrens, near the present Hope Valley Reservoir. Early one Sunday morning, Arthur Hardy, whose sheep-station at 'Shepley' (now Paradise) was then the furthest out on the Torrens, heard a cry from across the Torrens. 'Pushing his way through the dense growth in the bed of the stream he discovered an old shepherd who had been speared by the natives'.

An official report of the Inspector of Police, James Stuart, made on the following day, reveals details of the attack. Stuart reported that he had received information that 'a shepherd of Osmond Gilles, Esqu. had been murdered that morning by natives'. Stuart and the Police Superintendent had immediately proceeded to Gilles' sheep-station on the Torrens and there found the shepherd, William Duffield, lying on a litter dangerously wounded. Upon questioning, the shepherd stated that some natives had demanded sheep and when Duffield refused the demand 'he was struck a violent blow on the back of the neck with a waddie and fell senseless to the ground. The natives then proceeded to pull down the small clothes of the man and thrust a small spear into his body just above the pubes. When the shepherd recovered the natives had disappeared.

'He managed to crawl in his wounded state to the brow of a hill overlooking the river and called for assistance'.

This is when Arthur Hardy heard the shepherd's cry for help and came to his assistance.

The colonial surgeon arrived at the scene shortly after the police and ordered Duffield to be removed in a dray to the home of Osmond Gilles in Adelaide. The shepherd died of his wounds 48 hours later.

Tracked by the police for seven days, the native, George, was finally arrested near the Little Para River. At the trial which followed, 'George' was found guilty of murder and executed on a scaffold erected on the North Parklands.

Aborigines frequently passed through the district, sometimes from the River Murray, on their way into town. 'In Adelaide and neighbourhood, most of the men and women are supplied with some kind of covering. One may be seen wearing a shirt, another a pair of trousers. I remember observing a man whose only article of dress consisted of an old hat'.

In 1858 a group of 120 Aborigines from the River Murray passed through the district and set up an encampment near the S.A. Company's flour mill at Hackney. They had come into town 'to obtain supplies of various kinds, blankets, twine for nets, fishhooks and tomahawks'.

After 1845 such handouts became official and regular 'to protect them from the cold and at the same time prevent our wives and daughters being put to the blush as is now so frequently the case'.

To keep the natives out of Adelaide it was arranged to take rations out to certain collection points. One of these was at the Torrens crossing at Paradise. Local reminiscence has it that the Aborigines would hold a corroboree on the Torrens on the first night, then at Houghton on the second night before returning to the river.

Such issues of rations and clothing were later on made by local councils.

Reminiscences have been handed down to us of corroborees held on a district reserve near Tea Tree Gully, probably on Haines Memorial Reserve.* Lads from the villages gathered, at a safe distance, on the hillsides around the camping ground to watch the Aborigines performing their ceremonials by moonlight. The scene would be lit up on darker nights by long, flaming sticks held high by the dancers as torches. There is an excellent painting of a similar Kaurna corroboree at Burnside in possession of the Art Gallery of South Australia.

James Cronk, too, had his stories to tell. He retained his position as native interpreter until the end of 1840. The *South Australian Royal Almanack* of 1840 informs us that 'James Cronk, Native Interpreter' lived in Halifax Street. In 1842 he settled on a section of land he acquired at Modbury and built his home. In later life Cronk related stories of precautions taken by his wife and children against the possibility of marauding Aborigines during his absence. Items of garden and farm equipment would be placed inside the house and the doors locked.

Another story is told of Hannah Roberts and her children of *Greenwith*. On one occasion, when her husband Thomas was absent for some time from home, natives became troublesome in the Golden Grove area. Fearing trouble following an incident one day, Hannah Roberts waited until nightfall. It was winter and raining and the creeks were in flood when Hannah left her home to seek protection, carrying her baby, with the other children following on foot. Somehow she made her way under cover of rain and darkness across the range of hills to the home of her neighbours, John and Agnes Smart.

We need not vouch for the exact details of such stories — they were only too familiar in the early years of settlement.

One former camping and meeting place of the Kaurna tribes was by the Little Para where the present Snake Gully Bridge crosses the stream. Here there are permanent springs and waterholes. In 1848 two 80-acre sections (Sections 2174 and 2175), bordering the Little Para at these springs, were set aside as Aboriginal reserves. No doubt corroborees had been held for centuries on the small river flat below the present bridge. Such reserves, however well-meaning in intention, were of no use to nomadic tribes deprived of their hunting grounds. By 1853 the sections had been leased to Thomas Roberts of Golden Grove and after 1900 were subdivided into eleven smaller sections and sold.

There is little trace of the Kaurna people of the Adelaide Plains left today, apart from contemporary paintings held by the Art Gallery of South Australia and a fine collection of weapons of the Kaurna Tribe preserved in the South Australian Museum.

Among all the placenames in the district of Tea Tree Gully, only the

* v. Also, Reminiscences of Mrs. E.M. Everton. S.A. Archives.

name of the Hundred within which the district boundaries are situated (the Hundred of Yatala) and the name of a stream, the Little Para, remind us of the tribe which once roamed through the area. Yatala was the name applied by the Weira group of the Kaurnas to the area north of the Torrens, extending from Port Adelaide to Tea Tree Gully. The particular section of Yatala within our own district was known to the Aborigines as Kirra-Ung-Dinga — 'the place where the Red Gums grow by the creek' — referring it seems to the Dry Creek.

The literal meaning of Yatala is, according to early authorities, 'Water running by the side of a river' — perhaps referring to the Torrens in flood. 'It was', says Cockburn in his *Nomenclature of South Australia*, 'a favourite name with the authorities as far back as 1836. It was applied to a hundred, an electoral district, a Government schooner built at Port Adelaide, the labour prison, a paddle steamer'.

The Aboriginal word Para was applied very early, and to the confusion of subsequent generations, to three rivers, the Little Para, South Para and North Para, all rising in the Mt. Lofty Ranges. It now also applies to the new suburbs of Para Hills and Para Vista and will apply to the new reservoir on the Little Para River.

The word Para is a derivation of the Kaurna word 'pari' ('water'), a word which is incorporated in the Aboriginal name 'Karra-wirra-parri' (River of the Red Gum Forest) given to the river we know by its more mundane name of The Torrens.

16

A POLITICAL INTERLUDE

'exerting the fire of his eloquence'

Although in later years the district had, on occasions, its own resident men in parliament — men such as G.M. Waterhouse of *Highercombe*, who was Premier of South Australia from 1861 to 1863, and William Haines of Tea Tree Gully — no election ever aroused so much controversy in the district as the first, held in 1851. At the centre of the controversy was the fiery George Anstey.

The British Government in 1851 granted the new colony of South Australia its first instalment of self-government. The colony was to have a new Legislative Council consisting of eight members nominated personally by the Governor and sixteen to be elected by the settlers themselves. The settled areas were divided into sixteen electorates to return one member each. Our own district was included in the electoral district of Yatala.

There were few interested enough or with enough leisure time to seek political honours in 1851. In four districts no poll was needed as there was only one contestant. In our own electorate of Yatala, two contestants appeared — Richard Davies Hanson, an Adelaide attorney who had helped in London to plan the colony, and George Alexander Anstey of *Highercombe*.

The opening round in the struggle took place at the *Travellers' Rest*, Houghton, in March of 1851. It was a preliminary meeting only, held to confirm the nomination of Anstey, but it revealed somewhat less than unanimous support for that gentleman. Alexander McDonald of *Gaskmore Park* and Joseph Ind of Paradise and Thomas Battersby of Houghton spoke in favour of Anstey.

George McEwin of *Glen Ewin* spoke, at some length, against Anstey, and particularly against Anstey's support of State Aid to religion. He nominated a friend of his, David Randall, wine merchant of Adelaide, 'as a fit and proper person'. Robert Milne of *Drumminor* supported McEwin's nomination. Once again the rift in the interests of the northern and southern settlers of the district, centred around Anstey and Anstey's Hill road, came to the surface.

However, on a show of hands, Anstey was accorded the nomination. At a similar meeting at the *Wright's Road Inn*, Salisbury, Richard Davies Hanson received and accepted nomination.

At a well attended meeting held at the *Bremen Hotel*, Hope Valley, a fortnight later, both Anstey and Hanson were present to state their policies which differed basically only in detail. Anstey, with political acumen, appealed especially to the many Germans at Hope Valley by stating that he was in favour of the same rights for both German and English settlers. The chief complaint against him was the old one of having misspent public money on the road (Anstey's Hill) to his own home while Chairman of the District Road Board.

It was at a meeting at Salisbury in April that Anstey found once again that the strength of the opposition was based mainly upon his actions on the District Road Board. It was at this meeting that Anstey was accused 'of lying like a brown snake curled up under the cabbages of *Highercombe* waiting for an opportunity of darting out upon his prey' and of having 'withdrawn from the Agricultural Society of Adelaide merely because he had not been allowed to fix large placards to his exhibits'. The Salisbury meeting strongly favoured the election of Hanson.

Just prior to the election, news reached Anstey of the death of his father and he had to leave for Van Dieman's Land and was unable to take any further part in the election campaign itself.

Nomination day, to choose a representative for the District of Yatala, was held in the village of Houghton on Tuesday, July 2 — a long and muddy journey in mid-winter for people on the plains. 'The quiet and picturesque village of Houghton', wrote a reporter, 'presented a scene somewhat different from the ordinary aspect: a small but commodious husting being erected in front of the hotel while opposite to it waved one single banner with 'ANSTEY FOR YATALA'.

'As the hour fixed for nomination drew near, settlers from the different parts of the district poured into the village and by noon between fifty and sixty persons were present. The adherents of Mr. Anstey was distinguished by blue ribbons but none of Mr. Hanson's friends had mounted so much as a cockade'.

Because of the non-arrival of Mr. Hanson, the Returning Officer agreed to wait a further half-an-hour. When Hanson had still failed to show up, nominations began. The Returning Officer reminded the electors that 'they were met for the first time in the colony to represent their own wants and wishes'. The nomination of Anstey as a candidate was proposed and accepted.

At this point Hanson arrived, stating that he had been compelled to turn back for part of the way because of the bad state of the road. *(Cheers)*

'Till today', said Hanson, 'I had not known how bad were the roads'. Voice:- 'You've not had the gumption to make such roads as Anstey has!'

127

Another Voice: - 'But it's to his own house.'

Hanson said his principles were the same as Anstey's, except that he would give no support for State Aid for religion nor a State Church.

On a show of hands of electors Anstey received thirty-four votes and Hanson eighteen. As this was more than half Anstey's vote, Hanson was able to demand a poll. A day for the poll was set and the assembly at Houghton then applied themselves amicably enough to the food and drink 'provided by the worthy host of the *Travellers' Rest*'.

On election day on July 3, 1851, Anstey, still absent in Van Diemen's Land, was defeated at the poll. The polling places (all at hotels) and the figures are of interest:

Polling Places		Votes	
		Hanson	Anstey
Salisbury		87	25
Houghton		50	98
Walkerville ·		71	41
Adelaide		47	47
	Total	255	211

It was a victory, not so much for a principle, but for those people on the plains whose interests (and roads) had hitherto been neglected by Anstey.

Anstey did not return from Van Diemen's Land until July 18. In the meantime his friends had lodged a strong protest to the Governor, claiming correctly enough, that the election was invalid as Salisbury had not been gazetted within the requisite time as a polling place. The Governor, in his turn, declared the election to be valid, but following a petition headed by Anstey against the return, he diplomatically appointed Hanson to the position of Advocate-General and offered the vacant seat on the Legislative Council to Anstey. It seems that politics was a game of chess as long ago as 1851.

The proud — and in this case arrogant — Anstey refused the offer and demanded another poll. There was more — and more bitter — electioneering, with meetings at Houghton, Hope Valley, Salisbury, Gumeracha, Walkerville and Port Adelaide. Anstey's opponent in the second poll was William Giles, manager of the South Australian Company.

Once again Anstey was defeated — by 3 votes — and once again he protested, this time charging irregularities at the polling booths. Once again the Governor over-ruled the protest and Giles retained his seat.

The drama was not, however, quite played out. 'Mr. Anstey, like another Hannibal', wrote the editor of the *Register*, 'is exerting the fire of his eloquence and stirring up the electors of Yatala for a decisive victory, the expected triumph having been baulked'. Anstey decided to appeal to the Privy Council in England.

Just at this moment (September 1851) a dissatisfied member of the Governor's Legislative Council resigned. The Governor, Sir Henry Fox Young, despite his personal dislike of the Squire of *Highercombe*, once again nominated Anstey for the vacant seat. Even more surprisingly, Anstey accepted. The editor of the *Adelaide Times* expressed astonishment at the appointment, as 'Anstey had for years been the worst thorn in the honourable side of the Governor'. They suspected treachery on the part of Anstey. Here was a man who a few weeks earlier had said publicly of Sir Henry Fox Young, 'the official trickery of His Excellency was of a piece with the political treachery of the previous candidate — that one has abandoned religion and the other liberty — and both have been sold', now accepting a political favour from the Governor.

A poem, written in the political language of the day, which was often more intemperate and libellous then than now, appeared in the press:

TO G.A. ANSTEY, ESQU.

'He that entereth not by the door ... but climbeth up another way'.
(Vide — John X.)

The people's door! The people's door! The pass-way of the free!
Thou hast 'got in' that 'other way' which proves what thou wilt be:-
A lion caged, an eagle clipp'd — a spaniel fawning low —
To him of whom I've hear thee speak words dars't thou utter now?

Gone is thy independence — they manful fight and strong
Against whate'er thy wayward mind presented as a wrong
The locks in which thy strength once lay are sever'd from they head;
And shake thyself as thou wast wont, thou'lt find that strength is fled.

The *Times* need not have been worried. Anstey was hot-headed, arrogant and ambitious but he was not treacherous. True to his principles, he resigned from the Legislative Council just three days after taking his seat, 'so disgusted am I', he explained, 'with the doings of the present Council, with the utter neglect of the most important pledges and with the shameful preference of matters personal to themselves and to their pockets and prejudices'.

The seat that Anstey vacated remained empty for the rest of the session and the district of Yatala unrepresented.

Anstey never re-entered politics. It was a dramatic end to one of the oddest elections in South Australian electoral history. Anstey left South Australia within a few years, selling his beautiful estate at Highercombe in 1858 to George Marsden Waterhouse who became Premier of South Australia in 1861. Waterhouse, in turn, sold *Highercombe* to Robert Dalrymple Ross who was Speaker for many years in the House of Assembly. After some years in Tasmania, George Anstey returned to England and died in London in 1895 in his eighty-first year.

COPPER AND GOLD

'a little excitement'

Metal-mining in Australia began at Glen Osmond in South Australia in 1841 when Cornishmen discovered a lode of silver-lead ore in the side of the hill near the entrance to the glen. At that time the infant colony was on the verge of bankruptcy, largely because of land speculation. Insolvencies were common and unemployment widespread. There were nearly 2,000 men, women and children in Adelaide in destitute circumstances. There was talk of re-emigration — and more people were leaving the colony than arriving.

The mineral discoveries at Glen Osmond were however not rich enough to cause more than 'a little excitement'. With the announcement of a discovery of a rich lode of copper at Kapunda in 1843, a mining mania began which did not end until gold was discovered in the eastern colonies in mid-1851.

'Coppermania' and the discovery of gold were not without their effects in our own district.

In 1843, a promising lode of copper was discovered on the side of a steep hill at Montacute* and 'sharp Cornish eyes' were on the look out for rocky outcrops in the Adelaide Hills.

In his diary for July 1845, George McEwin of *Glen Ewin* recorded, 'Discovered indications of copper and lead and silver; let the mine to N. Fletcher and S. Clare who commenced work on the 28th April. Found the first solid piece of ore at 8 feet from the surface'. The mine, after five months of work proved a 'duffer' and on September 4, McEwin wrote in his diary, 'The miners left after a fruitless attempt on their part to obtain copper, having drove a level 22 fathoms and sunk a shaft 6 fathoms in order to intersect two different lodes and left without having done so in either case'.

It was the first of many other fruitless searches for minerals throughout the district and among the hills which followed during the next five years.

* The zig-zag road now known as 'The Corkscrew' or 'Corkscrew Hill' was built in 1843 to facilitate the removal of ore from the Montacute Mine.

But in August of 1845 on a visit to Adelaide, George McEwin saw something which was to be of real importance to South Australia and incidentally to many people in his own district. He recorded in his diary of August 21, 'Went to Adelaide. Saw specimens of the Monster Mine which was taken on Saturday'.

The Monster Mine was the lode of copper discovered by a shepherd near the Burra Creek, 100 miles north of Adelaide. Within a year the Burra Mine was employing nearly 500 men and had a population of nearly 2,000 people, many of them living in dug-outs in the creek.

The S.A. Mining Association was soon advertising for bullock-drivers and teams to cart the ore to Port Adelaide, and soon nearly a thousand teams, including many from our own district were on the track to Burra.

Thomas Roberts, a Cornish miner working at the Montacute copper mine on Fifth Creek in 1844, was engaged by the S.A. Mining Association prior to the discovery on the Burra Creek, to open up mineral sections on the River Torrens just above the present diversion weir across the river. The Mining Association engaged Roberts to investigate copper outcrops on the hillsides of two sections adjoining the river. It is interesting to note that John Green Coulls, blacksmith of Adelaide, great-grandfather of the present Leo Coulls of *Athelstone House*, Highbury, was engaged to supply Thomas Roberts (and his offsider Josiah Staunton) with mining tools, viz. 3 picks, one cross-cut saw, one axe, six gads, one wheel barrow, one maul, one set of iron wedges, one crow-bar, four files, and one brand, S.A.M.A.

The same Mining Association also acquired the steep sections of land immediately adjoining the southern side of Anstey's Hill Road. These sections were later worked, mainly in the gullies, by the Land and Gold Company of Adelaide in a search for alluvial gold.

When the S.A. Mining Association acquired the lode of copper which became the Burra Mine in September 1845, they sent Roberts and nine men to open up the mine and appointed him first mining Captain. They also engaged John Barton Hack, who had taken up the first Special Survey *(q.v.)* at Hermitage but had become insolvent because of land speculation, to cart the first load of tools and stores to the mine and to return to Adelaide with the first loads of ore.

Roberts remained at the mine for some months and early in 1846 was able to buy a section of land at Upper Dry Creek, near present day Golden Grove — Section 2147. In November 1846, he acquired section 2156 adjoining. Thomas Roberts had worked at the Greenwith mine, five miles south of Truro, in Cornwall, before arriving in South Australia in June 1839, with his wife and five children and his brother, Jonathon, and family on the emigrant ship *Sir Charles Forbes*. Thomas Roberts named his new property *Greenwith Farm*. Opposite is the little Greenwith Methodist Church, the building of which was begun in 1853.

Others from the district travelled the Burra road carting ore to Port

Adelaide. Among them was William Haines who later settled at Tea Tree Gully. At a gathering of old colonists in 1890 William Haines spoke of his experiences in bullock driving on the Burra Road.

The Burra Mine brought employment to thousands in South Australia and hastened a renewal of prosperity in the colony. It also led to a renewed search among the hills of our own district for mineral sections. In 1847, indications of copper were discovered on a rocky hillside above the River Torrens below *Highercombe*. A 69-acre section was surveyed (Section 5607) and the Enterprise Mining Company was formed with a capital of £3,000 to work the deposits of copper and lead on this section, and on other sections at Glen Osmond.

Mineral indications were found on section 5604 adjoining and other mineral sections were surveyed. Although work on these mines began in 1847 and ores were carted to the Glen Osmond smelters, the workings soon proved unprofitable and were discontinued in 1851.

All of this sporadic mining activity was suddenly disrupted by the discovery of gold, first in New South Wales and then in the new colony of Victoria. Such was the exodus to the mines that for a while Adelaide became a deserted town with wives and children left mainly in possession.

The dramatic discovery had dramatic effects in every district. The Kapunda Mine closed and the Burra Mine could only retain 100 of its 1,100 miners.

In our own district the exodus was just as great. The village of Houghton was almost deserted of men by the end of 1851. Most of them were unsuccessful as diggers and in March of 1852, the *Register* reported:

'A party of 14 men, residents of Houghton and the Little Para, have returned from the diggings unsuccessful and penniless and have begged their way back to the province overland.

These men returned, not from fear of hard work — for they were all labouring men — but simply from having failed to find gold. They represent the many hundreds who have left the province and would gladly return if they have the means'.

With the defection of postmasters along the North East line of road, postal services were discontinued in 1852 for three months to the towns of Hope Valley, Houghton, Chain of Ponds and Gumeracha. The *Register* newspaper then stated that 'considering the vast annoyance and inconvenience to which a large body of our subscribers in the N.E. district would be exposed by being cut off from postal communications', it had made arrangements for a regular weekly delivery of papers at its own expense and that it would also 'deliver and receive letters'.

At Hope Valley, first the storekeeper left and then the Postmaster, Mr. E.G. Day. 'There is not another Englishman within three miles upon that road capable of filling the office', stated the *Register*. As Day was also the Hope Valley schoolmaster, the school too was closed.

A letter* written by Day at the Victorian gold-fields in February of 1852 to Mr. Goldsack of Adelaide has been preserved. It reads:

The following circumstantial letter has been received by
Mr. S. Goldsack from Mr. E.G. Day of Hope Valley.

Forest Creek, Mt. Alexander,
February 21st, 1852

'Sir,

Agreeably to my promise, I take the earliest opportunity to furnish you with some particulars concerning the Gold-fields in the neighbourhood of Mt. Alexander to which such vast numbers of men of Adelaide have transported themselves, as a sure road to wealth, but that it is not so, many have found and are still finding to their cost; however, I write not to moralize, but to teach, by the statement of a few simple facts that my fellow colonists may at least have some antidote to the delirium of the worst form of 'Yellow Fever'.

The locality from which I write is called the 'Forest Creek', although most of the hills and flats have specific names, such as 'Golden Point', 'Adelaide Gully', etc. The scenery is much the same as in our own 'bush', rather thickly wooded with gum and stringy bark, with a wattle of a smaller leaf called silver-wattle.

The hills and flats between them have been very extensively dug into holes of different sizes, shapes and depths varying from a few feet to 25 feet. Considerable outlay of labour and capital have been necessary to carry out these mining operations and the instances are neither few nor far between where the final result has been in favour of the gold-seeker.

I have walked along this Forest Creek for some miles and the same appearance is presented to the eye. The bed of the creek is dry and dusty or filled with a yellow mud, the refuse of the 'washing'. Along the banks stand cradles and tubs, with hundreds of washers with large round dishes.

Since the drying up of the stream holes have been sunk on the banks to a depth of 10 to 12 feet, from these a good supply of water has been procured but these are fast drying up, owing to the continued dry weather; and we are daily in expectation of having the cry 'water, water' everywhere; and not a drop to drink. Along the line of the creek and up each flat, at the base of the hills, are the tents of the army of diggers. Those of the stores have white, tri-coloured and many coloured flags flying from the forks of their ridge-poles.

There are a few tents of doubtful character who ostensibly sell 'Lemonade' at sixpence a glass, but their real character becomes known when the Commissioner consigns them to a 'fiery trial' which converts their canvas to tinder and their 'spirits to pale blue flame'.

The first view of the diggings reminds me of an extensive fair, but a

* ex *Register* March 23, 1852.

nearer inspection suggested an idea more sad. The deep pits, so thickly strewn, seemed like so many empty graves.

Of the expense of living you may form some idea when I tell you that flour is sold retail at 5d. per lb.; butter is 3s.; cheese 2s.6d. per lb.; good black tea 2s. per lb.; ship biscuits 10d. per lb.; mutton, by the quarter 2s.6d. to 3s. each; candles 1s. per lb.; sugar 6d. per lb.

There is one respectable eating-house near the *Argus* office, where a good meal can be had for 2s. or a week's board for 25s. The price of a cup of coffee is 6d. and with a slice of currant cake 1s. A newspaper also from the aforesaid *Argus* office is 1s.

I must now say a few words on the profits of gold-digging and the necessary stock in trade.

It is undeniable that many have realized large sums and some few even now are clearing their £50 or £100 in the course of a month or 6 weeks, but the times are bad now.

Washing by the dish is a slow process and unless the stuff is very good, a man had better be working at his own craft as for the uninterrupted use of the cradle there is not a sufficiency of water. In this profession as in most others capital is necessary; or the possession of a plant of two or three large tubs, a cradle and dipper and several tin dishes, for which some £10 must be sunk, and in the event of sinking deep holes, in order to reach the rock where the gold deposit may be, buckets, rope and a windlass must be used. I heard of one party who had expended £60 in a Gold-digging outfit and their profits for a month had yielded some £36 per head.

The straight-forward honourable gold-seeker gets his license and applies himself in earnest to sinking hole after hole right down to the rock, in hope of finding a reward in a deposit of solid gold at the bottom; this hope is only realized by a few, the majority are disappointed; getting only stuff that will pay for washing by a cradle, or, get nothing for their pains.

Why these things are, the Theologian can perhaps say. There are many here who have realized considerable sums by 'Fossicking' as the phrase is, that is, they do not dig, but they peep about and get 'stuff' from good holes, which they wash.

Such is a brief sketch of the present condition of the Forest Creek Diggings. Things are not here what they seem in Adelaide. Getting to the diggings without a shilling in your pocket, over the license fee, is not a certain way to wealth, and many who have so come, with hundreds who have been better supplied, have dug and dug and have still been disappointed.

I am dear Sir,
Yours respectfully,
E.G. Day'

There were others from the district who travelled to the gold-fields.

James Cronk went to Forest Creek early in 1852 and sent home gold to his wife at Modbury with the first gold escort. William Haines, too, was at the diggings in 1851 and for a time enlisted in the police force at Castlemaine before returning to South Australia. Alexander Kirk, of *Kirklands* near the Little Para, was a successful digger. He 'took the gold fever' in 1851 and after six months at the Mt. Alexander gold diggings, he and his three companions 'carried home 40 lbs. of gold'.

Another successful digger was Robert Smart of Golden Grove. Smart arrived as a boy with his father and mother from Glasgow in 1839 on the *Ariadne*. The family settled at Golden Grove in the 1840s.

A party of men from Golden Grove, including Robert Smart, left for the diggings early in 1852. On the way the travellers were beset near the Coorong by a hostile group of Aborigines who took the ducks they had shot for food and demanded the white men's weapons. The party was saved by the timely arrival of another team of diggers.

Smart returned to Golden Grove after spending nine months at Forest Creek. In 1854, he married Miss Roberts, a daughter of Thomas Roberts of Golden Grove.

Among those who went to the diggings was Henry Tilley. The Tilley family of Wiltshire arrived in Adelaide in April 1851 on the migrant ship, *Asceola*. In 1853, Henry Tilley and his 13-year-old son John went off to the Victorian gold-fields. As Henry Tilley on his return was able to pay £800 for a 77-acre section of land (Section 2131) at Upper Dry Creek in 1854, we can assume that he and his son, John, were very successful as gold-diggers. The home Henry Tilley built on the section he named *Hillcott Farm**, after his native village of Hillcott in Wiltshire. The homestead survives to this day, close to a branch of Dry Creek, near the south-west corner of Yatala Vale Road and Golden Grove Road.

Descendants of Henry Tilley were to make continuing contributions to the service of local government over the next century. Among the descendants is John Garfield Tilley, the present Mayor of the City of Tea Tree Gully.

The exodus from the district had a widespread effect. There was difficulty in getting the harvest in, towards the end of 1852. 'The crops in the plains are luxuriant but many of the wheat crops are being cut for hay as a result of want of sufficient labour to reap it. Some farmers are turning their cattle into crops'.

Work on the district roads, too, was brought almost to a standstill and the Yatala District Road Board reported in October of 1852 that 'very soon after the news of the Victorian Gold-fields having reached the colony, it was found impossible to carry on works and only £26.7.3 was expended in the last quarter on roads' in the whole district.

Even in 1853 the Board of Education was still reporting that 'intensive

* The original 'Hillcott Manor Farmhouse' near North Newntown, Wiltshire, still exists.

migration to the gold-fields has produced much disarrangement' in district schools.

Robert Milne of *Drumminor*, Dry Creek, however was one farmer who was not despondent. 'The unprecedented influx of immigrants to the neighbouring colonies for the next year or two', he wrote in 1852, 'will open up such a market for the produce of the corngrower as will almost inevitably assure good prices' — a prophecy which proved correct.

During 1854, the district gradually resumed its normal tenor of life. From Houghton, in March, came the report that the 'Sabbath School which was discontinued in consequence of the exodus to the gold-fields has been reopened and 40 children are now in attendance'.

The postal service to the North-Eastern townships had been resumed in January 1853, although Hope Valley was still without a postmaster and a school teacher and mail for Hope Valley had to be collected or despatched from Houghton. However in April of 1854 a meeting, largely composed of German settlers, was held in the Bremen Hotel to 'consider the best means of reopening the school and Post-Office'. It was resolved to offer Pastor Kappler the school and schoolhouse 'on condition he vacate the premises in favour of an English teacher at any future time'. The school, however, remained without a teacher until 1856.

Despite the search for copper among the local ranges and for gold along the Torrens, the real underground wealth of the district finally proved to be not metal but instead, as we shall see, the more mundane deposits of clay, sand and building stone.

SECTION II
THE CENTURY AFTER

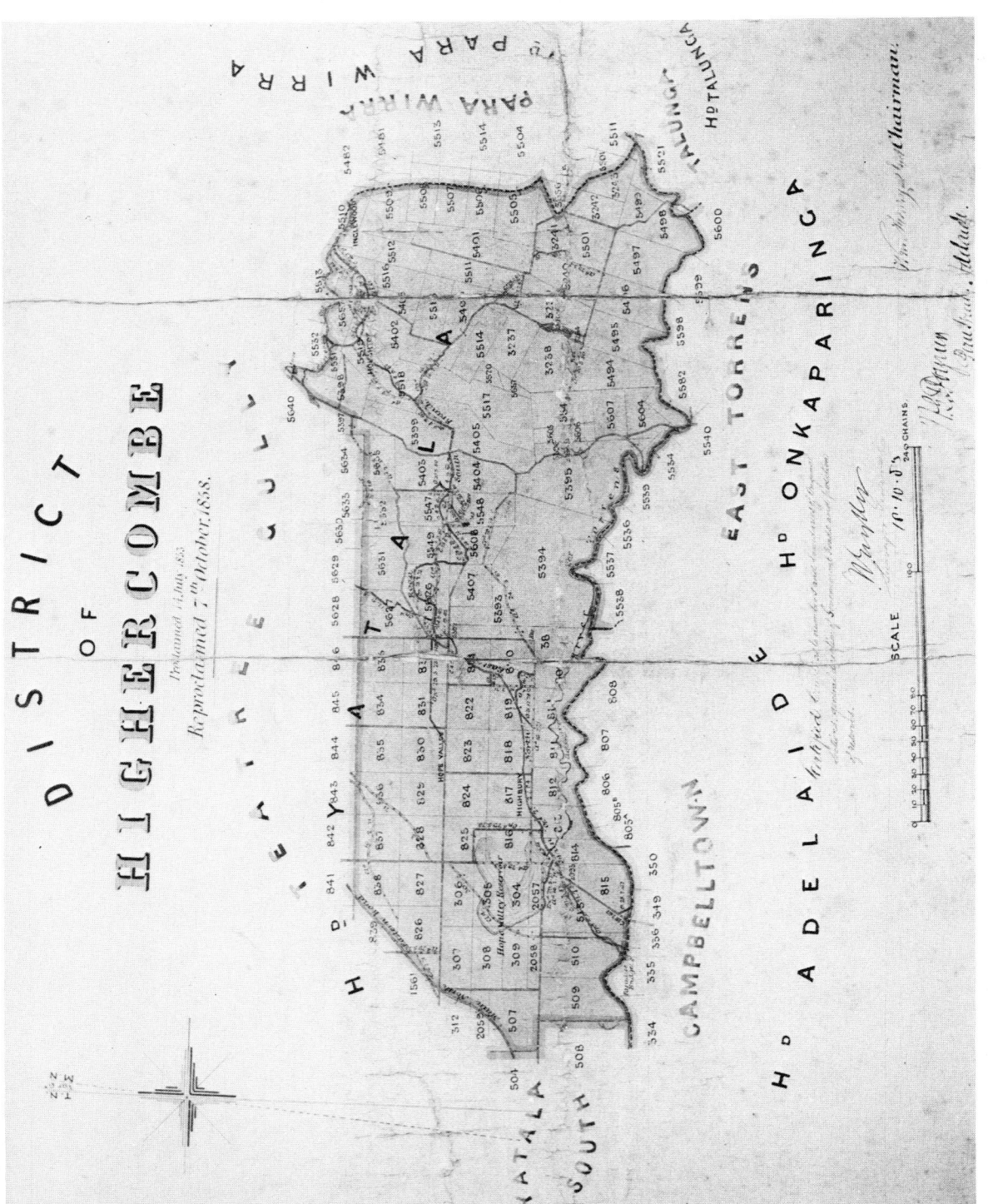

Map 8. District of Highercombe, 1858. The re-proclaimed district was the southern portion of the original (1853) District of Highercombe.

Highercombe District Council

Minutes of a meeting of Council, held at the "Bremen Hotel" Hope Valley on Tuesday August 2nd 1853 —

Present

Messrs Robert Milne, John Gollop, Henry Klapper, Joseph Ind, and George McEwin.

Mr Gollop moved and Mr Klapper seconded that Mr Milne be elected Chairman of the Council for the ensuing year, which was accordingly carried.

It was Resolved that the Chairman do cause an advertisement to be inserted in the "Adelaide Observer" newspaper inviting applications from parties willing to fill the office of Clerk.

Resolved — that a map of the District be procured as soon as the route of the Main North Eastern Road shall have been determined on by the Central Board —

Resolved — that the meetings of Council be held for the present at the "Bremen Hotel" Hope Valley and the "Traveller's Rest" Inn, Houghton, alternately

The Council adjourned until Monday Aug 15th 2 p.m.

signed. R. Milne Chairman

Item 2. Minutes of meeting of first District Council of Highercombe, August 15, 1853.

18

TOWARDS LOCAL GOVERNMENT

'bring a list of five gentlemen'

The district first gained 'a voice in its own affairs' in 1853. In May of that year a memorial signed by one hundred and nineteen 'owners and occupiers of land in and adjacent to Highercombe' was presented to the Governor, Sir Henry Edward Fox Young, asking him to constitute the first 'District of Highercombe'. The 'District of Highercombe' is now known as the District of Tea Tree Gully and its boundaries and area remain substantially the same as in 1853.*

The District was proclaimed on July 14, 1853 and five councillors, Messrs. Joseph Ind of Little Paradise; Robert Milne of Dry Creek; George McEwin of *Glen Ewin*; John Gollop of Houghton; and Henry Klopper of Hope Valley, held their first Council meeting in the assembly room of the *Bremen Hotel*, Hope Valley, on Tuesday, August 2.

When the new province of South Australia was constituted in 1834 by an Act of the British Parliament, provision was made for some form of local government when the population of the colony reached 50,000. This figure was reached by 1849 but it was not until November 25, 1852 that 'An Act to appoint District Councils and to define the power thereof' was passed. The Act gave to various districts power to tax themselves for the making and maintaining of district roads, bridges and public buildings; to grant timber, publicans', depasturing and slaughtering licences, and to establish pounds for the impounding of stray cattle and sheep.

Two factors had hastened the passing of the new Act. The exodus of man-power to the Victorian gold fields had brought the activities of the Central Road Board almost to a halt and had led to dissatisfaction with a single central road-making authority. Secondly, the districts were too large to be administered effectively — and as we have seen in our own district of Yatala, meetings concerning local roads might be held in places as far apart as Houghton, Hindmarsh and Salisbury. Indeed one of the resolutions of a public District Council was that 'the interests of those living in the hills and

* **Boundaries and area changed 1976 just prior to publication.** *(v. Chapter 36)*

Highercombe District Council 1906. **Standing:** L.to R. Cr. Nathaniel Packer, Cr. Thomas H. Possingham, Cr. John W. Newman. **Seated:** John Gollop (District Clerk), Cr.C.Hill (Chairman), Cr. William Ramsay.

Highercombe District Council taken just prior to amalgamation with Tea Tree Gully Council 1935. **L.to R.** Cr. W. Packer, Cr. A.T. Wakefield, Cr. L.J. Tolley, Cr. A. Hall. **Seated:** Chairman Cr. W.H. Ind, District Clerk B.L. Hill.

Governor, Sir Day Hort Bosanquet planting a tree after naming Haines Memorial Park, Tea Tree Gully, July 1909. Lady Bosanquet (right) and Miss Alicia Bosanquet (left).

Ephraim Haines (centre), plants a tree in memory of his brother William Haines at the opening of Haines Memorial Park, 1909.

those on the plains do not assimilate', an opinion shared by all sections of the large Hundred of Yatala.

The year 1853 saw the beginnings of local self-government in many districts. The first of the District Councils was Mitcham, established on May 10, 1853. Three more district councils — East Torrens, Onkaparinga and Hindmarsh — were proclaimed in the same month; two more — Angaston and Yatala — in June; and the District of West Torrens and the District of Highercombe in July.

The first move to establish a local District Council was made at a meeting held at the *Travellers' Rest*, Houghton, on Thursday, February 24, 1853. That enterprising man, Joseph Ind of Little Paradise, acted as Chairman. The meeting resolved to send a deputation of nine local men to attend a meeting of representatives of the Yatala Hundred on the following Monday.

The February 28 meeting was held in the dining room of the *Bird-in-Hand* Hotel, Dry Creek, and was chaired by Captain Charles Sturt, the erstwhile explorer, but in 1853 the Colonial Secretary. 'The long room was crowded to excess; many people were unable to gain admittance' reported Sturt.

Joseph Ind, backed by George McEwin of *Glen Ewin*, recommended the division of the hundred, as suggested by the Houghton meeting. It was generally agreed by all present that a district which extended 'from the hills to the Port township' was too large.

The outcome of the meeting was that two committees were elected — one to represent the hills and the other the plains at the next meeting. The newspaper report read:

TO REPRESENT

	The Hills		The Plains
Messrs.	G. McEwin	Messrs.	T. Abbott
	Robt. Milne		O. Lines
	Thos. Roberts		J.S. Duncan
	Thos. Crews		A.L. Lymburner
	Andrew Shillabeer		Daniel Brady

At the subsequent meeting of these representatives with the Yatala Road Board, held in the *Southern Cross Hotel*, King William Street, on March 12, Mr. McEwin expressed his belief once again that the people of the hills could have no community of interest with those on the plains. The plainsmen, too, said they would be glad to see the hundred divided. The Commissioners agreed. A line of demarcation, from the Torrens near the Paradise Ford to the Little Para, was, after lengthy discussion, agreed upon.

Ten days later the committee reported back to a crowded public meeting held at the *O.G. Inn*, Gilles Plains, where 'it was finally settled that the hundred of Yatala be divided into two districts'. George McEwin took advantage of the meeting to form a preliminary district committee for preparing a petition to the Governor and recommending five councillors.

All that was needed, it seemed, was to name the time and place of the district meeting. An advertisement was placed in the *Observer* of May 26 inviting all proprietors and occupiers of land in the new district to attend a meeting in the schoolroom at Houghton and asking each 'to bring a list of five gentlemen for whom he intends to vote for the first Councillors'. The advertisement also stated that it had been proposed and seconded by the preliminary committee that the name of the district be Highercombe.

The choice of Highercombe as the name of the new district appears puzzling at first sight. There was, however, perhaps little alternative. The title, District of Houghton, obviously would find little favour with the residents of Hope Valley or a District of Hope Valley with the Houghton villagers. As yet there was no township of Modbury, Tea Tree Gully or Golden Grove. *Highercombe* Estate was well known; it was private property and therefore neutral ground. George Anstey may possibly have agreed to the use of the name, although by 1853 he had left the colony, and neither George McEwin nor Joseph Ind had much respect for Anstey. The name may have been a sop to the villagers of Houghton who were supporters of Anstey and of his line of road to Hope Valley.

The meeting held in the schoolroom* at noon on Thursday, April 7, was livelier then George McEwin anticipated. When McEwin, as Chairman, put the motion of Joseph Ind:

'That the District Council Act be adopted for this district' it was promptly seconded by John Richardson of *Houghton Lodge*.

It was at this point that another faction in the schoolroom made itself heard. William Squibb, the village postmaster, seconded by Thomas Battersby, moved an amendment:

'That under the existing circumstances the inhabitants of the Houghton District at the present time deem it inexpedient to form a District Council until the main line [of road] be permanently fixed and the road rendered passable during the winter season'.

It was an expression of the bitterness of the feud concerning the rival lines of main road through the district — Anstey's Hill v. Tea Tree Gully. It was this continuing bitterness which contributed largely to division a few years later of the District of Highercombe into two council districts.

A vote, taken on Squibb's amendment revealed, to the confusion of the chairman, a majority of one for the amendment. It must have seemed to George McEwin and his committee that their months of effort to gain self-government for the people of the district were about to be brought to nothing by parochial pettiness.

After much confusion and a temporary adjournment of the meeting, sense prevailed. The amendment was declared out of order. Joseph Ind

* The schoolroom was the Union Chapel *(q.v.)*, the ruins of which still stand behind the present C.W.A. building in Houghton.

again moved that the District Council Act be adopted. This time it was carried unanimously.

Without further ado eleven men were nominated for District Councillors. They were: George McEwin, Howard Blyth, Andrew Shillabeer, Joseph Ind, John Gollop, Wm. Reeds Snr., Wm. Dunn, Thomas Battersby, Robert Milne, George McGilton and Robert Smith. Upon a vote being taken, Messrs. McEwin, Blyth, Shillabeer, Gollop and Ind were elected, subject to the approval of His Excellency, the Governor.

The District Council of Highercombe might have been proclaimed in June, at the same time as the District Council of Yatala, if two of the newly-elected councillors, Andrew Shillabeer of Gould's Creek and Howard Blyth of *Ladywood Farm* had not resigned. George McEwin was forced to call another meeting — this time at the *Bremen Hotel*, Hope Valley — to fill the vacancies. A mere handful of ratepayers attended. Joseph Ind took the chair but refused to act when he discovered that the two new nominees were not present. George McEwin determined no doubt to get his council, then took the chair and Robert Milne of *Drumminor*, Dry Creek, and Henry Klopper of Hope Valley were elected (in their absence) to replace Blyth and Shillabeer.

There were no further delays. The memorial of the 119 ratepayers was duly presented to the Governor; published in the *Government Gazette* of June 23, 1853, *(v. Appendix V)* and the District of Highercombe proclaimed in the *Government Gazette* of July 14, together with the appointment of the first Council — Messrs. Joseph Ind, Little Paradise; Robert Milne, Dry Creek; George McEwin, *Glen Ewin*; John Gollop, *Highercombe*; and Henry Klopper, Hope Valley. *(v. Appendix VI)*

It only remained for the councillors to arrange their first meeting and to elect a Chairman.

We can imagine that Joseph Ind and George McEwin, the two men who had been mainly responsible for establishing the council and had ridden long distances on horseback to attend the initial meetings, felt a considerable sense of relief and of satisfaction that the District of Highercombe was now a reality and its first Council formed.

19

LOCAL GOVERNMENT
DISTRICT OF HIGHERCOMBE 1853—1858

'rates must be paid in cash—not stone'

The five men who had been nominated at the April meeting of rate-payers in the schoolroom at Houghton to be first councillors for the district had all been active in local affairs. They had all been spokesmen for the district both in battles with the Central Road Board and in the formation of the new District of Highercombe.

They were all landowners, although by no means the largest land-owners. On later occasions they were to be accused, in the heat of debate, of self-interest. They were in fact men of great energy who had pioneered their own way in the new colony with little help and little capital but a great fund of determination. They lived on the land which they had cleared and fenced and into which they had driven the first plough. Now they had been chosen, by their neighbours and fellow-colonists, to take charge of the affairs of the district. It is perhaps forgotten that local government was South Australia's earliest form of self-government, free from the dictates of the British Parliament. Indeed, South Australia originated the principle of an elected local government and was the first of the colonies to institute it.

All sections of the new district were represented in the first council. The five men came from widely separated areas, although, as yet, there was no provision for district wards. On Tuesday, August 2, 1853 the councillors arrived at 2 p.m. — on horseback — at the *Bremen Hotel*, Hope Valley, to hold their first meeting and to elect the first chairman of the District Council of Highercombe.

Henry Klapper (originally Heinrich Klöpper, later Henry Klopper) of Hope Valley had taken up section 823 of 80 acres in 1849. By 1853 he held 268 acres of land in the district, including section 5626 below Anstey's Hill, which later became an important road metal and building stone quarry. The Klopper farmhouse, at the south-west corner of Valley Road and Grand Junction Road, was demolished in 1929.

The pleasant custom of naming individual properties was an early and useful one, although it is not so common today. John Gollop, who took up land near Houghton in the 1840s, named his property *Poundsford*. The name is still familiar in and around Houghton. John Gollop had early shown an interest in local affairs and in the 1840s privately constructed the first bridge over the Little Para, just below the present *Inglewood Inn*. The wooden bridge, referred to locally and by the Road Board as Gollop's Bridge, was finally replaced by the present stone-arch bridge in 1863. In 1844 Gollop rented a section of land near Houghton on which he grew wheat. By 1853, when he became Councillor, he owned six sections of land, an area of 318 acres. His son, John Gollop, also entered Council, in 1882, and was Clerk of the District Council of Highercombe for more than fifty years.

Robert Milne, as we have seen, rented land on Upper Dry Creek from the South Australian Company before he finally bought the property in the 1850s and built the two-storey home which has been known as *Drumminor* ever since.

The stories of the two other first councillors, Joseph Ind and George McEwin and of their descendants is threaded throughout the history of the district and of local self-government.

At the first meeting in the *Bremen Hotel*, Robert Milne was elected Chairman of the Council for the ensuing year. Only three resolutions were made at the meeting — one to advertise for a Clerk, another to procure a map of the district and its boundaries as defined in the proclamation, and a third deciding that the Council would meet on alternate fortnights at *The Travellers' Rest Inn*, Houghton, and the *Bremen Hotel*, Hope Valley.

At the next meeting held at *The Travellers' Rest*, five applications for the position of Clerk were considered and Edward Prowse was appointed to the position. It was a natural enough choice. Prowse had been second master of the Hope Valley School. In 1851 he had resigned to become first Clerk to the District Road Board of Yatala and had also become Surveyor of Roads a few months later.

The salary of the clerk was set at £150 a year — a very reasonable amount, it would seem, by 1853 standards. The duties of Edward Prowse were, however, onerous and involved him in some personal expense. Indeed, In November 1853, Prowse asked for and received a further amount of £10 'for the hire of the necessary horse accommodation in the assessment of the District'. Prowse had not only to visit and assess the value of each of the occupied sections of land in a district of over 47½ square miles before the close of the year 1853; he was also expected to collect the rates. Perhaps it is not to be wondered that Prowse handed in his resignation on January 3, 1854, just prior to the first annual election.

The first district assessment had been completed by the Clerk on November 28, 1853. Preserved in the clerk's meticulous hand-writing in the Assessment Book, the assessment and the list of district ratepayers and their holdings provide a valuable and interesting source of information today.

The assessment reveals that of the 30,720 acres of land within the boundaries only 22,803 were occupied by 1853. The assessed value, based on improved values, amounted to £10,846.18.0, and at a rate of 1/- in the £1, the rate was expected to produce the sum of £542.6.10½ from the 248 ratepayers in the district. However there was no time to collect the rates before the January election was upon the Council.

Since August, the five councillors had been busy seeking sources of income. They applied for and received proportion of the funds of the now defunct District Road Board for the Hundred of Yatala. The amount was small — a mere £33.6.8 — but it was followed by a grant of £250 from the government for preliminary expenses. Fees for timber and depasturing licences, and for public houses in the district, now had to be paid to the Council. By the close of 1853, receipts had been £324.6.8 and expenditure only £80.2.5 — leaving a satisfactory balance of £244.4.3. The only expenses had been for use of a room and the stabling of councillors' horses at hotels each fortnight; for the supply of stationery and stabling for the clerk's horse and payment of the clerk's salary. As Edward Prowse was not able to collect the rates before resigning, his salary was halved.

At the first annual meeting of the Council, called for 10 a.m. in the *Bremen Hotel* to elect three councillors in place of Klopper, Ind and McEwin whose retirement was required by the District Council Act, the Chairman, Mr. Milne, 'hoped that those present would all do their best to promote order during the day so that the District of Highercombe may that day show an example to other districts less harmonious in their meetings'. Council meetings it seems, have always had a tendency to generate heat. Although 'proper decorum was not always preserved' despite the Chairman's plea, the poll was satisfactorily concluded at 4 p.m. and the electors 'anxiously awaited the result without'.

Unfortunately for consequent peace and harmony in the district, three large land-holders, John Smart, Robert Halden and Richard Smith, by using plurality of votes according to the size of their holdings, were able to oust Joseph Ind and Henry Klopper. George McEwin, giving as his reason 'want of leisure to attend to the duties', had not stood for re-election, although despite this, one ratepayer cast a vote in his favour. The plurality of votes was questioned and found to apply only to special meetings, but His Excellency ruled that the election could now only be set aside by the Supreme Court.

The unfortunate aspect of the election was that the district now had very lop-sided representation. John Smart, Robert Halden and Richard Smith, Snr., all came from the same northern area of the district as the Chairman, Robert Milne. John Gollop still represented Houghton, but Hope Valley had no representation. The seeds of dissension among ratepayers

Modbury Methodist Girls' Club c.1910. **Back Row**: Dorothy Marrett, Rosa Marrett, May Holbrook, Minnie Buder, Alice Boord, Mildred Morriss, Myrtle Simcock. **Second Row**: Phoebe Westphal, Emily Mueller, Ivy Nelson, Mrs. Kemp, Ella Lloyd, Hilda Kelly, Maggie Papps, Grace Westphal, ... **Third Row**: Ethel Clayton, Miss C. Kelly, Mrs. M. Wake, Mrs. Broadbent and baby Betty, Mrs. Disher, Eva Newdegg, May Richardson. **Front Row**: Bessie Smith, Dorothy Roper, Lillian Lloyd, Elva Roper, Ethel Lucy, Hazel Broadbent, Sophia Buder.

Golden Grove folk c.1905. **L.to R. Back Row**: A. Bowey, W. Rehn, M. Maughan, J. Tilley, A. Robertson, Mr. O'Leary, A. Harper, Mr. Rankine, Mr. Maidment. **Front Row**: Mesdames. Tilley, Harper, Rehn, Smart, Miss Long, Mesdames A. Bowey and Rankine.

Annual 'Institute Day', Tea Tree Gully c.1908.

Group of Houghton girls and women outside of Houghton Rechabite Hall, September 1913.

were thus sown only one year after the formation of the first district council.

The answer — to divide the district into wards — was suggested at the next annual meeting of ratepayers, but the division into wards was not made until 1858. By then, however, it was too late to prevent the division of the district itself into two separate council areas.

Thomas Crews was appointed Clerk in place of Edward Prowse on January 11, 1854. His first duty was to call a public meeting of rate-payers to vote on the proposed rate of 1/- in the £1. An amendment of a rate of ¼d. in the £1 was moved at this meeting at the *Bremen Hotel*. The amendment was strongly supported by German farmers of Hope Valley. Voting was 109 for a rate of 1/- and 61 for ¼d. The ¼d. vote was virtually a protest by thrifty German farmers against being required to pay any rates at all. Among the list of rates still unpaid by the end of 1855 were many German names.

The years of 1854 and 1855 were progressive and busy years for the Council.

On June 25 tenders were called for fourteen contracts. The contracts themselves are a reflection of the tasks which confronted the district's first council.

Tenders listed were:

1. To construct a bridge across Gavin's Creek near Golden Grove.
2. To remove stumps and stones from Rowe's Hill near Golden Grove.
3. For the construction of a culvert and about four chains of metalling near Boase's Ford.
4. Removing fence and repairs at Gregory's Corner.
5. Repairing the road south of Wright's bridge.
6. For the construction of a bridge between Kelly's and Shaw's fence.
7. Repairing the ford near Cronk's.
8. For splitting and erecting a post and two-rail fence and the formation of a bank and ditch at the cemetery at Golden Grove.
9. Same at the cemetery at Houghton.
10. For the formation of a road at Hope Valley.
11. Repairs at Houghton ford.
12. Post and rails per hundred to be delivered at the Tea Tree Gully line.
13. Repairing a road at Dordoys.
14. Bridge over creek at *Drumminor*.

Some of the tenderers were William Hancock, Henry Tilley, Thomas Wright and William Reeds. In 1855 it was decided to insert all tenders and notices in the German language newspaper.

There were appointments to be made — stationmen for the different sections of the district roads, keepers for the public pounds, a health inspector, auditors for the council books, Justices of the Peace, trustees of the

151

local cemeteries and District Constables.

William Haines, who later became the district's first resident Member of Parliament, was appointed first keeper of the public pound erected by the council near the entrance to Tea Tree Gully. Fines for straying animals impounded were set down at 1/3d. for horses and cattle, 2d. for sheep and goats and 6d. for pigs.

The greatest achievement of the Council during 1855 was the erection of the council chambers — the first District Council in South Australia to do so.

The minutes of the council meeting held on May 28, 1855, state:

'The Clerk was directed to procure from Mr. Weir, Architect, by the next meeting, a rough sketch with the estimated cost of the most economical sort of building of a room for the use of the Council and district generally with 2 or 3 rooms attached. The Council were of the opinion that the room should be 30 feet long'.

The first meeting of the Council in their new quarters was held on November 26, 1855. The modest little building erected on a section of land near the entrance to Tea Tree Gully granted by the Government served as headquarters of the Council for the next 112 years. Now a building of historic significance, it serves as offices for the Works Overseer of the present Corporation.

The proposal to erect council rooms met with stiff opposition. Two public meetings — one in August and another in September — were called by ratepayers to question the council's decision. By this time the tender of Messrs. James Adds and John Mayers to erect the Council Room for the sum of £400 had been accepted and work on the building had begun.

The main complaint at the first protest meeting at the *Bremen Hotel* was that the expenditure of £400 had swallowed up one-third of the entire year's funds. The siting of the new building at Steventon (Tea Tree Gully) was questioned, but the new chambers were in fact centrally placed. A further objection was that an extra 3d. had been added to the rates.

In answering these objections it was pointed out that, for £400, the district had gained a Council House, a Court House and a public meeting place.

The protests at the second public meeting centred on the obvious fact that nearly all councillors resided in the same part of the district. A memorial praying for the division of the district into council wards was signed. To it was attached a request that ratepayers be permitted to supply stone in lieu of rates. Neither request was granted and the Council replied that 'rates must be paid in cash, not stone'.

Despite the outlay of money on the new council rooms, the balance sheet for 1855 was healthy. Expenditure had been £1,352.4.9½, but revenue had amounted to £1,579.14.2½.

In April of 1856, Thomas Crews resigned as district clerk and Thomas

Edward Cooke, a young man of 29, was appointed to the position. Cooke had been a storekeeper in Wellington Square, North Adelaide. He acquired, early in 1856, an acre of land in the new Steventon Estate where he built, in 1854, one of the first three stores in the new township, and later became its post-master. Before the Council Chamber had been completed Cooke had applied for the use of the cottage attached to the council office. Use was granted at a weekly rent of 2/- and on the understanding that Cooke would 'keep the rooms clean and take charge of documents and letters addressed to the Council'.

Cooke remained District Clerk and village storekeeper until his death in 1866 at the age of 40.

The Highercombe Council, like all councils, received its share of complaints. They differed only in kind from ratepayers' complaints of today.

The Hope Valley Germans asked whether they were not thought respectable enough to be considered for the position of Clerk. There were complaints against assessments, protests about road priorities, complaints about citizens blasting wood instead of chopping it, and charges that all the rates were being spent on the northern side of the district, particularly in the immediate vicinity of councillors' homes.

The balance sheet for 1856 reveals some interesting items of expenditure. Six cedar-stained chairs were purchased for the Council Chambers. (It is not stated how the councillors were seated for the three years prior to this.) A five-stalled stable for the Councillors' horses was erected and the Council Chamber plastered. In 1856, too, the Council purchased its first equipment — '2 wooden wheelbarrows, 2 picks, 2 shovels, and 1 crow-bar'.

As yet the Council had no 'road plant' of its own. The Clerk was directed to employ cartage where necessary 'at the rate of £1 per day for 2 horses and cart 'with man'; 6 bullocks and dray and one man, the same; and one horse, dray and man 15/- per day'.

The question of district wards became a very live issue early in 1858. The Council resolved in April that it would be advisable to resign office and call a meeting of ratepayers for the election of a councillor in each ward. The Clerk was asked to prepare a map outlining the boundaries of the new wards.

The meeting place for the elections in each ward on Monday, May 3, 1858 were advertised as follows:

'Ward No. 1   at the house of Mr. R. Smyth, Upper Dry Creek.
                 Mr. R. South, Chairman.
     2   At the Bremen Hotel, Hope Valley.
                 Mr. J.G. Coulls, Chairman.
     3   at the Travellers' Rest, Houghton.
                 Mr. W. Reeds, Jnr., Chairman.
     4   at the house of John Smart, Golden Grove.
                 Mr. W. Haines, Jnr., Chairman.
     5   under a gum tree on the District Road opposite the slip-panel leading to the residence of Mr. Robert Smyth.
                 Mr. J. Hunter, Chairman.'

Each councillor was to appoint his own Clerk for the day, to be paid £1.1.0 and expenses.

The five new councillors elected were — John Goodall, Ward 1; John Green Coulls, Ward 2; William Reeds, Snr., Ward 3; Charles Watson, Ward 4; and Robert Smyth, Snr., Ward 5. Charles Watson, storekeeper and farmer, of Golden Grove, was elected Chairman at the first meeting of the new council.

The much-needed improvement in representation did not however satisfy the residents and ratepayers at Hope Valley and Houghton. Nothing but a complete division of the District of Highercombe into two council districts would satisfy them. The main north-eastern road, via Teatree Gully, now by-passed the village of Houghton and the ratepayers of Hope Valley and Houghton realised that little money would be spent on the Anstey's Hill line of road, at least for some years. They wished to have their own rates and taxes spent upon their own roads.

In June of 1858 a meeting was held at Hope Valley 'to take into consideration the propriety of dividing the district into two and forming a district to be called South Highercombe'. A demarcation line between the two council districts was decided on and a council for the new district nominated.

In the *Government Gazette* of July 1, 1855 the following memorial appeared:

'Ratepayers of Nos. 2 and 3 Wards, after a patient trial of nearly five years, are unable to come to any conclusion than an apparent impossibility of an amicable working of the district as at present constituted; the interests of the North and South portions being in no way identical, and we therefore request that your Excellency will be pleased to cause the present district to be divided into two districts'.

A counter-memorial, petitioning against the division of the district was gazetted a fortnight later, complaining that the memorialists 'were merely playing at District Councils to ask for wards one month and separate councils the next', but the original petition was granted. The new districts — the District of Highercombe *(See Map 9)* and the District of Tea Tree Gully — were proclaimed on October 6, 1858. The final meeting of the original District of Highercombe was held in the Council Chambers on Monday, October 11, 1858. It was a brief session. The minutes of the previous meeting were read and confirmed, and a division of funds decided on.

After only five years, the old District of Highercombe was now divided, and remained divided for the next 77 years. In 1935 the two districts united again as the District of Tea Tree Gully, under compulsion, but with little protest.

20

DISTRICT OF TEA TREE GULLY 1858—1935

'now attending to clerical duties on two days a week'

Following 'an incessant commotion' both in and out of Council during 1858, which led to the division of the district in October of that year, the two newly-proclaimed districts settled down to a more or less hum-drum existence. The separate existence of the two district councils remained almost complete for the next 77 years. Occasionally the Tea Tree Gully District Council might politely request the use of the Highercombe District Council's road-roller or, less politely, the two councils might argue about who was responsible for which sections of boundary roads. Relations were, however, mainly amicable.

On some occasions co-operation was complete. One such notable occasion was the opening of Haines Perseverance Road on Thursday, May 20, 1880. Even then protocol was strictly observed, the opening ceremony, which consisted of breaking a bottle of champagne on the road, being performed under an archway exactly sited where the boundary line between the two council districts bisected the road. *(See Map 9)*

The problems of each council were the same — mainly that of road-making where no made roads previously existed. Another common problem was that of developing a permanent system of roads within the district and of satisfying, at the same time, the individual needs of ratepayers whose properties and farmhouses were widely scattered. New roads had to be opened through private property, and tracks to outlying farms fenced and made passable in winter. Metal placed on the road one winter had often disappeared beneath the Bay of Biscay soil before the next winter. It is to the credit of councillors during the first hundred years of local government that their minute books and letter books reveal so few complaints and even less litigation. The democratic process of biennial elections, retirement by ballot, and, if necessary, of public protest meetings, provided safeguards for ratepayers and safety-valves for letting off steam.

Occasionally ratepayers were even moved to show their gratitude to a Chairman who had, they considered, given outstanding service. When

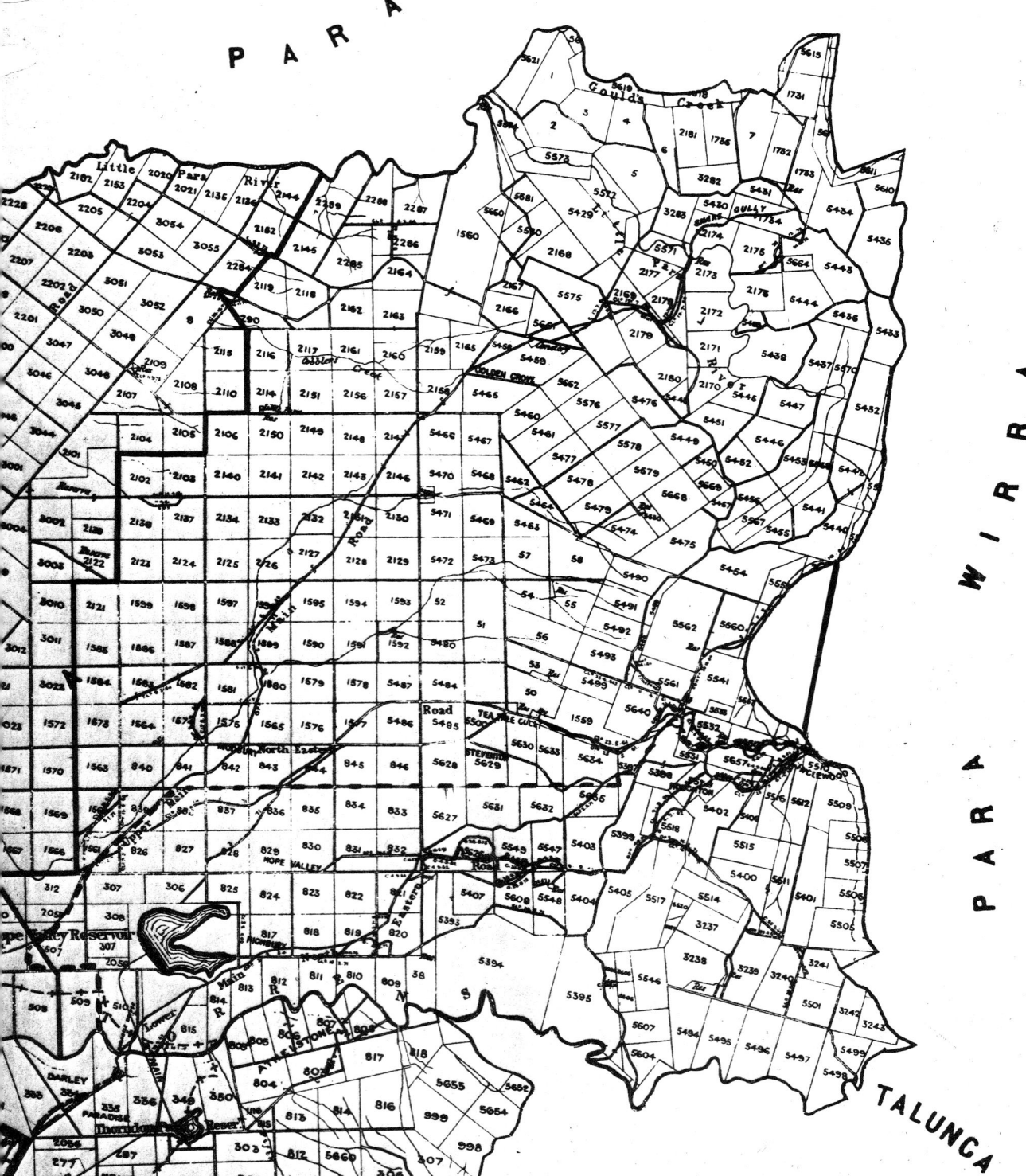

Map 9. (1877) Portion of Hundred of Yatala showing boundaries of District of Tea Tree Gully and District of Highercombe. *(cf. Map 8.)* S.A. State Library.

Robert Symons Kelly of Modbury announced his retirement in June 1862, after a two year term of office as Chairman of the Tea Tree Gully Council, he was given a surprise dinner by fellow citizens. 'Forty-four gentlemen sat down', we are told, 'to a sumptious spread provided by Mr. Stoneham, mine host of the *Modbury Hotel* and prepared by that chef-de-cuisine, Mr. Biggs of Hindley Street'. Four of the gentlemen — Mr. Tregeagle, Mr. Cooke, Mr. A.B. Murray and Mr. William Haines — made long speeches.

The result of 'the sumptious feast' and farewell was somewhat unexpected. Mr. Kelly was requested by ratepayers to again put in his nomination at the July elections and upon doing so was promptly re-elected for a further term of office.

Although the problems of each council district were the same and both had similar topographical problems of steep hills and a network of creeks to contend with, the area administered by each council differed greatly in size. The new District of Highercombe contained approximately 14 square miles, or 8,960 acres of countryside, while the District of Tea Tree Gully embraced some 34 square miles or 21,760 acres of country.

Because it included the villages of Hope Valley and Houghton, the smaller District of Highercombe was comparatively more populous than that of Tea Tree Gully. In 1861, with less than one-third of the acreage of the original district as proclaimed in 1853, its district population was 641. The population of the District of Tea Tree Gully, a district of twice the size, was 939.

If the District of Highercombe had the advantage of relatively greater numbers for its size, the District of Tea Tree Gully had two greater advantages. It had the money of more ratepayers, with the accompanying £ for £ government road subsidy, to spend on any one particular road. It also had possession, as a result of the division of the district, of the permanent Council Chambers built in 1855 in the new township of Steventon.

The District of Highercombe had, as we shall see, no permanent meeting place or Council Chamber of its own in its 77 years of existence.

The council chamber remained the meeting place and office of the newly-formed Tea Tree Gully Council until 1935 and then continued to be the home of the two re-united district councils until 1967.

The building must have been a crude structure to begin with. Its iron roof had to be rivetted down in 1860 following a wind storm. Until 1862, when a boarded floor was laid down in the large meeting room, the flooring was of compacted earth. In the same year tenders were called for ceiling, plastering and painting the main room. It was not until 1907 that it was thought necessary to grant the district clerk a cupboard in which to keep council books and papers. Finally, in 1916, a safe was purchased for £20 'to keep Council books in at the Clerk's residence'. In 1901, after some debate, a urinal was erected on the council land 'for the use of ratepayers'.

The council block was fenced in 1909.

The new District of Tea Tree Gully had been proclaimed on October 6, 1858 when five men — Charles Watson, Robert Smyth, John Goodall and William Haines, Jnr., and George Dickerson — were named first councillors. At the first council meeting held in the council rooms on October 11, Charles Watson, who had been Chairman of the previous District Council of Highercombe, was elected Chairman of the new Council of Tea Tree Gully. Watson, then 45 years of age and a batchelor, had been elected to represent the Golden Grove Ward in May 1858. In 1853 Charles Watson had built the first shop at Golden Grove and had become the village's first postmaster. In October 1854 he acquired section 5459 at Golden Grove for £420 — a large section of 131 acres. Here, opposite the present store at Golden Grove, he built the home where he lived until his death in 1893 at the age of 80.

The new Tea Tree Gully Council also retained the services of Thomas Edward Cooke as District Clerk, but his salary was reduced from £80 to £60 per annum. This included Cooke's duties as both Clerk and overseer. In 1866, following the death of Cooke, William Haines Jnr., at the age of 35, was appointed Clerk and remained in office for the next 37 years until his death in June 1902 at the age of 71. The position of Clerk was one which became more onerous with the passing of the years and with the enactment of Acts affecting all council areas throughout South Australia. Upon his appointment in 1866 Haines was granted the same salary as his predecessor — £60 per annum. In 1893, when Haines was once again re-appointed to the position of Clerk, the July meeting of Council resolved 'that Mr. Haines be appointed as clerk, collector of rates, registrar of dogs, granter of slaughtering and gun licences, secretary of the Local Board of Health; also Overseer of Works to the district' at the sum of £70 per annum — a rise of £10 in 27 years. It was not a princely award for a man who had, by 1893, become popularly known as 'The King of Tea Tree Gully', and had represented the District of Gumeracha in the House of Assembly from 1878 until 1884.

There were some meagre 'perks' for the Clerk. For instance, the Council cash book records that William Haines in July 1881 received the sum of £8.14.0 for the financial year — 'for registering 170 dogs, 1 shilling each: granting 1 slaughtering licence, 2 shillings and 1 gun licence, 2 shillings'.

In the year 1894, William Haines had, in addition to policing the noxious weeds, vermin, and dog acts, to implement the 'Sparrow Destruction Act'. The ubiquitous sparrow, imported into Queensland first in 1869, had spread to South Australia and in 1894 the whole colony was declared a Sparrow District. Councils were asked to institute vigorous measures for the suppression of the destructive bird. Poisoned wheat was supplied to the councils by Messrs. F.H. Faulding & Co., Adelaide, at 17/6d. a bushel for distribution to owners. More appealing, especially to small boys, was the introduction of a Sparrow Bounty.

Along with other district councils, both the Tea Tree Gully and Highercombe Councils advertised on notice boards throughout the districts that they would pay 'the following prices for the whole of the Sparrow Heads and Sparrow Eggs collected:

| For Sparrow Heads | 1/6 per 100 |
| For Eggs | 1/- per 100 eggs' |

To protect the poor clerk from constant harassment by boys, payment was not forthcoming for less than 50 heads or 100 eggs at any one time. Some district clerks insisted, for good reason perhaps, that eggs should first be 'blown'.

Although there was great concern felt in the district by fruitgrowers, and the Sparrow Act remained in force for the next forty years, and Councils continued to pay out for heads and eggs, the sparrow is still with us. Perhaps small boys grew tired of the contest. Perhaps there were fewer thatched farmsheds where birds might find a nesting place. Somehow we have learned to live with the sparrow.

As might be expected of a district which retained its farms, orchards, and vineyards for the century following settlement, the number of council assessments, as recorded by the assessment books, reveal no dramatic growth.

With the division of the district in 1858, the Tea Tree Gully Council found itself with 176 ratepayers on its books, leaving the Highercombe Council with 120 ratepayers. With a property assessment for the district of £9,496.13.0, the new Council reckoned upon an income from rates of £237.8.4½ for the year at the rating of 6d. in the £1. This amount would be doubled by the £ for £ government grant-in-aid. After 1874, when control of the main roads in the district was transferred to District Councils, rates were supplemented by a Main Road Grant.

During the 77 years of its life, the number of ratepayers increased steadily from the initial 176 to 360 in 1935, when, with the re-union of the two districts, the number of ratepayers in the amalgamated Tea Tree Gully Council rose suddenly to 795. Income derived from rates rose slowly from £237.8.4½ in 1858 to £274.16.3 in 1899.

The smallest annual income from rates was in 1860, when the rate was reduced from 6d. in the £1 to 3d. in the £1. This was as a result of a public meeting held in the Council Chambers in March of that year, when voting for an adoption of a district rate resulted in a majority of 24 for a three-penny rate.

With one variation of 8d., the rate remained at 6d. in the £1 until 1911. In that year the Council doubled its income by raising the rate to 1/- in the £1, amid outcries against the 100% increase, followed by a spate of appeals — a familiar enough story. In 1928 the rate rose to an all-time high of 1/5d, and the annual income reached a record £1,245.17.3 in 1931.

By that year the great depression, with its accompanying unemployment, was beginning to affect the ability of ratepayers to pay their rates. The licensee of the *Inglewood Hotel* had not been able to pay rates for three years, an amount of £3.7.6 per annum. The Clerk recommended that 'if the hotel was not doing enough business to pay rates it should be closed'. The hotel licence was saved when the hotel changed hands in 1933 and the accumulated rates of £9.18.5 were finally paid.

By the close of 1931 the arrears in rates reached a total of £227.10.7 out of a total rating of £1,139.9.11. In 1932, the Tea Tree Gully Councillors decided to bring a measure of relief to ratepayers by reducing the valuation of property in the district by an all-round 20%. The valuation was dropped from a total of £318,480 to £225,100 and the annual assessment from £15,924 to £12,755. The expected income from rates for the year dropped correspondingly from £1,245.17.3 to £903.9.7.

With the amalgamation of the two councils in 1935, the rate throughout the combined district was reduced to the 1934 Highercombe Council rate of 1/-, but the 20% valuation reduction was restored, so that the combined district valuation was £589,360, the assessment of rates £29,468 and the expected income from rates £1,684.9.4 for the year 1935-36. It is perhaps of interest to compare these figures with the figures current in the year of 1974-75 for what was virtually the same council area. The value of land in the district was given as — City: $39,905,770; Urban Farmland: $5,839,950; and the rates derived as $1,333,549. In reconciliation it must be remembered that in 1935 the number of ratepayers was a mere handful of 795. By 1953, a century after self-government, there were still less than 1,000 ratepayers in the district of nearly 50 square miles. In 1975, the same district issued more than 20,000 notices of assessment to ratepayers.

Apart from administering such local government Acts as the Width of Tyres Act, Thistle Act, the Sparrow Act, the Noxious Weeds Act, the main efforts and funds of the Tea Tree Gully Council were concentrated upon road making, with perhaps bridge building absorbing the second largest portion of available funds. Until re-union of the two councils in 1935, and then until 1953, the District Clerk was, except in a few instances, also Overseer of Works.

When John H. Tilley was appointed Clerk and Overseer in July 1906, it was expected that he would be 'at the Council Chambers half a day per week to attend to Council work' and on the road every other day in his capacity as overseer. By 1927 it was reported that the clerk was 'now attending to clerical duties on two days per week'.

The road-making equipment of the Tea Tree Gully Council in 1858 was almost non-existent. It seems to have consisted of two barrows — one for each of the two stationmen (permanent employees) of the council. The minutes of the Council meeting in September 1883 record the following request by the Clerk/Overseer: 'Will the Council have a new barrow made for the use of the stationmen. They have to get the loan of one for use'. *(Approved)*

Stationmen supplied their own picks, crowbars, hammers and shovels, although in 1877 it was decided that hammers and picks could be repaired 'at the expense of Council'.

The first major piece of equipment to be acquired by Council was a second-hand iron road-roller. In February of 1888 it was reported that 'the Government had given the council one of the Road Rollers formerly the property of the late Central Road Board, with the understanding that the district lend the roller to other districts in the locality free that may require its use'. The same report mentions the possibility of the Council being granted a free Road Scraper.

Council had no horse and cart of its own until 1903. Indeed, annual tenders were called for the supply of a cart and the use of one or two horses. In 1890 council minutes record that 'Councillor Tilley gave us some stone to help fill holes and also lent a horse and cart to cart the stone free'. In November 1903, after long and serious discussion the Overseer was instructed to purchase a medium draught horse for a spring cart and to advertise in the *Advertiser* for tenders for 'a spring dray 6 feet x 14 feet x 15 inches, to carry 1 ton; 1½ inch axles; closed sides, front and back; 1¾ inch flat tyre'. The successful tenderer was the Adelaide firm of Messrs. John & F. Holbrook, whose tender of £18.15.0 included a 'floor of Singapore cedar' for the cart.

Council, a few months later, decided that the new spring dray must be kept under cover and tenders were called for the supply of 'a galvanised iron stable and cart shed on the overseer's land'. The overseer was willing to have the shed on his property and 'to move it elsewhere when desired'.

By 1906 Council had come to the conclusion that their new piece of equipment was a costly failure. They now called for tenders 'for horse, dray, harness and shed as the new dray was not paying for itself'. A tender of £8 for the shed, £12 for the horse, harness £2 and dray £10 was accepted. Council then resumed its earlier practice of calling for tenders for a man, dray and horse for carting on the roads for the year. The tender of John Ross for 10/- per day for one horse and man or 13/- per day for two horses and man was then accepted.

A complete list of Council 'plant' as recorded by the Clerk in 1909 makes a fascinating comparison with the 'plant' required for road-making today. In 1909 it consisted of:

14 picks and 5 handles	1 tape
9 wheelbarrows (one without wheel)	1 spanner
3 drills	1 oil can
3 large hammers	1 stone gauge
1 fencing bar	1 back chain for Roller

1 steel crow-bar	2 lanterns
2 stone hammers	1 cash box
1 cross-cut saw	1 wooden box
1 x 1½" auger	1 iron safe
1 scraper	1 pair of calipers
1 hedge hook	1 official stamp
1 culvert cleaner	1 ring stone measure 2½"

The council also, by 1909, owned its own water-cart, roller and scraper.

Wages for council employees increased only marginally in the lifetime of the council. Wages for stationmen were 30/- a week in 1858. In 1909, fifty years later, wages for able-bodied men employed by Council full time were raised to 7/- a day and 6/- per day 'to all others not able-bodied'.

Ten years later, following World War I, wages rose to 9/- a day and returned soldiers were paid 10/6d. per day. By 1930, when the depression was just beginning, labourers were receiving 12/- and the foreman 14/- a day. Within a few years wages were reduced to 10/- a day (60/- a week) and both men and foreman placed on three-quarter-time. There was widespread unemployment throughout South Australia and applications for rations and relief, the clerk reported, 'were coming in wholesale' from district families.

Government relief — or 'the dole' as it became known — consisted of coupons (to the value of 16/3d. per adult per week at one stage) which could be exchanged in local shops for bread, meat, sugar, jam or honey, rice or sago, tea, raisins, and soap. Councils also dispensed 'Christmas Relief' to unemployed ratepayers, when men were given work for a day or two cleaning gutters and weeding footpaths in exchange for 10/- in cash.

Wages remained at a low level, and the hours of labour, at least until World War I remained long. Until then, all council employees were expected to be at work by 7 a.m. 'Knock-off' time was 5 p.m. 'except on Saturday when they may leave work at 4 p.m.; one quarter of an hour to be allowed each morning for lunch and one hour each day for dinner'. It was very close to being a 52 hour week. During and following the war, hours were reduced by an average of 1 hour per day to 47 hours a week, and remained at 47 until the 44 hour week became general during World War II.

The year 1926 was the greatest 'leap forward' in the history of the Tea Tree Gully Council — at least for the councillors, the clerk and the ratepayers. The Chairman at the time was Archibald D.N. Robertson of Golden Grove Farm, Golden Grove.

Early in the year Council was advised that it was intended to reconstruct the Adelaide to Tea Tree Gully road with bituminous concrete. Council also called for a quote for its first mechanised vehicle — a one-ton Ford truck to replace the council horse and dray. A quote of £179 was accepted and the Council made a down payment of £60 and agreed to pay the balance in 18 months. In August of the same year, shortly after the Adelaide Electric Supply Co. extended its mains to the district, a quote for lighting the Council Chambers was sought. Installation cost £4 and rental was 5/- per quarter.

Perhaps the most generally acceptable development was the arrival of piped water. In December of 1926, the District Clerk informed Council that pipes for a Tea Tree Gully water supply had been delivered along Perseverance Road and a start to lay the pipe was to be made immediately.

The twentieth century and the new age of technology caught up, too, with the district Clerk. Early in February of 1927 a telephone was installed in the Council Chambers and in November the Clerk acquired his first typewriter — a second-hand Remington purchased for £5.

In April 1933, Victor Spurgeon Bowen was appointed Clerk. For the next 25 years 'Vic' Bowen retained his position as District Clerk and Overseer and retired in 1957 at the age of 66.

Bowen took over at a difficult time in the history of the first District Council of Tea Tree Gully. The depression was already having a grave effect on council finance and the Royal Commission on Local Government Areas had just been appointed. Within two years 'Vic' Bowen found himself Clerk of the new Tea Tree Gully District Council, amalgamated again after a separation of 77 years.

BALANCE SHEET

OF THE

TEA TREE GULLY DISTRICT COUNCIL,

FOR THE HALF-YEAR ENDING JUNE 29TH, 1867.

Dr.   **Cr.**

	RECEIPTS.	£	s.	d.
1867.	Balance last Audit	85	6	4
	Rates	72	13	6
Feb. 25.	Reynolds and Johnson, Wood	0	15	0
March 11.	Richardson, Rent	12	0	0
	Goodall, Rent	8	0	0
April 8.	Taylor, Wood	3	0	0
May 13.	Warner, Wood	1	0	0
	Read, Rent	10	0	0
	Dog Fee	0	5	0
	Further Rates received	5	14	3
May 30.	Overdraft at the Bank	89	12	3½
June*	Rates since received	3	15	6
	Reynolds for Wood	0	7	6
	H. M. Government in aid of Subscriptions	7	7	7
June 29.	Interest due on Overdraft	1	6	9
		£301	**3**	**8½**

	EXPENDITURE.	£	s	d.
1867.	Mills, Smith, and James Dunn, Labour on Roads	34	13	0
Jan. 28.	Association of Chairmen	1	1	0
	Sherring, Printing Notices and Balance Sheets	1	9	0
Feb. 9.	Rawlings, Carting Stone	1	10	3
" 25.	John Gilmour, Constable's expenses	1	1	0
	John Smart for Stone, near Golden Grove	1	0	0
	James Dunn, Labour and Cartage, Hermitage	2	14	0
	Promissory Note to Bank	80	0	0
March 11.	James Dunn, Labour and Cartage	3	12	0
25.	James Dunn, Carting Stone	3	18	0
	Moschke, Hope Valley Road	10	0	0
	Cox, on account of Contract No. 1	22	0	0
	Reuben Coulter, Stone Carting	1	12	6
May	Petty cash accounts paid by late Clerk	6	11	6½
June	Mills, Dunn, and Smith, Labour on Roads	21	1	0
	David Mills, Cartage	1	5	6
	Mrs. Cooke, Implements, &c.	1	1	4½
	Daniell & Cox, balance on Contract near Whitmore's	7	14	0
	Special audit	2	2	0
	Auditors	2	2	0
	Balance in the hands of late Clerk	93	8	9½
June 29.	Interest due Bank on overdraft £98 12s. 3½d.	1	6	9
		£301	**3**	**8½**

* New Clerk commenced.

We have examined this Balance Sheet and find it correct, this 29th day of June, 1867.

CHAS. WATSON, } Auditors.
E. MITCHELSON, }

John Thomas Shawyer, Printer, 71, King William Street, Adelaide.

21

DISTRICT OF HIGHERCOMBE 1858 - 1935

'a private room with one table, six chairs and two forms'

The re-proclaimed District of Highercombe was reduced in size by the proclamation of October 7, 1858, from its previous 47½ square miles to a mere 14 square miles. For a few years, at least, the new Council felt that it had achieved the aim of its ratepayers in petitioning for separation and that their rates and taxes would now be spent on their own district roads. The villagers of Houghton and Hope Valley for the moment appeared satisfied. The Anstey's Hill Road, joining the two villages, might now also receive proper attention.

There were difficulties, however, facing the new councillors. With a mere handful of 120 ratepayers, the annual income to be expected from rates was less than £150. In 1860, when the ratepayers voted to reduce the rate from 1/- to 6d. in the £1, this income was halved. The balance sheet for 1861 showed receipts of £151, made up of rates (£76) plus a £ for £ subsidy, with an expenditure of £140 on public works and £11 for office expenses. The rate was restored to 1/- in 1862 and remained so until amalgamation in 1935. Not until 1874, when rates were supplemented by a Main Roads Grant, did the new Council have a worthwhile amount to use in road construction.

Upon separation from the District of Tea Tree Gully the new Council of Highercombe lost its meeting place and office equipment. One of the first purchases of the new Council was 'a fit box to hold books and papers'. It was not until 1932 that Council felt it necessary to purchase an office safe — a second-hand one costing £12.

The question of a Council Room remained a vexatious one throughout the lifetime of the second Highercombe Council. It was not solved until 1922, when the Hope Valley and Highbury Soldiers' Memorial Institute was built and the Council rented a room in the new Institute 'as a Council Chamber and District Office'. Even then, to appease the ratepayers of Houghton, Council felt constrained, from time to time, to hold meetings for the year in the old Schoolroom at Houghton.

BALANCE-SHEET for the Year ending 30th June, 1902, of the District Council of ....Highercombe.......

Amount of Assessment for 1901-2, £ 5,105 : 5 : 0.　　Amount derivable from Rate of Twelve pence in the pound, £ 259 : 5 : 3.

RECEIPTS.	£	s.	d.	Totals. £	s.	d.
Amount in Bank on 1st July, 1901	65	14	11			
Amount in Clerk's hand on 1st July, 1901	1	—	5	65	15	4
Amount of Rates for 1901-2 collected	238	10	0			
Arrears of Rates collected	—	—	—			
Amount received from Government as Grant-in-aid.......	65	14	3	322	4	3
LICENCE AND OTHER FEES—						
Amount received from Crown Lands Licences						
Dog Licence Fees	14	10	3			
Slaughter Licence Fees	1	5	0			
Gun and other Licence Fees	1	4	5			
Poundage Fees and Charges	6	11	0	15	19	8
* AMOUNTS DERIVED FROM OTHER SOURCES—						
Cemetery Fees — Rent						
Sale of Timber — Fees &c Plans						
Roads &c	6	11	0			
Bank Overdraft on 30th June, 1902						
Grand Total				410	13	3

EXPENDITURE.	£	s.	d.	Totals. £	s.	d.
Bank Overdraft on 1st July, 1901						
SALARIES AND OFFICE EXPENSES—						
Clerk's Salary and Guarantee Policy	11	10	0			
Ranger's Salary						
Wages to Overseer of Works	21	—	0			
Assessment Revising	16	9	0			
Advertising, Printing, Stationery, and Postage, &c.	2	—	0			
Auditor's Fees	2	4	0	54	14	9
AMOUNT EXPENDED ON PUBLIC WORKS—						
Construction, &c.	44	6	8			
Maintenance	124	11	9	198	18	5
MISCELLANEOUS EXPENDITURE—						
Election Expenses	3	19	9			
Travelling Expenses	19	18	0			
Legal Expenses						
Pound Expenses	1	6	0			
Bank Interest						
Destruction of Noxious Weeds						
Registration of Dogs (Rent)		8	5			
Board of Health Expenses						
Contributions to Charitable Institutions	1	1	0			
Contribution to District Council Association	1	1	0			
* SUNDRY EXPENDITURE—						
....	11	17	5			
....		5	3			
Balance in Bank 30th June, 1902	173					
Balance in Clerk's hands 30th June, 1902	40	13	10			
Total Balance in hand				213	1	11
Grand Total				410	13	3

MAIN ROAD FUND.

	£	s.	d.	£	s.	d.
Balance in Bank on 1st July, 1901	500	0	0	44	19	5
Amount received from Government as Grant for Main Roads	500	0	0			
Amount received from Government as Special Grant ...		2	6	500	0	0
	40	0	0	4	2	6
Grand Total				505	1	11

EXPENDITURE	£	s.	d.	£	s.	d.
Construction	560	19	0			
Maintenance	22	5	0			
Wages to Overseer of Works		10	0	583	14	4
Balance in Bank 30th June, 1902				1	4	4
Grand Total				505	1	11

We, the undersigned, Chairman and Clerk of the above-named District Council, hereby certify, that the foregoing statement of the Receipts and Expenditure of the District during the year ended 30th June, 1902, is true and correct in every particular.

Date July 11th 1902.

We, hereby certify that the foregoing statement of the Receipts and Expenditure of the District during the year ended 30th June, 1902.

Audited and found correct to date, 30th June, 1902.

.... Chairman.

.... Clerk.

.... } Auditors.

* Here state any items of Receipts and Expenditure not already stated.

Item 4　Balance Sheet of District Council of Highercombe, 1902.

The first meeting of the new Council was held on October 13, 1858 in the *Bremen Hotel*, Hope Valley. The new councillors, as proclaimed in the *Government Gazette*, were John Green Coulls of *Athelstone House*, Highbury, Wm. Reeds, Jnr., of Houghton, Heinrich Klopper of Hope Valley, Charles Kolwes of Hope Valley and W.H. Peryman of Anstey's Hill. John Coulls was elected Chairman for the ensuing year.

For a time the meeting place alternated between Hope Valley, Highbury and Houghton, the venue in each place being a room of the local hotel. A letter from the innkeeper, Mr. S. Pearce, of the *Travellers' Rest*, Houghton, in May 1862 offered 'to furnish a private room with one table, six chairs and two forms for the use of Council at two shillings per week'. The offer was accepted. However a request from ratepayers of Hope Valley was received two months later and the Clerk was asked 'to remove Council boxes to that place'.

In later years, to obviate this cumbersome method of satisfying local rivalries, the meeting place for the ensuing year was fixed at the first meeting of each council year. After 1878, when a new government school was erected at Houghton, the Old Schoolroom (previously also the Union Church) was vested in the Highercombe Council and was used by them as a Council Room, alternating annually or sometimes biennially, with the 'Council Room' at the *Highbury Hotel* or the 'Council Room' at the *Bremen Hotel*, Hope Valley.

For meetings with the District Council of Tea Tree Gully, when a neutral ground was required, a room at the *Inglewood Inn* was hired.

In 1918, under the Chairmanship of Councillor F. Hodges of Houghton, the resolution was moved 'That this Council is of opinion that a suitable Council Chamber should be provided in the district and that ways and means of providing same be considered by Council at a subsequent meeting'.

The campaign was a vigorous, well-conducted one and ratepayers were willing to sanction a special rate to raise the necessary money. Tenders received for erecting the building were, however, unexpectedly high and ratepayers too few and ultimately it was left to the Hope Valley and Highbury Memorial Institute Committee to build the hall in 1922 and to make rooms available to the Council as a District Office 'and for any meetings, elections and to supply lighting and fuel required for a lump sum of £3.3.0 per annum' — a generous offer readily accepted by Council.

Ratepayers of the village of Houghton had been the most voluble group in achieving the division of the first district council area in 1858. In 1861 another group of 32 ratepayers, many of them landholders in the Paracombe area and adjoining sections of the District of Para Wirra, petitioned in the *Government Gazette* of March 14 to establish a new 'District of the Para'. The spokesman for the breakaway settlers was William Weir, an Adelaide Architect, who had until 1860 held nearly 500 acres at Paracombe and in

1861 still held section 5401, a large section of 147 acres, adjoining present-day Murray Road along its eastern boundary.

The reason given by the Paracombe ratepayers was that they had little in common with either the district of Para Wirra or the district of Highercombe and that the upkeep of the more numerous roads of Hope Valley should not be their financial concern.

A much larger group of ratepayers from both the Para Wirra and Highercombe districts immediately petitioned the Governor not to grant the new District of Para. They pointed out that the new district had only 35 landholders and that the annual rates that could be collected would amount to less than £50. A strong opponent of the formation of a new district was the owner of the *Highercombe Estate*, the Hon. G.M. Waterhouse, who was later in the same year to become Premier of South Australia. Waterhouse suggested, as an alternative to division of the District of Highercombe, that the creation of five wards would give better representation — the wards to be named Para Ward, Houghton Ward, Highercombe Ward, Hope Valley Ward and Paradise Ward.

It was now the turn of the ratepayers of Hope Valley to lodge an objection to the idea of district wards. They stated that 'should the district be so divided, a great injustice would be inflicted on that portion of the district westward of the foot of Anstey's Hill, inasmuch as the thickly populated village of Houghton being able virtually to return three Councillors would thereby have the power of the purse of the district'.

It was stalemate. Neither the creation of a new district of Para, nor a division into wards was granted by the Governor. The matter was never raised again.

To us today, this attempt to fragment the district might seem to be an example of narrow-minded parochialism, but one must not forget that in the 1860s the distance between Hope Valley and Houghton or Paracombe presented a very real problem. The connecting roads were still unmetalled and for Councillors to negotiate Anstey's Hill fortnightly on horseback to attend meetings through hot summers and muddy winters and generally for a term of two years must have often been a stern test of their decision to serve as Councillors. The monetary reward for each attendance at Council meetings was, for nearly 70 years, 5/- per councillor. One district clerk, as we shall note, made the return journey between meeting places of the Council, fortnightly, for a record 52 years.

Although the Paracombe petitioners did not get their new district, the Highercombe Council did give more attention to their road problems. Settlers at Paracombe had two possible exits from their district — both unsatisfactory. One was via the present-day Murray Road to Inglewood and then down through Tea Tree Gully or, generally, via Houghton down Anstey's Hill. This involved an extra two mile journey from Paracombe to reach a main road to Adelaide.

Captain John Robertson of *Golden Grove*
— Officer-in-Charge of the Tea Tree Gully
Volunteer Rifles, 1897.

Leiutenant Frederick Christoff Newman
of *Water Gully* in the uniform of the
Mounted Rifles, 1897.

Pre-embarkation photo, Houghton 1915. **L.to R. Back Row:** Bob Coad, Les Pitman, Bill Clifton, Bob Drury. **Second Row:** Bill Drury, Angus Day, Clarence Possingham, Ern Chapman, Arn Chapman. **Front Row:** Jim Rehn, Albert Dearman, John Newsome.

Australia Day procession along the Main North East Road, Modbury, January 1919. The Kelly homestead is hidden by trees. At right is the home of Mr. and Mrs. Arthur Rehn. The procession is approaching the intersection at Reservoir Road.

The second exit road was from Paracombe down the Spring Hill road to the Torrens River and out through an unmade track through the Gorge. This track, long since closed, was too steep and rarely used except by early teamsters for hauling out red gum and blue gum logs from forests along the River Torrens. Only local families such as the Hurst, Crouch and Chapman families knew how to negotiate the Spring Hill Road.

Council decided then to open up a more direct line of road from Para-combe to the top of Anstey's Hill. This road was named in the 1860s Kangaroo Bottom Road and retained this name for over 100 years. It has recently been renamed Murphy's Road, after the old Houghton family of that name. Mrs. C. Murphy still occupies the house built in Murphy's Road by Mr. Murphy in the 1890s.

Kangaroo Bottom Road took its name from a swampy and wooded section of Anstey's original *Highercombe Estate* known, no doubt with good reason, as Kangaroo Bottom. The new road skirted the northern sections of *Highercombe Estate*. Much money, time and energy was spent over a period of 20 years in clearing, metalling and blinding the road, especially in its swampy sections. It however remained an unsatisfactory road, steep and often washed out, and to this day remains unsealed.

It was not until the 1920s that a suitable alternative to the Kangaroo Bottom exit road from Paracombe was opened. In December of 1921 a deputation of three men — Messrs. Ern. Chapman, Rol. Hannaford, and W.A. Crossman — all of Paracombe, was received at a meeting of the Highercombe Council. Following a meeting of 50 ratepayers, the three men had been appointed 'to express their desire to have a new road from Anstey's Hill running through *Highercombe Estate* and not have to travel on the steep grades of Kangaroo Bottom Road'. Many deputations and 8 years later, in December 1929, the new through road was opened and named Highercombe Road. The western end of the road, leading now to the Highercombe Golf Course and lined with magnificent pine and English trees, was once the private driveway to *Highercombe House*, originally the residence of George Anstey.

Other roads of early concern to the Highercombe Council were the Water Gully Road, the Black Hill Road from Inglewood to Houghton, the Houghton Hollow Road, and the road from Hope Valley along Grand Junction Road to the Ardtornish Corner, and the road to the new village of Modbury.

In 1874 the Anstey Hill Road became the responsibility of the Higher-combe Council and in 1930 received its first bitumen surface. Bitumen had first been used in the district in 1926 when approval was given to reconstruct the recently opened Gorge Road 'by the bitumen penetration method' from Athelstone to the Gumeracha Bridge. In the following year part of the Main North East Road bordering the district was sealed with bitumen. In 1929 a grant of £220 was given to Council 'to assist in surfacing with Colas or bitumen 56 chains on the Lower North East Road leading from the Paradise Bridge'. At the same time a 'Steam Roller, with driver, was loaned to Council at £3.10.0 per day all found'. The day of the motor car had arrived and the demands of its devotees had to be met. Metalled roads were good enough for the business of teamsters and residents but not for the new fad of touring and driving for the mere pleasure of movement and speed.

As early as 1912 a request was made by the Roads Board to the Highercombe Council and councils in general asking that when making or repairing roads the metal should be gradually sloped at the side 'to lessen the danger to motors'. In the previous year a letter had been received by the District Clerk from the Crown Lands Department offering to supply free of cost notice boards for tourists 'showing direction, distance and height of roads above sea-level' if Council was prepared to erect these. In 1922, at the request of the South Australian Automobile Association, entrance and exits to Houghton, Hope Valley and Highbury were marked with signs. In 1928 horse teams were limited to driving not more than three abreast and horse-drawn vehicles and bicycles required to carry a red tail light as well as white lights on either side. In 1930 Council erected the first four traffic signs to warn of schools and sought the help of the Tea Tree Gully police 'to warn Mr. R. Newman to moderate the speed of his new motor-lorry when travelling through townships in this district'. Mr. Newman apologised suitably to Council.

Road construction was by far the most important concern of council. These roads were almost entirely district roads. Until Dernancourt was laid out as a township in 1923 by the Department of Town Planning, the only township laid out as such was the 1841 Village of Houghton, a private township.

In 1863 'a number of ratepayers of Houghton having petitioned this Council to take under their control and management the roads, reserves and commons of the Village of Houghton' these were vested officially in the District Council of Highercombe and became the responsibility of Council.

Metal for roads was readily obtained from local quarries. It was carted from the quarries and stacked on the roadside ready for breaking down into 2½ inch gauge metal by stationmen using knapping hammers. The initial procedure was to crack enough stones to make a seat of road-metal, to cover this with a bag and to continue stone-cracking from this position. For this arduous task stationmen received, in 1860, 34/- per week. It would seem that the main distinction between stone-crackers on council road-gangs and convicts sentenced to stone-cracking in the prison quarries at the Yatala Gaol was that prisoners had to stand and received no pay except a prison pittance. On the other hand, prisoners on hard labour were required to crack no more than 1 yard of stone a day, whereas the road-worker, to keep his job, might be required to crack 3 yards each day. In addition, the council employee might have to wheel his barrow and tools from Hope Valley to

Houghton leaving home at 5 a.m. to begin work by 7 a.m. and wheeling his barrow home after a day's work, arriving home in the winter after dark and often rain-soaked.

For 20 years William Buder of Hope Valley kept the roadside water tables clear throughout the district of Highercombe. With his barrow and shovel, Buder might be seen anywhere on the roads from Houghton to the middle of the Paradise Bridge and in any weather. There was only one thing which Buder ever objected to and that was interference from any council official.

Day or casual labourers received 5/- per day and in addition had to find their own tools. Indeed, it was not until 1922 that Council felt it could afford to supply shovels and stone forks for day labourers. Stationmen were supplied, after the 1860s, with stone-cracking hammers, picks and shovels. In 1888 Council decided it would pay for the sharpening of picks and contracted with the Hope Valley Blacksmith, W.H. Nicholls, to sharpen picks as follows: 'sharpening 1/2d. per pick, steeling 1/-, and laying, 1/3d. including delivering all picks to men on work and conveying worn tools to the forge'.

In 1913, when wages were 9/- per day, the road men waited upon Council and 'respectfully' asked for a rise of 1/- per day. The request was not granted, Council deciding that 'in the event of men refusing, tenders were to be invited to spread metal by piece-work'. The overseer reported that 'after a few minutes deliberation, the men had agreed to go on with metal-spreading'.

By 1922 wages had risen but were still only 11/- a day and the working foreman (Mr. William Buder of Hope Valley) received an extra 1/- a day. During the depression years of the 1930s wages were reduced to 10/6d. per day for the foreman and 9/6d. per day for 'ordinary labourers'.

Over the years, metalling of the roads, generally of 12 feet width, proceeded a few painful chains at a time, although the bulk of Council contracts were of course for road-making. On occasions landowners offered to pay half the cost of metalling roads to their sections. Unsatisfactory contractors were dealt with by 'blacklisting'. One such contractor of Highbury remained 'blacklisted' for three years for supplying inferior quality metal.

Road-making equipment, throughout the life time of the Highercombe Council remained minimal. A shed, ten feet square, erected in 1888 at Houghton 'to house barrows exposed to the weather' sufficed to hold the Council 'plant' consisting at that time of 6 wheelbarrows, 12 picks and 12 shovels. The barrows were not replaced until 1905, when 6 new ones were purchased for 15/- each. Even by 1935 the 'Plant Statement' for the year recorded:

1	Road Roller	Value	£ 20
1	Water Cart		10
4	Wheelbarrows @ 5/-		1
	Picks and Shovels		2
		Total Value	£ 33

The most useful acquisition of Council in these years was a second-hand road-roller. Following the District Council Act of 1887 which disbanded the old Central Road Board, the equipment of the Main Roads Board was distributed among the various South Australian District Councils and Corporations. Mr. H. Pitman, Chairman of the Highercombe Council and the Clerk, John Gollop, were successful in acquiring a road-roller and took possession of it on March 28. Council minutes record that the roller was to be lent to neighbouring Councils free of charge, and money was set aside to have the 'Road-Roller repainted and the words Highercombe District Council painted on the front and back of it'. The roller, constantly repaired, was still in use at the time of amalgamation in 1935.

Electricity was first extended into the District of Highercombe in 1917, during World War I, when the Adelaide Electric Supply Company informed Council that it intended laying electric mains in Silkes Road, Paradise and extending 3 power poles into the Highercombe District to the premises of Mr. William Packer, market gardener, of Highbury. Electric power was used by William Packer to raise water from bores on his property for the irrigation of celery — a vegetable which Packer had introduced into the district in 1914. Electricity and irrigation made possible the celery industry in the Torrens valley. It was not until 1925 that electricity for lighting was extended into the district generally. A poll of ratepayers, held late in 1924, decided 107 votes for and 2 against the extension. The route of the extension was from Silkes Road, Paradise, by way of Highbury and Hope Valley to Tea Tree Gully. It was extended to Paracombe in 1930. The first street lighting began in 1926.

Both the District of Highercombe and of Tea Tree Gully were fortunate in having ready access to good stone for road-metal. On occasions stone was taken from outcrops on the district roads themselves. For a time the Council used a quarry off King William Road, Houghton, but with the building of the new school in 1878, protests were made against the continuation of blasting in the quarry and little further use was made of it except for building stone. The most extensive quarries were the Anstey's Hill Quarries of the Klopper family. The scars of these quarries are still plain in the gully at the beginning of the hill itself, on section 5626. Most of the roads of the District of Highercombe were constructed from stone supplied under contract from 'Klopper's Quarry'. Much good building stone, too, was taken from the quarry and used to build 'bluestone' homes in Adelaide suburbs and as kerbing stone. The Hope Valley Institute was constructed in 1921 from stone from the same quarry.

In 1912, Council agreed to the erection of a stone-crusher in their own 'Water Gully Quarry' in section 5549 to provide the gravel for the 'blinding' of roads in the district.

The Klopper family arrived in the district in 1849 when Heinrich Klopper took up section 823 of 80 acres at Hope Valley and began farming.

Henry Klopper was elected councillor of the first District Council to be formed in 1853. Until the Hope Valley Institute was built, Klopper's barn (and sometimes the hay shed) which stood until the 1930s at the north-eastern corner of present-day Valley Road junction with Grand Junction Road, was a centre for the dances and social functions of Hope Valley.

No summary of the work of the District Council of Highercombe would be complete without mention of its best-known clerk, John (to locals, 'Johnny') Gollop, of Houghton and reference to his record-breaking term of office.

The first clerk for the district was Josephus Longbotham, storekeeper and draper of Houghton. 'Longbotham's Draper's Shop' erected in the earliest days of the village, is still standing in Black Hill Road, Houghton, supported by the ivy which has almost overgrown it. Longbotham tendered his resignation as clerk in April 1860, and Councillor Peryman resigned to become clerk at a salary of £85 per annum. Peryman, also of Houghton, was a trained engineer. He had arrived in the colony in 1849 and soon after contracted to build the Pirie Street Wesleyan Church. Before taking up farming near Houghton, Peryman was City Surveyor and City Alderman. He died in 1864 after three years as clerk of the Highercombe Council.

John Gollop became Clerk of the Council of Highercombe on August 11, 1872, at the age of 25, and remained Clerk until his death on May 28, 1925, at the age of 78 years. 'For 52 years', recorded the *Adelaide Observer*, 'John Gollop was a faithful servant of the District Council of Highercombe' * — a record of office probably unique in the history of local government in South Australia. John Gollop wrote his last minute as Clerk one week before his death in 1925 and recorded that he had been granted six months leave of absence. Gollop was absent from Council meetings on only one occasion in his 52 years as Clerk. His salary had risen from £2 per

* Mr. L.G. Cocks of Hope Valley has supplied an interesting and descriptive sketch of the District Clerk whom he knew personally.
'John Gollop was a most efficient and capable officer — an Edwardian gentleman, small in stature but with a commanding presence.
He was always impeccably dressed and it seemed odd to see him measuring heaps of hard cracked stone on the side of muddy roads or checking the metal sizes through a 2½ inch steel ring.
He was nearly always dressed in striped pants, three-quarter length black cut-away coat, highly polished boots and a black hard hat with his beautifully trimmed grey beard — not a hair out of place.
In the cold weather he added a fine cloth overcoat with velvet cuffs and collar which he described as a Chesterfield.
Typical of his precise operating was his action at a declaration of the local council poll. Mr. Cocks and his mother were the entire audience and after getting some way through the official business of making the various announcements he discovered that he was wearing his hat. He doffed his hat, apologised and started over again from the beginning.
His hand-written notices calling for contracts, etc. were beautiful examples of old-fashioned penmanship'.

week upon appointment to £120 per annum in 1921.

The only occasion on which there appeared a difference of opinion between Clerk and Council was in 1920, when Council decided to split John Gollop's position as both Clerk and Overseer on account of his age. Gollop tendered his resignation, which Council quickly resolved not to accept. Instead they left their Clerk his title as Overseer and appointed a 'Working Foreman'.

The Gollop family had first taken up land south of Houghton Village in 1850 and named their property *Poundsford*. John Gollop, Snr. had been elected Councillor in 1853 of the first District Council of Highercombe. The home of John Gollop, the life-long District Clerk, and of his wife, Robina, stands next to the Methodist Church in Horn Street, Houghton.

Upon the death of John Gollop, Burgon Lambert Hill of Hope Valley was appointed Council Clerk and retained the position until amalgamation of the two districts in 1935.

At the final meeting of the District Council of Highercombe, held on April 29, 1935 the Chairman, William Henry Ind, grandson of the first Chairman of the first District Council of 1853, Joseph Ind of Balmoral, mentioned the absence of discord during his long term of office. The last resolution of Council was 'that a framed photo of Councillors be presented to the Hope Valley and Memorial Institute'.

A joint meeting with the Tea Tree Gully Councillors was subsequently held. At the meeting the Balance Sheet of the defunct District Council of Highercombe was presented.

It showed:

Previous Balance	£ 380. 2.	5
Receipts	26. 5.	2
	£ 406. 7.	7
Payments	328. 8.	5
Final Balance	£ 77.19.	2

22

DISTRICT OF TEA TREE GULLY 1935—1953

'a high state of cultivation'

In March 1935, after a division of the district which had lasted for 77 years, the District of Highercombe and the District of Tea Tree Gully were re-united. Although the re-union was a compulsory one, there was little district opposition to it. No protest against the enforced amalgamation was recorded in the final minutes of either of the two councils. In some parts of the State the 'forced marriage' of councils met with opposition, loud protest, petitions and expressions of strong disapproval.

Two main factors contributed to the decision of the Local Government Commission to recommend the reduction of the number of district councils in South Australia from 196 to 145. The main factor was economic. The 'black depression' of the 1930s had left councils struggling for funds. They had suffered a large reduction in road grants during 1930-31-32. Government subsidy on rates had been reduced and, at the same time, the list of unpaid council rates grew longer. In 1932 the Clerk of the Tea Tree Gully Council, Mr. V.S. Bowen, brought forward an amount of £186.15.2 of rates in arrears — nearly one-quarter of the total rates due.

Amalgamation, claimed the Local Government Commission, would prevent needless duplication of road plant, council offices, and staff. Certainly many council districts were too small to be viable. Council areas in South Australia ranged in size from an immense 1,534,400 acres to an absurd 270 acres, and in district population from 25,583 to a handful of 215 people. Numbered among the fifty-three councils with an annual revenue of less than £2,000 was the District Council of Highercombe. Its final annual balance sheet, published in the *Government Gazette* in June 1935, reveals 'grand total receipts' as being £991.16.5. It also revealed a sum of £196.5.9 in outstanding rates for the previous year.

Another factor was making it difficult for councils faced with a diminishing revenue to survive. The increasing use of expensive motorised machinery made amalgamation not only possible but necessary. Small councils could not hope to survive the new motor age, with its new demands for better roads and mechanised means of constructing them.

The motor-car was adding a new dimension to life — the dimension of mobility. Whereas in 1858 councillors made their way on horseback once or twice a month from Hope Valley to Houghton, or from Snake Gully to Tea Tree Gully, over dirt tracks to attend council meetings, by 1935 they were travelling by car over roads which were at least metalled. A few roads were even tar-paved.

The new District of Tea Tree Gully which was created by the proclamation of March 21, 1935 was virtually the first District of Highercombe as proclaimed in October, 1853. *(See Map 8)* The area of the district was increased marginally by the annexation of a few sections from the District of Para Wirra at Lower Hermitage. The recommendation of the Local Government Commission was:

'That portion of the district council district of Para Wirra be severed and annexed to Teatree Gully: that the district council district of Teatree Gully, as altered, and of Highercombe be united and named the district council district of Teatree Gully and the assessment for rates be based on annual values'. *(v. Note 1.)*

For the first time, by determination of the Commission, the district council was now divided into wards. The five wards were also named and defined. In addition it was laid down that the Teatree Gully and Torrens wards should have two councillors each, and the Highercombe, Glen Ewin and Modbury-Golden Grove wards one councillor each.

Nominations for the election of the seven councillors required were to be submitted to the district office by Saturday, June 8, 1935. The councillors of both council districts all retired from office but were eligible for re-election. They were: William Henry Ind, Herbert Hancock, Leonard James Tolley, Allan Hall, William Packer, Andrew Thomas Wakefield, Owen John Griffiths, William Hannaford, Norman Keith Gogler, and John Henry Tilly. Tolley, Packer and Griffiths did not seek re-election. Unopposed, Gogler and Hancock became first councillors for Teatree Gully ward; Tilley for Modbury-Golden Grove ward, Hall and Ind for Torrens ward and Hannaford for Glen Ewin ward. Only in the Highercombe ward, where Frederick Hodges and Andrew Wakefield contested the seat, was an election necessary. This was held in the old Union Chapel at Houghton on July 6, 1935 when Wakefield was duly elected.

The formalities of amalgamation were now over. Presiding over the complexities and technicalities involved in amalgamation, uncomplaining and seemingly unruffled, was Victor Spurgeon Bowen, Clerk, Overseer and general factotum of the old and of the new district council of Teatree Gully. It

Note 1. The change in title format from 'Teatree Gully' to 'Tea Tree Gully' came later.

was fortunate indeed that a man of Bowen's ability and temperament was on hand to cope with the changeover. In the days before typists and typewriters (there was one second-hand one in the Council Chambers in 1935), Bowen's penmanship must have been a great asset to him. His generous, flowing handwriting make the minute and assessment books of council a comparative pleasure to read if one must perform that tedious task. Only John Gollop, Clerk of Highercombe Council for 52 years, could match the minutes of Victor Bowen for clarity and legibility. Brevity, too, was fortunately the soul of Bowen's minutes.

At the time of writing, V.S. Bowen, now in his 85th year, lives in retirement with his wife in Bowen Road, Tea Tree Gully.

'Vic' Bowen was born at Maylands in 1892, one of a family of six boys and two girls. He gained his formal education at the Norwood Public School and Adelaide High School. He arrived with his family in the district in 1913 and at 22 years of age began dairying on his own on the same property where he now lives in retirement. In World War I, Bowen enlisted and served with the 43rd Battalion A.I.F. He was on active service from 1916 and returned home on Christmas Day, 1919, complete with a Military Medal awarded for distinguished services, and went back to dairying, and in 1925 married Evelyn Mary Allen.

In the June elections of 1923, after serving as auditor for a few months, Victor Bowen was elected Councillor, and in the following year, Chairman. He retired from council in 1925 but was again nominated and elected as Councillor and then as Chairman in June 1930.

Towards the end of 1932, the Clerk, R.S. Ross, resigned. Immediately, Bowen, still a councillor, announced his resignation in order to be able to apply for the clerkship. There were 22 applications for the position — a sign of the continuing depression. Applicants asked for salaries ranging from £260 to £120 per annum. 'Vic' Bowen asked for 'award rates'. Three local men — Chamberlain, Bowen and Tilley — were considered for the position and at a special meeting held in October 1932, Bowen was elected Clerk and Overseer at a salary of £12 per month — 12/- a month above the award rate.

In 1947, paper work began to catch up with the clerk. 'Vic' Bowen was granted permission to be in attendance at his office at the Council Chambers on three full days each week and on Saturday mornings. On Tuesdays and Fridays he became district overseer again. In the year that he retired — 1957 — 'Vic' was still the only official office staff, although he occasionally called his daughter in to help him on the second-hand typewriter.

A year after the amalgamation of the two council areas, South Australia celebrated its centenary of settlement. Celebrations there were but they were reasonably sober. The death of one King during the year and the abdication of another in the same month as the main centenary celebrations in December perhaps helped to dampen down festivities. The State was just

179

climbing out of the worst depression in its history and 11,000 men were still unemployed. On the European horizon the dark clouds of war were blowing up again. In 1936 Hitler had just come to an understanding with Mussolini, the dictator of Italy. The storm of World War II would break within three years, but in the meantime South Australia celebrated the fact that it was 'no longer a young country'.

Apart from special 'Arbor Days' in the seven district schools (with a combined enrolment in 1936 of less than 300), special church services and a little centenary pageantry at local floral and agricultural shows, there is little record concerning the passing of the centenary year in our own district. Among the old colonists attending the centenary Commemoration Day dinner at Glenelg were three elderly district residents whose life span had been virtually the life span of the colony — John Ross of Golden Grove, James Gosden who had been born at Tea Tree Gully in 1844, and F. Hancock of Tea Tree Gully who had been born in Adelaide in 1837 in its first year of settlement.

After 100 years of settlement how different was the district in appearance from when the first settlers moved into it? The people who had inhabited it so casually for 30,000 years before settlement had all gone, leaving scarcely a trace. The nomads had been displaced by settlers; the kangaroos, wallabies, dingoes and native fauna by sheep, cattle, rabbits and foxes; exotics were now preferred to the indigenous native flora. Nearly 150 varieties of introduced weeds had been declared noxious and the battle for their eradication was a never-ending one for councils. The most common pest in the cultivated areas of the district remained the Scotch thistle and the European artichoke.

The axe and the plough of the settlers had transformed the landscape. The greatest transformation was not so much in the destruction of its trees and natural vegetation but in the change from open countryside, through which the Aboriginals had passed freely like dark shadows, to a countryside enclosed with hedgerows and fences, patterned by agriculture, vineyards and orchards and dotted with farm houses. In many cases they were the farmhouses of families which had pioneered the settlement of the district. Of the 200 or so family names listed in the first assessment book of the first District Council of Highercombe in 1853, nearly 100 still remained in the assessment book in 1936.

The city, in 1936, was still distant. In 1910 a Houghton correspondent had written to the *Observer* advising Adelaide residents, 'If you are wanting a holiday come to Houghton. If you are pining for a sight of green hills, lovely dales and verdant valleys, make a tour of Houghton and its beautiful environs. From Anstey's Hill the buildings of Adelaide and the surrounding hills seem to be stretched out like an octopus endeavouring to clutch within its ever-expanding feelers as much as possible of the vast plains on which it lies'.

Highbury Hotel, c.1920 (Licensee Mrs. C.M. Cocks) — building now demolished.

General view of the township of Tea Tree Gully, 1910.

Arbor Day gathering at Tea Tree Gully, July 1913. Post Office (old *Highbury Hotel*) in background.

An early photograph of Steventon (Tea Tree Gully) taken prior to 1880 before the *Highbury Hotel* became the Post and Telegraph Office. Blacksmith's Shop (shingle roof) in foreground.

But by 1936 the suburban octopus had still not reached the district and would not do so for another 20 years.

Since the establishment of the six early villages of Houghton, Hope Valley, Steventon, Modbury, Golden Grove and Inglewood, only one new community had developed. This was at Paracombe where closer settlement as a result of the subdivision of the Paracombe sheep station in 1901, had created the need for a school, and a post-office, a church, a recreation ground, and a community hall. By 1936 the Paracombe blocks were in full production. Most of the Paracombe blocks had been planted with fruit trees — the majority with apples and pears. In 1908 a reporter visiting the new subdivision had written: 'A prolific district. A thousand acres that a few years ago carried 1,000 sheep and one man to look after them, since the Government has become landlord, now carries 33 familes. In the present season 30,000 cases of apples will be produced within a radius of three miles, 20,000 for export to London'.

By 1936 Paracombe had its own fruit-packing shed and by 1939 had added cold-storage, capable of handling 96,000 cases of fruit.

Other subdivisions, such as those of Dernancourt and Vista, were merely extensions of the early townships, and even by 1953 had added only some 400 residents to the population of the district, and gave no hint of the tidal wave of population to come in the following 20 years.

'The district', said an official centenary report of 1936, 'is situated twelve miles north of Adelaide with an area of 50 square miles, and is a fine tract of agricultural land in a high state of cultivation, the growth of wheat and culture of the vine being particularly attended to, whilst a few sheep and cattle are kept by various farmers. Teatree Creek — a small stream of fine water — flows through the bottom of the gully and past the township of Steventon, which lies within the district. There are 2,200 residents in the district'.

The 17 years from the centenary of the State to the centenary of local government in the district were uneasy ones, broken by the 6 years of World War II.

The war, which had remained distant in 1939 and 1940, suddenly came to Australia's own back doorstep with the entry of Japan into the arena and the fall of Singapore in February 1942. The reaction was immediate and the measures taken, urgent. As in other local government areas, and in Adelaide, street lights were 'browned out' throughout the district by painting the globes black or by shading the lights. As there were few street lights in the district, except at some intersections, one or two in the townships, and three at the Paradise Bridge, this incurred little hardship.

Signboards throughout the district were taken down and stored in the Council shed and the marking of bridges for military purposes was required by defence authorities. A local Volunteer Air Observers' Corps was established and a telephone installed in the back room of the Council Chambers for the use of observers who manned the post for twenty-four hours a day. Consideration was given by Council to the establishment of Emergency Fire Services and First Aid Posts. By the end of 1942, the threat of invasion had receded and Council was able to announce: 'Normal lighting can now be resumed in the district except that no lighting be visible from sea'. Signposts were brought out again and re-erected.

The war brought shortages and food rationing. The rationing of petrol was severe and the sight of motor-vehicles lumping their own 'gas-producers' on their backs became common. Fuelled by coke and belching smoke and occasionally fire, the 'gas-producers' were allotted sign-posted cleaning areas in the district and found themselves banned altogether in the summer months.

The surrender of Japan in September of 1945 held a portent for radical and rapid change within the district, quite unrealised at the time.

In the meantime, to mark the end of the war, Council called for a minute's silence at the next meeting in memory of the fallen, an observance which continued for the next 20 years. A list of names of men and women of the district who had served during the war was compiled. It contained the names of 254 men and 20 women. Eleven had died on active service.

Memorials for the fallen of World War II took a more practical and useful form than the crop of statues and war trophies which had followed World War I.

At Houghton, the trustees of the Houghton Masonic Lodge transferred to the Council of Tea Tree Gully the triangular area of land in the centre of the township to be developed as a memorial to the men and women of Houghton who had served.

Early football matches in the village had been played on a flat piece of land — the 'butcher's paddock' — off Cemetery Road.

Following World War II the Houghton, Inglewood and Hermitage Soldiers' Memorial Park Inc. was formed to develop a more adequate playing field and a parcel of land was bought from Ray Johns and an oval developed. It was an expensive task involving the changing of the course of the creek and extensive bull-dozing and earth works. The new Houghton Recreation ground was opened on September 29, 1947.

A proposal for a Memorial Drive at Tea Tree Gully was submitted to Council in 1949 and in 1950 the War Memorial archway and drive was officially opened by the Premier of South Australia, the Hon. Thomas Playford.

Three people — Mr. Short of Dulwich and Mrs. Lloyd Milton and Mr. Claude Ellis of Tea Tree Gully — gave land in order to enable the 440 yard drive to be taken through to Haines' Perseverance Road and to Haines' Memorial Oval. William Haines, upon his death in 1902, had left two pieces of land to the people of Tea Tree Gully 'on condition that they should be available as recreation grounds for all time'. One piece had become Haines'

Memorial Park, the other the Tea Tree Gully oval. Pine trees, with brass memorial plaques, were planted on either side of the roadway to make a memorial drive to the oval. The original memorial archway, built by Mr. Hedley Neale, had later to be raised following its partial demolition by a high load on a truck.

Other recreation grounds too were, wisely, being set aside as a result of the efforts of various Progress Associations and individuals. In 1946 the South Australian Brewing Company asked the Council to accept as a gift on behalf of the Hope Valley and Highbury Progress Association a triangular piece of land opposite the *Highbury Hotel*. It was to be developed as a Memorial Oval. Previously it had been the site of saleyards and of stables for the *Highbury Hotel*. Following the location by Messrs. Wicks and Packer of a more suitable site for a recreation ground, Council rejected the offer of the Brewing Company 'as the area was not large enough for an oval' and, in 1947, accepted the trusteeship of the present Hope Valley Oval. The oval had been the gift of Councillors Wicks and Packer.

The Trustees of the Modbury Recreation ground, too, were able to find funds to improve their site; and in November of 1948 came the dedication of the Paracombe Soldiers' Memorial Archway.

The Paracombe Memorial Oval had been officially opened in December 1922, after World War I, when the Premier, Sir Richard Butler had taken the bat, and Mr. Reuben Chapman had bowled the first ball on the new cricket pitch. On the same day the Governor, Sir Alexander Hore-Ruthven had set in place the foundation stone of the Soldiers' Memorial Hall.

However, debate concerning the use of district recreation grounds, vested now in the Council, was fierce and frequent at council meetings.

Until 1948 grounds could not be let on Sundays for public picnics, although at Tea Tree Gully footballers 'could practice between the hours of 8 and 11 a.m.' The Tea Tree Gully Tennis Club was to be permitted to practice on Sundays 'provided there are no organised games and everything is conducted in the proper manner'. The distinction between 'organised' and unorganised games was perhaps too fine a one to have much effect.

Even in such a remote area as Hermitage, the Tennis Club had to seek permission to play Sunday tennis. Permission, after much thought on the part of Councillors, was granted 'under strict supervision, two local persons, approved by Council to be appointed and be responsible for the good conduct of players and see that only local players use the courts'. The permissive society, it seemed to some councillors, had arrived. Finally, in 1950, Council permitted what it could not prevent, public picnicking on recreation grounds on Sundays.

Local Government in the district was approaching the end of its first hundred years of responsibility for district affairs. There was the retirement from office in this period of two councillors who had given long years of service. In 1943 William Henry Ind of *Balmoral*, a grandson of Joseph Ind who had been a councillor in the first district council in 1853, retired after 25 continuous years as councillor and Chairman, and A.G. Dearman succeeded him as Chairman. Ind's father, William Henry Ind, Snr., had himself been Chairman for 19 years.

A year after the retirement of Ind, John Henry Tilley of Golden Grove, grandfather of the present Mayor of the City of Tea Tree Gully, retired after a period of 22 years of service as Councillor, Chairman, Auditor and Clerk.

Preparations were made for the centenary of the district council to be held on Saturday, July 18, 1953, part of the celebrations to be the planting of 1,200 pines on the council reserve at Tea Tree Gully.

Invitations were sent to Mr. and Mrs. Roy McEwin of *Glen Ewin* and to Mr. and Mrs. David Ind of *Balmoral* to attend as descendants of members of the first 1853 district council. Among the invitations sent out to various other dignitaries and residents, perhaps the most remarkable one was that to Mrs. Robert Gilmour, then living with her daughter, Mrs. E. Heitmann, at Tea Tree Gully. Born at Hope Valley in 1852, one year before the first council was formed in the district, Emma Gilmour was now 101 years of age and was still walking to the Baptist Church each Sunday morning. Her great age served to remind people of the relative youth of the State — she had lived through its first century of local government.

Her father, James Hill, a veterinary surgeon, had arrived in the colony in 1840 and had settled on section 824, Hope Valley, in 1842. Hill had been a butcher, 'vet.', and postmaster in the village and Emma had for a term, as a girl, been postmistress, riding to Hope Valley with the mail bags. After the death of her husband and until the age of 74, Mrs. Gilmour had been midwife to nearly 400 of the district's children. She had delivered more than 100 of them without a doctor at hand.

Although she was unable to attend the Council centenary because of indisposition on the day, Emma Gilmour lived another year and died at the age of 102. Perhaps the passing of Emma Gilmour as much as the completion of the first hundred years of local government, symbolised the end of one era and the beginning of another and very different one for the district. The relative tranquility of more than a century was about to be disturbed nearly as suddenly and permanently by another invasion, just as the age-old tranquility of the original inhabitants, the Aborigines, had been shattered with the coming of the first migrants in 1836.

STEVENTON AND INGLEWOOD

'King of Tea Tree Gully'

Until 1854, there was no sign of settlement at the entrance to Teatree Gully. Indeed the section of land where the village of Steventon began to take shape in 1854, remained unsold until mid-1852. It was a small section of 42 acres, sandy and cut deeply by the Teatree Gully Creek, where it emerged from Teatree Gully itself. 'The sand at the foot of Teatree Gully was heavy hauling for our four bullocks', wrote William Flavel in 1842 and there would have been little improvement by 1854.

There was still, in 1854, no official line of road from the gully to Hope Valley. The unfenced track lay through private property. At a public meeting held at Houghton in June 1853, George McEwin stated that although this track intersected a great agricultural district it was the worst road in the province and that he had experienced difficulty at times in getting to Adelaide, even on horseback.

The unofficial road was a busy one, carrying loads of hay and firewood from Gumeracha to 'the mills, malthouses and brickyards at Hindmarsh, Bowden, Walkerville and North Adelaide'. McEwin, leading a deputation to the Central Road Board late in 1853 to request that the line of road from Teatree Gully to Gilles Plains be declared a main line of road, stated that on his way in to Adelaide that morning he had passed 25 loaded drays.

Two other persistent arguments favoured the Teatree Gully line of road, rather than the Anstey's Hill line. One was the presence of water in the gully itself. The other was that the line provided a direct route to Port Adelaide.

One other argument used was that there was in course of erection at the entrance to the gully a flour mill 'and grinding of wheat could be effected better there because of the abundance of fuel'. The remains of the mill, still quite a substantial building, stands facing the North East Road on the southern side where it enters Teatree Gully.

McEwin's deputation and its petition, containing the signatures of 250 settlers from Golden Grove, Teatree Gully, Hermitage, Houghton, Chain of

Ponds, and Gumeracha, were evidently sufficient to convince the Central Road Board. In January 1854 the new line of road from Gilles Plains, through Hope Valley and across to the present North East Road and along to the entrance to Teatree Gully was gazetted, 'the said intended road to be sixty feet in width'.

A month later the 'Southern Branch of the North Eastern Road', 'commencing at *Balmoral* on the River Torrens' and passing through Hope Valley to Houghton via Anstey's Hill was gazetted a main line of road.

In April of 1854, a continuation of the North Eastern Road 'from the Gorge of the Teatree Gully to Gumeracha' was gazetted. The unofficial road via Teatree Gully, in use at least since 1840, had now become official.

The effects of this belated decision of the Central Road Board were immediate and important. Within the next few years, three new embryo villages — Steventon, Inglewood and Modbury — came into existence.

Two men were responsible for the development of the village which from its very beginning was as often called Tea Tree Gully as it was Steventon.

In August 1853, William Haines, Snr., of the North Road, Enfield, acquired section 5500 at the entrance to Teatree Gully from Edward Millsteed. Haines paid £140 for the 42 acres which Millsteed had been granted one year before for £42. Perhaps Haines gambled on a favourable decision of the Central Road Board in paying such an amount for the small, sandy section and foresaw the section as a site for a village. Perhaps the erection of the flour mill had influenced his decision. Whatever his reason, William Haines, Snr., can be regarded as one of the founders of the village of Teatree Gully.

Haines, a gardener, had arrived in South Australia on the *William Mitchell* in August 1840, from Troubridge in Wiltshire, with his wife and six children. The family was almost penniless upon arrival and for a time lived in a tent in Emigration Square, close to the River Torrens, where the Adelaide Gaol was later built. For a time William Haines was employed in a Government garden, established on the banks of the Torrens, to provide vegetables for Government House. In 1846 he was given the lease of the land which had been acquired in 1839 near the Torrens for the first Botanic Gardens. He was placed in charge of the gardens and with the help of two of his sons, Ephraim and William, grew vegetables and planted fruit trees. In 1852 Haines and his family moved to Teatree Gully 'to start market gardening'. 'There was', stated William Haines, Jnr., in his reminiscences, 'but one house there in the area, a one-roomed building occupied by a man being engaged in constructing the Tea Tree Gully Mill'.

The section that Haines acquired 'to start market gardening' was section 5486, now occupied by the St. Agnes shopping centre. In the following year Haines acquired the section at the entrance to Teatree Gully itself, selling five acres of it to his son William Haines, Jnr., and retaining

22 acres. By 1854 the assessment book shows he had a 'house, good garden and land'. Two of his sons, Ephraim and William, Jnr., now married, each had a house and garden on the same section.

It was William Haines, Jnr., who became so closely identified with the development of the township and district, who later entered Parliament and became popularly known as the 'King of Tea Tree Gully'.

William Haines, Snr., died in November 1863, and was buried at Houghton cemetery beside his wife and a daughter, both of whom had died early in 1862.

Steventon, the original name of the township of Tea Tree Gully, was given its name by John Stevens in 1854, when he acquired a large section (Section 51) of 227 acres adjoining Haines' section at the entrance to the gully. The section, hilly, scrub-covered, and until 1854 unoccupied, was purchased by John Stevens for £633 and named Steventon Estate. Steventon Estate, bounded today by Haines and Grenfell Roads, and Elizabeth and Walter Streets, was acquired by Stevens for subdivision.

It is unlikely that John Stevens ever lived in his village of Steventon. Stevens was a pioneer colonist and a miller by trade. He had arrived in the colony in 1838 and in 1840 built a small, wind-driven flour mill in Adelaide to grind some of the first wheat grown in South Australia. In 1842 he erected a steam flour mill at Noarlunga and soon afterwards became the manager of the South Australian Company's Mill, close to the Torrens at Hackney. He remained manager of the mill almost until the time of his death in 1871 at the age of 54.

John Stevens first acquired land in the district in 1850, when he bought two unoccupied sections of land near present-day Vista. By 1853, when the first district council was formed, Stevens had acquired section 5629, adjoining Haines' section on the south. Part of this irregular section (See Map 10) speared into the very entrance to the gully itself. It was on this triangular spear-head of land that the *Highercombe Hotel* and the village store (now the North East Highway Restaurant) were built in 1854.*

Both Stevens and Haines seem to have anticipated, in 1853, the official gazettal of the North Eastern Road in 1854. It was a gamble on the part of both men perhaps but the chances were very much in favour of the old line of road being accepted officially.

If the new village of Steventon was a late arrival in the district, its development was perhaps the more rapid for that very reason. There was an obvious need for a village in the northern section of the district and where better than on waste land where the main road from Gumeracha and beyond emerged from the hills. It would become a staging place for traffic to and from Adelaide. It would provide a communal centre for the northern settlers who had no shops, schools, post offices or churches closer than Hope

---

* Previously thought to be 1849. Further research shows 1854 as the correct date. There was no semblance of any village until 1854.

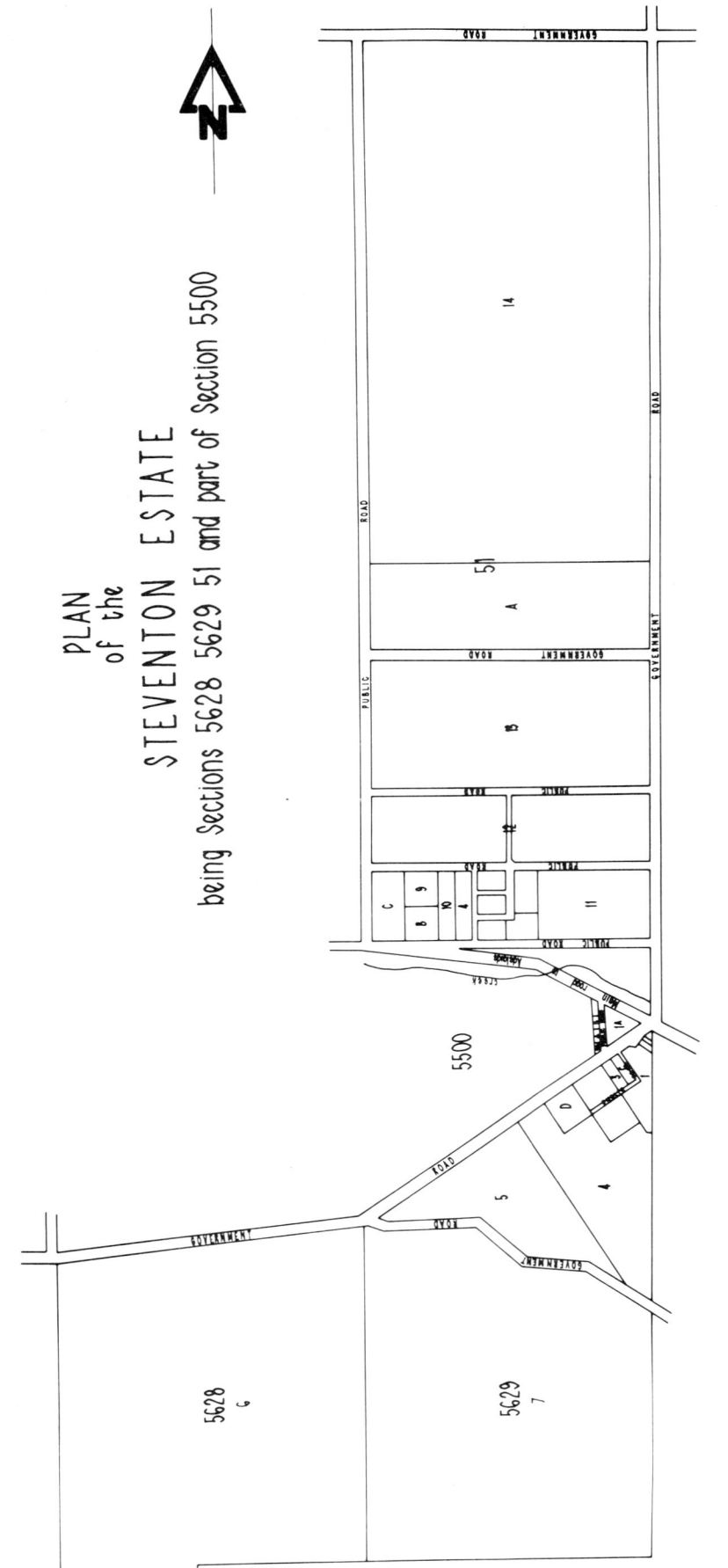

PLAN of the STEVENTON ESTATE

being Sections 5628 5629 51 and part of Section 5500

Map 10a Plan of Steventon Estate as laid out (1854) by John Stevens *(see plan opposite on p.191 for details)*. Maps - Department of Lands, South Australia (re-drawn by Engineering & Town Planning Section, City of Tea Tree Gully).

Enlarged portion of Sec. 5629

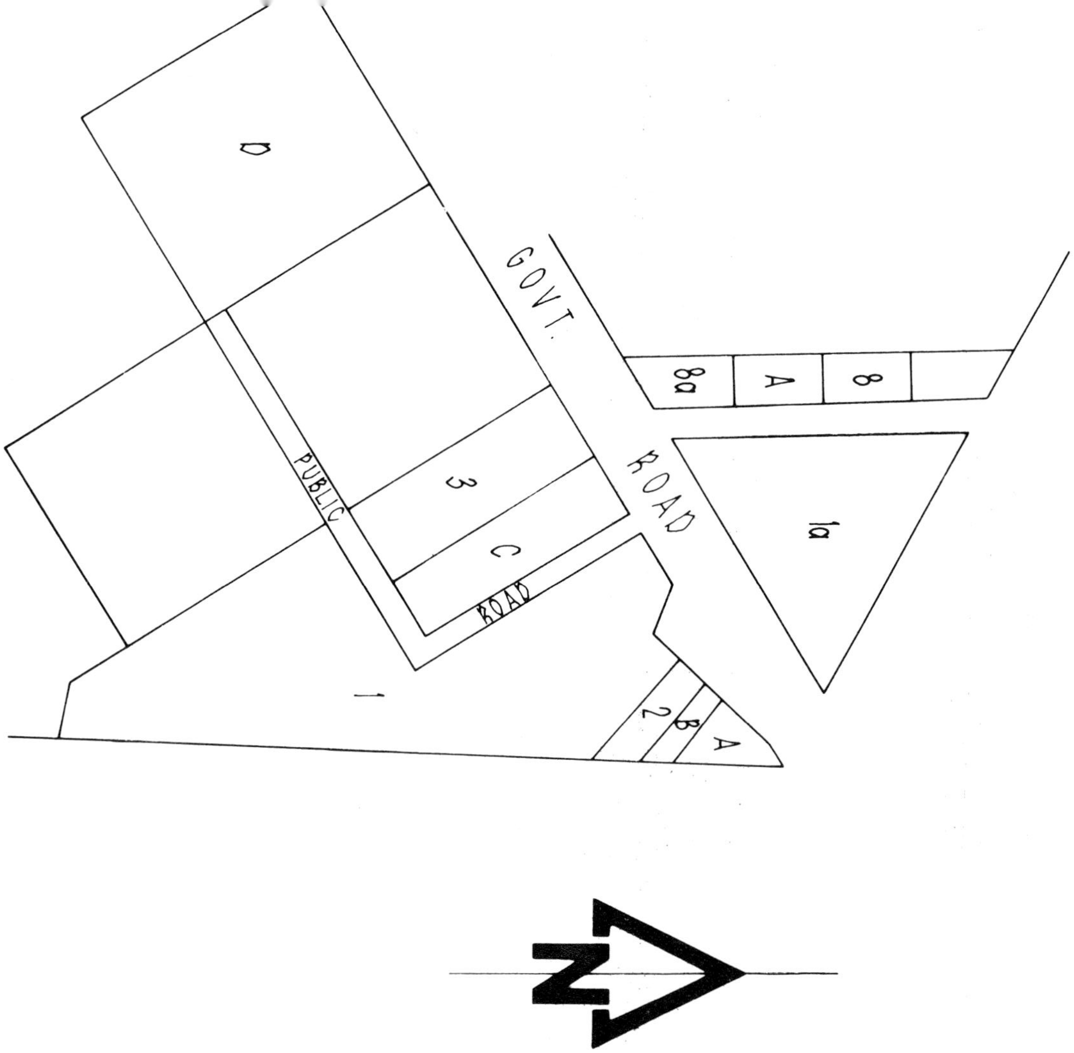

No.	Section	Name	a	r	p
6	5628	Opie	86	2	19
A	Do		71	1	32
7	5629	P. D. Prankerd	13	3	0
5	Do	Do	12	0	5
4	Do		0	1	20
3	Do	Wm Haines	0	0	11
2	Do	Opie	1	2	14
1	Do	Cooke			
A	Do	Collison			
B	Do	Cooke			
C	Do				
D	Do				
E	Do				
1a	5500	Wm Haines	0	2	29
8	Do	Thos. Edwd Cooke	0	0	12½
8a	Do	Do	0	0	13½
A	Do	Cooke			
9	51	Jas. Wicks	1	0	0
10	Do	Thos. Knuckey	1	0	0
11	Do	John Hicks	6	2	30
12	Do	Geo. H. Parr	16	3	8
13	Do	Do	32	3	4
14	Do		128	2	30
A	Do	J. Forster			
4	Do	T. Knuckey			
B	Do	Wesleyan Chapel			
C	Do	Rickard			

Map 10b Details of section 5629, Township of Steventon (Tea Tree Gully) with names of occupiers in 1863.

Valley or Houghton. Indeed the public buildings erected within the first ten years after the establishment of the village were to prove adequate for the following hundred years.

Although situated in the corner of one of the sections of the gully itself, (Section 5630) the flour mill undoubtedly qualifies as Steventon's first public building. Named the Tea Tree Gully Steam Flour Mill, its construction was completed in 1853 by its owners S. Camper & Co. of Adelaide. In the following year the mill was bought and managed by the miller James Hunter. Water for the steam mill was drawn from the springs in Tea Tree Gully. In the 1860s part of the springs became the property of George Dickerson, the supply of water became inadequate and the mill literally ran out of steam. For many years the building was used as a grain and chaff store.

In 1881 Richard Montague Ellis took over the mill for his butchering business and built a home just east of the mill. Later, his son, Claude Oswald Montacute Ellis, dismantled the third storey of the mill and used the stone to build his home and butcher's shop on the western side of the mill. The butchering business was transferred back to the mill by Dick Ellis in 1946 when he, in turn, took over the family business and continued the third generation of butchering in the Ellis family. A room on the ground floor served for a time as a barber's shop. The present owners of the old 'Tea Tree Gully Steam Flour Mill' are Mr. and Mrs. Don Allnutt.

Within a few weeks of the official recognition of the North Eastern line of road through Teatree Gully, the walls of two new public buildings began to rise — the *Tea Tree Gully Inn* and the *Highercombe Hotel*. The smaller *Tea Tree Gully Inn* was completed first and on March 13, 1854 the District Council of Highercombe granted William Bailes a publican's licence. The 1½ acres of land on which the *Tea Tree Gully Inn* was erected cost its purchasers £100.

At the same meeting the councillors considered an application from Thomas Pearce for a licence for a public house in Tea Tree Gully to be called the *Black Tiger*. The application was refused 'as the house was incomplete'. In June, Thomas Pearce, son of Samuel Pearce, the licensee of the *Travellers' Rest Inn* at Houghton, appeared again before the councillors for a publican's licence. Mr. Bailes, keeper of the *Tea Tree Gully Inn* also appeared 'not to oppose the applicant but to assure the Council there was not sufficient business to support one house', much less two.

The council however 'was of the opinion that such a fine building as Mr. Pearce's was deserving a licence'. Pearce had by now decided to name his hotel the *Highercombe Hotel*.

Bailes was correct — there was not enough business to support two houses. Within a year Pearce had become insolvent and Bailes had left for a more profitable location. Both hotels changed licensees almost annually for the next few years. In 1860 William Haines, Jnr. became the licensee of the

Highercombe Hotel and later purchased the land and building from John Stevens. The building closed as a public house in 1877, the year before William Haines entered Parliament. Drinking space in both hotels was very limited — the bar of the *Highercombe Hotel*, twelve feet by five feet, would have been crowded with ten customers.

Like most country hotels, both hotels in Steventon had a large Assembly Room which, in the days before Institutes, could be used for public functions. What must have been the first dance in Tea Tree Gully was held in August 1855 in the Assembly Room of the *Highercombe Hotel*. 'A Select Ball' read the advertisement, 'will be held at the *Highercombe Hotel* on Monday, 20th August. Double tickets 5/- to be had at the bar'. The Assembly Room at various times came into service for electoral meetings and annual Lodge dinners.

In 1880 the little bar was transformed into a Post Office and Telegraph Station and the Post Office remained in occupation until 1963. For a brief period the building was in use as office and library accommodation for the Tea Tree Gully District Council. Finally, in 1967, the building became the home of the Tea Tree Gully Branch of the National Trust and the repository for historical artefacts and documents of the district. Happily its preservation as a permanent district historical and folk museum is now guaranteed.

By the end of 1854 the new village of Steventon had two inns and four shops. Two of the 'shops' had disappeared from the assessment books by 1855 but two were destined to continue in business for many years. One of these early buildings now forms part of the present North East Highway Restaurant.

Steventon's first shop was the blacksmith's shop of John Opie. It was situated, understandably, at the entrance to Teatree Gully itself, on a small triangle of land at the northern spearhead of section 5629 *(See Map 10 Allotment A)* Opie, previously an Adelaide blacksmith, paid John Stevens the large sum of £90 for the small triangular block. Following Opie's death in the 1860s, William Boyle became the village blacksmith.

In August of 1854 Thomas Edward Cooke, a storekeeper of Wellington Square, North Adelaide, acquired Allotment B of Section 5629 *(See Map 10)* leasing it for £10 a year with the right to purchase for the sum of £110. The block of land is described in the deed of registration of 1854 as being 'next to Opie's, the Blacksmith's Shop lately erected there and fronting a piece of land reserved by John Stevens for public use'. This reserve later became Haines Memorial Park.

In 1858 Cooke's new store became Steventon's first postoffice. Cooke died in 1866 at the age of 40 and his wife leased the general store. In 1881 William Dunn, Snr.,* and his family moved from *Gordon Bank*, the property near *Glen Ewin* acquired by George Dunn in 1845, and took over the store at Steventon. William Dunn, Jnr., became the storekeeper and the

* Dunn, Snr., died at Houghton in 1906 in his 92nd year.

business remained in the family until 1911. It then passed into the possession of the Ellis family but returned to the Dunn family through the marriage of Miss Olive Ellis to Walter Dunn. After more than a century, the building ceased life as a village store in 1961.

Tea Tree Gully's first baker appears to have been Charles Rumps whose bakehouse was situated, in 1872, on section 5500 facing the Main North East Road. The bakehouse was taken over in 1884 by Ernst Heitmann, and the family carried on the baking business for the next 75 years. The bakehouse and residence opposite Elizabeth Street are still standing but their demolition seems imminent.

In 1855, against the wishes of councillors from Houghton and Hope Valley, the Council Chambers were built at Steventon, close to the entrance of Teatree Gully. It seems certain that the Council Chamber was the first to be erected by any council in the colony and the building in Haines Road is still a useful council structure.

A month after the completion of the Council Rooms the Wesleyans of the district held opening services in their new chapel. The building, 'an elegant little place of worship', was situated on the southern boundary of Steventon Estate, close to the corner of what is now Walter Street and Elizabeth Street. 'A chapel bell cast expressly for the purpose', continued the report, 'has been presented by John Stevens, Esquire, and will occupy the stylish turret in a few weeks'.

Attempts were made, too, in 1855 to erect two more public buildings to provide for the needs of the district — a public school and an Institute. The efforts met with little success. The Council did not feel justified 'in appropriating the funds of the district for the purpose of erecting a school-house', but gave its approval to a Miss Elizabeth Carter to conduct a school in the Wesleyan Chapel.

Funds too were collected to establish an Institute in the village. William Haines, Snr. gave a piece of ground for the site and in 1858 the foundations of the building were laid out. Monday, August 23, 1858 was a great day in the village. The foundation stone of a new Institute was to be laid and a new cutting opened through the summit of the road through Teatree Gully.

'The villages of Highercombe and Steventon,* beautifully situated at the entrance to the gully and commanding a bird's-eye view of Adelaide in the distance, were decked out at almost every point with bunting, ranging from the Union Jack down to the most florid of all possible red handkerchiefs'. During the morning a battery of muskets fired off from the top of the hill and at 12.30 p.m. a carriage-and-four arrived with the guests of honour from Adelaide.

* The reporter himself was uncertain of the exact name of the village. There are other occasional references to the section of the village north of the North East Road being designated Steventon and the southern section being named Highercombe.

194

Butcher's shop of Richard Ellis — formerly the Tea Tree Gully Flour Mill. L.to R.: Jim Ellis and Richard Ellis with his grandson, Merlin Dunn, c.1900.

W.H. Stevens (closest to horse) stands outside of his bootmaker's shop at Tea Tree Gully with his son and some customers. The shop later became Miss Gilmour's grocery shop.

An early photograph of Steventon (Tea Tree Gully) taken prior to 1880 before the *Highbury Hotel* became the Post and Telegraph Office. Blacksmith's shop (shingle-roof) in foreground.

Gathering at the Tea Tree Gully Institute on Carnival Day, January 1918.

The first ceremony was the laying of the foundation stone of the new Institute. 'A bottle containing the names of the trustees, of the donor of the ground and of the gentleman who laid the stone, together with the coins of the realm, was deposited under the corner-stone' and the assemblage 'of 300' people gave three cheers. The building unfortunately got no further than its foundations. The people of Tea Tree Gully were not able to summon up such enthusiasm again until 1896 when the foundation stone of the present Institute was placed in position.

By 1866 the *South Australian Gazetteer and Road Guide* included a description of the new village which stated:

'STEVENTON, or TEA-TREE GULLY (Co. Adelaide) is a postal township in the electoral district of Gumeracka, and under the control of the Tea-tree Gully district council. It is situated on the Tea-tree gully creek, the Little Para river being 3 miles N.E. of the Tea-tree gully, which is situated at the foot of the Gawler ranges. The district is an agricultural one, wheat being the chief product, whilst the culture of the vine is particularly attended to. The farmers are also in the habit of grazing sheep and cattle, but only in small numbers. There is an iron ore mine about 1 mile S.E. of the township, and 5 good freestone quarries in the neighbourhood. There is also a flour mill (Mahon's). The nearest places are Modbury, 2½ miles distant S.W.; Houghton 2½ miles E.; Golden Grove, 4 miles N.W.; Hope Valley, 3 miles S.W.; and Inglewood 3½ miles E. With Modbury, Houghton, and Inglewood, as also with Adelaide, 12 miles S.W., there is communication by means of Rounsevell's daily mail coaches. Steventon has a post office, a district council chamber, used also as a local court, a Wesleyan and a Baptist chapel, each containing 150 sittings, a licensed day-school, a lodge of the M.U. of Oddfellows' [the Highercombe] and a Forresters' court [the Tea-tree gully]. The hotels are the Highercombe and the Tea-tree gully. There is a licensed carrier in the town, and a booking-office for Rounsevell's coaches to Adelaide or Port Mannum. The township is very prettily situated, and commands a fine view of the gulf and the plains. It is elevated about 500 feet above the level of the sea, and a view for 70 miles N. may be had on a clear day. To the E. of the township there is a range of mountains, whilst to the N.W., and S., the country is of a gently undulating character. The population is small and scattered'.

New Year's Day, 1867, saw the first recorded New Year celebrations in the village. 'nearly all the people here turned out and retired to a nice little spot near the residence of Mr. John Opie where they amused themselves to their heart's content in some old English games.

'Towards evening the ceremony of naming the place was gone through. Miss Elizabeth Coulter, a young lady born near by, after breaking a bottle of wine on a heap of stones, declared the name of the place for the future, Glen Opie.

'There was great cheering afterwards for Mr. and Mrs. Opie and Miss Coulter. Then all went home hoping to live to see the return of many as happy New Year Days'.

It had taken only twelve short years for the new village of Steventon to become a community.

The same *South Australian Gazetteer* of 1866 also described the two other villages which had emerged as a result of the official recognition of the North Eastern Road through Teatree Gully.

The description of the tiny village of Inglewood takes only three lines in the *Gazetteer*:

'INGLEWOOD (Co. Adelaide) is a small village on the Para River, lying 3½ miles from Steventon. It has a scattered agricultural population, and 1 hotel — the Inglewood'.

When the North East line of road from the Teatree Gully gorge to the Chain of Ponds was gazetted, the residents of Houghton discovered that a proposed deviation in the main line of road would by-pass their village. The three mile deviation began at the Houghton Hollow entrance and joined up with the old line of road again at the foot of the Black Hill Road. It is the deviation which we travel on today.

The residents of Houghton were enraged, particularly when they discovered upon presenting their petition against the deviation, that the deviation had already been confirmed in the *Gazette* of November 9, 1854. The village storekeeper, Josephus Longbotham, the butcher, William Reeds, and Thomas Battersby, the wheelwright and Samuel Pearce, licensee of the *Travellers' Rest*, drew up the petition. George McEwin of *Glen Ewin*, then a member of the Central Road Board, defended the proposed deviation, stating that the road via Anstey's Hill would still pass through Houghton.

A letter in reply signed 'An Old Roadster', however, was more to the point. He referred to 'the cutting off of this well-established village, leaving it a lonely monument of folly and fault'. The 'Old Roadster' was correct — the deviation did seriously affect and inhibit the growth of Houghton.

In 1856, the Governor re-examined the proposed deviation but decided that as the new line of road would be more advantageous to the public 'the long-agitated question may now be considered to be finally settled' and the construction of the deviation began.

Two men saw the possibility of profiting by the deviation. One was William Reeds, the Houghton butcher, through whose sections the road would pass. He claimed compensation of £1,500 for the 6 acres of his land to be taken by the road. At the hearing held before a jury and a crowded audience in the Tea Tree Gully Council Chamber, Reeds claimed that the dust blowing from the road would injure feed and the traffic would frighten the sheep and cattle kept there for slaughtering.

In the event, Reeds was given £91 for the 6 acres of land and a sum of £500 for severance of his sections.

The second man to seek to profit by the deviation was Firman Deacon, a publican of Franklin Street, Adelaide. In 1857, when the dust of argument had been settled, to be replaced by the dust of road construction, Deacon acquired 5 acres of land from Reeds for £225. Here in 1857 he began to build a hotel, close to Gollop's Bridge where the Black Hill Road from Houghton and Adelaide met the main North Eastern Road via Teatree Gully.

Casting around for a name for his new inn, Deacon hit upon a novel incentive. The facts were later vouched for by Robert McEwin. 'In 1857 the hotel was being built by Mr. Deacon who offered the men on the job five gallons of beer if they could find a suitable name. That evening they had a talk in camp and one of them suggested Inglewood (after the Inglewood in Cumberland). The others approved and when the owner next arrived the men had painted the name in large letters on a board which was nailed to a scaffold opposite to the bar door. The men got their beer and the hotel its name'. In 1858 when there was some subdivision and sale of land in the area, the location was given as Inglewood. Deacon found no reason to object, especially as in 1859, he sold the rest of his 5 acres of land to the 'Permanent Land and Building Association', retaining the hotel and renting it to its first licensee, John Randall, for a weekly rental of £3.

Inglewood did not grow into a village. It remained a wayside stopping place, mainly for thirsty teamsters or for those who needed the services of the local blacksmith, John Pitman, further west along the road.

A small store was built opposite the inn. In 1864 its owner, Antonio Francesco, opened another 'handsome stone building selling hardware, draperies and groceries close to the *Inglewood Inn*. In January 1865, the new store was 'reduced to ashes' and Francesco returned to his old store opposite the inn.

It was not until 1869 that Inglewood was listed as a postal town. The first census for the Inglewood as a separate district was taken in 1871, when the figures given were 22 houses and a population of 107.

Map 11 District map, 1915, giving the names of some individual homesteads. S.A. State Library.

24

MODBURY

'cranking in through my sections'

The establishment of the village of Modbury was entirely unplanned and fortuitous. Indeed, until 1856, there was no likelihood of subdivision or of closer settlement in the area.

There was a possibility of a village developing at Ardtornish corner, where Grand Junction Road once met present-day Valiant Road. The Ardtornish School had been erected here in 1847 and soon became a focal point for the neighbourhood. The school building was in regular use through the next 10 years for day and evening classes, church services, political meetings and social functions, until the village of Modbury began to emerge in 1857-1858. It served the function of an Institute and had a small library of some 200 books for public loan.

The Ardtornish corner became a focal point, too, for traffic on the Main North East Road in 1855. Previously the Main North East Road (as originally planned by Colonel William Light) ended at the junction with present-day Blacks Road at Gilles Plains. Travellers then went north along Blacks Road to Grand Junction Road and so along to Hope Valley; or along present-day Lyons Road to Hope Valley.

In 1855 a new line of road was opened from the Gilles Plains end of the Main North East Road 'passing diagonally through the sections belonging to Mr. R. Halden' to the Ardtornish School corner.

This extension of the road became known as Halden's Hill. Even as late as 1935 the section was still referred to in the district council minutes as Halden's Hill* and not, as it is today, as Holden Hill.

However, Ardtornish corner did not get an opportunity to develop into a cross-roads village. In the following year the line of the Main North East Road was again extended, diagonally from Ardtornish corner across agri-

---

* There can be little doubt that the present name Holden Hill is a misnomer. The unfortunate error probably occurred when a name was being sought for the new subdivision. Robert Halden had acquired the sections of land in the 1840s and the family farmed the sections now known as Holden Hill.

cultural sections 841 and 842 to meet the road to Golden Grove.

The gazettal of this new line of road brought the Central Road Board into direct conflict with the owner of the sections — Robert Symons Kelly. Kelly immediately brought an action against the Board protesting against the new line of road through his property and seeking recovery for the value of the land taken from him.

Kelly expressed his feelings publicly in a letter to the Adelaide *Register*. 'There was', he wrote, 'already a good road to Tea Tree Gully along his southern boundary [present-day Wright Road] and now the Central Road Board must come cranking in through my sections'. This would split his farm, take 5½ acres of his best land, separate his house from the Dry Creek and from his main well and bring the main traffic to Gumeracha almost past his door.

All of this was true enough, but the Road Board considered Kelly's claim for compensation — £1,000 for 5½ acres — 'preposterous'. The jury in the case travelled out to view the locality before reaching their verdict. Back in court, it was suggested that Kelly could perhaps divide his land and sell it as a township at great profit. Kelly claimed the laying out of new townships in the colony had been overdone but thought 'a public house might perhaps answer well at one of the angles of the road'.

In the event, the jury awarded Kelly a severance payment of £310. A road was fenced through his wheat paddocks and the Main North East Road finally took the line of road from Gilles Plains which we now follow today.

There is no doubt that Robert Kelly was genuinely distressed at finding his orderly and productive farmlands, the result of 14 years of hard pioneering work, so ruthlessly bisected. Kelly was, however, an intelligent and energetic man and set about turning his loss to advantage.

He foresaw that the new line of road would create an important new set of cross-roads where the Main North East Road would meet the road from Dry Creek (now Montague Road), the road from Golden Grove and the road from Tea Tree Gully. Better perhaps, as the jury had suggested, to have a new village developing close at hand than at Ardtornish corner.

Kelly actually set about encouraging the development of such a village on his land. Within three years a little settlement had emerged and had been given the name Modbury by Kelly himself. An analysis of the first assessment book of the District Council of Highercombe reveals the gradual emergence and outlines of the village.

The first component was the blacksmith's shop of Ludwig Koop who, until 1857, had been for many years the wheelwright at Hope Valley. The blacksmith's shop remained on the same site in Modbury for the next 80 years, the last 'village blacksmith' being George Wilkey. By 1939 mechanisation had largely replaced horse power and the war had created a shortage of materials and the 'smithy' closed.

The second component of the new village was a public house, built in

1858, a few chains east of Koop's wheelwright's shop — an understandable business combination in the days of teamsters. It was the hotel to which the name Modbury was first applied and it is almost certain that Kelly, a builder by trade, constructed the two-storey hotel. In September of 1858, Mr. William Stoneham applied to the district council for a general licence for a public house 'to be called the Modbury Hotel'. Stoneham became the first licensee but Robert Kelly retained ownership.

The first village shop in Modbury, owned and probably built by Kelly, was also opened in 1858, alongside the blacksmith's shop. The shopkeeper was John Wyatt.

In the following year another little shop was opened by Edward Mitchelson in the cottage he had built for himself on three quarters of an acre of land he had acquired from Kelly in 1855, shortly after the gazettal of the new line of road. The little shop, facing present-day Wright Road, had become Modbury's first post office, at least by 1863, and Mitchelson became Modbury's first post master.

Kelly was no mere opportunist — he was also a public-spirited man. He had taken an interest in the establishment of local government in the district and from 1860 until 1862 was Chairman of the district council. In 1863 Kelly donated a piece of land for the establishment of a Wesleyan Chapel in the new village of Modbury, stipulating that the chapel, when erected, should be used as a licensed day-school. In 1865 he also gave a piece of ground close to the new chapel as a recreation ground, where in January 1867, the people of Modbury held their first New Year's Day gathering — 'a picnic, festival, public meeting and a cricket match' with afternoon tea laid out in the new Wesleyan Chapel.

The *South Australian Gazetteer* of 1867 describes Modbury as:

'a postal village situated on the Dry Creek, and is in the midst of an agricultural country where wheat and hay are extensively grown. With Adelaide, 9 miles S.W., the communication is by daily coach. Modbury has a post office and 1 hotel — the Modbury. The resident magistrate is R.S. Kelly, Esquire, J.P.'

Like many South Australian pioneers, Robert Symons Kelly was a young man when he arrived in the colony. At the age of 22, Kelly, still single,* arrived at Port Adelaide on February 9, 1839, on the emigrant ship *Platina*, a barque of 303 tons. Among the 70 assisted migrants travelling steerage with Kelly was Elizabeth Wakeham and her brother, John, of the parish of St. Budeaux, near Plymouth. John Wakeham, like Kelly, was a builder by trade. Perhaps Robert Kelly knew Elizabeth before his departure from England or perhaps a romantic attachment developed on board ship during the long voyage out. In March 1840, Robert Kelly and Elizabeth

* Not as a married man as previously thought.

Wakeham were married in Trinity Church, North Terrace.

Robert Symons Kelly was born at Modbury in Devonshire on November 30, 1817. His family were descendants of the Kellys, of Kelly in Devonshire, 'where the head of the family had resided since the days of Henry II'. He was educated at Hoe House School, near Plymouth, and was a brilliant scholar. He served his apprenticeship as a builder and in 1839, after reading, as he later said, 'glowing accounts of the sunny south' sent home by Dr. Wyatt, decided to emigrate.

Upon his arrival in Adelaide, then as Kelly later said, 'a collection of huts', Robert obtained his first job with the firm of Messrs. East & Breeze, who were then building the Adelaide Gaol and Government House. He later joined the building firm of Borrow and Goodiar.

In Adelaide, following his marriage, Kelly and his wife first lived in Devonshire Place, where they rented a cottage for £10 per annum. Kelly also owned Lot 605, facing what is still known as Symonds* Place. The *South Australian Almanack* of 1841 records that Robert Symons Kelly, Carpenter, was then living in Symonds Place, Adelaide.

In 1842 Kelly must have decided he could afford to take up farming. He purchased an 80-acre section at Upper Dry Creek for which he paid £220 — a measure not only of the young migrant's success in the new colony but of the agricultural quality of the section.

The house which Kelly began building for himself and his wife in 1842, and where he lived until his death in 1893, was fortunately saved from imminent demolition in 1974 by a young couple, Robert and Ros Phillips, who have restored it and preserved its original features. Restoration has revealed that the house was constructed in three stages — the rough random walls of the original cottage contrasting with the dressed stonework and loftier rooms of the later additions.

Kelly named his home *Trehele* after another *Trehele*, a manor house south of Exeter in Devon. The name later became written as *Treehill*, but the property was known generally as *Modbury Farm*.

As a farmer Kelly was successful but seems to have had no ambition to expand his holding beyond the purchase of another 40 acres in 1850, and a further adjoining 80-acre section in the 1870s. The Kellys had no children to provide for.

Later, Robert Symons Kelly persuaded his brother in Devon to allow his three sons to migrate to South Australia. Two of Kelly's nephews, Albion and Robert Symons, duly arrived to work on their uncle's farm at Modbury. Understandably, considerable confusion of the namesakes has resulted, especially as the two Robert Symons Kelly were referred as R.S. Kelly, Snr. and R.S. Kelly, Jnr., and have subsequently been considered as father and son. It was R.S. Kelly, the nephew, who built and occupied the two-storeyed home facing Main North East Road near its intersection with

* The land title records refer to 'Robert Symonds or Symons Kelly, of Adelaide, Builder'.

Reservoir Road.

Descendants of R.S. Kelly, Jnr. and of his brother Albion, continued to occupy the Kelly homes and to farm the properties until the 1950s.

Kelly, Snr. was a scholar of diverse interests far removed from farming. He served the public interest with distinction, locally as Chairman and councillor of the district council and in Adelaide as a member of the Central Road Board on which he served for seven years with George McEwin of Hermitage as his colleague. He was twice nominated by people of the district to contest the electoral seat of Gumeracha but was defeated, evidently to his relief.

In his private life he was a mathematician of repute, delighting in supplying calculations for railway engineers, professors with a problem, road-designers and stock-brokers baffled by problems of foreign currency. He became well-read in heraldry, antiquarian lore and English Literature.

It is recorded that Kelly, on one occasion, attended a get-together of lawyers in Adelaide and joined in their legal discussion. 'I thought Kelly a country yokel', said one lawyer afterwards, 'who had strayed in by mistake and never was I more surprised in my life to find that we were the country yokels'.

Robert Symons Kelly died in September 1893, at the age of 76. His wife, Elizabeth, had died six months earlier. Both wife and husband were buried in the North Road Cemetery.

'The cortege', stated the obituary of R.S. Kelly, 'which included a considerable number of vehicles, left the residence of the deceased gentleman at Modbury and proceeded thence to the cemetery, the gathering at the grave being large. The burial service was read by Archdeacon Farr, and the mourners included R.S. Kelly, Jnr. and A. Kelly [nephews], J. Robertson, E. Mitchelson, W. Trenoweth, R.E. Lucy, G.W. Sudholz, J. Quinlin, W. Bowhey, J.W. Sudholz, S. James, T. Lawrence, W. Powell, E. Cartwright, W. Cole, R. Thompson, J. Holbrook, F. Carter, C. Weston, J. Nelson, J.H. Cronk, R. Morris, J.E. Martin and H. Mortimer' — in fact all of Modbury, it might be said, was present at the graveside.

The two most colourful and now almost forgotten events in Modbury's rather subdued history are perhaps best related verbatim from the newspaper reports of the day.

One was the construction of the steamboat *Mosquito* from a huge red-gum tree felled close to Dry Creek, in a paddock just east of present-day Kelly Road.* The Adelaide *Observer* carried the story in its issue of April 11, 1857:

'On Thursday at noon the inhabitants of Adelaide were agreeably sur-

---

* Local reminiscence has it that the *Mosquito* was constructed under the red-gum tree which now stands in the grounds of the Modbury West Primary School.

prised by the unexpected appearance in the streets of a steamboat drawn by 10 pairs of bullocks.

The vessel had been built by Mr. Wm. Masson of Dry Creek near the Ardtornish Estate assisted by his two sons and was intended for the Murray trade. She is 50 feet in length by 13 feet beam and is calculated 25 tons burthen.

Mr. Masson intends to proceed to Milang with the vessel by way of Macclesfield and on arrival the engine will be fitted in the boat ready for plying on the Murray.

Various conjectures were made by numerous spectators who saw the difficulty of its being conveyed through the hilly district lying between Glen Osmond and the plains beyond Strathalbyn. We hope that the undertaking will be accomplished without any unforeseen difficulty. Mr. Masson is a cautious man and has ten bullocks in reserve in case of accident'.

A notice in the *Observer* of April 25 announced the successful launching at Milang:

'The little steamer, recently built at Dry Creek and conveyed overland to Milang was launched on the 21st instant on the waters of the Murray'.

The *Observer* of May 2 gave the full details of the launching:

'Milang this day has been enlivened by the successful launching of the steamer lately built by Mr. Masson of Dry Creek. The launch was accomplished in a rather novel manner.

On drawing near the lake Mr. Masson caused a pine road to be constructed and as the carriage was drawn forward the pines were drawn from the back wheels and placed in front which operation was carried out until the boat was drawn about 50 feet into the lake when the connecting poles were cut and the fore body of the carriage was drawn from under the head of the boat when the fore part immediately floated; then passing the tackle to a bolt passed through her kelson, she was drawn off the back carriage and launched in first-rate style.

During the time the boat was passing off her back carriage she was christened by Mrs. Brook *The Mosquito* amidst much cheering.

The launching of the boat may be looked upon with great pleasure by colonists. It has proved that we have men of judgement as shown by the carriage of her hull over the hills without a scratch, the successful launching and last but not least the accurate calculation of her draft of water. Mr. Masson said her draught would not be over one foot, though many declared his calculation would prove a failure. I have much pleasure in forwarding her exact draft taken this day, namely, forward 4½ inches; aft 7 inches; midships 11 inches'.

It is recorded* that the shallow draught of the *Mosquito* enabled her

* *RIVER BOATS* by Ian Mudie (Rigby Ltd.) pp.67-68.

Modbury Hotel 1872 — Licensee, James Butler.

Blacksmith's shop, Modbury c.1913, with William Wake on right.

Above: Modbury folk at the opening of the Modbury Institute (now St. John Ambulance Centre) April 1906. **Below**: Sir John and Lady Downer about to leave after opening the Modbury Institute, April 1906.

to open up the shipping trade on the Murrumbidgee. The 50 foot steamer set off up the Murray, with Masson at the wheel, in August 1857, and entered the Murrumbidgee on September 1. Masson determined to push on and to 'secure himself and party the credit and glory of having first navigated successfully with steam this noble river'. Masson reached Balranald, 82 miles up river, before snags blocked progress.

The *Mosquito* ended her days on the lakes near Milang and in 1860, says Mudie, 'was converted to a schooner and spent the last years of her life in sail'.

The second noteworthy event in the early history of Modbury was the village's first football match. Played in 1862 against the Adelaide Football Club, which had then recently been formed, it was not only the first match to be played in the district but one of the earliest to be played in the colony. Fortunately the match was of sufficient interest for the *Observer* to report it in great detail in their issue of September 6:

'On Saturday afternoon, 30th August, a match was played at Modbury, a village situated 9 miles North East of Adelaide, by 20 members of the Adelaide Football Club against an equal number of the Teatree Gully and Modbury Club. The contest was, we believe, the result of a challenge from the latter.

The Adelaidians hired one of Rounsevell's omnibuses which started from the *Globe Inn*, Rundle Street, shortly after 1 o'clock and arrived at its destination in an hour's time.

The country footballers were awaiting their opponents and looked eager for the fray. The necessary preliminaries having been arranged, the sides were marshalled under Mr. T. O'Halloran [Adelaide] and Mr. J. Robertson, Captain of the Teatree Gully Rifles and the 'tug of war' commenced.

The ground on which the game took place was exceedingly rough. It looked — in fact very like, if it were not in reality — fallowed land. This gave the yeomanry an advantage over the townsmen who had always been in the habit of practising on level soil. The lovely weather conduced to swell the number of spectators who were very numerous and among whom were several ladies.

After about an hour's hard play one goal was made by O'Halloran's side but being disputed by their competitors it was not counted. After another hour the Adelaidians succeeded in making a goal about which there could be no question. Much cheering followed the event and now commenced some desperate play.

It was clearly a contest between strength and science.

About a quarter after 5 o'clock a loud shout proclaimed the victory of the Adelaide Club, another goal having been secured. It was at first called into question but after a little explanation the country club admitted they had been fairly beaten'.

It should be recorded that the match was played without an umpire. At a return match played at Modbury a year later there were again 20 players a side and no umpire. Although the game was kept going until sundown no goal was recorded.

At the dinner which followed in the *Modbury Hotel*, the Captain of the Adelaide Club stated that 'all he regretted was the absence of umpires without whom he thought it impossible to conduct a match properly'. Captain John Robertson in replying said he did not agree 'respecting the need for umpires'. It is interesting to speculate what might be the result today at Modbury — or at Football Park — if no umpire were to appear.

Modbury did play a return match in Adelaide, this time with only fifteen players; both sides, the report states, 'fielded two blackfellows each'. Perhaps sport provided South Australia's first opportunity for the integration of black and white. On the football field, at least, Aboriginals had a chance of being treated as equals.

Kelly's village of Modbury, established in 1857, felt no reason for much further expansion. A public school was erected in 1881 and an Institute in 1906.

In 1907 a reporter visiting the area wrote, 'Modbury is a quiet little country village with its store, machinist's shop, chaffmills, Methodist church, schoolroom and hotel. It is most pleasantly situated in rich undulating country, lightly timbered, and though there are not very many residences, all the buildings indicate substantial prosperity'. The 'machinist's shop' was Koop's old blacksmith's shop, the village blacksmiths in 1907 being Fred and Jack Wake.

The reporter might have written an identical report at the end of another 50 years. In 1957 there were still only 62 houses in Modbury and wheat was still being harvested on Kelly's sections, where within a few years the fertile soil would disappear under the bitumen, concrete and brick of the Tea Tree Plaza shopping centre and the Civic Centre of the new City of Tea Tree Gully.

25

BRIDGES, CUTTINGS AND ROADS

'ladies and gentlemen on horseback'

It would be difficult to over-estimate the value of bridges and roads to early pioneers. It is not surprising to find that the opening of a new road or bridge, or even of a cutting, was rarely taken for granted, but was considered a cause for rejoicing and celebration.

The history of the district of Tea Tree Gully, with its ranges and the innumerable creeks of its foothills, is rich in stories of the christening of cuttings, bridges and special roads. The names bestowed on these 'triumphs of engineering' — such names as Snake Gully Bridge, Perseverance Road,* Breakneck Hill Cutting — have often remained after their stories have been forgotten. But who today remembers Kolwes' Cutting, Gollop's Bridge, Kangaroo Bottom Road, Stoneypinch Rise, or their location.

Kolwes' Cutting, on Valley Road, between Hope Valley and Highbury, is too insignificant today to warrant notice. One man, with a bulldozer, could now construct the cutting in a day or two. Yet, in 1870, slicing off the top of the rise using only pick and shovel was an achievement important enough to local residents to call for some celebration.

'At 7 p.m. vehicles and pedestrians proceeded to the centre of the cutting when a young lady broke a bottle of wine against the rocky slope and named it 'Kolwes' cutting'. The party then proceeded to visit the worthy host of the *Highbury Hotel* who treated them liberally'. The party later returned along the road to continue the evening with a social gathering at the *Bremen Hotel* at the expense of Councillor Kolwes. The main toast of the evening was 'Success to the Villages of Hope Valley and Highbury'. It was a warm evening in January, and the toasting of Councillor Kolwes and his cutting continued until early morning.

The practice of using bottles of wine to christen road engineering works was a general custom in the early days of the colony. Locally, bottles of wine continued to be smashed against bridges, cuttings and roads, and even buildings, with great gusto.

* See Chapter 28 for an account of its construction.

The earliest such ceremony recorded was the 'Opening of the Great Cutting at Teatree Gully' on Monday, August 23, 1858. The steep pinch at the summit of the gully road was a well-known hazard to early travellers and required extra horses to surmount it and great care in descending it. With the opening of a cutting, stated Captain Freeling at the dinner held in the *Teatree Gully Hotel* following the ceremony, 'the agriculturists of Gumer-acha, now in winter as well as in summer, could convey their produce to Adelaide without the loss of wheels or of bullocks, and the whole debris of transportation which formerly lay here and there upon the road'.

The village of Steventon, 'beautifully situated at the entrance of the Gully and commanding a birds-eye view of Adelaide in the distance ... and the blue waters of Gulf', was then four years old. The village and district had decided to take a holiday for the occasion.

On the day of the opening the village 'was decked out at almost every point with bunting, ranging from the Union Jack down to most florid of all handkerchiefs. During the morning a battery of muskets from the crown of the hill reminded the inhabitants that the day was to usher in some important event and the people were on the tiptoe of expectation and excitement'.

At 12 o'clock a carriage-and-four, full of notables from Adelaide, escorted by local carriages and 20 to 30 horsemen, came into view. After a brief pause to permit Captain Freeling to lay the corner-stone of the new Steventon Institute* 'the whole of the assemblage, now numbering about 300, male and female, proceeded in procession up the gully for about a mile and a half to the new cutting'.

The procession halted in the centre of the cutting. Miss Davidson, who had been chosen to 'christen' and name the cutting, stepped down from her carriage. Elizabeth Davidson, 'one of the fairest young ladies in the district', the 18-year-old daughter of Thomas Davidson, farmer, of Houghton, was no doubt the envy of all the other girls present, when she took the bottle of wine and hurled it against a wall of the cutting. It took a second hurl to break the bottle before she could declare the cutting open and name it the Teatree Gully Cutting.

Elizabeth Davidson had been chosen for the very good reason that she had been the first girl to be born in the district. Her parents had arrived in the colony in 1839 and her father had been engaged by Thomas Williams on his Hermitage estate where Elizabeth was born in 1840.

No doubt Elizabeth remembered for the rest of her long life the 'christening' and the sound of the crowd cheering her and the echo of guns firing from the top of the cutting above her. Elizabeth Davidson died in 1925 in the suburb of Knightsbridge. Her brief newspaper obituary (as Mrs. George Inglis) indicates that the great day in her life had never been forgotten.

A public luncheon was laid out in the *Highercombe Hotel* for local citizens and a ball held in the Assembly Room at night. Across the road at the

* This early institute was never completed.

Highways steam-roller at Houghton c.1929. Driver W. *(Bill)* H.T. Phillips and W. *(Bill)* Hannaford standing alongside. Note the chain steering of the front roller.

Bins and crusher of the Highways Quarry alongside of Main North East Road in Teatree Gully 1914-16, with steam-engine hauling a road-metal 'train'.

Paradise Bridge, built in the 1880s to replace an earlier wooden bridge. The iron 'bow-string' bridge was itself replaced by the present bridge in 1957.

Employees and 'road-plant' of the District Council of Tea Tree Gully c.1925. Walter Dunn on extreme right of group.

Teatree Gully Inn 100 official guests sat down to 'a sumptuous supply of poultry and various meat delicacies' and 'a liberal allowance of wines — sherry, port, claret, and ultimately of champagne'.

The champagne was reserved for the speeches and toasts where credit for the completion of the cutting was given to, or claimed by, various dignitaries of the Road Board, Members of Parliament, and Councillors.

Only a brief and belated toast was drunk to the person who probably deserved the greatest credit, Charles Bennett, the contractor.

Bennett, a Houghton farmer, who had contracted to make the cutting more cheaply than the original tunnel which had been proposed (the final cost was £3,750), used novel methods to dislodge the 35,000 cubic yards of rock and earth. He sank six shafts along the length of the proposed cutting at the summit. A chamber was dug out at the bottom of each shaft, sufficient to hold eight kegs of gunpowder each. The action of 'the six grand blasts of gunpowder' in dislodging the earth 'was perfect in each instance'.

The cutting today is pock-marked by the gougings of pipe-clay quarries, dug out in the 1880s to manufacture drain pipes and some of South Australia's earliest toilet-pans. When completed in 1858, it was a neat cutting 516 feet long, angled at 45°, and supported by masonry work at its base. Its greatest depth was 52 feet.

Five years later came the completion of another 'triumph of engineering', one which was not only of local interest but, for its magnitude at the time, aroused the interest of the whole colony. This was the opening of a cutting through Breakneck Hill, just beyond Inglewood. Wednesday, March 18, 1858 was a day long to be remembered by settlers in the district. Three road works — the cutting itself, a stone bridge at Inglewood and another at Chain of Ponds — were christened on that day and named. Three more bottles of wine were ceremoniously sacrificed.

Except for its bitumen sealing, the cutting through Breakneck Hill remains the same today as when it was completed more than a century ago. It is a rewarding historical experience to alight from a car, climb to the summit overlooking the 80-foot cutting, and to imagine the manual labour involved in separating the vertebrae of the mountain ridge using no more than pick and shovel, barrow and dray, and gunpowder.

The work began late in 1859 and was completed early in 1863. Charles Bennett, having successfully completed the Teatree Gully cutting, was given the contract. Bennett, however, struck harder rock than he had in the cutting of Teatree Gully, was forced to use large quantities of blasting powder, and finally was employing 120 men in his endeavour to finish the cutting. Early in 1860 Bennett was forced to relinquish the contract which was then taken over by Mr. S. Pearce of Houghton. Pearce, too, lost money on the contract, even though his fine for exceeding the contract time was remitted by the Central Road Board.

There were many Breakneck Hills in various parts of the colony, named so with ample reason. The particular incident which earned the name for the local Breakneck Hill is not recorded, apart from the information that 'the hill was so named from a bullock breaking its neck during descent' some time in 1850. A newspaper item of 1855 tells us that 'some repairs have been affected at Breakneck Hill on the North East Road' but that 'wheels of waggons need to be locked even with a pair of very staunch pole bullocks'.

The residents of Houghton and settlers on the North Eastern line decided at a public meeting that the completion of such an immense undertaking as the cutting provided a reasonable excuse for indulging in a monster celebration, and they planned accordingly.

At noon on March 18 an omnibus, lent by Mr. Rounsevell and loaded with dignitaries from Adelaide, arrived at Houghton Hollow, drawn by eight horses. At the summit of Teatree Gully the vehicle had taken aboard George McEwin and his daughter, Mary, who was to christen the cutting. A party of horsemen met the omnibus and ceremoniously conducted it through Houghton Hollow, which was lined with vehicles and 'ladies and gentlemen on horseback', and a group of mounted and armed volunteers in full uniform. Followed by hundreds of men, women and children on foot, the procession, 'with banners held aloft, passed through Houghton, disappeared over Black Hill Road and descended to the *Inglewood Inn*.

Here was assembled 'a crowd of men, women and children all in holiday attire, some on foot, some on horseback and some in vehicles'.

The Hope Valley German band, crowded on to a single vehicle, somehow managed to strike up 'a lively air' and Miss Lillecrapp, daughter of an old district resident, descended from the omnibus to christen the new stone bridge over the Little Para. 'Triumphal arches' of foliage and flowers spanned the bridge and festooned its stone walls. A bottle of wine hung suspended ready for Miss Lillecrapp. As the bottle smashed against the wall, the crowd, now swelled to nearly 1,000 gave an immense cheer, and the Teatree Gully Rifles loosed three volleys into the air.

The 'Inglewood Bridge' as it was christened, built by Mr. T.C. Haynes for £519.13.0 and replacing John Gollop's earlier wooden bridge, still carries traffic over the Little Para at Inglewood. The beautiful stone-work of the bridge is best visible from the creek-bed itself.

The new bridge duly christened, the procession moved on towards Breakneck Hill itself, picking up horsemen and vehicles at every point 'as if emerging from concealment'. Horsemen dashed ahead to mount the hill on each side of the cutting where they could peer down at the ceremony below. Across the highest point of the cutting a Union Jack was suspended, marking the halting place for the cavalcade, now with its horsemen, banners and followers presenting an almost mediaeval scene of pageantry.

Finally Miss McEwin dismounted, approached the suspended bottle of wine and 'dashed the fragile vessel to pieces against the rock, naming the work 'Blyth's Cutting'. A sigh of satisfaction rose from the crowd, followed by immense cheering and shouting. Order was restored only when the band struck up the National Anthem, a signal for silence and for all the men present to doff their hats and the ladies to shush their children.

Dramatically the silence was broken by the firing of volley after volley from Captain Robertson and his Teatree Gully Rifles, which echoing and reverberating around the cutting made the horses 'start and prance'.

The crowd, on horse and foot, exited from the cutting under more triumphal arches and headed for the new Chain of Ponds Bridge, where Miss Lillecrapp hurled another bottle of wine to destruction and the volunteers fired off another triple *feu de joie*.

The festivities now began in earnest. Back at Blyth's Cutting huge canvas tents had been erected, and two smaller tents, one for the sale of liquor and one for the sale of fruit. The crowd had by now increased to nearly 1,500, most of whom stayed outside of the tents to enjoy themselves while the official speeches and self-congratulations, aided by good colonial wine, got under way inside. It was not until 6 o'clock that the crowd finally dispersed and the officials 'resumed their seats in the omnibus and started for town'. The day had not only demonstrated the ingenuity of colonial engineers but the capacity of colonists to make the most of an occasion.

'Blyth's Cutting', named after the Hon. Arthur Blyth, Treasurer during the Premiership of G.M. Waterhouse of *Highercombe Estate*, did not retain its official name. Sensibly, local settlers preferred the more colourful 'Breakneck Hill Cutting', a name still current among older residents of Inglewood and Paracombe.

The completion of two other local bridges in these early years were greeted by local settlers as major achievements in the civilisation of their district.

The opening of the Paradise Bridge in August 1857, made settlers using this line of road to Adelaide independent for the first time of the winter vagaries of the River Torrens.

The opening of a bridge over the Little Para River at Snake Gully in February of 1874 united the outlying settlers north of the Little Para with the main section of the district of Tea Tree Gully.

We remember that Joseph Ind, in 1850, had named his little hotel the *Paradise Bridge Inn* in anticipation of the proposed construction of a bridge close by. It was not until August 13, 1857, however, that a bridge was constructed and opened for traffic across the Torrens. The MacDonnell Bridge was a wooden structure, supported by three graceful arches and four stone piers. It had a clear waterway over the Torrens of 180 feet. The final cost of the bridge was £6,300 and the contractor was Jacob Pitman.

Pitman and William Holden, who named Hope Valley and became its first post master, arrived in the colony on the *Trusty* in 1838. Jacob Pitman built his own house in Rundle Street East and is recorded first as a 'Builder and Piano-tuner'. He taught shorthand for a time but later contracted for and superintended the building of the first Adelaide Post Office and the first railway bridge over the Torrens. His bridge at Paradise 'was of superior workmanship and a credit to the colony'. It was severely tested a week after opening for traffic by a great flood which almost reached the decking 'but it sustained no damage'.

His Excellency, Sir Richard MacDonnell, accompanied by a cavalcade of officers and gentlemen, arrived on horseback to conduct the ceremony. The christening process consisted of breaking a bottle of champagne over the hand-rail and calling out 'The MacDonnell Bridge'. After declaring the bridge the handsomest in South Australia, the Governor and his party retired to tents pitched on the river side where they 'discussed a champagne lunch'. Meanwhile the band played to the crowd and a battle of rocks and road metal raged across the river between rival factions of boys from Magill and the local 'Paradisian boys'.

The day finished with a banquet in the *Glynde Inn* and a victory, we are told, for the Paradise boys.

In the 1880s a new, iron 'bowstring' bridge was built to replace the earlier wooden MacDonnell Bridge. The present concrete construction bridge was erected in 1957.

In 1863 two other bridges, 'Tilley's Bridge' at Modbury and 'Smart's Bridge' at Golden Grove, were opened, 'Smart's Bridge' with a bottle of colonial wine from Mr. Smart's vineyard.

When the boundaries of the District of Highercombe were outlined in 1853 one small group of settlers found themselves isolated. These were the settlers north of the Little Para, occupying the steep, hilly sections between the river and Gould's Creek, which formed the northern boundary of the new district. There was no connecting road between these outlying sections and the rest of the district. Settlers wishing to attend district meetings either made their way on horseback through private property or made the round journey via One Tree Hill and Salisbury and the Bull and Mouth Road to Golden Grove.

Robert Smyth occupied nearly 1,000 acres of higher land south of Gould's Creek, Joseph Gould himself occupying the choicest sections astride the creek. Some 400 acres of the steep sections along the Little Para were occupied by Reuben Richardson of *Cumberland Farm*. Another early settler in this area was Alexander Kirk. Both *Kirklands* and *Cumberland Farm* are still farmed today by descendants of the same families.

A road through Snake Gully was opened on Monday, August 10, 1859. A crowd, including 'most of the farmers of the neighbourhood accompanied by many of their wives and daughters' assembled at McPharlin's Hill at the summit of the gully at 11 a.m. The procession proceeded down the hill to the creek crossing, although the track was as yet too steep and narrow for vehicles.

Charles Watson, Chairman of the district council called on Miss Jane Roberts, daughter of John Roberts of *Greenwith*, Golden Grove, to christen the road. Jane, we are told, 'dashed a bottle of wine on the ground saying 'I name this the Snake Gully Road'. Following the speeches and toasts 'a number of young people stayed to enjoy the pleasure of a dance upon the green'. The new road, said Mr. Watson, would save 7 miles for settlers taking produce to Adelaide.

The initiative of the settlers in raising £318 to construct the new road through private property in 1857 led to its official recognition by the Central Road Board in the following year.

For many years the road remained a primitive one and the crossing of the Little Para in Snake Gully hazardous. The discovery of a gold-field* near Williamstown in 1868 gave district settlers an added excuse for claiming that the traffic via Snake Gully warranted the construction of a bridge. To convince the necessary politicos, Mr. Percival Gaylard, Chairman of the District Council of Tea Tree Gully, invited them 'to a sort of picnic at the Gully of Snakes' when 'the excellent luncheon provided by Mr. Gaylard appears to have been quite convincing'. In 1871 a grant of £1,000 was voted by the South Australian Government to build a stone bridge over the Little Para.

A contract was let to Mr. James Coad of Chain of Ponds on March 11, 1873, and the corner stone of the bridge was laid on Saturday, May 3, when a document was placed under the stone with coins and newspapers of the day. The document read:

'The corner-stone of this bridge was laid by Miss McEwin, daughter of Mr. Robert McEwin on this 3rd day of May, 1873. Miss McEwin was escorted to the spot by Percival Gaylard, Esquire, Chairman of the District Council of Tea Tree Gully. Mr. C.F.G. Ashwin is the Surveyor of the North East District: Mr. James Coad the Contractor: Mr. Horner the Clerk of Works. Sir R.D. Hanson is the Acting Governor of the colony.

Signed: Wm. HAINES
Clerk of the Tea Tree Gully District Council'

No bottle of wine was broken on this occasion. Instead Miss McEwin 'in a firm voice declared the stone properly laid' and the gathering of settlers cheered.

It was almost a year later before the bridge was opened for traffic. Built on a foundation of solid rock, using solid freestone, the structure remains sound after 100 years. Fashioned from a freestone quarry opened nearby, one of the largest ashlars measured 6 by 4 feet. Although too narrow and perhaps not substantial enough for modern traffic, the bridge remains a monument to colonial workmanship. Its preservation should be a matter of

* The Barossa Gold-field, discovered October 1868.

State concern. Its handsome proportions, as seen from the creek bed, attracted the notice of newspaper reporters at the opening ceremony on Saturday, February 14, 1874.

A large marquee had been erected for the occasion alongside the bridge. Above it floated two banners, one inscribed 'Welcome to Snake Gully' and the other 'Advance Australia'.

Despite the hot summer day, more than 200 settlers had arrived for the opening ceremony. Miss Gaylard, whose father had been responsible for the bridge grant, headed the procession across the bridge and broke the christening bottle of wine on the causeway. Two inscribed memorial stones, their wording still decipherable today in the parapets of the causeway, commemorate the opening. At the speechifying and toasting held in the marquee, Mr. Coad the contractor said that 'he had done his best to make the bridge a strong one and hoped it would last for ever'.

Descendants of some of the earliest pioneers in the sections north of the Little Para are still in occupation of their family lands today.

Reuben Richardson and his wife arrived in South Australia from Cumberland on the *Baboo* in March 1840. For a few years he was in the police force but resigned to take up farming on Gould's Creek. After carting ore to Port Adelaide from the Burra mines, Richardson took up the sections astride the Little Para and established *Cumberland Farm*. In the first year of farming in 1853, during the gold boom, wheat was 21/- a bushel and in that year Richardson reaped 1,700 bushels (all the reaping being done by hand at 10/- per acre) and was no doubt able to pay for his 387 acres of land.

In 1858 Mrs. Richardson was killed when the spring cart in which she was returning from Adelaide hit a stump when she was nearing home and overturned. We are told Mrs. Richardson often took farm produce to town alone in the cart.

Richardson leased his farm in 1868 and returned to Cumberland for a time.

At the time of his death, Richardson had increased his holding of land to several thousand acres 'stretching from the North Road through to Mount Gawler'. *Cumberland Farm* and its orange orchards, still owned by the Richardson family, will disappear within a few years under the waters of the Little Para Reservoir, now under construction.

Shillabeer Road, on the district border at Sampson's Flat, is a reminder of another early pioneer family. The picturesque remains of *Attyford*, the family home, still stand alongside Gould's Creek on Shillabeer Road.

Andrew Shillabeer, his wife Sophia and their 8 children, arrived in the colony in the ship *Brightman* in December 1840. Shillabeer, a butcher by trade, quitted his butchering business within a few years and took up land along Gould's Creek, part of the original Special Survey of Hack, and began a dairy farm. In 1849, Andrew Shillabeer lost an arm when two young steers he had yoked to his dray took off at top speed and overturned the cart. Shillabeer's arm, badly fractured, had to be amputated and much of the work of the farm had to be done by his wife and children. Shillabeers continued farming at *Attyford* * until recent years.

Perhaps the most indomitable of the early pioneers of this isolated section of the district was Alexander Kirk. Born in the parish of St. Margo, in Dumfriesshire, Scotland, Alexander Kirk, at the age of 21, emigrated to South Australia in 1839 in the ship *Lysander*.

In an interview given to a reporter at his home, *Kirklands*, in 1906 at the age of 88 (he died in 1912), Alexander Kirk recalled that his first job upon arrival was helping to make the Old Port Road and to excavate the wharfs at Port Adelaide. His single-man's sleeping quarters was a wooden barrel. The only house available for the 20 men was a weatherboard house. Driven by desperate straits, Kirk explained, he had emulated Diogenes. There was one advantage of the half-tun (100 gallon) cask; it could be turned in any direction to keep out the cold wind at night.

Later, Kirk bought some cows and 'squatted' on land at Campbell's Springs on the Little Para. At that time, recalled Kirk, the native kangaroo-grass was so high that the cattle were hidden when lying down.

The 'squatter' having no horses, had to carry his butter on his shoulder for 12 miles to Adelaide for exchange 'of boots, groceries, etc.' which he carried home in the same way.

In 1844, Alexander Kirk married Clementina Smart, the 18-year-old daughter of another district pioneer, John Smart of Golden Grove.

To build a home on the new section of land which he had purchased, Kirk, with the help of his bride, felled 'a noble red gum tree', sawing the uprights, rafters, and floor-boards over a saw pit.

In 1851, Kirk with three others 'took the gold-fever' and walked overland to Mt. Alexander, near Bendigo. The journey took 5 weeks. After working for two months with no result, the three came upon a gold-bearing layer. For another 6 months they dug until they were finally flooded out and returned to South Australia, this time by coach, with 40 lbs. of gold in their boxes. Alexander Kirk, like many settlers in the district, carried copper between Burra and Port Adelaide to supplement his income.

For many years Kirk was a member of the Tea Tree Gully Council. His wife, Clementina, died in 1909 at the age of 83. Alexander Kirk, on his 90th birthday, managed a five-mile walk over the hills with his son-in-law. He died in 1912, at the age of 93.

The original slab homestead of *Kirklands* built in 1844 still stands and, close by, the stump of 'the noble red-gum tree' which supplied the timber for its construction. The present owner of *Kirklands* is Allan Kirk, now 84.

* The remains of *Attyford* are still to be seen near the creek on Shillabeer Road, towards the northern end of the gully.

The fact that Allan Kirk can remember his pioneering grandparents and was 21 years of age when Alexander Kirk died, has a significance which should not be overlooked. It strongly underlines the comparative youthfulness of the state of South Australia, and the continuity of the pioneering days of the district into the present.

The tiny, head-high pioneer home of *Kirklands*, only two generations removed from the young Scottish couple (Clementina Smart was born in Edinburgh) who built it, remains an important and visible link with the very beginnings of the settlement of the district and of the colony.

26

SCHOOLS

'. . . the rudiments of a sound and liberal education . . .'

The first of the district schools to be established was the little school*
of William Riccardo Squibb in the village of Houghton. It is uncertain when
Squibb first opened his school but his obituary of 1885 states that 'what is
now called the Old Schoolroom was built for him as a place of worship on
the Sabbath and a school during the week'. Squibb was both preacher and
teacher. He came to the colony with his family in 1839 from London where
he had at different times been an actor, preacher and schoolmaster. In Adelaide he was employed 'in the Government school' for about 4 years before
coming to Houghton in 1843. Soon after his arrival, the little building
known as the Union Chapel was erected by the people of Houghton for use
as a church and school, and William Squibb became the village's first preacher and schoolmaster.

In June 1848, in accordance with South Australia's first Education Act
of August 1847, Squibb submitted a return to the Board of Education giving
details of the children attending his school. Squibb was evidently seeking to
qualify for the new government grant to licensed teachers. The rate of payment was an amount 'not exceeding twenty pounds per annum for the first
20 scholars and not exceeding one pound per annum for every additional
scholar, no amount to exceed forty pounds per year'. It was the beginning
of the acceptance by government of its responsibilities in education and
which, by slow steps, finally led to education becoming compulsory in 1875
for children to the age of 13 and, in 1891, to education in government
schools becoming free.

Squibb's 1848 return, written in flowing longhand, gives the names of
26 scholars. Five of the children — William and Jane Tregeagle, Samuel
Philp, and James and Sarah Ellis — were from Teatree Gully. Those from
Houghton Village are given as Samuel Hart, Pasco Hart, Elizabeth Reeds,
Mercy Williams, Florence Williams, Jane Florence, Olive Florence, Ellen

---

* The building, now derelict, stands today behind the premises of the Houghton Branch
  of the Country Women's Association.

Florence, Eliza Davidson, Jane Davidson, Joseph Squibb, Daniel Squibb, Emma Squibb, Henry Carn, John Harmer, Mary Hall, Mary Sambell, Susannah Sambell, Lucy Sambell, Amos Crouch and Hezekiah Crouch.

The form was signed, as required by the Act, by a group of parents — Thomas Davidson, Henry Ellis, William Philps, John Tregeagle, James Sambell, T. Williams, Mary Florence and Thomas Hart — and countersigned by George Anstey of *Highercombe*.

Anstey, along with the more affluent of the district, preferred household tutors and governesses or private schools for his children to the rough and tumble of public schools. In many of the outlying sections of the district children received no education at all except whatever their parents were able to give them.

Unfortunately, for Squibb, the Act of 1847 required the teacher to find 20 children above the age of 6 years before a grant was forthcoming. Squibb's return showed only 19 above age — 7 children were under age, one scholar, Florence Williams, being only 2 years old. 'The application', replied the Colonial Secretary, 'could not be entertained'. The letter of the law evidently could not be bent, even for one child less than required.

William Squibb taught for another 2 years. Early reminiscence has it that the children proved too unruly for Squibb — 'he did not fall readily into the new system of education' — and he retired to the quieter life of village preacher and postmaster.

In October 1850, a petition was forwarded to the Colonial Secretary from 19 parents residing in Houghton and district stating that they were desirous of placing their children under the tuition of Mr. Richard Nicholls, Schoolmaster of Houghton, and that they could guarantee the attendance of 43 children over the age of 6 years. The appointment was approved. By the beginning of 1853, when Patrick Maitland took over from Nicholls, the school had an enrolment of 45 children and was a licensed school.

By June of 1853, Maitland had left for the Victorian goldfields with a group of 14 men from the village.

His place was taken by George Needham in July 1853. Except for a short period Needham remained the Houghton schoolmaster until 1870. His stipend then was £64 per annum, although his wife received a small amount of £5 per annum as sewing mistress.

Houghton considered itself fortunate to have a person of Needham's ability and qualifications. 'Not every country village', said George McEwin, President of the District Schools Board of Advice in 1855, 'had the advantage of a graduate of the university as a teacher'.

The Union Chapel had become somewhat derelict by the mid-1870s. Both Methodists and Congregationalists had moved out into new church buildings of their own. With the passing of the Education Act of 1875, the Government began to erect its own schools and in 1877 began the construction of the Houghton Public School on a site donated by R.D. Ross of

Pupils of the Tea Tree Gully Primary School, September 1917 — sixty-two children in Grades I - VII in charge of Headteacher Mr. Alfred T. George (left). Mrs. George (centre) was the sewing teacher.

Houghton Primary School children, c.1915 — L.to R. Back Row: Mrs. Melbourne, Charlie Newman (monitor), Arnold Wright, Will Curtis, Claude Chapman, Doug Wellington, Frank Newman, Kevin Keane, Eric Murphy, Colin Johns, Millie Strachan (Mrs. Melbourne's housemaid), Mr. Melbourne (Headmaster). Second Row: Malcolm Hodges, Tom Foley, Ivy Robinson, Dorrie Alcorn, Ivy Rehn, Jean Goodwin, Amy Carpenter, Marg. McEwan, Lila Appledore, Marg. Wellington, Doris Carbins, Addie Humphris, Jessie Robinson, Ernie Churchett. Third Row: Gertie Humphris, May Foley, Phyllis Newman, Billy Melbourne, Florrie Murphy, Nell Keane, Ethel Churchett, Muriel Newman, Dorothy Robinson, Hazel Alcorn. Front Row: Jack Alcorn, Ray Nicholls, John Rehn, ... Wellington, Laurence Goodwin, ... Crabb, Bruce Rehn, ... Mildren, Don Robinson, Cyril Murphy, Harold Carbins, ... Crabb, Jim Murphy, Keith Chapman.

Houghton Primary School c.1922 — Mr. Fred Mullet, Headteacher (top left). **Back Row:** Ron Clifton, Ray Carbins, Rex Bagshaw, Don Robinson, Max Alcorn, Len Keane, Bill Veale, Jack Alcorn. **Second Row:** Pearl Johns, Annie Kester, Mabel Murphy, Evelyn Brealey, Gladys Robinson, Violet Johns, Jean Chamberlain, Mamie Pitman, Rena Clifton, Eddie Curtis. **Third Row:** Hazel Carbins, Marj. Pitman, Lorna Nicholls, Doris Lambert, Doris Smith, Gwen Phillips, Violet Roberts, Ina Gilmour, Elsa Nicholls. **Front Row:** Victor Edwards, Ern Carpenter, Bruce Clifton, Gordon Roberts, Alick Goodwin, Annie Kester, Jack Lambert.

Children of the Hope Valley Primary School ready to leave for their annual picnic c.1919.

Highercombe, adjoining the Houghton Common. The foundation stone was placed in position by Miss Ross on Wednesday, February 13, 1878, and the building and residence was completed later in the year at a cost of £910.

One of the complaints of the first Board of Education in South Australia in 1851 had been concerning 'the considerable number of teachers who, emerging from every possible position of society, have embarked in the business of tuition'. The Board was equally concerned about the schoolhouses, often 'absurdly so-called, in some cases, serving at the same time various domestic purposes, in others little better than stables'.

Most of the district's early schools were adequate structures, although the little Hope Valley School, erected in 1849, was so neglected that by 1880 William Haines, Chairman of the local district Board of Advice, described it 'as scarcely fit to keep pigs in'. Hope Valley, however, got its new school in the following year.

The years 1848-1849 saw the completion of two more district schools — the first on the Ardtornish Estate of the Maclaine brothers and a second at Hope Valley, little more than a mile away, and both on Grand Junction Road.

There was as yet no District Council and no provision in the 1847 Education Act for any building grant. The burden of erecting churches and schools fell directly on the settlers themselves, in 1849 still clearing and fencing their own land. Sensibly enough, the one building was made to serve as both church and school in these early years of settlement. At Houghton, Hope Valley, Ardtornish, Golden Grove, Tea Tree Gully, Hermitage and Modbury, school buildings served the double purpose, at least for some years.

Whatever their use on Sunday, the schools were open during the week to children of all denominations. Indeed, the new Education Act of 1851 stipulated that in schools receiving grants towards the erection, upkeep, and payment of teachers' stipends, there was to be no religious bias and 'no denominational catechism', thus upholding one of the principles on which the colony was founded — the separation of church and state.

Another burden which fell upon settlers was that, as far as possible, schools were to be self-supporting by the payment of fees. Teachers, licensed by the Board of Education, were now guaranteed a minimum salary of £40 per annum, in place of the previous £20, with a maximum of £100 per annum, according to the number of their scholars. In addition they were allowed to retain the school fees, a matter of 6d. a week. Many parents, however, especially those with large families, were unable to find the weekly amount. As a result a considerable number of children of poor, apathetic, or indigent parents, 'were rarely or never sent to school'.

Irregularity of attendance was the greatest bugbear of teachers. It led directly to education becoming compulsory in 1875, when it was revealed that only 53% of South Australian children between the ages of 5 and 14 could both read and write and 20% could not read even the simplest primer.

Mr. Needham of the Houghton School spoke strongly at a public meeting in the Houghton schoolroom about 'the great irregularity of attendance of children' and 'the indifference of parents on the supposed necessity of employing their children in domestic or farming occupations'.

Mr. E. G. Day, schoolmaster at Hope Valley, expressed himself even more forcibly in a letter to the Adelaide *Register* in July 1853, entitled 'Apathy of Parents', concerning the Golden Grove School.

'The erection of a schoolhouse, the appointment of a master and the sending of their children to school when they do not happen to want them at home, is not all the inhabitants of a district have to do. There are many parents who never visit a school unless it be to make a complaint.

I have been led into these reflections by having recently attended the half-yearly examination of pupils attending the [Golden Grove] school conducted by Mr. W.H. Humpage.

The children, mostly girls, were assembled in the schoolhouse at 10 o'clock and passed a very creditable examination, exhibiting considerable and accurate knowledge of the subjects in which they were examined.

The master was hoping that a large attendance of parents would enable him to urge upon their attention certain matters such as the punctuality and regularity of their children, but would you believe it, Sir, only one mother arrived and that when the exam was half over ... The attendance for six months has not averaged more than 3 days per week'.

One must report, however, that attendances of parents and friends at these annual examinations rapidly improved in district schools and, indeed, examination days often became festive occasions for both children and parents. It was reported in the *Register* of December 1870, that at the annual examination of Mr. G.H. Reinhard's school in the Houghton schoolroom nearly 100 visitors were present. Some 36 boys and 38 girls were put through their academic paces in the morning but were rewarded with a picnic in the gardens of the *Highercombe Estate* in the afternoon, and an evening of magic lantern slides in the schoolroom, accompanied by much eating and 'regaling' throughout the day.

Even in 1851, the examination of pupils of the Ardtornish School was well attended 'by a numerous and highly-respectable assemblage of visitors and parents. Afterwards the children sat down to a repast of plum and seed cake, bread and butter, tea and coffee, and regaled themselves to their heart's content'. The children we are told had 'tastefully decorated the room with evergreens'.

The Ardtornish School had, perhaps, the best reputation for scholastic achievement of any of the district schools, due largely to the efforts of Charles Kerr who remained in charge of the school from 1857 until it closed in 1874. 'The schoolhouse', stated a report of 1849, 'contains two rooms inclusive of the schoolroom and 3 acres of ground for the exclusive use of the master. The number of children is 64 attending at present inclusive of 2 boarders'.

As early as 1846, Angus MacLaine applied for a Government grant to build a school at Ardtornish 'for education and religious services'. Three acres of land were donated by MacLaine and the school placed under the superintendence of the Adelaide Session of the Church of Scotland. The schoolhouse was erected at the corner of one section of the Ardtornish Estate. The corner, today the north-west corner of the intersection of Grand Junction and North East Roads, became known as 'Ardtornish Corner' and the building remained a landmark for 60 years.

It is not certain who was the first schoolmaster of the Ardtornish School. It did not prosper until the appointment of Mr. F. Tullack. In April 1849, it was reported that 'this school which lately was all but extinct has been rescusitated by the diligent efforts of Mr. Tullack, the recently appointed teacher'. A meeting was held in support of Tullack 'at which 300 persons assembled when subscriptions were raised for completing the building'. Unfortunately, Tullack, although grateful for such support, became homesick and returned to England in May. The Committee advertised for a married man 'whose wife could attend the girls' department' and Robert McTaggart was appointed master. McTaggart was replaced by Augustus Winter in 1852 and tenders were called for flooring the Ardtornish School 'with Singapore Cedar — Room 30 feet x 15 feet'. On January 19, 1857, Mr. Charles Kerr of Morphett Vale was appointed to the school. Kerr, before he arrived in Australia, was formerly a teacher in Newhaven, Scotland.

An inspector's report of 1860 described the school at Ardtornish as a very useful school conducted by an energetic master in a good and well-furnished building. Kerr also conducted evening classes from 6 to 9 p.m. each day 'for the improvement of youths and adults'. The stern Scottish elders, however, insisted that the evening classes should not be 'mixed males and females'.

Kerr was a popular teacher and had the support of the parents. Following the morning's examination in November 1866, 'the children were liberally entertained with cake and tea and dismissed to play for the afternoon' while the 200 parents and visitors sat down to a spread, interspersed with items from the choir of St. Andrew's Church. 'Everyone was happy and returned home at a late hour'.

The school came to a sudden end in 1875 when the Ardtornish Estate was sold and became part of the Beefacres Estate. The school was converted into a woolshed 'where once wool-gathering of another kind used to be practised'. Maclaine, however, then resident in Scotland, did not forget the children of the district. He set aside from his estate the piece of land where the present Hope Valley school now stands, donated it free to the Board of Education, together with an amount of £100, insisting only that the school retain its old name of 'Ardtornish'.

If the Ardtornish School had a strong Scottish flavour about it, then the first Hope Valley School, a mile further along Grand Junction Road, had an equally strong German flavour in its teachers, pupils and instruction.

Many of the settlers in Hope Valley were Germans and two of the initial trustees of the school were Heinrick Klopper and Frederick Kolwes. The schoolroom was erected in 1849 on part section 824, on the southern side of Grand Junction Road, almost opposite present day Parcoola Avenue. William Holden, who gave Hope Valley its name, had donated an acre of land which was to be divided into 3 lots 'to be used for a play-ground, a school and garden, and a cemetery'. Today only the old cemetery remains, the newer section of the cemetery occupying the site of the original school and playground.

Great satisfaction was expressed at a meeting at the school in April 1850, that 'whilst so many parts of the province were destitute of any means of education that a school had been established and a number of children, not less than fifty, were regularly taught the rudiments of a sound and liberal education'. Mr. Holden, after stating that the building had a two-fold purpose — 'the education of youth and the spreading of the gospel' — gave those present an opportunity for showing practical interest 'by permitting the plate to circulate among them'. The rattle of the collection plate was no doubt subdued 'by the deep and melodious tones of an harmonium lent for the occasion'.

But the school soon ran into difficulties. From its commencement until 1854 it had 3 schoolmasters, Mr. Dempster, Mr. Prowse and Mr. E.G. Day. Prowse had resigned to become clerk of the District Road Board and, in 1853, Edward Day left for the Victorian gold-diggings. It is related in Day's biographical notes that while living at Hope Valley 'it was Mr. Day's unfailing custom to walk to the city each Sunday and after conducting three services at Carrington Street to walk back home to Hope Valley at night'.

With the departure of Day, the school was in trouble. The migration of teachers to the gold-fields resulted in the closure of many licensed schools. The miserable pay of a schoolmaster, 'less than that of an untrained farmhand', did not encourage teachers to stay.

At the emergency meeting held in April 1854, it was suggested by the Germans present that the trustees, Messrs. Masson, Cronk, Blyth, Cole, Klopper, Kolwes and Wark, invite Pastor Kappler to reside at the schoolhouse 'with a view to him opening a German day-school'. A proviso was made that 'he vacate the premises in favour of an English master at any future time on receiving 6 months notice'.

The school did not surface either in newspapers or in Board of Education reports until 1866 and was often lacking a teacher. In 1866 the school gained its first licensed teacher, Frederick Sivkovich, but the school laboured

Hermitage School pupils, 1912 - **Back Row:** Alec Wilkey, Bert Colebatch, Harold Dunn, Maurice Verrall, Ivor Clifton, Clarence Verrall, Albert Dunn, Lindsay Clifton, Don Bagshaw, Harry Millar. **Second Row:** Ray Millar, Ron Thomas, Pearl Neale, Daisy Dunn, Doris Warner, Elsie Dunn, Myrtle Millar, Nell Thomas, Roy Dunn, Keith Wilkey. **Third Row:** (girls) Amy Millar, Hazel Clifton, Gertie Millar, Grace Clifton, Irene Wilkey, Gwen Johnson. **Fourth Row:** Raymond Verrall, Len Warner, Ivy Stevens, Evelyn Millar, Teacher-in-Charge - Miss Daisy Neale, Audrey Millar, Coral Clifton, Rene Verrall, Alex Clifton. **Front:** Geoff Millar, Harold Dunn.

Houghton School, Arbor Day - August 1906. With umbrella (left) Treasurer, A.H. Peake, M.P., with umbrella (right) Premier Hon. Thomas Price.

Houghton School, Arbor Day - September 1913. **L.to R.** Marg. McEwan, Emily Murphy, H. Homburg, M.P., Pearl Newman, Mr. John Newman, Hilda Hannaford, Jean McEwan, Ruby Pitman, Amy Carpenter. (Girls at right) - Phyllis Newman (presenting buttonhole), Addie Humphris, Marg. Wellington, Ivy Robinson, Jessie Robinson.

Houghton School, Arbor Day - September 1913. 'Naval' Guard-of-Honour for Governor's wife, Lady Day Hort Bosanquet. L.to R. Frank Newman, Claude Chapman, James Jones, Eric Murphy, *Mick* Jones, Jim Murphy (with flag), Malcolm Hodges, Ern Churchett, Ray Johns, Alf Carpenter. 'Officer' in front Harry Armitage - son of Headmaster. Holding out flag - Mary Drury.

under a dual language system where children of German parentage often began school with little knowledge of even conversational English. An 1873 report commented that 'considering most of the advanced pupils have to learn arithmetic, grammar, and geography in two languages from two sets of books' they acquitted themselves well.

Sivkovich remained in charge of the school for 10 years and was replaced by Wilhelm Schulze. Schulze remained to take over the new Hope Valley school built on Maclaines's land and opened in 1881 with an attendance of 31 children. The schoolroom with its teacher's residence attached was completed in late 1881 at a cost of £820.5.5. It is still (1976) in use as the office, staff room and library of the Hope Valley school.

The new Ardtornish School* had become necessary in 1875 when the Ardtornish Estate was sold. It was also necessary because of the disgraceful state of the original Hope Valley School.

A deputation to the Minister of Education in 1880, led by William Haines, Chairman of the District Board of Advice, urged immediate action. The brick floor of the Hope Valley School was in pieces and 'in such a state that the children were liable to break their legs'. The mortar between the timber slabs which composed the walls had broken away 'leaving great gaps through which winds found entrance, and the place altogether was not fit to keep pigs in'. Haines urged the erection of two new schools, one at Modbury and the other at Hope Valley.

The school was formally opened on Wednesday, December 7, by Mr. R.S. Kelly as a member of the local school Board of Advice. The contractors were two local men, E.R. Gilmour and M. Kaske, and the freestone came from the Anstey Hill quarry of Heinrich Klöpper. The children walked in procession, 'headed by a small band of music', from the old school to the new one.

Early in 1849 a few settlers in the Golden Grove area met to consider 'the erection of an edifice for the purpose of religious worship and secular education'. An incentive was supplied by Adam Robertson of Golden Grove House who presented an acre of his land to the committee. Settlers subscribed an amount of £53 and it was reported in October of 1849 that a room 30 feet long and 15 feet wide was rapidly approaching completion and that it was expected that the school would be opened within a fortnight.

Subscriptions lagged however and it was not until March 20, 1850 that the school was opened with a religious service conducted by the Rev. R. Drummond in the morning and by the Rev. T.Q. Stow in the afternoon. The new schoolhouse was filled with the neighbouring settlers and their families 'who all rejoiced in seeing themselves and their children within reach of the

* The new school at Hope Valley was officially designated the Ardtornish School, as requested by Maclaine, until 1915, when a notice appeared in the Education Gazette officially changing the name to Hope Valley.

moral and religious instruction of which so many of them had long been deprived'.

The subscribers were liberal and ecumenical in outlook. 'They do not intend to restrict the use of the building to any particular sect and will be happy to hear any preacher professing the great Christian principles'.

The first licensed teacher of the school was William Humpage. In November 1852, the school had an attendance of 8 boys and 18 girls, a discrepancy in the sexes which Humpage attributed to 'the boys being required to assist their parents during harvest'.

In 1852 an additional room was added as a residence for the teacher and in 1853 the parents celebrated the abolition of the debt with a tea meeting. 'The bread was made from Golden Grove wheat, the fruits which enriched the cakes were grown in the same locality, the butter and cream from Golden Grove dairies and the honey from a colony of bees attached to the spot'. One can sense in such simple rejoicings the thankfulness of pioneers in having 'made it' in their new colony and in having succeeded in taming a strange and harsh wilderness, and making it productive.

By 1870 the number of children attending the school had risen to 50 and Mr. John Robertson requested that another room be built, 'as it was thought desirable to separate the boys and girls'. However, it was finally decided to use the schoolroom for additional rooms for the teacher and his family and to build a separate schoolroom 31 feet by 21 feet. The schoolroom was completed ready for opening in 1871, and the building remained unaltered until its closure on July 28, 1961.* In that year the number of children attending was 24, a few less than when the school opened in 1850.

From at least 1860 until 1869, a school was conducted in the Greenwith Methodist Chapel on Golden Grove Road, by Mrs. E. K. Ghrimes. For a time the school was known as the Upper Dry Creek School and the average number of scholars attending in 1863 was 22 — at 6d. a week, scarcely a 'self-supporting system', although Mrs. Ghrimes, as a licensed teacher, received an annual salary of £64. Mrs. Ghrimes, trained in Queen's College, London, had opened a school in Victoria Square, Adelaide, in 1843, where she instructed pupils 'in the elements of English, French, Drawing and Music', and 'gave private lessons in crochet'.

We know little about the Greenwith School but it can be recorded that its only teacher, Mrs. Elizabeth Ghrimes, was well liked. In January 1863, when it was reported that her only surviving child, Lacy, was likely to recover from a kick from a horse, it was 'to the delight of her pupils by whom she is much beloved and to the joy of everyone in the district'. Perhaps the joy was the more genuine as during a diphtheria epidemic a few months previously, three of the children who had died were those of the teacher herself. They were buried in the same month in the Golden Grove cemetery.

* Both school and schoolhouse are now private property.

Another little school which concerns the district was the Precolumb School near One Tree Hill. The building, now derelict, was erected early in 1863 as both church and chapel, and began its life with a church service on Sunday, a morning tea on Monday and a picnic half holiday in the play-ground when 'Kiss in the ring was played, old and young all mixed in to-gether'. The Precolumb School was attended mainly by children from One Tree Hill, but children north of Snake Gully, the Richardsons, Shillabeers, Gaylards, walked over the hills to attend it. It closed in December 1938.

The children of Lower Hermitage were able to attend their own school after 1869, instead of walking to Houghton. Their schoolroom was the little Wesleyan Chapel erected in 1867. The first teacher of the Hermitage School was Mary A. Cole. As the building was west of the Little Para River and most of the children (rarely more than 20) lived east, across the little river, a swing bridge was constructed for the children. The old schoolhouse closed in July 1929, when Miss Bertha Rofe and her children moved to their new departmental school further up Warner's Road. This school, too, closed in September 1941, when the attendance fell to less than 6. In 1941, in the second year of World War II, little one-teacher schools all over the state were being closed. The day of the school-bus had arrived. The last teacher at Hermitage was Joyce Pemberton. Both school buildings are still in existence on Warner's Road.

Tea Tree Gully did not get its first school until 1856, two years after the village of Steventon began to take shape. In May 1855, Mr. T.E. Cooke, storekeeper, and other inhabitants of Steventon, memorialized the district council requesting the erection of a schoolroom. Council replied that 'they could not feel justified in appropriating the funds of the district for such a purpose but would use their influence with the Board of Education' and 'also allow a building to be erected on the reserve belonging to the district'. The schoolhouse was, however, not erected until 1870.

The Steventon (Tea Tree Gully) School opened in the new Wesleyan Chapel shortly after its completion in late 1855, with an attendance of 8 boys and 17 girls under the supervision of a licensed teacher, Miss Elizabeth Carter. In November 1856, a Council Minute records that Miss Carter had been granted the use of the new Council Chambers as a schoolroom 'until the Chapel was plastered'. A government report of 1860 suggests that Miss Carter had some difficulty in controlling the older boys.. It stated that, 'the school was a very orderly and well-conducted school' but that 'the older boys in the neighbourhood attend the school at Houghton'.

In 1869 the residents of Steventon bestirred themselves, under the in-fluence of William Haines, Jnr., and found a site for a schoolhouse — a piece of land which had been donated in 1854 by William Haines, Snr., as a site for an institute and library.

The new school was built on the foundations of the proposed 1855 institute which had never been completed. The building was finished and ready for occupation in April 1870, and the District Council had forwarded a request to the Board of Education for a cheque for £112 — half the cost of the building.

The Council, in whom the building was vested, also had the power to appoint teachers. It called for applications and received nine. The 9 teachers presented themselves to the district councillors and a gathering of 50 parents in the Council Chambers. After questioning, the teachers retired, a ballot was taken and Mr. Samuel Cozens was found to have an absolute majority and became the first schoolmaster of the new Steventon School.

Cozens had a sound educational background and had a unique collection of Australian shells and botanical specimens and of Australian bugs and beetles. He lectured on his collection to raise money for the school fittings. By the close of 1870 the number of scholars had increased from 19 to 74, 'including 20 evening scholars', due to the efforts of Samuel Cozens.

The school retained its name of Steventon until 1874, when the name was officially changed to Tea Tree Gully. The 1870 schoolroom still forms part of the present Tea Tree Gully Primary School.

Children from the Modbury and Upper Dry Creek district walked to the little schools at Hope Valley or Ardtornish Corner until they finally had their own village school in April 1864. R.S. Kelly of Modbury had stipulated, in giving land for the erection of a Wesleyan Chapel, that the building should also be used as a schoolroom. A teacher had been appointed but the Board of Education had refused a licence for the new school — it considered the Ardtornish School close enough. Local parents decided to continue the school and to find the teacher's salary themselves. In the following year, the school was licensed. The teacher at the time was Sarah Ann Wyatt, who conducted a school of some 33 children.

The school continued in the Wesleyan Chapel until 1881. It was suggested in 1880 that a larger school be established between Modbury and Hope Valley to replace the closed Ardtornish School and the disreputable school at Hope Valley. William Haines, Chairman of the local schools Board of Advice, advised against the idea, mainly because 'the black soil between the villages would be impossible for children to negotiate in winter'. The new Modbury School and residence* was completed in 1881 at a cost of £965.10.6.

After 1875, partly because of 'a continual outcry against irregular attendance coming from all schools', attendance at school between the ages of 6 and 13 became compulsory.† The government took over from councils

* Both Schoolroom and schoolhouse, on Montague Road, Modbury, still exist.
† In 1867, the average attendance of children in seven of the eight district schools was 178 from an enrolment of 261.

and parents the responsibility for the erection of school-buildings and for the appointment of teachers. There were outcries of 'Socialism' but the Government of the day replied, 'That the nation should interfere to educate its youth is now an established fact'. Many of the old village school buildings in the District of Highercombe and District of Tea Tree Gully were gradually and thankfully handed over legally to the Education Department.

Fees were not, however, immediately abolished. With education becoming compulsory, each child had to go to school, with or without fee, and a distinction was soon drawn between those children who arrived with their weekly 6d., or without. 'The child comes to school branded as a pauper' said William Haines, whose job it was, as Chairman of the District Board of Advice, 'to keep a sharp look-out to see that too many children were not put on the free list whose parents were able to pay'. In 1891, Education became free as well as compulsory.

Another of the duties of the local Board of Advice, which in 1881 consisted of George McEwin, William Haines, R.S. Kelly, Henry Klopper, Charles Watson, Edward Mitchelson and Sir. R.D. Ross of *Highercombe*, was to examine cases of undue severity in the punishment of children. Beating of children was not common — it was confined to individual teachers. 'Most teachers', observed Haines, 'appear to give great satisfaction to parents ... but even angels cannot please everyone'. After all, enquired Haines, 'What is the use of having a schoolmaster unless he can maintain discipline in his or her school?' — a rhetorical question needing no answer.

School 'crimes' remain largely the same today but school 'criminals' are not subjected to the same type of instant persuasion once used to encourage them to give up their evil ways.

The 'Punishment Book' (compulsory in public schools until a few years ago) of one local school reveals some well-remembered types of crime and punishment prevalent in sterner days: and also some fine distinctions.

Name:	Offence:	Punishment:	Date:
-	Use of bad language	2 on left hand	-
-	Habitual use of b.l.	4 on left hand	-
-	Deliberate and continued bad language	6 cuts	-
-	Laziness and untidiness	2 cuts	-
-	Stealing chalk (repeated offence)	3 across thighs	-
-	Bullying	3 across left hand	-
-	Using a water-pistol on girls' dresses	2 handers	-
-	Stealing cane from school (this was boasted about)	3 cuts	-
-	Blackguardism	2 on left hand	-

237

This, let it be said, was a year's tally.

The village schools of the district proved adequate, in size at least, for almost the next 100 years. In 1867 there was a total school population of less than 300 in the eight district schools. In 1953 the average attendance in the six remaining district schools was 282. By 1973, twenty years later, 11,000 children were attending schools in the same local government district.

The last of the village schools to open was the Paracombe School. The subdivision of the Paracombe sheep station in 1901 into blocks for intensive farming and orchards suddenly raised the level of population. The first school was opened on June 5, 1910 in a room of the Paracombe Congregational Church. The teacher was Edith S. Edwards, appointed at a salary of £78 per annum, with a class of 28 children. Children in the upper 4th and 5th classes, however, still had to walk to school at Houghton until the wooden departmental building was erected a few years later.

The first of the new Primary schools, built expressly to accommodate the growing tide of children of migrant parents moving into the district after 1960, was the Banksia Park Primary School. It opened in 1965 with an enrolment of 310, the equivalent of the number of children in all district schools less than 10 years before.

Meanwhile the older schools began to bulge and then overflow into temporary buildings, and children, for the first time in the history of the district, were able to obtain secondary education without having to leave the district to do so, when Modbury High School opened in April 1965 with an enrolment of 99 first year students.

27

CHAPELS AND CHURCHES

'An elegant little place of worship'.

A Government census conducted in mid-1855 throughout the colony gives us some information concerning the numerical strength of the various religious denominations of settlers in various districts. The population of the district of Highercombe is shown as 1,440 — 582 children under 14; 217 young people between the ages of 14 and 21, and 641 adults.

Adherents of the various denominations are shown as:

Church of England	501
Church of Scotland	125
Roman Catholic	97
Wesleyan Methodist	229
Congregationalists (including Independents and Baptists)	69
The Presbyterian Free Church	23
Other Presbyterians	10
Other denominations	137
Lutherans	146
Religion not specified	101
No religion	2
Total	**1440**

Only one church building existed in the district in 1855 at the time of the census — the Union Church at Houghton, built in the 1840s. This is not surprising perhaps as Houghton was the most populous village in the district and the earliest to develop its community life. In various other parts of the district, church services — and on occasions, weddings and baptisms — were being held in homes or in buildings which served as schools during the week and places of worship at the week-ends. Some attended church services in the city. George McEwin recorded in his diary of Saturday, April 26, 1847:

'Went to Adelaide with Mr. McLaine's dray and 14 bushels of wheat to grind. Slept in town all night and went to church in forenoon. Returned home in the evening'.

We learn from the diary of Edward Day that it was his unfailing custom, when living at Hope Valley, to walk to the city each Sunday and, after conducting three services at Carrington Street New Church, to walk back home at night. There were others, no doubt, who also rode or walked into Adelaide, or up to Houghton, to attend a church service — there were those indeed who threw in their lot with denominations other than their own rather than forego the opportunity of public worship.

Between 1855 and 1875 all denominations had at least one church building of their own within the district, with two exceptions — the Church of England and the Roman Catholic Church. Lack of numbers and the scattered nature of the population perhaps is sufficient to explain the lack of a Roman Catholic Church. On the surface it is more difficult to explain the lack of any Church of England in the district — at least until 1886. The census figures of 1855 reveal an overwhelming proportion of Church of England adherents.

The answer probably lies in the fact that our pioneers came mainly from a land where there was an Established Church of England and where adherents of the Established Church had long been accustomed to already-established and state-supported churches. The dissenting non-conformist churches in England were accustomed to having to build their own churches and to financing their own ministers. In the new colony, with no state aid for religion, at least after 1851, no established church, and a large non-conformist population, the non-conformists were the most vigorous builders of chapels. Another early South Australian census also indicates that the non-conformist churches had a far higher attendance percentage than the Church of England.

The earliest church building in the district was 'a little smoky hut' in the village of Houghton, built in 1841, where the Congregationalists held their first services. It is of interest to note that among the preachers, lay and clerical, who rode up from Adelaide on horseback to conduct services was Mr. John Martin, the Rundle Street draper.

'A few years later the Episcopalians, the Wesleyans and the Congregationalists joined together and built a place of worship called the Union Chapel on an allotment given by John Morphett, the people themselves carting the stone, sand, burning lime, sawing the timber, splitting the shingles for the roof; and so the place was built and properly floored'.

The opening services of the Union Chapel were conducted by Thomas Playford, great-grandfather of Sir Thomas Playford, Premier of South Australia from 1938 to 1965.

The ecumenical nature of the Union Chapel was confined mainly to its building; the services were sectarian and held at different times. There were other 'Union' churches in the early days of the colony. The motivation for union was unfortunately mainly economic. When, for various reasons, the sects separated to build their own churches in the same village, the financial strain on settlers became a burden, chapels remained uncompleted and growth was inhibited.

In the first few decades, the ecumenical spirit was however strong. A typical example of this feeling was the statement made by those subscribing to the building of the first school and chapel at Golden Grove in 1849. The building was to be entitled the 'Union Chapel' and 'the sentiments of the subscribers are as liberal as their acts would indicate.

'They do not intend to restrict the use of the building to any particular sect and will be happy to hear any preacher professing the great Christian principles which prepare men for future happiness in that house where there are many mansions'. A similar liberality was evinced by the trustees of the little wooden schoolroom and chapel at Hope Valley.

At Houghton, the Anglicans, because of lack of adherents, withdrew their support from the Union Chapel. In 1851, with the departure of so many villagers for the gold fields, church services were abandoned and not resumed until 1854 when William Reeds, Josephus Longbotham and Mr. Crews waited upon the Rev. T.Q. Stow of the Congregational Church in Adelaide, to ask for a regular preacher to be supplied by the Home Missionary Society.

In 1864 steps were taken by the Wesleyans to build their own chapel, a gift of a piece of land was accepted from Samuel Pearce, licensee of the *Travellers' Rest Inn*, and in January 1865, a building tender of £323 was approved. There were troubles and delays — poor workmanship resulted in a decision to dismiss the contractor, demolish the partly built walls and to call for new tenders. The tender of an Adelaide builder, William Bundey, of £454 was then accepted and the church was completed and opened for service on Sunday, February 25, 1866.

In 1874 the trustees of the Union Chapel conveyed the building to the District Council of Highercombe for use as a licensed school on condition 'that Council pledge to keep the property for the same purpose as it has always been used, viz. — Day and Sabbath School, the preaching of the Gospel and all other meetings for the benefit of the inhabitants'.

Spurred on by the lack of an independent building and also by the fact that Mr. and Mrs. George McEwin, lacking a church of their own Presbyterian faith, had decided to join their congregation, the Congregationalists determined to build their own church. The foundation-stone of the church was laid by Mrs. George McEwin in August 1875. Built at a cost of some £600, the church was opened free of debt.

The 'Union Chapel' continued in use as a public day-school and Sunday School, the Education Department being responsible for its upkeep until a new Houghton school was erected in 1878. The old chapel then reverted to the District Council and lived many subsequent lives as a Rechabite Hall, a Salvation Army barracks,* Council Chambers, and a Polling place and, later, as a meeting place for the Football Club, Improvement Association, and Labor Union.

In the 1880s permission was granted to Mr. W. Kitchingham to use the old chapel for his dancing classes. To the Rev. W.R. Squibb this constituted sacrilege. He petitioned Council to have the classes stopped. Incensed youths replied by showering Squibb's roof with stones (his house was next to the chapel) and the dancing lessons came to an end.

Squibb was not an ordained preacher.† Nevertheless, for many years, he regularly conducted services in the Union Chapel. Post master, store-keeper, curator of the cemetery, teacher and preacher, William Squibb was widely known throughout the district. The village delighted in his eccentricities and remembered them with affection long after his death.

In 1910, the following story appeared in the *Observer* of July 18, concerning the Rev. Squibb:

'The little building opposite was once the Union Chapel. The floor sloped to the front door and the pulpit was on wheels stayed with wedges. It was the custom to read out next Sunday's text on the previous Sunday so as to allow time for preparation and study. One day 'Arise and go to Nineveh' was announced for the following Sabbath.

When that day arrived there was a good muster of lads in the front pews — a gratifying sight to the minister — and it was with a feeling of satisfaction he stood up to deliver the discourse. But he had only pronounced the few words — 'Arise and go to Nineveh' — when the pulpit began to move and increasing in speed every second crashed into the front door. The lads had withdrawn the wedges by means of string which they had pulled at the right moment'.

Knowing that it was Squibb's habit to read from the Bible each Sunday at the point where he had previously left off, two lads on another legendary occasion, waited for an appropriate chance and pasted two pages together. Getting to the last sentence on the page one Sunday, Squibb read, ...'and Esther was' — and, turning the page, '50 cubits high'. Squibb turned back puzzled and finally announced — 'If the Lord says so, must be so' — and read on. +

The historic Union Chapel, perhaps the oldest of the state's surviving chapels, stands today abandoned and derelict behind the C.W.A. Hall in Houghton. In 1956, the original Bible used in the chapel was placed in a glass case in the Congregational Church.

* New barracks were later erected at Hope Valley on what is now known as Barracks Road.
† The title of Revd., however obtained, was usually accorded him, and regularly used by him.
+ A further legend, still current in Houghton, based on a real incident reported in the *Advertiser* of March 1, 1861, and replied to by Squibb in the issue of March 6, has been described in *Tea Tree Gully Sketchbook*, p.53.

Greenwith Methodist Church, Golden Grove. The church, built in 1863, originally had a slate roof.

Tea Tree Gully Baptist Church - erected 1862.

Left: This photo of the original Hope Valley Methodist Church was taken in its centenary year — 1967.

Below: Playtime at the Hermitage School c.1925. The little school was originally erected to serve as the Hermitage Methodist Chapel.

The second chapel to be built in the district was the Wesleyan Chapel at Steventon. A correspondent referred to its location as Steventon, Teatree Gully, and wrote, 'The above really elegant little place of worship was opened on Sunday last when three sermons were preached; those in the afternoon and evening by Rev. Spencer Williams. The chapel was quite full at each service and literally crowded in the morning.

'A Public Meeting was held on Monday and notwithstanding the heavy rains, about 90 persons sat down to tea. The meeting was addressed by ministers and also by Messrs. Haines, Virgo, Swann and Cooke. The collections were very liberal — £57.17.4 and promissory notes £65.8.0.

A chapel bell, cast expressly for the purpose, has been presented by J. Stephens, Esqu.† and will occupy the stylish turret in a few weeks'.

The building, partly demolished in the 1960s, was situated on Walter Street, just east of Elizabeth Street. John Stevens' bell at present rests in the Methodist Manse, pending the erection of a new Methodist Church at Tea Tree Gully.

On Sunday, May 11, 1862, three sermons were preached in the Wesleyan Chapel, Steventon — one Baptist, one Wesleyan, and one Independent — in aid of the building fund for a new church in the same neighbourhood — the Tea Tree Gully Baptist Church. A successful tea-meeting and fund-raising effort followed on the Monday evening, and a new chapel was opened later on March 29, 1863. Baptists had held services in their homes as early as 1858, often in the home of Mr. Job. Mills. Finally William Haines, Snr., had given them the use of a cottage in Tea Tree Gully when the congregation had increased. The new Baptist Chapel was supplied with ministers from the Ebenezer Chapel in Lefevre Terrace, North Adelaide, a chapel built in 1843 by the 'English' Baptists.

The little chapel — 36 feet long and 24 feet wide — often proved too small for its congregation. In 1913 the construction of a larger church — 41 feet wide and 25 feet long and with two vestries — was begun by Fisher Bros., contractors. A foundation-stone was laid by Sir Charles Goode on Saturday, October 11, and the new church opened on January 24, 1914, with addresses by Goode. Charles Goode, the founder of the drapery firm of Goode, Durrant, & Co., was a fervent supporter of the Baptist Church.

The new church was named the Medcalf Memorial Church after the Rev. F. Medcalf, minister-in-charge of the original church from 1887-1890. The 1862 chapel, unchanged in external appearance, now serves as a Sunday School and general meeting place.

Although services of various denominational groups in the district were being held in buildings which served as both schoolroom and chapel, the next building expressly designed to serve as a church was the Greenwith Chapel on Golden Grove Road. The chapel, built by local adherents of the

† A reporter's error. Should read J. Stevens.

Primitive Methodists, took its name from Greenwith Farm, the original farm of the Roberts family on Golden Grove Road.

The Greenwith Chapel had its origins in a meeting held on June 9, 1863 in the home of a member of the Roberts family. According to the *Australian Christian Commonwealth* of 1914, services in the locality 'were first held in a wine cellar on the property of Mr. Thomas Roberts'. An offer by Mr. Paul Roberts of half an acre of land was accepted at the meeting and five trustees — Jonathan Roberts, William Roberts, George Robinson, Charles Smart and Charles Watson — accepted office. On June 30, 1863 tenders were called for the masonry work and the tender of George Robinson for '2/6d. per yard' was accepted. Robinson was a tenant farmer of Adam Robertson of Golden Grove and a church trustee. Church records* show that Robinson carted stone for the walls from nearby creeks and that bricks for the quoins were brought up by bullock wagon by members of the Salisbury Methodist Church at £2 per 1,000. The original slate roof has in recent times been replaced with an iron roof. Mrs. Thomas Roberts of *Greenwith Farm* laid the foundation-stone of the church.

The opening services of the church, 'a neat and commodious place', were held on the Sundays of November 15 and 22, 1863, when sermons were preached by Rev. Thomas Braithwaite of Salisbury. A trustees' report presented at a tea-meeting held in the chapel on Monday, November 23, indicates that the total cost of the building and furnishings was £173.

At the same time as the Greenwith Chapel was under construction, the Wesleyans of Modbury had begun the building of a chapel on land presented to them by Robert Symons Kelly, the founder of Modbury.

A public meeting was held in 'Mr. Hutton's barn' on Monday, June 29, 1863 to raise funds for Modbury's first church and it was decided that the building should be on a similar plan to the Steventon Wesleyan Chapel 'but larger'. More than 100 residents attended the public meeting and tea and subscribed £90 towards the building.

At the opening service on Sunday, March 13, 1864 the building was crowded and many had to join in the service as best as they could from the outside. The choir from the Tea Tree Gully church lent their services, bringing their harmonium along in a dray for the occasion. The first services in the new chapel were conducted by the Rev. N. Bennett in the morning and the Rev. John Watsford, of the Pirie Street Wesleyan Church. Watsford, in 1865, initiated the first moves for the establishment of Prince Alfred College.

The cost of the building was £220. Following a violent local thunderstorm in October 1924, the building was unroofed and in 1926 was replaced by a brick building on the same site. Before 1970, the new building had be-

* v. pamphlet, *Greenwith Methodist Church Centenary Celebrations*, compiled by Mrs. Melva Neale, 1968.

come too small for its congregation and on December 5, 1971 a new church on Montague Road, almost opposite the old one, was opened for service.*

The Cornish influence at Golden Grove centred around the Roberts family of *Greenwith Farm*. The Scottish influence in the same area centred around the Robertson family of *Golden Grove House*. The impetus to build a Presbyterian Chapel at Golden Grove derived from a gift of an acre of land by Captain Adam Robertson in 1849 'for the purpose of religious worship and secular education'.

The first service in the new building was conducted early in 1850 by South Australia's first Presbyterian minister, the Rev. Ralph Drummond.

The building continued in use as schoolroom and church until 1866, when the present church was erected on an allotment of land diagonally opposite, donated by John Robertson, son of Captain Adam Robertson. Built at a cost of £552.2.7., the Golden Grove Presbyterian Church† was opened on Tuesday, June 26, 1866, in stormy weather. The church, designed by the Gawler architect, Daniel Garlick, was built, said a reporter on the opening day, 'with an eye to the useful rather than to the ornamental'. What he did not know was that the original design had, with true Scottish caution, been curtailed 'to save expense'.

We are told that a document placed under the foundation-stone included the names of the original Trustees — John Robertson, Robert Smart, James Daw, Robert McEwin, Robert Smyth, Jnr., Alexander Kirk, James Campbell, and of the Building Committee — John Robertson (Chairman), Robert Smart (Treasurer), John Smart, Snr., C.F. Smart, David Daw, Robert McEwin, Robert Smyth, Snr., John Byers and Peter Little, John Johnston (contractor), C. Walters (builder), Wm.B. Coston (Secretary).

Another little building, erected as both chapel and schoolroom, was the Hermitage Wesleyan Chapel. The Chapel, now used as a storage room for apples, is to be found at the foot of Warner's Road, off Upper Hermitage Road. Its secluded situation made it difficult for strangers and visiting parsons to locate. It is recorded that in 1904, the Rev. W. Potts of Adelaide was expected for afternoon service. Missing the morning coach from Adelaide, the minister mounted his cycle and headed for Houghton. Upon arrival there he was given a horse and directions for finding his way to Hermitage. Potts missed the track and finished up at the Golden Grove Presbyterian Church just as the service there ended. Re-directed to Hermitage, he finally found himself back at Houghton and in despair and too late to conduct any service, mounted his cycle and set off for Adelaide, reaching it in time to conduct his own evening service. On other occasions local preachers walked from Chain of Ponds to conduct services.

* For a fuller history of the original Modbury Wesleyan Church, *v. Modbury, 1840-1926* by Dean Stringer.

† For some subsequent history of the church, *v. 1974 Information Booklet*.

The building of the little chapel was a community effort, like that of the Union Chapel at Houghton. 'Let members of our Church and builders of chapels and churches take a lesson from those who dwell amid the mountains and in the bush at Hermitage', wrote a reporter who had arrived to witness the laying of the foundation-stone by Mrs. Warner on July 17, 1867. Before the end of the day '2 gentlemen had kindly promised to find materials for roofing and to pay for its erection: stone, sand and water were in abundance nearby free of cost'.

Services had been held by the first settlers in a room of Mr. and Mrs. William Neale's home and in Warner's home for many years previously and Mr. John Warner had presented land for the chapel. A large tent was erected on the site for the ceremony of laying the foundation stone and for the tea-meeting and public meeting which followed. The sum of £29 was raised and because of the voluntary labor on the building, this amount enabled the chapel to be opened free of debt. 'It was a grand day at the Hermitage and one long to be remembered by those residing there'. The little building remained unfloored until 1879.

For the settlers of Hope Valley and Highbury there were problems — no sect except the Lutherans had sufficient numbers to finance a building of its own. The early leaders in local affairs — Holden, Pitman and E.G. Day — belonged to the 'New Church' group in Adelaide; while the Wesleyans and Church of England adherents were too few in number to do anything but meet in private homes. The Lutherans — numbering more than 100 — were penurious and uncertain of their future.

The answer found was perhaps the only one possible — for the community to combine and erect a building which, as William Holden stated at a meeting held in April of 1850, would have 'a two-fold purpose — the education of youth and the spreading of the Gospel'.

During the gold-rush, as we have noted, the German residents secured the use of this small wooden schoolroom for day-school and for church services.

By 1866, local Methodists at Hope Valley felt that they were able to undertake the building of a church of their own, especially as a Captain James Stephenson had offered them 'a beautiful site of land'. A meeting was held on February 20, 1866 at Hope Valley under the chairmanship of the Rev. James Maughan, the founder, in 1862, of the Methodist New Connection Church in South Australia.

After inspecting the site, the meeting of nearly 100 local residents adjourned 'to the little log chapel' (in 1866 mainly used by the Lutherans and known locally as the 'Anybodies Chapel') to consider 'ways and means'. The amount of £75 was raised that evening and with the promise by the Central Road Board of free stone from their quarry on Anstey's Hill road, work on the building was begun in March and the foundation-stone laid by Maughan in May 1866, followed by 'a two-hour sermon in the 'Anybodies Chapel'.'

The church trustees, however, discovered that they had built upon Maughan's enthusiasm rather than on a solid congregation, and by 1870 there was only a handful of members. The church, 'a beautiful little Chapel, built in the Gothic style', was finally saved from extinction in 1876 when it was taken over by the Primitive Methodist Society who paid £140 for a building which had originally cost £300.

The closing service of this church was held on September 30, 1973, following the opening of a new Hope Valley Methodist Church and the building, a little colonial treasure, was sold — a Bible, Kerosene Lamp and Bell being retained 'as a permanent link with the old building'.

Although numerically greater in strength than any other denomination, adherents of the Church of England were scattered to a greater extent throughout the district. Generally speaking, they were landowners rather than villagers.

We have seen that at Houghton the local Anglicans combined with the Wesleyans and Congregationalists to build the Union Chapel, but later withdrew their support — probably during the gold-rush period.

In the 1860s Canon Farr, who had arrived in the colony in 1854 to take up his appointment as second headmaster of St. Peter's College, built a holiday home for his wife and children in the hills above Tea Tree Gully and named it *Brightlands*.

'The bullock dray was timed to arrive at St. Peter's the last day of term and set off again early next morning for *Brightlands* piled with rolls of bedding, blankets and wraps, boxes of linen and stores and the nurse, 'Sophy', seated on top with the younger children around her. The boys rode their ponies alongside and drove the cow and Jack Harmer, who lived on the property, was in charge of the whole caravan. It took four hours to cover the distance'.*

During his holidays at *Brightlands*, Canon (later Archdeacon) Farr held service occasionally in the Baptist Chapel at Tea Tree Gully or in the Methodist Church at Houghton.

'On occasional Sundays, service was held in the sitting-room at *Brightlands* and there were brought all the Church of England babies in the neighbourhood to be baptised. A little wooden font was kept for the service. The pet parrot meanwhile whistled 'Oh, don't I love my Nancy' on the verandah and at least once a calf wandered in through the back door'.

At Hope Valley, the Rev. E.K. Miller of St. George's Magill, was invited in 1853 to hold Anglican Service at *Gaskmore Park* (now *Bickham Grange*) then owned by Mr. Edward Clark. The drawing-room of the house 'being full of furniture and ornaments', the first service was conducted in the gar-

* v. *Early days at St. Peter's College - 1854-79*. A biographical sketch by G.H. and Julia Farr, Adelaide, 1936.

249

den in a weather-board building with a canvas top. 'Within a few Sundays an afternoon congregation of from thirty to forty persons attended'.† In 1855 the congregation shifted to a small mud and straw building erected on a site of two acres given to them at Campbelltown, where St. Martin's Church of England was built a few years later.

A further attempt to establish a church for local Anglicans of Hope Valley was made in 1883, when 'Lot 197, Highbury, was given for church purposes by owners of the township'. The site proved unsuitable and in 1886 Miss Dordoy of Highbury donated an area of section 819 for church purposes, but no church has as yet been built on the allotment.

Strong efforts were made in 1886 by local Anglicans of Tea Tree Gully to finance the building of their own church. Canon Green of the Anglican Mission Society gave lectures on 'Courtship' in the Tea Tree Gully school-room in aid of the building fund, and a half-acre of land fronting Haines' Perseverance Road (lots 8 and 9 of section 5629) was obtained from Mr. P.D. Prankherd, land agent of Adelaide, for £15.

Plans for a Mission Church, to be known as St. Wilfred's, were drawn up by William K. Mallyon,* a banker and amateur architect responsible for planning many of South Australia's early country churches. Mallyon designed an incomplete church with transepts and Sanctuary only. The church was not completed until 1969, when a novel design managed to blend modern materials and methods with the early building in the completed modern church.

The foundation stone of St. Wilfred's was laid on Saturday, April 17, 1886, by R.D. Ross, of *Highercombe*, Speaker in the House of Assembly at the time. The building was of local Tea Tree Gully sandstone and was completed in July of 1886 by a local contractor, Charles Tovey, for a contract price of £294. The price included the seating.

Tea Tree Gully made the day a festive occasion with welcome banners in the streets of the village and 'Hitherto the Lord has helped us' inscribed on a banner leading to the church.

At the open-air service which followed the laying of the foundation-stone, Bishop Kennion thanked the local Baptists 'for having hitherto allowed Anglicans to use their chapel'.

On Sunday, August 1, 1886, the Bishop of Adelaide conducted the dedication of St. Wilfred's and the opening service. On October 10, to make up for lack of previous opportunity, 10 children, ranging in age from 16 years to a few months, were baptised — four of them the children of Walter and Adelaide Beames and five the children of John and Annie Shield.

In 1887, the churchwardens were able to announce 'that the stable had been built at a cost of £14 — not including the roof, the gift of Mr. Lucy'.

---

† *Forty-seven years Clerical Life in South Australia*, Rev. E.K. Miller, 1895.
* *W.K. Mallyon, 1850-1893*, by M.E. Fenton, Adelaide, 1971.

The stable (still standing) was built to house the horse and trap of visiting clergy from St. George's, Magill.

The last of the early churches in the district to be built was the Paracombe Congregational Church. Once again the building of the church was a communal effort, all the building stone being donated by Mr. R. Lloyd and much time and labor by such local residents as Andrew Wakefield, Reuben Chapman and James Hurst.

From 1904 until 1907 services had been conducted in the home of Mr. and Mrs. Reuben Chapman. The new church was opened on May 1, 1910, and until 1915 the building was used on week days as a public school by the Education Department. In 1921 it was proudly announced that with the help of the Houghton Church, the Paracombe congregation had managed to buy 'a pony and trap for the pastor', the Rev. C.A. Hawke.

No Catholic Church was built in the district until the late 1960s when St. David's Church opened in the new Parish of Tea Tree Gully. The main denominational strength in the district in its first 100 years continued to reside in the non-conformist churches. With 14 churches and chapels in a district with a population of little more than 2,000, congregations were often small and on some Sundays it is recorded, non-existent. The financing of some churches, especially in the year of depression, was often a heavy burden borne by the few.

28

ROYAL MAIL

'. . . like a king receiving homage from his subjects'

On Thursday, April 30, 1921, George Carter drove the Gumeracha coach along the North East Road for the last time. At Tea Tree Gully, travellers on the coach waited while the ostler, Walter Beames, quietly changed horses just as he had done for the past 35 years. With a crack of the whip, the coach was off and an hour later turned into the stables of Graves, Hill & Co. in Pirie Street,* Adelaide.

This journey from Gumeracha marked the end of an era for Adelaide. The Gumeracha coach was not only the last coach along the North East Road. The coach-service from Gumeracha to Adelaide was also the last line of coaches from Adelaide to go off the roads.

In earlier years, before the days of telegraph and telephone, it was the Royal Mail coach which linked townships together. It brought letters, newspapers and passengers and a 'whiff' of the world outside.

'In the seventies the event of the day was the departure of Hill & Co.'s coaches from the booking office at the Criterion Hotel, opposite the town hall, where many people gathered to see Her Majesty's mail leave for country towns.

At half-past two the first coach would be seen coming around the corner of Flinders Street where the stables were situated. This was the Mt. Lofty — Mt. Barker coach, drawn by five grey horses.

Then came the Gumeracha — Mt. Pleasant coach. Beside the driver sat an ostler from the stables whose duty it was to stand at the horses' heads while the coach was being loaded — the driver never left his seat'.

The arrival of the coach at the staging-places along the road, where horses were changed for the next stage of the journey, had its fixed rituals no less than the departure. On the Adelaide to Mt. Pleasant run, horses were changed twice, one at Tea Tree Gully before tackling the hills, and again at Gumeracha, after the steep haul through the hills.

* In Flinders Street in the 1870s.

'At every stage the driver sat there like a king receiving the homage of his subjects. Men rushed to the heads of horses. The 'steady there with that mare' from the driver was sufficient to make every ostler careful as though they were handling the property of an Emperor ...

When the time of departure arrived and the relay of horses was ready to be harnessed no one dared disturb the driver or suggest it was time he was on his seat. He knew his business. In his own good time he mounted leisurely to his seat, exchanging a word here and there as he climbed the wheel, the horses were harnessed to the coach, the reins passed to the old coachie, the men leaped from the horses' heads, there was a wild plunge, a crack of the whip and off the coach rattled to repeat the performance anew of each successive stage'.

It was not until William Rounsevell & Co. took over the mail service on the north-eastern route to Mt. Pleasant in 1861, that resident ostlers were installed at Steventon (Tea Tree Gully) and Gumeracha. William Gardiner was the first ostler at Tea Tree Gully. The stable then passed into the care of Frank Jolly and on May 11, 1886, Walter Beames, at the age of 32, took over the management of the stables of Hill & Co. The blacksmith's shop and stables of Hill & Co. were situated across the road from the first Council Chambers, and behind the *Tea Tree Gully Hotel.*

In his 35 years as ostler, only once did Beames receive any serious injury from the horses he handled, although he stated that 'he could not remember the number of times his horses tried to write letters on him'. On one occasion, however, he failed to detect 'a slight difference between a strange horse in the pole' and threw a trace over him with the result the horse let out with both hind legs and Walter went to bed for 5 weeks 'to think it over'. When the stables closed in 1921, Beames retired and later settled at Clarence Park. He died in 1936 at the age of 82 in the same week as Hill & Co.'s old stables in Flinders Street were demolished.

The earliest postal service in the district began on October 1, 1848. Until then local settlers had to post or collect letters themselves from Adelaide's first Post Office. In 1848, a memorial was signed by 144 residents 'in the vicinity of Houghton, Chain of Ponds, Gumeracka, and Reedy Creek (Tungkillo)' asking for a mail service. In September it was announced that the tender of James Chambers had been accepted 'provided postmasters could be found to do the duty gratuitously'.

Although no volunteer postmaster could be found at Gumeracha, the resident manager of the Reedy Creek Mining Co., Mr. B.T. Solly; Thomas Battersby, storekeeper of Houghton; and Oliver Philp, Publican of Chain of Ponds, undertook the position and early in 1849, William Holden of Hope Valley offered his services, too, as postmaster.

The primitive mail service continued for a few years, mail and a few hardy passengers being conveyed in an open spring cart. In winter, when the bush track became impassable to anything but bullock-teams, the mail was carried on horseback, the contractor being liable, as before, 'to the fine of shillings for every ten minutes late'.*

The gold-rush which began in late 1851 brought an end to this weekly service. Unable to reach its subscribers, the *Register* newspaper announced in March of 1852 'to the inhabitants of Hope Valley, Houghton, The Chain of Ponds, Gumeracka, Mt. Torrens, Reedy Creek and the adjacent districts' that it had made arrangements for a regular weekly service of its own and would be prepared to deliver and receive letters. The *Register* by such means managed to survive the gold-rush where other newspapers succumbed.

The driver of the unofficial mail-cart was George Smith who had announced when the postal department — 'for reasons of economy' — discontinued the service in January that he would continue 'to run his cart as heretofore'. Smith had been employed as mailman by James Chambers from the time the service began and continued to do so when the service resumed again officially on January 1, 1853. Chambers' contract price for the run was £160 per annum.

Smith became a legendary figure, carrying the mails in the winter by pack-horse 'which, owing to the rough state of the track, had often to be led for many miles through the hills'. 'The Torrens in flood many times endeavoured to block his progress' and George Smith 'had often to swim creeks and rivers in carrying out his duties', among which was an obligation to average 6 miles per hour between towns.

Smith continued as mailman on the North East Road until 1861, when William Rounsevell put a daily coach on the road to Gumeracha and announced a reduction in fares. George Smith's reply to this competition was to purchase a new 'omnibus' and to announce that the new coach, *Defence*, would also run daily between Gumeracha and Adelaide.

A price-war followed and the fares were reduced by Rounsevell from 3/- to 2/6d. for the full journey to Gumeracha. Two months later the *Defence* advertised reduced fare:

* The time table laid down for the journey in the spring cart, leaving Adelaide at 10.30 a.m. was as follows:

Postage	Distance from Adelaide	Post Town	Time of Arrival	Postmaster
4d.	7	Hope Valley	Mon.Thurs. 11.30am	William Holden
4d.	15	Houghton	1.00pm	Thomas Battersby
4d.	22	Chain of Ponds	2.00pm	Oliver Philp
4d.	26	Mt. Torrens	6.00pm	George Dunn

Government Gazette, 1850, p.203

Houghton and district folk ready to leave Houghton for the Oakbank Race Meeting — 1890.

Blacksmith's shop, Inglewood c.1890.

Hill & Co.'s
last coach to
Birdwood (via
Teatree Gully) about
to leave Adelaide, April
30, 1921. Driver, George Carter.

Old *Highbury Hotel*, Tea Tree Gully. The building served as a Post and Telegraph Office for nearly 80 years. It is now a National Trust Folk Museum.

Between Adelaide	- Steventon	1/-
	- Houghton	1/6d.
	- Gumeracha	2/-
	- Blumberg	2/6d.
	- Mt. Pleasant	3/-

In March 1861, George Smith's omnibus came to grief in descending the last stretch of the road into Houghton. The driver lost the reins during the descent and in a desperate attempt to recover them, fell off the coach. The driverless vehicle plunged into the embankment and capsized, killing one passenger and injuring others.

A few weeks later came the final blow. Rounsevell, who, with his new coaches, had captured most of the mail contracts in South Australia, succeeded in securing the Mt. Pleasant mail contract. Before long Smith withdrew the *Defence* from the road. He became postmaster at Gumeracha and his son, Walter, joined the service of his father's competitors.

By 1858, the mail coach had abandoned the old route via Payneham, Hope Valley and Anstey's hill in favour of the route via Walkerville, Gilles Plains and Steventon. Hope Valley was isolated and until a post office was established at Modbury in 1863, the township received its mail from Houghton.

At Houghton, the Rev. W.R. Squibb had replaced Thomas Battersby as postmaster. Squibb had abandoned schoolteaching in 1853 for the quieter life of village storekeeper. Stories concerning Squibb's eccentricities still survive in Houghton to this day. Returning from Hope Valley one hot day with the mail bags slung across his horse's neck, man and horse finally reached the summit of Anstey's Hill. Squibb reined in his horse, took the mail bags from around the horse's neck and placed them on his own. 'Thou'st borne t' heat and burden of the day', he explained to his horse, 'now I'll carry un for'ee'.

Squibb remained the village postmaster until a year before his death in 1885 at the age of 79. He was a familiar figure to drivers and regular passengers on the line and in later years waited for each coach (there were 4 daily) to arrive with his bundle of religious tracts ready for distribution to unsuspecting passengers.

Thomas H. Possingham followed Squibb as postmaster at Houghton and the postal agency was kept by the family for the next 80 years in the general store originally built by John Possingham in 1857.

For a short time during the gold rush Hope Valley was without an official postmaster. Holden left the district in 1851 and the schoolmaster, E.G. Day, who took over from Holden, left for the diggings early in 1852. Hope Valley was still without a postmaster by 1854 and it was probably during this period that Squibb became the mailman for Hope Valley. It is also most likely that during the same period James Hill, butcher, of Hope Valley became unofficial postmaster for Hope Valley.

We know that Hill was officially appointed postmaster at least by the early 1860s. The postal agency of Hope Valley remained in the Hill family for the next century — a unique record of postal service.

James Hill, his mother, his wife, Mary, and their small son and daughter, along with a brother, John, and his wife, a sister and a cousin, all from Devon, England, arrived in the *Brightman* from Plymouth in August 1840. After 2 years in Adelaide as a butcher, Hill and his family moved to Hope Valley where he had acquired 4 acres of section 824 for £12 from William Holden. James Hill set up a business as a butcher, practised as a local veterinary surgeon, and by 1850 had built a two-storey family home on the site of his temporary home facing Grand Junction Road.

After becoming official postmaster at Hope Valley, James Hill undertook other postal contracts and in 1866 was delivering the Hope Valley mail to Mitchelson, the postmaster at Modbury, taking the mail on from Modbury to Charles Watson, postmaster at Golden Grove, and returning with mail from Modbury and Hope Valley. The mail contract for the year was worth £44.10.0. Very often it was Hill's daughter, Emma, in 1866 a girl of 14, who rode to Modbury with the mail bags or who acted as postmistress at her father's shop at Hope Valley.

After the death of James Hill in 1876, the appointment was transferred to his son, Charles, who remained postmaster until 1906. The site of the post office then transferred to the home of Burgon Lambert *(Bert)* Hill, eldest son of Charles Hill. Bert Hill's wife, Gertrude, then became postmistress, retiring from the position on June 30, 1961.

Charles Watson, as has been noted, became first postmaster at Golden Grove. Watson, a batchelor, was born in Dumfriesshire, Scotland, and came to Australia in 1847. In 1848 he came to Upper Dry Creek, as Golden Grove was then known, and began a small carrying business, selling goods to local residents, until he had saved enough to build a small wooden store opposite the present store in Golden Grove. He took wheat for local farmers to be ground at Dinham's Mill on the Torrens near Highbury and obliged farmers by delivering and collecting mail at Hope Valley before becoming postmaster at Golden Grove. Watson died in 1893.

The site of the Golden Grove Post Office varied from time to time following Watson's death. The annual allowance was small — a mere £6. For a time the Presbyterian Minister undertook the duties at the manse. Later Miss Hughes, the schoolmistress, conducted the postal service at the Golden Grove School. Upon her retirement, the post office returned to the village. Mrs. A. Ross, in 1909, ran the postal service in her private home before it was finally transferred back to the store.

By 1858 Steventon had its first postmaster, T.E. Cooke *(q.v.)*, and Modbury, E. Mitchelson *(q.v.)*. Inglewood was not listed as a postal town

Sid and Perce Lokan fitting a new shoe to their draught-horse c.1925.

Mr. & Mrs. Richard Smith of *Surrey Farm*, Yatala Vale Road, with their son Howard (driver), and Victor trying out their new Ford car, Registration No. 2776 (c.1912).

David Bowman stands by his new bus purchased in 1942 — then the only public transport in the district.

Bowman's Bus Service — the fleet of twenty-four buses with their drivers and Jack and Milton Bowman on the Highbury Oval, 1970.

until 1869.

Although the district, beginning with Houghton, had official post-masters from the earliest days, no official post office was built by the Postal Department in the district. With one exception, post offices were all agencies conducted generally as part of a store.

The exception was the *Highercombe Hotel*, which was acquired by the government in 1879 and was opened as a Post Office and Telegraph Station on Thursday, May 20, 1880. Built in 1854, the *Highercombe Hotel* closed as a public house in 1877. In 1878 its owner, William Haines, was elected Member of Parliament for the District of Gumeracha. Discreetly, in September 1879 Haines arranged for a petition signed by 48 residents of Tea Tree Gully to be presented to the Minister in charge of the South Australian Post and Telegraph Department praying the government 'to establish a Telegraph and Post Office at Tea Tree Gully in the buildings which the Government recently proposed to purchase'. Haines had not taken long to learn the art of political manoeuvering. His most effective debating point was that the telegraph wires already passed through the township on their way to the river port of Mannum.

On the same day as the new Post Office and Telegraph Station was opened, another of Haines' favourite projects — a road linking Tea Tree Gully with the Lower North East Road at the foot of Anstey's Hill — was given official recognition.

It was a great day for the township. William Haines on that day was truly 'The King of Tea Tree Gully'. 'The township was decorated with bunting and a triumphal arch, bearing the words, 'Welcome to Tea Tree Gully' were erected across the main road leading into the township'.

Haines was given the honour of declaring the building open. Among the official guests was Charles Todd who had erected the first telegraph line in the colony in 1855 between Adelaide and Port Adelaide and in 1872 had been responsible for the overland telegraph line linking Adelaide with Port Darwin and the world beyond. In the Tea Tree Gully Post Office, Todd set up a new device called the telephone. He had used it once before at Port Augusta to demonstrate its possibilities. Although Adelaide did not get its first telephone exchange until 1883, the residents of Tea Tree Gully were already having their first experience of this modern wonder. 'Conversations were held with the head office. The Post Office clock [in Adelaide] was distinctly heard to strike much to the astonishment of the residents'.

A procession, led by Rounsevell's drag, then set off along the new road to the boundary line between the district of Tea Tree Gully and the district of Highercombe. 'The road is exceedingly rough', wrote a reporter, 'and although several large cuttings have been made, no metal has been laid down, as it is thought that the gravelly nature of the soil will do away with the necessity for metal'.

Another archway has been erected at the boundary line and here Miss

Tregeagle, a daughter of John Tregeagle, the earliest settler in Teatree Gully, broke a bottle of champagne on the roadway and 'amid cheers named the road 'Haines Perseverance',' and declared it open for traffic. The name 'Haines Perseverance Road' had justly been retained.

There was a great improvement in the style, safety and comfort of the coaches after 1866. In that year it was rumoured that Cobb & Co., the great Victorian mail contractors, intended setting up a branch in Adelaide. In December of 1866, W. Rounsevell turned over to Cobb & Co. their entire establishment in Adelaide and their plant and property throughout the state.

Cobb & Co.'s coaches were strongly built to withstand the rough roads of the time. Greater comfort was achieved by mounting the body on heavy leather strapping, resulting in a swaying rather than a jolting movement over rough roads. Comfort, however, was a relative matter as the board seats inside the coach were without upholstery. In summer the inside passengers stifled and in winter the outside passengers, riding on top, froze.

There was another hazard for inside passengers. 'At present', wrote 'An Unprotected Female', Houghton, 'they have the greatest difficulty in making the driver hear and are carried distances varying from 100 yards to a third of a mile to say nothing about bawling themselves hoarse, smashing their knuckles, breaking parasols and umbrellas in knocking against the roof and upsetting their fellow passengers in struggling to open the door'.

The improvement in style and safety were largely due to government 'interference'. Royal Mail coaches now had to have more powerful brakes on the back wheels and were brightly painted, 'the undercarriage and wheels yellow, the body red and lettered 'V.R. Royal Mail' in gold'. As on other mail runs, the Adelaide — Tea Tree Gully — Gumeracha coach had a dicky-seat built over the back steps for the guard who had charge of the mail. 'As one of his duties consisted of collecting loose letters from roadside post offices and making up mails to be dropped further along, he was furnished with quite a young post office on the coach'.

'To add a proper dignity he was equipped with a bugle and garbed in a scarlet coat, which gave to the coach a glory that was almost imperial'. The bugle was sounded when approaching each township.

Such style and luxury had, as usual, its price. In 1868, Cobb & Co. raised its fares throughout the state. On the north-eastern run the fares to Modbury and Steventon increased by 6d. to 2/6d., and to Houghton by 1/- to 3/6d. Travel itself was a luxury not to be undertaken lightly or wantonly. For most working families, with an income of little more than £2 per week, the cost of public transport was prohibitive.

Soon after 1900, a new form of public transport began to appear on the roads and the question was being asked, 'Is the horse doomed to be ousted by the petrolized car?'

In 1907 it was reported — 'John Hill & Co., livery stable proprietors, have added another car to their stables, and now have three cars on hire, a 24 h.p. Mitchell, a 10-12 h.p. De Dion, and a 10-12 h.p. Talbot'.

The new form of transport made people impatient with the old. Speaking of the heavy coach traffic in the holiday season along the North East Road to Mt. Pleasant, the Houghton newspaper correspondent wrote — 'It is ridiculous that such a tremendous area of country has to depend on an antiquated stage coach passing over the worst kept roads in the state'.

The Tea Tree Gully correspondent in 1912 was ready to write the epitaph of the coach. 'The days of coach travelling, in the district, appear to be drawing to a close. Two motor charabancs go to Mannum and return daily in addition to the ordinary coach. Messrs. Graves, Hill & Co. are running one motor and Mr. Raphael of Adelaide the other. The mails are still being carried by coach but it is understood they will shortly be conveyed by motor'.

It was, however, to be another 9 years before the last coach drew up at the *Tea Tree Gully Hotel* and Walter Beames made his last change of horses.

For many years, mail and papers were delivered to the people of Lower Hermitage on horseback. From 1917 until 1930, in all weathers, on three days a week, Mr. Ray Millar of Lower Hermitage arrived at 8 a.m. at Warner's to begin his mail round. From Warner's there were pick-up points along the road for each house, the box marked by a stone if it contained letters to be posted. The round finished at Possingham's Store, Houghton, and the delivery was made on the return trip timed to reach Warner's at 11 a.m. It was an official postal service for which Millar was paid £2.2.0 a month for the delivery of letters. Residents along the track paid an additional 2/- a year for the privilege of having their newspapers delivered. When the Hermitage School shifted in 1930 and Warner's was no longer central, the service ceased. Millar* was presented with a watch inscribed in recognition of his 13 years service by residents of Lower Hermitage.

Records appear to indicate that Modbury was the first township in the district to be blessed with a telephone. In August 1904 a special meeting of 'influential residents' took place in the Tea Tree Gully Institute, with Dr. W.T. Angove as Chairman, to petition the Deputy Post Master General for an extension of the telephone to Tea Tree Gully and Blumberg (Birdwood) from Modbury where a public telephone was already in service at the store and post office of H.E. Marr.

By 1908, the service had been extended to Tea Tree Gully and two subscribers, Dr. Angove and R. McEwin of *Glen Ewin*, had telephones. Three years later there were 6 subscribers — now with telephone numbers allotted to them —

* Information supplied by Mr. Ray Millar.

Angove, Dr.	Tea Tree Gully	2
Hall, Henry	”	3
McAree, Dr. J.V.	”	7
McEwin, R.	”	1
Pitt, A.E. *Alice Vale*	”	6
Pitt, A.W.G.	”	5

and the local charge was 2d. for each three minutes. In 1911 Houghton was connected by telephone and had two subscribers —

Houghton Hotel	Houghton	2
Maughan, Marinus	”	1

In the following year Golden Grove Post Office, and in 1913 the Hope Valley Post Office, were supplied with a public telephone. By 1930, Tea Tree Gully had 26 subscribers and Houghton 38, but neither Modbury nor Hope Valley had an exchange. Highbury had no telephonic communication until 1922.

It is worth noting that it was not thought necessary by Council to grant the District Clerk a telephone until 1927.

29

STONE AND CLAY

'. . . enough stone to build a city.'

Many of Adelaide's finest mid-Victorian public buildings had their origin in the quarries of Tea Tree Gully. Perhaps only the quarries at Glen Osmond supplied more tonnage of building stone to the city. Even then the Glen Osmond stone was more likely to be used as undressed rubble for side walls or ashlars of squared stone for filling in between the corner quoins of brick or of dressed freestone. Tea Tree Gully freestone was often reserved for the main facades and ornamental dressings of buildings. Occasionally, new public buildings, where design rather than economy was the main object, were built almost entirely of freestone from Tea Tree Gully. Three such buildings were the Adelaide Town Hall, the General Post Office, and the Supreme Court in Victoria Square, all completed between the years 1863 and 1872. 'The Post Office', wrote a reporter in 1869, 'will be one of the handsomest of our buildings and the stone-facing used is the finest yet quarried in South Australia'.

Looking at the three buildings today and their massive stonework it is difficult to believe that one quarry supplied the amount of stone needed for their substantial superstructures. Freestone dressings for many other notable buildings which have become part of Adelaide's heritage — St. Peter's Cathedral, St. Francis Xavier's, Stow Memorial, Flinders Street Baptist, the Mitchell building of the University of Adelaide, Scots Church, North Terrace — and of other now demolished buildings, also came out of the same quarry.

The quarry which supplied most of the freestone was the Glen Ewin quarry, first opened in 1856 by the Adelaide building firm of English and Brown. Thomas English came to South Australia from Cumberland in 1850 with his brother-in-law, Henry Brown. The two men set up in business as builders, trading under the name of English and Brown. English retired from the firm in 1865 upon his election to the Legislative Council, but the firm continued for many years as Brown and Thompson, retaining the Glen Ewin quarries until 1882 when the supply of suitable building stone began to fail.

The Glen Ewin quarry consisted of some 20 acres of section 5640 at Upper Hermitage belonging to George McEwin. The quarry site was acquired from McEwin early in 1856 by English and Brown, and opened up to provide stone for the first portion of St. Francis Xavier's Cathedral. 'The structure will consist of uncoursed rubble stone with cut stone facings of fine freestone from Teatree Gully. The foundation stone from the same quarry is a fine specimen containing about 30 cubic feet. Only a portion of the building will be erected for the present, extending from the chancel northwards about 80 feet'. By October of 1856, English and Brown were able to supply stone to other builders 'of the first rate quality for Ashlar Work, Cornices, Sills, Quoins and Steps to any dimensions. The working of the stone has been found to cost only half that of any other colonial stone for the same purposes. Samples may be seen at the yard, Waymouth St., or at the Cathedral, St. Francis Xavier's, Victoria Square'.

The use of stone as a building material became common in South Australia, at least by the 1850s. One reason was the absence of the vast forests of stringy bark of the eastern states. Another reason was the presence of good stone in the Adelaide hills face, within easy reach of the new capital.

In 1850, a colonist noted the likelihood of a trend towards using stone and wrote, 'The demand for stone for the projected roads here is fast bringing to light a vast number of good quarries and more will be discovered yet. This is proof in opposition to the preposterous ideas 'that there is no good building stone in South Australia'.' What was brought to light was not only good hard 'bluestone' for the cheaper random stone for walls, but good 'freestone' — sandstone which could be quarried, cut and shaped without splitting.

The three main early sources of stone, both for quarrying and building, were at Glen Osmond, Dry Creek and Tea Tree Gully.

A variety of materials were used in the construction of the earliest homes in and around Adelaide. One of the earliest substantial homes in our own district was that of Thomas Williams of Hermitage. This was a portable wooden building, pre-fabricated in sections in England, shipped in crates and re-assembled on site in 1840. At Ardtornish, as we have noted, the family spent their first year in a tent and even the wealthy George Anstey 'first pitched his tent in a forest of sheoaks' at *Highercombe* while his home was being built in 1841'. Houghton's first blacksmith, George Barrass, first set up business 'in the shell of an old hollow gum tree'. A common type of settler's home was one of red-gum slabs, such as that of Alexander Kirk, cut from the nearest tree, the gaps caulked with a mixture of straw and mud. The Boord brothers of *Freshford*, below Highbury, stated that at first 'they lived under rocks or in wurlies' on their section on the Torrens. Even as late as 1893 their homestead had a thatched roof 'beautifully cool in summer'. Wooden shingles, imported from Tasmania or split in the forests of the Mt. Lofty Ranges, were extensively used for roofing, even of larger buildings, until galvanized iron roofing became less expensive in the 1860s. A photo of the village of Houghton taken in the late 1860s, shows the shingle roof of the *Travellers' Rest*. Such shingle roofs were not dismantled but later merely covered over with iron.* During the demolition of Possingham's General Store at Houghton the original shingle roof was again revealed when the roofing iron was removed. The original slate roof of the Greenwith Methodist Church came from a nearby quarry, while the slates for *Drumminor* and the home of R.S. Kelly at Modbury were probably imported from Wales. Pisé houses, with their thick walls of straw or cow manure and mud were common enough. One of the few remaining today is that of Miss Iris Payne in Payne Street, Hope Valley. Whitewash has protected the century old walls from the eroding forces of wind and rain.

The census returns of 1846 show that of the 159 houses in the Little Para Survey, which was then the most populous section of the present district, 41 houses were of stone or brick, 68 of wood and 50 'of other materials or tents'.

The use of stone however soon became more general throughout the district. As early as 1840, outcrops of stone along the Torrens on the property of Charles Gooch, near Paradise, were used to build 'the dwelling house, cottage, barn and stockyard'. It was soon realised that the hills face might not only provide stone for local buildings and roads, but provide an inexhaustible storehouse of building stone and road metal for the city.

In 1850 the Government opened quarries on Dry Creek, where it reserved a section of 160 acres 'containing a supply of the best quality stone for building and road-making'. Stone from the quarry was taken to the Adelaide Gaol for prisoners to break, until it was decided that it might be more sensible to take prisoners to the quarry. In 1854 the Yatala Labour Prison was erected and by 1855 the *Government Gazette* was advertising building stone at 5/- per cubic yard and road metal of 4 inch gauge at 4/6d. per cubic yard and 2½ inch gauge at 6/- per cubic yard.

Early in 1856 a public meeting was held in the council room at Steventon 'to consider the propriety of forming a tram road from the Teatree Gully to the Dry Creek Stockade'. Both Mr. Milne, the Chairman, and George McEwin stressed the fact that the purpose of such a branch line would be to convey not only corn and timber but the large quantities of local stone then beginning to be used in the buildings of Adelaide. There was in the neighbourhood of Glen Ewin, said George McEwin, 'enough stone to build a city'.

The tram line 'on which one horse would be able to draw twelve tons on rails instead of 1½ tons by road' would join up with the loop railway line then being constructed to the stockade itself from Dry Creek Station.

* At the time of publication *Bristol House* in Houghton was being re-roofed with split shingles.

The meeting was followed in 1857 by a memorial of ratepayers of the north-east district, asking for 'the extension of the Dry Creek Branch of the Adelaide to Gawler Railway to the foot of the Teatree Gully'. The Surveyor General felt that although such an extension was justified, the railway terminus should be 'at the N.E. corner of Section 844' as the ground rose too rapidly beyond that. The debate concerning the line is interesting if only for the contributions of R.S. Kelly to the mathematics of the new line and the relative power of horse v. steam traction. If the line had been constructed the terminus station would have been at the south-west corner of the intersection of North East Road with Tolley Road. This site, from 1844 to 1846, was occupied by the district's shortest-lived hotel, the *Shepherds' Rest*. Oddly enough the site did become a terminus, not for any railway station, but, nearly a century later, for Bowman's Bus Services.

John Stuckey of Modbury, in 1858, again advocated that the terminus should be at Tea Tree Gully because of 'the inexhaustible quarries of splendid building stone now used in all the best buildings: viz. Catholic Cathedral, Bank of South Australia, Government House, Parliament House, Railway Station, and many of the first-class buildings of North Adelaide'.

In 1863, it was stated by the Adelaide *Observer* that the Glen Ewin Quarry 'supplied a stone hardly to be exceeded for durability and general colour and appearance. It also works well and will no doubt come into general use'. Skilled stonemasons received high wages and were in such demand by 1864 that they felt confident enough to strike for an extra 6d. a day. Their claim was met and their wages rose to 9/- per day.

At the Exhibition, held in honour of the visit of the Duke of Edinburgh in 1867, 'among the principal objects of interest was a large block of free-stone from Messrs. Brown and Thompson's Glen Ewin Quarry, measuring 4'3" x 4'1" and 2'7" in depth, weighing over three tons, on top of which were built quoins of various finish showing the different styles of workmanship and surmounted by a carved keystone representing a monster female head. This is the stone intended to be used in the eastern end of the passage between the Insolvent Court and the Police Court'. The keystone can still be seen in position in the building, now known as the Supreme Court.

The case for a railway to Tea Tree Gully was revived at Parliamentary level in June 1878, this time by the 'King of Tea Tree Gully' himself, William Haines, then Member of Parliament representing the District of Gumeracha. Once again the main argument used was that if the Government would extend the Dry Creek line to Tea Tree Gully there could be obtained a supply of stone which 'would last for untold ages, not only of building stone and ballast, but of the best freestone'. By this time, another fine quarry had been opened on the south side of Teatree Gully itself by William Bundey, an Adelaide building contractor and later, from 1883 to 1886, Mayor of Adelaide. Bundey had opened the stone quarry on section 5397 in 1868 to supply freestone for the Magill Orphanage. There were smaller quarries, too, in

Teams loaded with pipe-clay from Whiting's Mine ready to leave for the Adelaide Pottery
Co. at Brompton c.1920. L.to R. Drivers: Bill Lokan, Bob Lokan, Ern Lokan and Spencer Roberts.

Exploratory drilling at Hope Valley (c.1920) by S.A. Coal and Briquette Co. testing the
depth of the Hope Valley coal-seams.

Allan Whiting (left) and a visitor at the poppet-head in April, 1962, shortly before the clay-mine closed.

Poppet-head of Whiting's Mine c.1920. **On Top:** Fred Whiting. **On Stand:** Keith Hawke, ... **On Load:** L.to R. E.A. Whiting (mine-owner), ... , D. Goodes, ... , Ern Lokan, Spencer Roberts, Eddie Lokan, Bill Lokan, Bob Lokan, ... **On Ground: Mr. Jones, Secretary, Adelaide Pottery Co.**

the gully and nearby, supplying road metal to the Tea Tree Gully Council. The railway, said William Haines, 'would be connected with everyone of the ten or eleven quarries' in the gully and the owners 'would make their own sidings to it on their own narrow gauge'.

The Teatree Gully Railway Bill was introduced into Parliament in August 1878, and, after debate, had its third reading in October when the Bill was passed by a majority of 3. One main argument against the construction was the double handling of stone. Teamsters, it was said, were able to cart the heavy stone direct from the quarries to the building site. William Haines however pointed out the expense of maintaining the road between the city and Teatree Gully 'which was cut up almost entirely by the stone traffic'.

No money was forthcoming for the line. The cost of the line was undoubtedly the main reason. The 'inexhaustible supply' of good freestone from the Glen Ewin quarries began to fail by 1882.

The question of a railway line was raised again briefly but vigorously in 1911, when the Government was investigating a suitable route for a line to the River Murray. Mr. William Hannaford of Paracombe was the enthusiastic supporter of a Torrens Valley Railway 'to enter the gully on Mr. Farr's property, go through a tunnel to Constantia [Lower Hermitage] belonging to Mr. Van Senden, then proceed along the banks of the Little Para to Inglewood, pass through another tunnel near Breakneck Hill, go round Millbrook and cross the river at Gumeracha Bridge'. Another route suggested and inspected was via the Torrens Gorge.

Hannaford founded and became Secretary of the Gumeracha Railway Vigilant Committee. This time it was not the cartage of stone which justified the claims for the railway but the 5,000 cases of apples grown at Paracombe and the 15,000 cases of jam produced each year at *Glen Ewin*. The railway finally went to Mount Pleasant, but via a branch line from Balhannah Junction.

Road-metal quarries in the gully became more profitable than building-stone quarries. In 1888 George Hannaford took over Bundey's quarry and supplied road metal to the Tea Tree Gully Council. 'Hannaford's Quarries' became the subject of a Royal Commission in 1918. Conspiracy between the lessee, W. Egan, and the Engineer of Roads and Bridges was alleged. In 1912 the quarry had been leased to Edward Tregeagle, who like Hannaford had his home in the gully. Tregeagle supplied stone to the Tea Tree Gully Council for 3 years. The quarry lay idle for a time, until large quantities of road-metal were required in 1915 for reconstructing the Port Road. In cycling through the gully Mr. Egan, a dental mechanic of Geelong, had noticed the quantity of the stone and had acquired the lease of the quarry from George Hannaford 'as a venture'. The findings of the Commission were not conclusive of anything much except that blasting operations in the quarry were a nuisance to residents in the gully.

James Hannaford also opened a 'bluestone' quarry in the gully, known as *Little Gully Quarry*. This tough bluestone was used for kerbing suburban streets and building surburban homes.

The District Council of Highercombe opened a road-metal quarry at Houghton Common early in the 1860s. In view of the fact that the quarry was on 'common land' Council moved in September 1877, 'that all stone required from the Houghton quarry for the use of district roads or for the use of ratepayers in the district for building and paving in the district be not charged for'. When however a new Houghton Public School was also built on the Common in 1878 and stones began to rattle on the roof, blasting had to cease.

The Council however, had another source of good road-metal. This was at Anstey's Hill where a local farmer, Henry Klopper, had opened up quarries. Most of the road-metal for the District of Highercombe came from Klopper's quarries and building stone for many homes in Prospect. Henry Klopper died in 1888 but his wife and sons carried on the quarrying business. In 1905 the Kloppers sought permission to open a freestone quarry close to Anstey's Hill. It was from this site that stone for the Highbury and Hope Valley Institute was quarried in 1921. The quarry was abandoned in 1927.

The last of Adelaide's buildings to be constructed of stone from the district was the War Memorial Hall of St. Peter's Collegiate School, erected in memory of the 1,100 old scholars who had enlisted in the services in World War I. 'The building', stated a report of the laying of the foundation stone in 1921, 'will be of freestone, taken from a quarry belonging to the school at Tea Tree Gully'. The quarry was 5 acres of section 5634, the section which had supplied William Bundey with the stone for the Magill Orphanage in 1868.

The Memorial Hall was not opened until September 1929, but over the years provided much needed work for local teamsters. The Lokan brothers of Tea Tree Gully carted most of the stone for the Memorial Hall. Indeed, the six Lokan brothers by 1921 had established the largest cartage business in the district and their teams from 1912 on were carrying wine to Port Adelaide, pipe-clay to Bowden, almonds to the city and quantities of hay to the Lokan chaff mill on the North East Road. The first of the Lokans, Martin Lokan, is shown as occupying section 844 on the North East Road as early as 1861 and William H. Lokan as occupying section 1578 where the chaff mill was later built, by 1875.*

On April 25 (Anzac Day) 1922, a Cross of Sacrifice, paid for by women of South Australia, was unveiled in Pennington Garden, Adelaide. The cross, a copy of an original erected at Clane, Wiltshire, is of Tea Tree Gully stone, the base of granite from Palmer.

Dean Stringer, in his brief history of Modbury, relates how two Modbury men, Spencer Roberts and Eddie Lokan, were required to cart the

---

* For further details of the family see *Modbury, 1840-1926*, Dean Stringer, 1971.

granite.

'When they arrived at the quarry several large boulders weighing from half to one ton were loaded by hand on Mr. Lokan's flat-top trolley. The large stone approximately 12 feet long, 3 feet high, and 2 feet 6 inches thick which now forms part of the base and seat of the monument was to be loaded on to Mr. Robert's trolley.

The only personnel available to load the stone which weighed 6 tons 19 cwts. was one stone mason and two teamsters. The only equipment used to load the largest slab of granite on the trolley was two hand jacks. It took the three men almost ten hours before it was in position on the trolley. Unfortunately the terrain was extremely rough from the quarry to the road. A distance of less than 200 yards was covered when Mr. Roberts ran over a large stone which caused the slab of granite to roll off the wagon. Tired and disheartened, they returned to Modbury with an empty wagon.

However two days later they returned, re-loaded the granite slab and delivered it to its destination'.

The freestone for the Cross of Sacrifice was cut from the same vein of stone from which the foundation stone of St. Peter's College Memorial Hall was quarried. 'The stone is of especially durable character with an artistic grain which the winter rains will develop', wrote a contemporary reporter, quoting the words of the contractor, Mr. Walter Torode.

The cross stands 38 feet high and the arms of the cross stand in alignment with the altar of St. Peter's Cathedral. The stone for the cross, as well as for the base, was carted by Spencer Roberts and Eddie Lokan.

As early as 1849 a sample of clay from the Teatree Gully had been examined in Adelaide and it was stated — 'the clay is remarkably white, very plastic and although neither so fine nor so pure as the porcelain clay from Cornwall, it might possibly become so after careful processing'. No use, however, was made of this particular clay deposit until 1920. In that year the Adelaide Pottery and Drain Pipe Co. sought permission from the district council to remove the stone wall of the Teatree Gully Cutting 'for the purpose of removing fire-clay' — some 1,000 tons of it — for making fire bricks.

The first real opportunity to make use of the district's immense deposits of clay came in 1878.

In that year the South Australian Parliament passed an Act which provided for the introduction of a sewerage and deep drainage system for the city and suburbs. Adelaide became the first city in Australia to construct such a system.

Miles of drain pipes were needed and it was expected that these would come from England. In 1880, Mr. George Marks of Hindmarsh, seeing the opportunity for a local industry, established a drain-pipe works at Hindmarsh. He succeeded in obtaining a small order for drain-pipes and upon testing it was found that the colonial pipes made by Marks easily withstood pressures which shattered imported English drain-pipes. Within three years Marks' establishment was employing 40 men and many boys in his sheds and kilns at Hindmarsh. The firm later became *The Adelaide Pottery and Drain Pipe Works Ltd.* of Brompton and held the annual contract for Government supplies of earthenware pipes and fittings.

The clay used by Marks and the Adelaide Pottery Co. was a mixture of one part of white clay and two parts of red clay. 'The latter abounds in almost unknown quantities on Mr. Marks' own property, but the white clay had to be carted from the vicinity of Teatree Gully'.

The clay mining industry, established in the 1880s, has grown into the modern large-scale industries of Hallett Brick Industries Ltd. and P.G.H. Industries at Golden Grove.

As well as using Teatree Gully clay for sewer and drain pipes, Mr. Marks also began the manufacture of that other necessary adjunct of modern living — closet pans. 'The pans are quite up to the quality and shape of the English pan, and the cost is 9s.6d.' The pottery also turned out 'jars, stone-bottles, breadpans, etc. in any size or colour'.

Until 1962, when modern open-cut methods were employed, clay was mined by deep-shaft mining. The last of these clay mines was employing 10 men when it closed in April 1962. In charge, as foreman, was Allan Whiting, today retired and living with his wife on Whiting Road, facing the old mining area, now open-cut, where he began mining with his father at the age of 13. Even at the age of 6 years, before school, Allan Whiting, and sometimes his sisters, would lead around the horse which drew the buckets of clay up the shaft to the poppet-head. Originally the buckets were made of bullock-hide, replaced later by woven wicker baskets, made especially for the purpose by the Institution for the Blind, and then by iron skips.

Henry Whiting and his family had come to South Australia from Cornwall in the 1860s. By 1974 Whiting had a house and 5 acres of land on section 846 and was probably already mining clay on the property. By the 1880s 'Whiting's' clay mine was busy supplying Mr. Marks with white clay for the manufacture of Adelaide's drain-pipes. We know that from 1922 the Lokan brothers had as many as 9 teams on the road each day, taking clay to the pottery works of the Adelaide Pottery Co. at Brompton. By 1920, the 5 or 6 horse teams, each pulling a load of 6-8 tons, were hauling as much as 50 tons of white clay each day to Coglin Street, Brompton.

There were many other clay-mines in the St. Agnes area supplying good clay to the Adelaide Pottery Co. Some of the finest white clay, hand-picked for quality, was taken to Bennett and Koster's potteries at Magill for the manufacture of jugs, basins and 'toilet-sets', and to Worthley's on the Port Road from the clay mine of Norm. Lambert and Harry Parry.

Henry Kempson and Roy Kirkham also owned and supervised clay works in the St. Agnes area from the early 1900s. Henry Whiting's son, Ern became manager of the 'Whiting' clay-mines for Adelaide Pottery Co., and

Allan was foreman of the mine when P.G.H. Ltd. took over in 1962, bringing to an end nearly a century of family mining.

The last mine had reached 100 feet and drives were still following the 'veins' of good clay. In the final stages of the mine, the shafts were lit by electricity, the clay hauled to the surface by electric winches and jack-hammers were being used underground. Until 1946 the clay was dug out by 'hard yakka' using pick and shovel, the men working by the light of a candle held by a 'spider' thrust into the clay wall. Timbering of the drives and shafts was necessary and later it became compulsory to timber a second shaft within the main shaft to protect the men descending the vertical ladders from the pit-head.

Ventilation of Whiting's clay-mine was achieved by a 100-foot funnel of canvas with a vane of canvas suspended at the pit-head to direct fresh air during the night, especially in the summer months, down the shaft. One of the first jobs of Mrs. Allan Whiting after their marriage was to construct a new 100-foot funnel on her sewing machine for her husband's mine. A change of wind direction during the night meant getting up and going across to the mine to re-position the vane. The funnel was replaced by a compressor after World War II.

Although the stone quarries and the clay mines provided much needed work for the labouring men and teamsters for many decades there was little return to the district as a whole. No railway arrived despite Parliamentary approval and the dream of William Haines for 'an earthenware manufactory' in the district was not realised until long after his death.

The Glen Ewin quarry was closed soon after 1880, one of its last uses being to provide stone for extensive additions to the *Glen Ewin* residence of George McEwin.

Kirkham's mines now lie under the St. Agnes shopping centre. Kempson's clay mines, now filled in, have become the site for a council park adjoining Whiting Road and tended by Mr. and Mrs. Allan Whiting. The 'Whiting' mines, across the road, have become open cuts. Alongside, other open cuts where once clay was mined, are ending their useful life as rubbish dumps, later in turn to become council recreation reserves.

Load of almonds from *Surrey Farm*, Yatala Vale Road, crossing the 'Albert' Bridge, Adelaide, 1914. Driver, Howard Smith.

Lunch-break on Gregory's Farm, Modbury, 1904.

30

AGRICULTURE

'The sweet smell of new-mown hay'.

The problems that emigrant farmers and would-be farmers faced when they first began to move into the districts around Adelaide were daunting.

Apart from the sheer physical problems of clearing the land, constructing some sort of a dwelling and tilling unworked and unyielding ground, there were the more puzzling problems of pioneering agriculture in climatic conditions completely 'topsy-turvy' to all previous experience.

'When the first colonists arrived, the country was parched up, the ground hard baked and apparently unworkable. For some time the early settlers were content to sit down with the conviction that agriculture on such a soil and with such a climate was impossible'.

In 1906, Mr. G. Holden, son of William Holden who took up section 824 in 1842 and named it Hope Valley, wrote in his reminiscences of *Hope Valley Pioneers** 'The early settlers used to mow the long grasses — kangaroo, spear, barley, and silver grass — for hay. The district was covered with forests of giant gums, sheoak and wattles and from Teatree Gully — so named because of the dense growth of native teatree all along the course of the creek there — on to the River Torrens, there were thousands of yuccas or grass-trees. Birds were very numerous, and it was a common thing to see a dozen wild turkeys, great fellows 20 pounds in weight, marching along.

Cockatoos were in thousands, and blue mountain, grass, cockatoo, shell, rosella, and other beautiful parrots, parakeets, quail, laughing jackasses and many other native birds were also plentiful'.

Not all the present district was so well forested — there were the 'Bald Hills' beyond Golden Grove then as there are now. But, in season, natural grasses were abundant everywhere.

Alexander Kirk who kept dairy cattle in the 'Bald Hills' area before it was surveyed, stated, 'At that time the kangaroo grass in the district was so high that the cattle were hidden when they lay down and the dairy yield of

* *Observer*, October 20, 1906, p.3.

277

the herd was heavy'. At Beefacres, close to Hope Valley, 'Ned' Bagot fattened his cattle in the 1850s upon the native grasses. 'The land was then in its virgin vigour, and the cattle fattened rapidly upon the rich succulent and nutritious grasses that there abounded'.

The tendency in the first decade of settlement was to leave the foothills and plains to the flocks of sheep and their shepherds and to grow wheat in the more English conditions of the valley of the Torrens and the damper soil of the hills. The Beefacres Estate remained a sheep and cattle station until well into this century, carrying between 3,000 and 5,000 sheep, herds of Shorthorn cattle, pedigree bulls and a particularly fine stock of stud Clydesdale mares, paddocked on the springs and green grass of the leakage from the Hope Valley Reservoir.*

Until sections were fenced with post-and-rail, or 'live fences' could be grown, the sheep were folded each night.† Even as late as 1862, it was reported that Mr. Milne of *Drumminor* 'not having fenced all his farm with sheep-proof fences is seldom able to allow his sheep out at night'.

Following the gold discoveries in Victoria, and the consequent demand for South Australian wheat, the district came rapidly under cultivation. By 1857 statistics for the District of Highercombe show that of the 30,720 acres in the district nearly 26,000 were occupied and that there were 4,464 acres under wheat, 219 under barley and 815 acres cut for hay. There were two flour-mills in the district — Dinham's on the Torrens and the Teatree Gully Steam Mill, although the two mills also served farmers in districts south of the Torrens and east of the Little Para.

Although the 'Reaping Machine' had been invented by Ridley in 1843, Robert Milne in reply to a questionaire in 1854, stated that 'no new or improved agricultural implements had been introduced into the district'. Another district farmer had replied, 'Reaping machines are injurious to the land, fill it with weeds and prevent good crops. Hand reaping is best'. Even as late as 1874 large areas of crops in the district were being cut for hay with a scythe. The mowing was done by piecework, 'being let to men at prices ranging from 13s. to 25s. per acre'. 'Formerly', wrote the reporter, 'a good many women used to assist their husbands, but that practice is now on the wane'.

The gathering and binding of the sheaves was still done by hand until the 'Binder' came into general use after 1890. The first local trial of a mechanical 'Twinebinder' took place in October 1886, on the farm of Henry Klopper at Hope Valley. Present at the demonstration were such local farmers as 'Messrs. Marrett, McEwin, Watson, Kolwes and Parks'. 'The machine did all the work in splendid style, cutting very close to the ground and not missing a single sheaf during the whole afternoon'.

* For a full description of the Beefacres Estate consult *A Visit to Beefacres, 1882,* in the South Australian Collection of the State Library.

† Driven into yards made of movable hurdles and watched over by a shepherd camped in a movable hut alongside.

Hay paddocks, Modbury, 1910.

Freebairn's (formerly Sudholz's) Chaff Mill, 1906. The chaff mill was situated at the junction of Black's Road (upper left) and the Main North East Road.

Golden Grove and Yatala Vale Show Committee, 1918. L.to R. Back Row: F. Newman, A. Robertson, J. Tilley, W. Lucy, B. Manley, F. Maidment, A. Harper. Second Row: A. O'Leary, F. Gregory, W. Wake, M. Maughan, J. Papps, J. Ross, H. Smith. Front: G. Rehn, P. Maxwell.

Arthur Tilley harrowing at *Hillcott Farm*, Golden Grove.

Robert Milne, of *Drumminor*, was perhaps the district's most progressive agriculturist. Born near Aberdeen, he had obtained a thorough knowledge of Scottish farming before arriving in South Australia. By 1862, stated a report, the greater portion of the wheat crop on Milne's property was being reaped by machine and thrashed with a thrashing machine. Milne was the first farmer in the district to use fencing-wire and apparently the first to construct catchment dams.

An interesting agricultural and community development in these early years was the annual ploughing match. The first of these was held 'on a section of Bay of Biscay land belonging to Mr. R. Milne' on Tuesday, August 14, 1860. A large crowd had assembled on the ground by 10 a.m. 'Nestling in the hills to the east', wrote the reporter, 'appeared the village of Steventon'.

The rules of the ploughing match were specific — 'each man or boy to plough half-an-acre in furrows not to exceed 9 inches in width or 5 inches in depth'. The time allowed was 5½ hours, the teams to start at 10 a.m. For bullock teams competing, one bullock-driver was allowed, but no assistance was permitted to ploughmen with horses.

A gun was fired at 10 a.m. and 7 bullock teams and 16 horse teams set off across the paddock to make the first furrow. The spectators filled in time with quoit-playing, a football match and other 'hilarities' while the weary ploughmen plodded up and down the paddock for the next 5 hours, their only incentive a free ticket to the dinner at the *Modbury Hotel* that night if they completed the course or a first prize of one of 'Tuxford's best single ploughs' for men or of £4 for boys.*

Not to be outdone, the farmers of Hope Valley organized a ploughing match for the District of Highercombe. 'A very numerous and highly respectable meeting of farmers and other gentlemen' met at the *Bremen Hotel* early in September, with J.G. Coulls in the chair, Robert Halden, treasurer, and the District Clerk, H.W. Peryman, as secretary.

The first Hope Valley Ploughing Match, held on September 20, 1860 on the land of Mr. Heinrich Klopper behind the *Bremen Arms*, was not a great success. The entrance fee of 5/- was perhaps too high: only a few ploughmen entered the contest. The ground, too, proved unsuitable 'with many stumps to contend with'. But it was a beginning and 50 people sat down to dinner and speeches at the *Bremen Hotel* in the evening.

The annual ploughing matches which followed took on more and more of a festival atmosphere during the next few years with sideshows, 'Aunt Sallys', greasy poles, foot racing and wheelbarrow races. There were booths on the grounds and dinner in the hotels in the evening.

To vary the tedium of watching 5 hours of ploughing, mowing matches were introduced — 'each man to mow ½ an acre of crop in 2¾ hours and prizes to those who cut their section best and laid it out best for tying up'.

* See Footnote p.282

Occasionally there were exhibitions of horses and stock, one held at the Ardtornish Farm belonging to Messrs. R. and C. Smart in 1867 being attended by 'a large crowd of both sexes'. The three agricultural districts, Modbury, Hope Valley and Golden Grove combined on this occasion. A committee consisting of Dr. Bosch and Heinrich Klopper of Hope Valley, and William Haines of Tea Tree Gully, conducted a programme of sporting events for parents and children.

In 1873, following a ploughing match in which there had been more hard drinking than ploughing, the annual ploughing matches lapsed. Instead, annual rural picnics for the combined districts of Highercombe and Tea Tree Gully became popular for a time.

Under the leadership of Mr. John Robertson of *Golden Grove Farm*, an active branch of the South Australian Agricultural Bureau was formed at Golden Grove and held regular meetings in the Golden Grove Schoolroom.

One of the first scholars of St. Peter's College, John Robertson, after leaving school, took up farming and vine-growing on his father's property at Golden Grove. Like Milne at *Drumminor*, Robertson treated farming as a science. The two men were the first in the district to advocate the use of Peruvian Guano and of bonedust from Burford's factory in Grenfell Street

* The published list of the twenty-three ploughmen and of the owners of the teams probably contains the names of most of Modbury's farmers in 1860

		OWNER	PLOUGHMAN
BOYS' CLASS (under 16)	*	T.D. Harris	Henry Baker
	*	W. Roberts	Emanuel Roberts
		John Goodall	Walter Goodall
		Patrick McCabe	James McCabe
MEN'S CLASS		R.S. Kelly	Luke Hunt
		R. Milne	John MacKay
	*	Robt. Halden	James Magarey
		Geo. Foulis	G. Foulis (Jnr.)
		R. Milne	W. Herring
	*	R. Halden	Alex. Halden
		Geo. Johnstone	Disqualified
		Joseph Ind	J. Ind (Jnr.)
	*	James Cronk	J. Storer
		Mrs. Roberts	W. Hudson
		R. Halden	R. Halden (Jnr.)
		H. Bussenschutt	H. Bussenschutt
	*	John Warner	J. Warner
		Chas. Raikes	Joseph Parson
		W. Cooper	R. Cooper
		Richd. Smith	F. Smith
		A.M. Goodall	P. Ryan
	*	Thos. Reid	Wm. Day
		Mrs. Westphall	H. Westphall

MEN'S CLASS 1st PRIZE	Geo. Foulis
BOY'S CLASS 1st PRIZE	Emanuel Roberts

* Bullock teams.

to fertilize and revitalise their farmlands. Robertson played a leading role in district affairs, serving as Councillor and Chairman of the Tea Tree Gully District Council. He was a member of the Royal Agricultural and Horticultural Society and its President from 1893-1894. John Robertson died at his residence at Golden Grove at the age of 60 in 1896.

The Golden Grove Agricultural Bureau continued as a vigorous body, making visits to Roseworthy Agricultural College and inviting experts to speak at their meetings.

The interest thus stimulated bore lasting results. It led to the formation in 1911 of the Golden Grove and Yatala Vale Agricultural and Horticultural Society, 'a remarkably keen, enthusiastic and patriotic' group of local farmers. The Society is still active today and conducts its annual Show on the same grounds as its first Show in March 1912.

The Show was held on land leased from Messrs. Tilley Brothers for 21 years at a peppercorn rental. For the first Show the perishable products were accommodated in a marquee but by 1913 'a substantial wood-and-iron pavilion 50 feet by 30 feet had been built, a new fence had been erected and the arena had been planted with couch grass'. The 'zealous and efficient secretary' was Mr. W.W. Wake. It was a district affair with exhibitors from all district areas and a programme of ring events.

We read that Mrs. M. Maughan 'tabled a beautiful collection of preserves', that 'Mrs. G. Rehn's jellies were beyond cavil', that 'Mrs. Ross's pickles were excellent', and that 'Mrs. A. Roberts triumphed with her eggs'. There were collections of apples from Messrs. R. McGilton (Hermitage) and Geo. McEwin & Sons and displays of dogs, machinery and farm implements. The Show Society has held successful Agricultural Shows each year since 1912.

The agricultural development of the district followed the normal pattern in the colony, until the advent of large areas of vineyards altered the local pattern of cultivation and the growth of the city led to a demand for large quantities of chaff and hay for fodder.

The earliest and largest of the local hay-farms lay partly inside and partly outside of the present district, at Gilles Plains, with its chaff mill at the junction of the North East Road and Black's Road. Large quantities of hay from the Modbury-Golden Grove district were chaffed here. The hay farm of Mr. J.W.A. Sudholz was the largest in the colony in 1874, with 900 acres under crop yielding 1,800 tons of hay. The whole of the crop was cut by scythe and at harvest time 128 men were employed on the farm, with many women, boys and girls engaged in tying sheaves in the fields.

Indeed in 1874 the drive along the North East Road lay through hay fields almost all the way from the *Maid-and-Magpie Hotel* and in November, a reporter on his way out to the Sudholz Chaff-mill, wrote, 'the sweet smell of new-mown hay has pervaded the air around the city at every turn during the last few weeks'.

By 1907 the scene had changed little, except for ᴛʜᴇ ᴀᴅᴠᴇɴᴛ of the motor-car. 'A drive in the early morning on the road from Adelaide to Mt. Pleasant', wrote a reporter in that year, 'whether by motor-car or any other kind of private vehicle, may be a delightful commencement of a holiday, but if enjoyment of scenery is the object, the box of a Hill & Co.'s coach is to be strongly recommended. With a substantial, well-hung vehicle, a spanking team and a capital driver, the tourist may dismiss anxiety, and will find objects of attraction along every mile of the road.

When the suburbs [of North Adelaide and Walkerville] are left behind there is a straight run for some miles along the Gilles Plains. Down to the right lies the Torrens Valley, with its luxuriant orangeries, vineyards and fruit plantations, and beyond it rich country stretches to the foot of the ever-beautiful hills.

A wide and cultivated expanse lies to the left, where heavy crops of hay and cereals are grown, and in front the road rises till it disappears over the crest of a gently sloping hill [Holden Hill]. From that point there is a splendid panorama, including Adelaide and its suburbs.

Modbury ... is a quiet little country village ... pleasantly situated in rich, undulating country, lightly timbered and though there are not many residences, all the buildings indicate substantial prosperity'.

Fifty years later, in 1957, the scene was little changed, except that 'the sweet smell of new-mown hay' was now accompanied by decidedly more motor-car fumes, and the road was bitumen. The last chaff-mill on the North East Road — Lokan's Chaff-mill at Modbury — had closed in April 1950.

It should perhaps be recorded that in the present year of 1976, along the Golden Grove Road, are still to be seen the last remaining haystacks of the district — those of Bruce Willison, John Tilley and of Don Neale at Golden Grove. At Golden Grove in February could be seen a solitary field of stooked hay.

31

HORTICULTURE

'. . . the whole district is something of a fruit bowl.'

More interesting and unusual than the district developments in agri-culture were those in horticulture. These developments, which later gave the district an industry and considerable stability, began to take place very early in the valley of the Torrens and then in the hills area.

It has been related how the report of Dr. Imlay and Mr. Hill in 1838, following their discovery of the Torrens Gorge, led to the early settlement of the sections of the district bordering the Torrens. It was from this area that Joseph Ind brought in his loads of watermelons to sell to the thirsty citizens of Adelaide until the first trees of the colony came into bearing. The Boord brothers of *Freshford*, below present-day Highbury, planted their first fruit orchard in 1839. Within a few years wheat-growing on the river flats ceased and gave way to the vineyards, orchards and vegetable gardens which still occupy some of the original river-front sections today.

The most astonishing transformation of the landscape, however, was that which was taking place on the *Highercombe Estate* of George Anstey.

'At that time [1840] when nothing more ornamental than a cabbage plant was procurable in Adelaide beyond the products of our native forests, Mr. Anstey was receiving packages by the best means available from Europe and elsewhere and raising around him in his mountain home the choicest ornamental plants of England and warmer climates. In the avenue leading to the house and the plantations around it, there are in addition to pines of a score of different kinds, oaks of six or eight species, acacias, hollies of four varieties, oranges, lime-trees, olives, walnuts and an endless variety of choice flowering shrubs'.

Writing in 1862 of his visit to *Highercombe*, by that time the domain of the Hon. G.M. Waterhouse, Premier of South Australia, Ebenezer Ward* was impressed by the magnificence of the driveway which began 'at a white chase gate', where the present road to Paracombe and the Highercombe Golf Links branches off the Anstey's Hill road. 'Side by side with English oaks,

* WARD, Ebenezer. Newspaper reporter, later M.P. for the constituency of Gumeracha.

elms, sycamores, hollies, thorns [now clothed with May blossom], laburnums, acacias, and bay trees, are pines in almost endless variety'.

Much of this driveway of English trees shades the public road today, although the orchards, pleasure gardens, walkways and vineyards, planted in Anstey's time and developed by Waterhouse and Ross, have now been replaced by the open landscaping of the Highercombe Public Golf Course. 'The house', wrote another visitor in 1871, when *Highercombe* had become a showplace familiar to many people in Adelaide, 'may be fittingly described as surrounded with fruit-bearing hills and vales. The former are covered with apple, pear, peach, cherry and other fruit trees and the valleys are planted with nut-trees and pines. In the flats [once occupied by tea-tree] orange trees are planted. There are gooseberries, rhubarb, asparagus, raspberries, black, white and red currants in abundance.

The ground rising from the flats is principally taken up with nuts of various kinds, comprising the hazel, cob, Barcelona, filberts, walnuts and chestnuts. There are also two hills planted entirely with walnut and chestnut trees. ... The process of gathering must be something to recall recollections of nutting rambles in England. Women and children [from the village of Houghton] go out to the different nutteries with their provisions and there spend the day in picking nuts and putting them together at various spots whence they are collected by the fruit van'.

Among the vestiges of the early plantations still remaining on what was once the *Highercombe Estate* are some of the oldest exotic trees in South Australia. We know that the magnificent deodara cedar, a native of the Himalayas, which grows close to the lake, was planted in 1842. We also know that somewhere under its thick bark is embedded the initial 'A' for Alfred, Duke of Edinburgh, which he carved when he visited the estate on his official visit to South Australia in 1867.

At *Glen Ewin*, George McEwin was developing vineyards, orchards and a nursery which, although less elaborate than the estate of his previous employer, George Anstey, were destined to provide the district with its first industry — jam making.

McEwin said in 1863 that he had been led to the selection of the steep section where he established himself and his family in 1844 from a resemblance in the gorge to some 'bonnie glen where in early life he sported'. By 1861 *Glen Ewin* was well on the way to becoming one of the more important vineyards and orchards in the colony. The *Glen Ewin Nursery* was advertising several thousand young fruit trees for sale; cuttings of vines; and gooseberry, currant, raspberry and strawberry plants. In that year George McEwin was President of the South Australian Agricultural and Horticultural Society. His early two-roomed cottage had been enlarged in the spring of 1859 by the addition of 4 stone rooms — 2 upstairs and 2 downstairs, built of freestone from his own quarry.

Glen Ewin Jam Factory, 1864, with George McEwin standing in front with hoe, (left) Rev. John McEwin (son) and four daughters, Mary, Margaret, Jessie and Elizabeth (right), and workmen.

Employees of *Glen Ewin* Jam Factory, c.1904.

Mr. and Mrs. George McEwin and family outside of *Glen Ewin* homestead, probably a few years after its completion in 1880.

Glen Ewin - The homestead and factory today.

In 1862 came the incident which led to the establishment of the enterprise which continues at *Glen Ewin* to this day.

Robert McEwin, in 1900, related how as a lad of 14 it was his job to take fruit from *Glen Ewin* for sale to fruit shops in Adelaide. 'He took a load of plums into the city and hawked the fruit all day to no avail. He then gathered the street urchins together and, taking them into the Park lands, upset the fruit and told them to help themselves'. On the following day his father, who was in Adelaide at the time, sent home a supply of sugar, tins and a copper which was set into a room carved out of the hillside rock and skillion roofed. The copper, a large one, could take 200 pounds of fruit at a boiling. 'The fruit thereafter', recorded Robert McEwin, 'was turned into jam'.

Painstakingly, each evening, George McEwin recorded the beginning of his enterprise in his diary.

GEORGE McEWIN'S DIARY

SECTION 4. GLEN EWIN

December 13th 1862 (Saturday) Commenced to make jam today with my new copper which I have got set at the old Wine place at the Rocks. Paid £2.5.0 for the copper & £1.10 to the old man for setting it. Bricks £1.10.0. Iron work 10/- Total £5.15.

Put the fire on at 10 a.m. and had to wait till 2 p.m. before the water boiled. Then put on the Gooseberries 100 lb. with 66 lb. Sugar, 2/3, Boiled them well and made 150 lb. Jam (Very good). Loss by evaporation 10 per cent.

Monday, Decr 15th Preparing for another charge tomorrow have got 120 lb. Gooseberries prepared by carefully sorting them in a riddle.

Monday, 21st Decr 1862 Prepared Apricots by quartering and taking out stones. In all 128 lbs. Weight of stones 13½ lb. and 90 dozen being equal to 8½ per lb. Put in 7/8 of Sugar or 112 lb. Total in boiler 240 lbs. Boiled well and when dished have 116 — 2 lb. tins & 1 one lb. tin full. Counts 233 lbs. Jam.

Wednesday, 24th Decr Had 22 galls of Gooseberries from Gumeracka this morning. Very poor .. and with a good many spoilt ones amongst them. Sorted them the best way we could. Had 147 lbs. Gooseberries to which I put 98 lbs. Sugar or 2/3 the quantity. Boiled it long and well and filled tins as follows:= 245 lbs.

75 — 1 lb. tins		75 lbs. of Jam
56 — 2 lb. tins		112
7 -- 3 lb. tins		21
8 — 4 lb. tins		32
	Total	240 lbs.

Cost of Fruit 33/- Sugar 34/8½ = 67/8½ = Cost of Jam per lb. : 3d¼ and $\frac{8}{15}$ of a farthing.

Quantity formerly made		350
Add todays —		240
	Total	590 lbs. Jam

289

Saturday, 19th March, 1863. Finished labeling Jam tins. Have been nearly a fortnight over them. Found a great many leaky ones particularly Apricot. Mary, Margaret, Jessie & Elizabeth, Robert, John and Self all employed over them.

Wednesday, 24th March, 1863. Finished packing the Jam. In all 90 cases — Total weight 8,481 lbs. Loaded two of Williams' drays ready for starting in morning.

Thursday 25th March, 1863. In Town today, and saw the Jam delivered to Messrs. D.& J Fowler to whom I have sold it all @ 8d¼ per lb.

Tuesday, 30th March, 1863. Commenced Wine making today. Hot & thundery. Smart shower in evening. Made Blk. **Hamburgs.** Fine crop. Filled a 300 gall. cask. Have 2 . . . full yet. Had Pearces machine and crushed with stalks. Took out stalks over the Fermenting Vat with a riddle. Measured the Specific Gravity of must this morning with Gardiners Instrument. It indicated 111.50. Very good for Black Hamburg.

George McEwin's jam-making enterprise flourished. He increased the size of his own orchard to 100 acres and was soon beginning to purchase fruit locally. With confidence in his own ability and in the future of the young colony, McEwin built himself in 1864 a new jam factory and began to look for markets interstate and overseas. In 1870 he gave a series of lectures in Adelaide to the Chamber of Manufactures on the encouragement of the dried and preserved fruit industry. He had already set out himself to introduce the horticultural products of South Australia into India.

His business at *Glen Ewin* prospered so well that in 1880 he was in a position to make extensive additions 'of nearly a dozen rooms' to the family home at a cost of £2,000.

The industry had become a large scale one by the time of George McEwin's death in August 1885, at the age of 70. Mrs. McEwin had died during the previous year. It was only in the last few years of his life that George McEwin found time to relax and, as a botanist of repute, to indulge in his favourite hobby — microscopy and the study of plants. One of his proudest possessions was the silver medal presented to him in his later years by the Scottish Arboricultural Society for a paper on the natural forests of South Australia. George McEwin's life and that of his hard-working wife remains one of the finest examples of pioneering in South Australia — the contribution of McEwin to the horticultural life of the young colony was enormous and his life-story awaits a biographer.

Robert McEwin, at the age of 38, took over the family business which has continued under the name of Geo. McEwin & Son ever since. Other members of the family who have had direct control of the company have been Roy McEwin (son of Robert), Gordon *(Bro)* McEwin (eldest son of Roy), and Glen and Greg. McEwin who today manage the enterprise created by their great-grandfather.

The *Glen Ewin* business advanced year by year under Robert McEwin who bought out the Kent Town Preserving Company and the preserving machinery of D.& J. Fowler, Ltd. and established a branch of *Glen Ewin*

This early woodcut of the 'Model Nursery' of C.F. Newman & Son, was used to illustrate the original catalogue of plants.

When this photo of *Water Gully* was taken (c.1900) Newman's 'Model Nursery' was a thriving establishment. Today, little remains but crumbling walls.

Right: Mary Ann Maria Newman, wife of Charles Frederick Newman, founder of *Water Gully* Model Nursery. The photo was taken in Mrs. Newman's 79th year.

Below: Charles Newman (centre) founder of the 'Model Nursery' with his son Frederick Charles (right), and a visitor (left). c.1910

at East Adelaide. Between the two establishments the firm produced 52,290 cases of jam in 1900 and tins of *Glen Ewin* jam found their way to the furthest shearers' hut in South Australia and was a staple of troops fighting the Boer War in South Africa.

The greatest impact of the enterprise was, however, within the district around *Glen Ewin*.

In the season of 1904 the company purchased (much of it from local growers) 10,000 bushels of plums, 10,000 cases of apricots, 1,500 cases of quinces, 1,400 cases of pears, 300 of peaches, 800 of figs, 500 of apples, along with 100,000 lbs. of raspberries, 20,000 lbs. of blackberries and 7,000 lbs. of mulberries from other areas. Thirty men, 10 girls and 10 boys were employed full time in the factory and in the summer 'almost all local teams were engaged in carting hundreds of tons of sugar, tins, cases and coals to or from *Glen Ewin*.

There were other small local jam manufactories. The best-known of these was the little jam factory of Marinus Maughan at *Ingleside*, near Houghton, making *Ingleside* brand jams. Maughan and McEwin were friends, but the friendship became strained somewhat on one New Year's Eve when Robert McEwin overpainted the gates of his friend's factory with the sign '*Glen Ewin* Jams'. Maughan promptly added the words 'Are Rotten' to the sign and left it there for some months.

Maughan, like McEwin, was a leader in local affairs and for a time was Chairman of the District Council of Tea Tree Gully. His little jam factory, today the property of Mr. A. Schultz, now provides cool storage for apples.

Local growers in the district were not able to cope with the appetite of the jam factories for fruit, and fruit came in from places as far afield as Angaston, Gumeracha, Mount Torrens, and the South East, with raspberries from Victoria and black currants from Tasmania. Today, with most of the district orchards going out of production, fruit for *Glen Ewin* is brought in from the modern, large-scale orchards of the River Murray irrigation areas. Jam, itself, once the great standby of every working-class family, has lost favour and *Glen Ewin* remains the last of the jam manufactories of South Australia.

One section of the district which relied for a time upon the *Glen Ewin* factory was Paracombe. The Paracombe Blocks by 1908 were beginning to come into full production. 'A 1,000-acre district that a few years ago carried 1,000 sheep and one man to look after them, since the Government has been landlord, now carries 33 families'.

Originally the property of John Richardson, the property had later become the *Paracombe Park Estate* of W.H. Brooks. Brooks had sold the Estate in 1873, advertising it as '1,269 acres of splendid grazing land with a frontage of 2 miles to the River Torrens and containing several never-failing Springs, the property being undoubtedly auriferous, as good gold specimens have been found on it'.

In 1901, the government of Sir Frederick W. Holder, had taken over the Paracombe Sheep Station, by then the property of Alexander Borthwick Murray. The Paracombe Station had been managed by Mr. McLachlan. The station house, stockyard and stables faced the main road between present-day Head Road and the main road from Inglewood to Paracombe, opened in 1901. The woolshed of the original station is now on Allotment 567, close to the coldstores. The estate of 1,244 acres purchased by the Government for £5,816, was subdivided into 60 blocks in February 1901, and the 'blockers' were allotted their land under perpetual lease in April 1901.

The blocks varied in size from 7 acres of richer land to 93 acres of scrubbier land. Although partly fenced by the government, much of the land had to be cleared before orchards could be planted. By 1908, however, the apples and pears were coming in to payable production and within a radius of 3 miles 30,000 cases of apples were being produced, 20,000 cases for export to London.

One of the best export varieties grown was the Dunn's seedling. Dunn's seedling was first grown by William Dunn while working on Anstey's Estate at *Highercombe*. The apple had been exhibited in Adelaide in 1846 and had taken first prize as a new variety. The Agricultural and Horticultural Society had named the new variety *Dunn's Seedling*. In the same year Anstey forwarded to Queen Victoria 'a cask of Dunn's Seedling apples, a cask of wine and a gold brooch' made of gold found on Anstey's property. The apples, not wrapped but placed in a cask, reached England safely. The wine, placed in two casks one inside the other with the space between filled with sawdust, also arrived in good condition.

Dunn, in 1845, purchased 30 acres of steep land belonging to George McEwin and named his home *Gordon Bank*.* There he worked up thousands of his seedling trees and sent them interstate and to Tasmania.

The local apple export industry did not really come to life until the time of Frederick Hodges of Houghton. In 1904 the first consignment of 350 cases of mixed apples was despatched from Houghton to overseas markets. By 1912, with the orchards of the Paracombe blockers in full production, 30,000 cases of prime apples were being exported from the district under the supervision of Hodges.

It was calculated that such a consignment consisted of some 6,000,000 apples and would turn the scales at 500 tons. It also used 3½ tons of tissue paper, 2½ tons of 'wood wool' for packing, ½ ton of nails and ½ ton of hoop iron. In 1912 the 'blockers' were receiving 3/6d. to 4/- a case for apples in the orchard — a good price for 1912.

The figures for the jam season at *Glen Ewin* were impressive too, with the factory turning out 700 cases of jam a day and using, in a season, 600 tons of sugar, 200 tons of coal, 400 tons of local wood and 40,000 cases of

* *Gordon Bank* residence survives and can be seen below Range Rd. at Upper Hermitage.

empty tins from Simpson's metal works in Adelaide. It was an exception in these years and until World War II to see a local farm without its few acres of fruit trees. 'The whole district is something of a fruit bowl', wrote a reporter in 1913.

One of the larger orchards was that of A.E. Pitt* at *Alice Vale* on Lokan (now Milne) Road. *Alice Vale*, bounded by present-day Hancock Road, Milne Road and Harris Road, was in 1892 the largest orchard in the state, consisting of 35 acres of pear trees and 30 of apple trees in full bearing.

Despite difficulties and set backs, and even opposition, a community developed at Paracombe, with its own school, church, post office, oval and hall. In 1934 the 'blockers' formed their own Fruitgrowers Association and soon afterwards formed a co-operative society and built their first packing shed. Coldstorage was added in 1939 and additions made in 1940 and 1954. The Paracombe Packing Shed and Coldstores are now capable of holding nearly 100,000 cases of apples and pears when full, but with the district increasingly going out of fruit production, supplies of apples and pears from 'outside' districts have become necessary for survival.

Water Gully today is no more than an obscure gully in the hills face off Perseverance Road and now owned by the Engineering and Water Supply Department. Few know of its whereabouts or of its story.

The gully opens out below Anstey's Hill, from the summit of which a steep driveway descends to the valley floor. At the end of the driveway, invaded by creepers and exotics, are the ruins of 'The Model Nursery' and of *Water Gully*, once the home of Mr. and Mrs. Charles Newman and their family of 8 sons and 6 daughters.

Charles Frederick Newman was born in Hamburg in 1834 and together with his parents, a brother and 2 sisters, arrived in South Australia on the *George Washington* from Bremen in September 1844, along with 181 German migrants in the steerage. His father, Carl Vincent Neumann (anglicised in the 1850s to Newman) originally held a few acres of land at Hope Valley before he acquired 24 acres of section 5516 adjoining Black Hill Road in 1850.

Charles Newman was one of the many young men from Houghton who joined in the gold rush to Victoria. He met with little success. Following his return he acquired in 1854 the 68 acre section which was named *Water Gully* because of its natural springs. He began to clear the gully of its heavy timber and to lay out a garden and orchard. By 1855, Newman had built a house on his property. Then, in 1857, in Trinity Church, Adelaide, he married Mary Ann Maria Bales. Evidently young Newman liked to do things in an orderly way.

In 1866 Charles Newman purchased two steep sections (5548 and 5608) on the southern side of Anstey's Hill in the name of the Land and

* A.E. Pitt & Sons were importers and exporters of fruit and had a shop in King William Street, Adelaide.

Gold Company. Sections adjoining *Water Gully* itself were later added until the property covered nearly 500 acres.

'The Model Nursery' of *Water Gully* was established in 1875. Newman had begun to exhibit exotic flowers in exhibitions in Adelaide at least by 1871, and a sketch made of *Water Gully* in 1870 shows hothouses already in existence, so we can assume the nursery was well established before it was named 'The Model Nursery'.

The nursery became the centre of family activities at *Water Gully* and quickly acquired a state-wide reputation for the variety of rare and delicate exotics available from its hothouses. 'There are', stated a report of 1889, 'six hot-houses full of valuable plants, amongst which we may mention 300 varieties of orchids, several of which have been hybridized by Mr. Newman who makes a specialty of these rare and beautiful plants'. Three shadehouses built of stone enclosed an area of 8,000 square feet. 'The ferneries contain the largest collection in the colony. The open grounds contain a magnificent rosary of 400 varieties of rose ... There are 90 acres of fruit trees from which scions are used for grafting and budding the nursery stock. The nursery stock comprises 500,000 apple, plum, cherry and other fruit trees; 100,000 orange trees and vines [which are chiefly muscatel], 100,000. Mr. Newman is continually importing new varieties from all parts of the world and supplies the trade, both local and inter colonial'. Newman also established an extensive nursery, 'The Victoria Park Nursery' at Perth, in Western Australia.

The annual catalogue of plants available at *Water Gully* or from the family shop at 17 Rundle Street, Adelaide, in 1894 ran to 187 closely printed pages. Typically, with mid-Victorian tastes favouring ferns and exotics, the calendar lists few indigenous Australian shrubs and trees.

In June 1899, Charles Newman was killed in a fall from a horse while riding home from a council meeting. Newman had been councillor and Chairman of the District Council of Highercombe for many years.

He had not only been a nurseryman but a florist and regular exhibitor in the Royal Agricultural and Horticultural Society's autumn shows. In the year that he died the show report stated, 'As has been the custom for years, Messrs. C.F. Newman & Son annexed nearly all the principal awards for floral designs, wreaths and bouquets, and swept the boards with a very fine collection of orchids'. Perhaps the report was the most fitting tribute Charles Newman and his wife could have wished for. Mrs. Newman carried on the nursery with the help of her sixth son, Frederick Christoff Newman. The eldest son, Charles William Louis Newman, managed the business in Western Australia.

Early in 1913 a tremendous and widespread rainstorm swamped Adelaide and large areas of the state. At Tea Tree Gully two inches fell in half-an-hour and hail damaged the glasshouses at 'The Model Nursery'.

In October, as the Newman family were about to sit down to a birthday dinner, a storm, centred on Anstey's Hill, broke over *Water Gully*. At Tea Tree Gully vineyards and orchards were stripped of their leaves and hail shattered windows in most homes and in the post office, institute and churches.

The storm had a disastrous effect upon 'The Model Nursery'. Within 20 minutes almost every pane of glass in the six glass houses lay smashed and most of their contents — orchids, ferns and palms — washed away. The flood of water coming down the valley swept away two glasshouses and a protecting wall, and in the Nursery on the southern side of Anstey's Hill, two years stock of fruit trees were washed out within a few minutes.

The nursery struggled back into existence again, but perhaps never really recovered from the destruction of 1913. In 1925, Mr. F.C. Newman and his wife left *Water Gully* and began their own nursery in the Teatree Gully itself. Another son, Mr. Harry Newman from Western Australia came to manage *Water Gully*. 'The Model Nursery' continued in the name of C.F. Newman & Son until the death of Mrs. C.F. Newman in 1932, when it was sold up.

Mr. and Mrs. F.C. Newman continued the florist trade in their Gully nursery. Following the death of 'F.C.', Mrs. Newman, her daughter and son-in-law carried on the business.

Today their nursery in Teatree Gully, now specialising in camellias, continues the name of C.F. Newman & Son. It is managed by a great-grand-daughter of the original owners of *Water Gully*. Mrs. Doris Newman, who remembers the flood of 1913 and who helped her husband to establish the nursery in the gully now, at 85, still finds pleasure in potting plants for her daughter.

The few remaining walls of *Water Gully* will be preserved by the E. & W.S. Department, and the few exotics from 'The Model Nursery' which now grow wild in the gully will be encouraged to survive.

The last new industry in the field of horticulture to be introduced into the district was celery-growing in the Torrens Valley area of the district. Its first exponent in this area was Mr. M. Packer who made his debut into this field of market gardening about 1914. It took some time, however, for Adelaide to acquire a tast for this native of the marshes of the African coast. As it needed summer irrigation it was not grown extensively until electricity became available in the Torrens Valley in 1917. Packer, at his own expense, brought electricity across the river to his property bordering the Torrens near Reid's Road in 1926 and began to concentrate on the growing of celery, first for the interstate market and then for Adelaide.

The clearing of the native forest and undergrowth to make way for productive crops and orchards was the natural accompaniment to settlement. What is more difficult to explain was the antagonism of settlers to almost all native flora and fauna, resulting in its replacement, at least around homes and townships, by exotics and aliens. There was obviously nostalgia in this practice, and the need to have at least some touch of one's native land that 'would be forever England' — or Scotland. The craze for all things exotic did not abate until after World War II.

One of the earliest attempts to re-establish native flora was by Mr. L. Wicks at *Freshford*, originally the property of the Boord brothers. It was reported in the *South Australian Naturalist* in 1929 that 'Mr. L. Wickes devotes his hard-won leisure to the cultivation of native flora. Callistemon [bottle brush], Boronia, Hakea, Elaeocarpus and many other species have taken kindly to their new habitat'.

As a result of the deliberate policy of the R.D.C.,* the large-scale planting of indigenous native trees and shrubs is now giving the suburban areas of the district more of an Australian aspect than they have possessed since the land was first cleared for agriculture.

* R.D.C. = Realty Development Company, responsible for many new housing subdivisions in the district.

32

VINEYARDS, VIGNERONS, AND VINTNERS.

'I cannot doubt that the grape . . . will become one of the staples of South Australia'.

In a lecture given in Adelaide in 1839, less than three years after the colony was founded, George Stevenson said, 'Looking at the peculiar adaptation of the vine and considering that the soil between Adelaide and the mountains, especially on the rising slopes, is so admirably fitted for the purpose, I cannot doubt that the grape, at no distant period, will become one of the staples of South Australia'.

Stevenson's words were prophetic. The vine adapted itself readily to its new habitat and 'the rising slopes' have proved to be the last refuge of Adelaide's earliest vineyards.

When Stevenson gave his lecture, he already had vine cuttings from Cape Colony and from Sydney in his North Adelaide gardens. The first vineyards of John Reynell and Richard Hamilton were already planted. In the following year the South Australian Vine Association was formed and imported 57,200 cuttings of vines from Cape Colony for distribution among its members.

George McEwin, after leaving the employ of George Stevenson in 1843, to lay out Anstey's gardens at *Highercombe*, entered in his diary of Friday, December 15:

'All day sharpening stakes with Joseph. Warm Day. There are nearly 2,000 vines young and old in the garden, 500 of which are two years old and the others three years'.

Planted in 1840 and 1841, the *Highercombe* vineyards were among the earliest vineyards in South Australia and certainly the earliest in the present district. They did not go out of production until the 1920s.

In August 1845, less than a year after leaving Anstey's employ, McEwin entered in his diary that he had commenced to plant at *Glen Ewin* vine cuttings of the following varieties — 'Lachryma Christi, Tinta or claret, Muscat of Alexandria, Early Blue Muscatel, and White Constantia'. McEwin also tells us that he had obtained the vine cuttings from the Hermitage gardens of

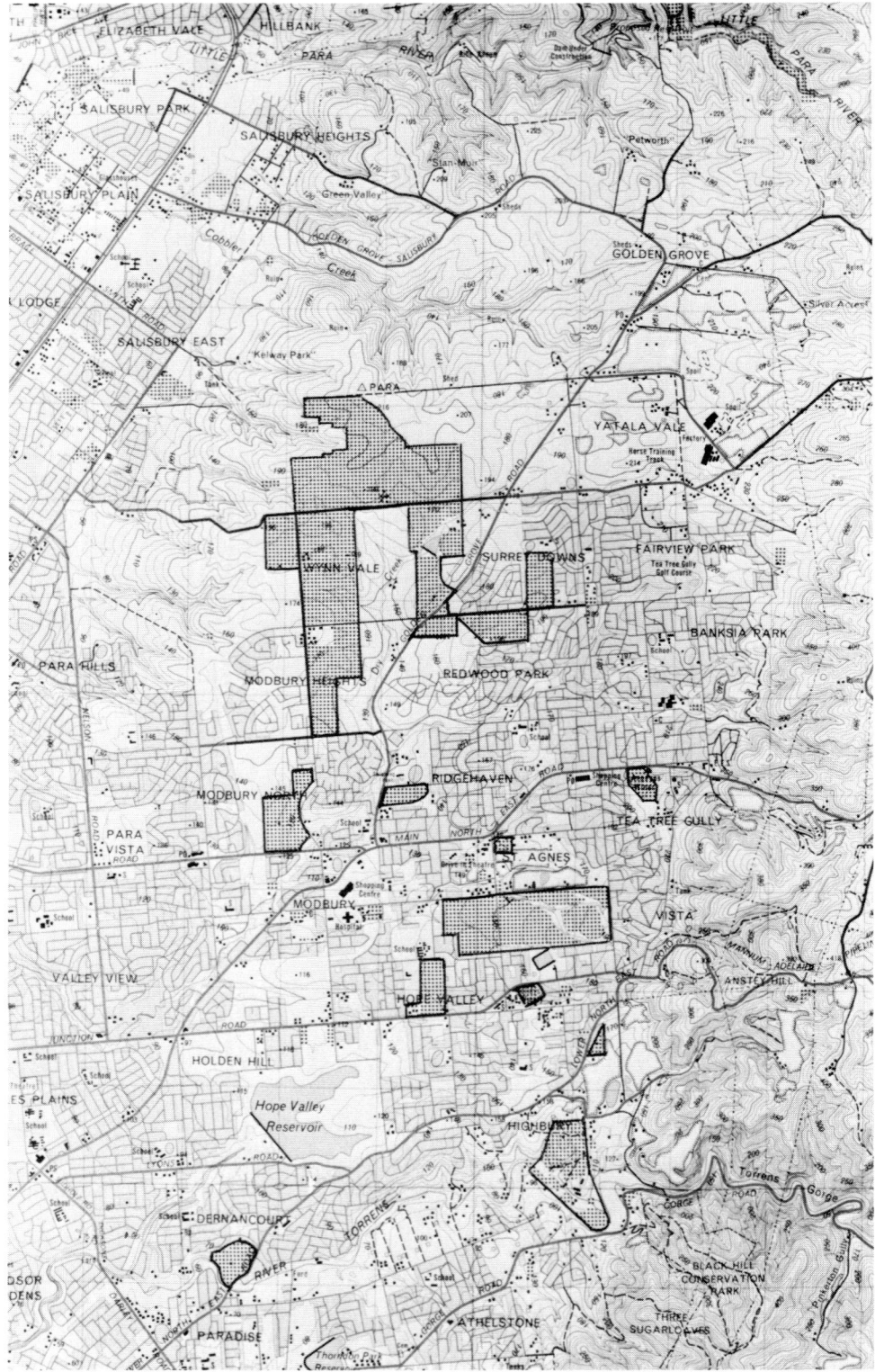

Map 12 Topographic map of District of Tea Tree Gully (1970). Areas of vineyard (and orchard areas adjacent to River Torrens) are shown by dotted sections. Department of Lands, South Australia.

Thomas Williams, his neighbour. Williams, too, had a small vineyard and intended to produce wines for his own table.

The *Hermitage*, *Highercombe* and *Glen Ewin* vineyards prospered and the *Observer* of March 1844 announced 'Several hundred gallons of wine will be produced this season from the South Australian vineyards of:

Mr. Anstey	Highercombe
Mr. Barker	North Adelaide
Mr. Davis	Reedbeds
Mr. Duffield	Echunga
Mr. Randall	Gumeracha
Mr. Stead	Milton Grove [Paradise]
Mr. Stevenson	North Adelaide
Mr. Williams	Hermitage'

In the *Observer* of May, George McEwin announced that he had from 15,000 to 20,000 vine cuttings and rooted vines 'from the Camden Vineyard ready for sale'.*

At the Adelaide Agricultural Exhibition of February 1846, table and wine grapes were exhibited by Williams of *Hermitage*, Anstey of *Highercombe*, and Joseph Ind of *Paradise*.

McEwin's diary tells us that in April 1854 he had casked nearly 100 gallons of wine. 'Our wine cellar is rather small', he wrote, '— intend building a larger one before next vintage'. By 1862, the vintage had increased to 1,000 gallons, mainly Frontignac.

Early in 1843, before McEwin left North Adelaide to take up his new position at Anstey's, he published *The South Australian Vigneron and Gardeners' Manual*, the first horticultural work to be written for South Australian climatic conditions. In it he gave simple and precise directions on how to plant a vineyard, how to choose the site and the subsequent management of the vineyard. McEwin was only 28 when he compiled his manual.

The manual was valuable and popular and was subsequently reprinted in 1871 in an edition revised by McEwin. Recently the Public Library of South Australia has re-published the first 1843 edition of the book in facsimile.

McEwin advertised his *Glen Ewin* Wines in the 1871 edition — 'These wines are sweet, rich and generous and are very suitable for Invalides. Frontignac [White] ... 20s. per dozen. Shiraz [Red] ... 16s. per dozen'.

But by 1881 there were family doubts about the morality of making wine. Temperance and Total Abstinence Societies were gathering converts, especially in non-conformist circles. As leaders in the Congregational Church at Houghton, both George McEwin and his son, Robert, felt constrained to abandon the making of wine. Following an encounter with a drunken employee, Robert McEwin expressed his concern to his father. Acting on their

* **The vineyard of Sir William Macarthur of Camden, New South Wales.**

convictions, father and son released the bungs from their wine-casks that day, allowing most of the wine to drain away. No more wine was made at *Glen Ewin* and the family concentrated thereafter on jam-making.

We know that *Glen Ewin* wines were on sale at local hotels in the district and at the Wine Depot of Henry Noltenius, 75 King William Street, Adelaide. In March 1867, two travellers on horseback sighted what they took, in the dusk, to be 'a spectre motionless near a huge gum tree in the sandy soil which lies between the Paradise Bridge and Anstey's Hill'. They fled up Anstey's Hill to Houghton, 'a very pleasant picturesque village nestled in the hollow of the Hills', and rushed into the *Travellers' Rest*. There they refreshed themselves 'with a goblet each of what Host Pearce informed us was McEwin's choicest shiraz'. Their nerves steadied, they moved on to the *Inglewood Inn* and repeated their performance, and so by increasingly unsteady progression continued to their destination at Mt. Pleasant.

By 1857 when G.M. Waterhouse purchased *Highercombe Estate*, Anstey's orchards and gardens had become a showplace of exotic trees, and pleasure gardens and walks and the vineyards were flourishing.

George Marsden Waterhouse, son of a Cornish Methodist Minister, had arrived in South Australia in 1843. In 1857, when he acquired Anstey's property of some 1,100 acres, Waterhouse had become a Member of Parliament, representing the electoral district of East Torrens in South Australia's first House of Assembly. From 1861 until 1863, Waterhouse was Premier of South Australia. In 1866 he sold *Highercombe* to Sir R.D. Ross, M.P. and went to live in New Zealand, soon to become Premier there.

Both Waterhouse and Ross extended the vineyards at *Highercombe* and the successive vineyards were known, until they were finally grubbed out in the 1920s, as 'Anstey's', 'Waterhouse's' and 'Ross's'. The vineyards were of 11 acres, 22 acres and 30 acres respectively. It was eventually found that the earlier vines had been planted far too closely — 2,700 to the acre — and these were gradually replaced. The varieties of grape favoured were the 'Verdeillo, Reisling and Stein', from which Highercombe White was made and 'Shiraz, Carbonet, and Madeira', which yielded the Highercombe Red.

In 1863 the old cellars were considerably enlarged. The new building, 60 feet by 30 feet, was built close to the side of a steep hill and its completion was marked by something of a Bacchanalian evening with a 'profusion of wine' for the workmen on the estate and their families and the builders. Dancing for the 80 guests began at 6 p.m. and went on until after midnight, interspersed only by more of the best wine from the cellar 'and cake'.

Close by the cellars was a magnificent and immense weeping willow, planted in 1844 by Anstey from a cutting of a willow planted at Napoleon's grave in St. Helena.

By 1871, there were 30,000 gallons of wine held in store in the cellar, in casks ranging from a huge one of nearly 2,000 gallons to 6-gallon casks. The annual vintage in the time of Sir R.D. Ross was from 8,000 to 12,000 gallons.

Sketch of *Brightlands*, Upper Hermitage.

Brightlands the holiday home of Archdeacon G.H. Farr and his family at Upper Hermitage was built in the 1860s.

Anstey's wine-cellars and vineyards, Highercombe c.1920.

Lokan brothers with their teams carting wine from Angove's cellars to Port Adelaide.

Highercombe Estate had been presented by John Baker, mine-owner and politician, to his daughter upon her marriage to Robert Dalrymple Ross. Ross died in 1887 and in 1896 the estate of 1,063 acres and the residence were sold to Lorenzo Charles Goodwin.

There were still 35 acres of vineyard under cultivation producing, according to the sale notice, 'Highercombe Wine superior to many wines of the highest class'. Goodwin leased the vineyards to T.C. Angove, and following the sale of the estate in 1925 to the Chapman Brothers, the vineyards were allowed to fall into disuse and the cellars were dismantled, the great casks being hauled out of the valley by teamsters to find a new home, the largest of 2,000 gallons in the cellars of D.A. Tolley, and others in Angove's cellars.

The roofless walls of Anstey's and Waterhouse's wine-cellars, still substantial, may possibly survive to serve as a reminder of the district's earliest vineyard.

By 1867, it was possible for the *South Australian Gazetteer* to state that 'the growth of wheat and the culture of the vine are particularly attended to in the district'. But the vineyards, so far, were all located in the steep, hillier areas. After 1867, came the vineyards of the 'gentler slopes'. Of the twelve wine-growing areas in the Adelaide district in 1877, the vineyards of West Torrens were producing the most wine, with Burnside and the Highercombe — Teatree Gully vineyards making the next largest contribution.

Some of the earliest vineyards of the foothills and slopes were small plantings, the vintage being stored in house cellars for private consumption. John Smart of *Golden Grove* and Robert Milne of *Drumminor* had substantial wine cellars, although they would not have considered themselves vignerons. The assessment book of 1874 shows that there were at least 12 family vineyards in the district of Tea Tree Gully. There was also a licensed wine-shop in the Teatree Gully itself, where James Hannaford or his wife sold bottles or casks of local wine in a room of their house. The wine-shop was first licensed in 1870.* The *S.A. Vinegrower's Manual* of 1892 lists the vignerons in the district of Highercombe as ROSS, KLOPPER, TOLLEY, IND, AUSTIN, BOORD and PACKER, and in Tea Tree Gully as SMYTH, HARPER, HAWKER, MILNE, SMITH, MC EWIN,† GAYLARD, ROBERTS, BYERS, ANGOVE, HALL and WICKES.

The largest of the private vineyards was that of Canon Farr,+ at *Brightlands*, the family holiday resort of Tea Tree Gully. The home was perched high on the first tier of the range with an immense view over the Adelaide Plains and Gulf of St. Vincent. The stone cellars were situated at the entrance of the gully below and the vineyard, a few acres, clung to the steep

* The little building still stands in the gully almost on the edge of the main road.
† Robert McEwin, brother of George McEwin.
+ *v. Chapter 27* for information concerning Far and *Brightlands.*

southern flank of the valley. A flying-fox conveyed the grapes from the terraced vineyards to the cellar. Too steep for a horse, the soil between the rows of vines was cultivated and weeded by 'Canterbury hoes'.

In the 1880s, the cellars of *Brightlands* were leased to Dr. W.T. Angove of Tea Tree Gully, together with the 5 acres of Farr's vineyard on the steep slopes alongside the cellars.

The incentive for Angove's interest in wine making may have been provided by his appointment in June of 1887, shortly after his arrival in the district, as medical officer to attend to the poor and destitute of the district at a salary of £8 per annum. Wine was recommended by medical men of the time for their patients and Dr. Angove may have merely been following the example of South Australia's earlier medical vignerons — Dr. Christopher Rawson Penfold and Dr. Alexander Charles Kelly — in growing their own wine for their patients.

District Councils had the power of appointment of medical officers to attend to the destitute of the district. In 1875, 3 ounces of gin per day were being prescribed by Dr. Bosch of Tea Tree Gully to destitute patients. In 1877, following the sudden death of Dr. Bosch, Dr. Max Neubauer the new medical officer, sought permission from council to grant one bottle of wine per week to his destitute patients. When Mr. W.H. Nicholls, licensee of the *Travellers' Rest* at Houghton, forwarded a half-yearly account for £3.5.0 for supplying 13 bottles of wine ordered by Dr. Neubauer for one of his patients, the Destitute Board of Adelaide complained. The District Council was asked to endeavour to provide colonial wine in place of imported wine.

Council minutes reveal that they approved of Mr. George McEwin's wine at 1/6d. per bottle and also forwarded a sample of the wine of H.J. Coulls at 1/- per bottle.

Dr. Hartley Dixon, who followed Dr. Neubauer as medical officer for both district councils, favoured whiskey for his destitute patients. He was reprimanded in 1883 by council for ordering half-a-pint of Irish Whiskey and half-a-dozen eggs per week to the same Houghton patient who had, back in 1875, consumed 13 bottles of imported wine at council's expense.

Dr. William Thomas Angove began practice at Tea Tree Gully in 1887. He was born in 1854, second son of Thomas Angove, a mining 'Captain', at Mount Pleasant in Cornwall. Following graduation from London Hospital in 1875, Dr. Angove practised medicine for a time at Mildern Hall. In 1880 he married Miss Emma Carlyon and soon after migrated to South Australia. In 1912, with his wife, he returned to England and entered the London Hospital again with the idea of extending his professional experience. Shortly after arrival in England, Dr. Angove became ill and died on March 25 at the age of 58.

At Tea Tree Gully, Dr. Angove had been a familiar figure, visiting his patients on horseback or by buggy until he acquired his first 'horseless carriage' — an imported American 'White Steamer' — a vehicle which could run

Above: Dr. William Thomas Angove, medical vigneron of St. Agnes, Tea Tree Gully.

Left: Douglas A. Tolley with his cellar-manager, John Ramsay at the Hope Valley winery c.1922.

A view inside the Hope Valley cellars of D.A. Tolley, 1898, with the cellar-manager, Mr. George Shields.

Employees of D.A. Tolley Ltd., 1925. **Back Row:** K. Hawke, P. Lokan, J. Lokan, R. Lokan, L. Lokan, O. Tregeagle. **Front Row:** G. Lambert, S. Lokan, R. Ramsay, L.J. Tolley (proprietor), R. Reeves, J. Lambert, A. Rawlings.

100 miles on a tankful of water and which took only a quarter of an hour to get up steam. The boiler of the 'White Steamer' was located under the driver's seat. In 1907 Dr. Angove purchased his second car — a 10 h.p. De Dion — registration No.77. The registration number is still in use by Thomas W.C. Angove, grandson of Dr. Angove and managing director of Angove's Ltd., Renmark.

Dr. Angove's obituary tells us that he was 'a familiar figure in yachting circles and had with his own hands built several yachts at Tea Tree Gully. He was also a keen ornithologist and had one of the finest collections of birds' eggs in Australia'. Following his death in 1912, Mrs. Angove presented his collection of 278 varieties of eggs, collected on expeditions as far afield as the West Coast, to the South Australian Ornithological Society. They now form part of the collection of the South Australian Museum.

By 1893, Angove had 30 acres of wine grapes in production on his own sections of land, with another 20 acres planted. He prided himself upon his Cabernet wine and the vintage of 1903 included 2,000 gallons of Cabernet. In that year Dr. Angove had 100 acres of vines, 60 acres in bearing and, following a luxuriant vintage, produced 10,000 gallons of wine in his own cellars.

Before Dr. Angove's death in 1912, the hobby which had begun in the *Brightlands* cellars to provide wine for himself, his friends and his patients, had become the business enterprise of Angove and Sons. In 1910, the doctor's eldest son, Thomas Carlyon Angove, began pioneering wine-growing in the Renmark irrigation settlement. After World War I, the distillery at Renmark began to produce the brandy named by 'Carl' Angove, St. Agnes Brandy, after the St. Agnes vineyards of his father at Tea Tree Gully. Sometime prior to 1907, Dr. Angove had named the vineyards after the little village of St. Agnes, near his last home in Cornwall.

Little wine was bottled at Tea Tree Gully. The wine, mostly sherry after 1920, was casked and transported by local teams to the wholesale stores of Port Adelaide for shipment to London.

Grapes from other local vineyards — from the *Surrey Farm* vineyards of R.C. Smith on Yatala Vale Road, from the *Warboys* vineyards of Henry Hall, across from Angove's own vineyards, and from the old *Highercombe* vineyards, leased from L.C. Goodwin — were vintaged in the St. Agnes cellars.

Henry Hall was the second son of George Hall of Norwood, the founder of the firm of George Hall and Sons, Cordial Manufacturers. Retiring from the firm in 1888 because of ill-health, Henry Hall acquired 38 acres of land on section 5484 and began to lay out vineyards, assisted by two of his sons, Frank and Arthur.

Arthur, after a year in Roseworthy College, obtained a position with Angoves at Renmark in 1910 as a distiller. In the '20s Arthur Hall became manager, wine maker and distiller at St. Agnes and continued in that position until his retirement in 1950. Living today with his wife at William

Street, Tea Tree Gully, Arthur Hall can remember walking to the wine-cellars at *Highercombe* to superintend the vintage. He can also remember painful rides over rough roads on the back of 'Carl' Angove's motor-bicycle to Renmark.

Both Arthur Hall and Perce Goodes, who succeeded him as vineyard manager and later as manager at St. Agnes Cellars, were experts in the making of sherry. Perce Goodes, who retired in 1972 at the age of 71, saw two important innovations during his 50 years with Angoves — one was the contouring of vineyards in the district to prevent run-off. The second was the change in public drinking habits during the 1950s from fortified wines to table wines.

Driving up to Houghton in 1911, a reporter wrote, 'At Hope Valley I saw the vineyard of Mr. Douglas Tolley, which is situated on a sloping hillside, from which a beautiful view of Adelaide and the Gulf is seen. The wine-cellars are of the latest construction; some of the largest wine-casks in the state are to be seen there. In fact, all the appointments of this vineyard are of the latest date. Hope Valley Vineyard is worked in conjunction with* the Angas Park and Phoenix Park Distilleries of Angaston and East Adelaide, and special prizes have been taken for the wines and brandy for which the firm of Tolley is famous'.

Douglas A. Tolley and his brother, Ernest, together with the London Distiller, Thomas Scott, purchased the Phoenix Distillery at Stepney in 1888 and thereafter traded in the name of Tolley, Scott and Tolley. Both brothers had been pupils of Scott in his London distillery, where they had been 'inducted into all the arts and secrets of the distiller'.

Albion James Tolley, the father of Douglas Austral and Ernest Alfred (there were 6 sons and 4 daughters in the family), migrated to South Australia from England in 1853 with his wife, son and 3 daughters, in the *Gypsy*. He began an importing business in Adelaide. It was while the family was on a return visit to England that Douglas Austral Tolley was born in the village of Chertsey, near Richmond, in Surrey.

In 1891 Douglas Tolley purchased a section of pasture land at Hope Valley and began a vineyard as a hobby. By 1903 the vineyard covered 95 acres and the hobby had rapidly grown into a business, with successive plantings each year.

The building of the cellars and winery began in 1892. 'The winery which is splendidly built', wrote *Rufus* of the *Register* in 1903, 'is kept scrupulously clean and reflects great credit on the manager, John Ramsay. The cellar is ceiled with finely fluted galvanized iron, sawdust being placed above it and the temperature has never been known to go above 70 degrees ... There are bins for the bottles and a perfectly appointed office and samp-

* Actually the Hope Valley vineyards were the private venture of D.A. Tolley with no financial connection with *T.S.T.*

ling room. The claret and chablis we tasted were first class. This year [1903] 14,000 gallons of wine were made'.

Douglas A. Tolley did not live at Hope Valley. At the time of his death in 1932, he was still Chairman of the firm of *T.S.T.* at Stepney, which he and his brother, with Thomas Scott, had founded in 1888. A section of match-board lining retained now in the offices at Hope Valley, has inscribed on it in pencil, 'Record trip Stepney to Hope Valley 8/3/10 'Jimmie', 35 minutes, Big Buggie'.

Leonard J. Tolley, son of D.A. Tolley, expanded the family enterprise and, following his marriage, lived at Hope Valley, taking an active part in district affairs. He was a councillor for the District of Highercombe at the time of its amalgamation with the District of Tea Tree Gully in 1935. Two sons, David and Peter, attended the Hope Valley School.

Casting around for a name for a new family boat sometime in the 1930s, Mr. Len Tolley christened it *Pedare* -- a name formed from the first two letters of the names of his 3 sons, Peter, David and Reg. The name was subsequently given to a new Tolley vineyard in Ladywood Drive, Modbury, and in 1941 the name was applied by Len Tolley to the firm's premium wines.

Peter, David and Reg. Tolley, together with Peter's son, Christopher, still trade under the name of Douglas A. Tolley Pty. Ltd. In an era of take-overs, both Tolley's of Hope Valley and Angove's St. Agnes Wines at Tea Tree Gully remain family wineries, with supervision of the winery and wine-making firmly retained in family control.

Two late-comers to the ranks of local vignerons and wine makers were Samuel Wynn and C.F. Hodges.

The little cellars of C.F. Hodges, on Tolley Road, were established in 1914 by Gilbert Shield to vintage grapes from his own vineyards. Shield had gained experience as a vigneron and wine maker with both Tolley's and Angove's. The area under vines was small — some 38 acres — and the vintage (the largest no greater than 13,000 gallons) was crushed, processed and stored in ground-level sheds on the property. Only ports and sherry were produced. Charles Hodges, a nephew of Shield, who had worked in the cellars from 1936, took over the cellars following the death of Gilbert Shield in 1950. The cellars finally closed in 1966 and the vats and puncheons were disposed of.

David Wynn, third son of Samuel Wynn, who had first begun wine-making at the *Romalo* cellars at Magill, established the *Modbury Estate* vineyards in the mid-1940s. These were followed later by the *Huntersfield* vineyards nearby.

The firm of S. Wynn & Co. purchased *Surrey Farm* — 561 acres of undulating farmland fronting Yatala Vale Road (then Surrey Road). The vineyards — 'the largest non-irrigated vineyard in Australia to that time' — were planted to ensure an adequate supply of table wines. Following World War II and the arrival of migrants from European countries, the use of wine as an accompaniment of food increased rapidly. Wynn's met the demand by marketing wine in returnable half-gallon containers — the now familiar 'flagon'.

At *Modbury Estate* a dam, designed by the Water Conservation Branch of the Department of Agriculture to retain some 22,000,000 gallons of water, was constructed across Dry Creek and became for a time a source of anxiety to those living on farms below it. Some 40 acres of vineyard were irrigated, with good results. The vineyard manager responsible for the success of the vineyards and of the irrigation scheme was J.L. (Jock) Williams, an ex-Roseworthy Agricultural College wine-maker. Foreman for 16 years with him was 'Jimmy' Lewis of Modbury, a pruner of expertise.

Almost without warning, early in 1975, after almost 90 years of skilled nurture and planning, virtually the whole of the district's vineyards came under sentence of death. In April the South Australian Government Land Commission announced that they would acquire the vineyards of the four major wineries at Modbury, Tea Tree Gully and Hope Valley.*

There were strong protests from the vignerons who would be deprived of a valuable source of fine wines needed for blending with wines from their vineyards in other districts. The loss of traditional family vineyards was keenly felt. Protests, too, came from families new and old in the district. The destruction of the vineyards not only meant the loss of jobs. It would also deprive the district of the green carpet laid down each summer over the foothills from Hope Valley to Golden Grove which soothed the eyes on hot days and gave the district its distinctive character.

Unless there is a last minute reprieve, the vineyards will disappear under an expanding suburbia. The historic cellars of Dr. Angove and Douglas Tolley and their recently constructed tasting rooms will remain, surrounded by a few token acres of vineyard. But the district for the first time since Anstey planted his vineyard in the 1840s will produce no more wine.

---

* Approximate land holdings acquired in April 1975, were: WYNN 160 hectares (400 acres) ANGOVE 90 hectares (220 acres) ST. PETER'S COLLEGE 30 hectares (71½ acres) TOLLEY 49 hectares (120 acres) PENFOLD 65 hectares (161 acres).

33

WELLS, WATER WORKS AND RESERVOIRS

'8 shillings a day for 8 hours work'

Although the Hope Valley Reservoir was completed in 1873, residents of Hope Valley and Highbury did not themselves get reticulated water until 1927. Residents of Tea Tree Gully and Modbury were a little more fortunate — they had a water supply by 1882, although in summer the supply was often reduced to a useless trickle.

Hope Valley residents felt it was a dubious advantage to have at their back door a picturesque artificial lake holding 750 million gallons of fresh water, but unavailable for their use.

It was a different story along the valley of the Torrens from the Gorge to the Paradise Bridge, where for 3 miles on either side a miniature irrigation colony developed. By 1893 twenty or more steam-pumps drew water from soakages, springs and water-holes in the river in summer to irrigate the vegetable gardens, orchards and orangeries of the river flats. The steam-pump on the property of J.G. Coulls was capable of raising 18,000 gallons an hour, distributing it over some 15 acres of garden through half-a-mile of galvanized piping. Wagon loads of wood were needed to feed the steam boilers. 'Each engine was equipped with a siren operated by steam and it was the engine driver's duty to blow starting time 7 a.m., dinner hour noon, and 6 p.m. 'knock-off' time'. It was not until after 1925 that electricity and oil began to relieve the steam-pumps of their burden.

Adelaide relied from its infancy upon the River Torrens for its water supply, supplemented in the summer months by numerous wells. We see 'a succession of water-carts passing through the rough and dusty streets of the primitive city ... on their way to the Torrens. This, in summer time, was merely a succession of pools. It was from these that the water supply for Adelaide and the suburbs had to be dipped. It was carted to the homes of immigrants for 1s.6d. or 3s. a load and then stored in buckets, tubs, barrels or tanks'.

Just as Col. William Light had laid out his city close to the Torrens, so settlers in our own district chose sites for their first homes along the

Torrens or the Little Para or close to springs of Gould's Creek, Cobbler's Creek or the many branches of the 'Dry' Creek. The supply was supplemented from wells.

Well-sinkers were in great demand. James Cronk of Modbury claimed to have sunk the first well in the colony — behind the sand-dunes of Holdfast Bay — in November 1836, while awaiting the arrival of Governor Hindmarsh. He later sank two wells — one in Halifax Street and another in Gilles Street — and stated that he made £3 per week by supplying houses with water at 1/- a load.

Maurice Preston of Hope Valley, in the 1850s, 'and his wife, sank a well 100 feet deep: the good lady pulled the rock with a windlass as her husband cut it away'. We read that Preston was also 'an excellent fencer and hutbuilder and of such exceptional strength that he once carried a full bag of flour from Adelaide to Hope Valley, a distance of 9 miles'.

Sinking a well at Tea Tree Gully and Modbury could, as often as not, be unproductive. William Haines, in a Parliamentary Debate in 1879, stated that 'the people had sunk wells to a depth of ninety feet without reaching water' and at Modbury well-water was too salty for domestic use. The problem was partly solved after the 1860s when galvanized iron roofing and guttering could be used to feed water into underground tanks, although few working men could afford the cost of an iron roof.

The permanent springs in the Teatree Gully itself had been invaluable to teamsters since 1839 when the first track was put through the gully. 'It is the only water available from Gumeracka Bridge to town' stated R.S. Kelly in evidence in 1865.

After 1854, when the village of Steventon began to emerge, the springs became valuable to local residents. The springs were included in the road laid out through the gully by the Road Board in 1842 but, because of incorrect surveying, were in fact proved later to be on the private land of George Dickerson, who acquired the gully section in 1855. Residents of Steventon found that they had lost the run of the water and that Dickerson was able to demand payment of 1/- a year from families using water from the springs. 'People go miles for water there', Kelly said in evidence.

The district council disputed Dickerson's claim to the springs. Just below the springs, in 1860, council considered the erection of a public trough for cattle and arranged for a tree on the reserve to be felled and for a large wooden trough to be hollowed from its trunk at a cost of £5.

In 1862 and 1863, the residents of Steventon, with good reason, petitioned the Government not to confirm the wrongly surveyed road and if necessary to purchase the springs from Dickerson and make them available free for public use.

The Government finally in 1865 set up a Select Committee of the House of Assembly to report upon the proposed Teatree Gully Water Reserve.* Evidence was given by R.S. Kelly, William Haines, John Tregeagle,

* The report (Parliamentary Paper No. 107 of 1865 and No. 135 of 1865-66) contains much interesting information on the early history of Steventon and Teatree Gully.

Torrens Gorge Weir in 1908. The weir was erected in 1857. There was no road through the Gorge until the 1920s.

The Township of Millbrook in 1913. The road and bridge now lie under the water of the Millbrook Reservoir. The store, post office, school and nineteen houses were demolished in 1918 prior to inundation.

Above: Aerial view taken over Paracombe and Highercombe c.1960.

Left: Aerial view over Hermitage, and Golden Grove (centre left). The Snake Gully Road and Bridge can be seen crossing the Little Para (upper left). Department of Lands, South Australia.

George McEwin and John McGilton and by George Dickerson himself. The final report of the committee was predictably in favour of the petitioners and a Water Reserve was declared and part of the springs made available for public use. Dickerson was offered £150 in compensation but refused to accept it, firm in the belief that the spring was legally his. 'I did not buy it to sell', he told the Commission, 'but to be my own inheritance and my children's children'. He consented however to allow the public use of one of the two wells fed by the springs. Council's plans for piping water from the springs on the Water Reserve† were not however revived again until after Dickerson left the gully in 1876.

By 1855 the population of the city of Adelaide had reached a total of 18,259 and, in summer, when the Torrens ceased to run, water-carriers were not able to supply citizens with more than a few gallons of well-water a day. Reservoirs and piped water became a necessity.

Adelaide's first reservoir was at Thorndon Park. Work was begun on the reservoir and on a weir and headworks in the Torrens Gorge in 1857. Adelaide received its first piped water on December 28, 1860 when water was ready for distribution to North Terrace, Rundle Street, Pulteney Street and Flinders Street.

A few days before the water was turned on, a trial demonstration was given from a water-plug close to St. Paul's Church, Pulteney Street. Only a few officials, passers-by and the usual group of stray children were present to watch as the 1 inch nozzle directed a stream of water over the roof of the church. It was a convincing display of water-pressure.

The little reservoir, with a capacity of a mere 142,000,000 gallons, was barely able to keep the taps of Adelaide and North Adelaide running in the summer months and a second reservoir became necessary.

Because of its underlying clay beds, a site at Hope Valley was finally chosen and work began on the construction of the reservoir in 1869. The site was a double valley, and part of E.M. Bagot's Beefacres Estate.

It was estimated that the surface of water in the new reservoir would cover 170 acres and that its earthern embankment would impound some 1,000 million gallons — enough to extend the supply of water to the main centres of population and industry around Adelaide — Walkerville, Port Adelaide, Glenelg, Hindmarsh and Brompton.

The estimated cost of the reservoir works which included the raising of the height of the weir in the Gorge and the construction of 3¼ miles of open aqueduct from the weir to the reservoir, was £75,000.

The estimates might have proved reasonably correct but for one un-forseen eventuality — upon completion it was discovered that there was a serious leakage of water from the reservoir. Rumours of a great disaster were rife, especially among farmers and gardeners whose homes lay below

† Still a reserve today.

the embankment.

'A few months after water from the weir was allowed to flow into the new reservoir', wrote a reporter in August 1873, 'considerable anxiety for the stability and safety of the works was excited by the discovery of a persistent leakage through the ground at the foot of the dam'.

The reservoir, after supplying water during the summer of 1873, was drained in March 'in order to admit of a careful examination of its bottom' — as the reporter put it. The subsequent correction of the trouble took 6 months, added £50,000 to the original cost and reduced the capacity of the reservoir by one-quarter.

Another factor which added to the final cost was the exorbitant recompense demanded by proprietors of land through which the aqueduct channel had to pass. 'They exacted the uttermost farthing that they were able to claim. Ledges of rock upon which nothing could grow suddenly became desirable freehold and strips of clayey soil skirting the rises overlooking the Torrens acquired almost fabulous value'. Evidently the pastime of 'soaking the government' was not unknown among our pioneers.

The construction of the aqueduct called for quite precise engineering skills. The average fall from weir to reservoir was no more than 1 foot 9 inches per mile. The weir had to be raised 12 feet to provide enough fall. For the first half-mile the water was led through 42-inch iron pipes (made in Wales) following the precipitous cliffs of the gorge. The pipe then crossed the Torrens by an aqueduct bridge on stone piers. A few hundred yards beyond this, the water flowed via an open aqueduct, pitched with masonry 12 inches thick. The aqueduct skirted around the sides of hills and valleys and passed through three tunnels before emptying into the reservoir itself.

The whole of this work remains in use today. The contractor for this section of the work, Mr. William Walker, ran out of money long before completing the aqueduct. He was unable to pay his men and work stopped. Finally the government completed the job at its own expense.

Tenders for the construction of the reservoir itself were called for in March of 1869. There were several tenderers but the lowest tender, that of Messrs. Fry Brothers of Kapunda, was accepted. Ten minutes after the expiry of time, a tender for £5,000 less than that of Messrs. E. & R.E. Fry was received.

The contract price was for £35,467. When one looks at the reservoir embankment today, the amount seems incredibly small, even allowing for the equally small weekly wages of those years — at the reservoir, 6/- a day for drivers and gangers and 5/6d. a day for pick and shovel men.

For the amount of £35,467 the Fry brothers were to raise an embankment nearly half-a-mile long and 70 feet from the floor of the valley. The breadth of the embankment was, at its greatest, to be 355 feet with a uniform width on top of 17 feet. Little excavation was required in the reservoir but the embankment had to be flagged (pitch-paved) to a depth of

12 inches on its inner side and through the centre of the embankment a core of puddled clay, 8 feet thick at the top and some 50 feet thick at the bottom was required to prevent soakage. In addition, the Frys' contract included the building of a valve-tower and its outlet works. The valve-tower was to be 59 feet high and fixed in cement descending to 16 feet below ground.

The district council, if one can judge from its minutes, showed little interest in the construction except to ask for a special grant of £200 for repairs to local roads being cut up by the traffic engaged in building the reservoir and aqueducts. Local farmers, too, complained that the Fry brothers were depriving them of their usual labourers. The earthworks were commenced just before harvesting in Christmas, 1871.

For the local working-men, however, the building of the reservoir was a windfall of regular work. Because of harvesting, only 150 men were at first employed on the site but this rose, after harvest, to the full complement of 240 men.

The site works were extensive. A semicircle of stables was set up to house the 60 horses belonging to the Fry brothers, who also employed a further 60 local horses and their drivers. Behind the stables were built a carpenter's shop, a wheelwright's shop and a blacksmith's shop. There was also at the works 'a wine-shop, where under the name of colonial wine a liquor is vended of which very little is needed to make those who partake of it unfit for the performance of his hard job'.

The pug-mill was the centre of activities. Clay for the wedge of pug in the embankment was brought on a tram-line from 'a splendid clay deposit found just outside the embankment'. At the mill the clay was pulverised, puddled with water and delivered to the embankment in 'dobbins'. These were odd-three-wheeled trucks, the third wheel at the rear being swivelled so that the vehicle did not have to be turned. There were no shafts; when the truck was emptied, the horses were led around and the traces hooked to the rear of the truck. Five hundred tons of pug were delivered each day to fill the core of the embankment where it was rolled with 'punning rollers' imported by Frys from Melbourne.

Aqueduct and reservoir were completed towards the end of 1872 and water was allowed to flow into the reservoir. It was only a matter of a few weeks before the 'serious leakage' at the base of the embankment was noticed.

In March of 1873 the water was released and the reservoir examined. The cause was, however, found in the laboratory of Mr. Mair, Engineer-in-Chief of Public Works. It was discovered that the natural clay bed underlying the reservoir itself was permeable under pressure.

The answer was to puddle the bottom of the reservoir itself with compacted clay to a depth of some 6 feet at the deepest part of the reservoir. The extra work took 6 months, cost the Government an extra £50,000 and considerably reduced the holding capacity of the reservoir.*

* Today its capacity is 765,000,000 gallons.

Wages, too, had risen to 7/- a day and in August 1873, a deputation waited upon Mr. Fry asking him for '8 shillings a day for eight hours work'. At a meeting of some 50 labourers held in the *Paradise Bridge Hotel*, Joseph Ind expressed the opinion that '8s. for 8 hours' work was too much and those who asked that were men who did not want work'. Fry himself was more conciliatory — he could not pay the men more than 7/- a day but would agree to shortening the hours of work from 8½ to 8 hours a day after October 1. It was a little enough compromise, as the government of the day was about to adopt the eight-hour working day. October 1, 1873 saw the introduction of the eight-hour day in South Australia but it was still a six-day working week.

In 1875-6 nearly 10,000 trees were planted around the reservoir and along the aqueduct channel and within a few years transformed the area into a Sunday afternoon tourist attraction and picnic area. The Highercombe Council asked for a special road around the reservoir 'for use by persons out for drives from Adelaide'.

The Hope Valley Reservoir remains a very essential reservoir. Enlargement of the aqueduct in 1954 enable it to feed up to 40 million gallons a day into the reservoir and an increase in the height of the embankment in 1881 gave the reservoir its present-day capacity of 765 million gallons.

The River Torrens was called on to fill an even larger reservoir — the Millbrook, although it was a struggle for the small stream until supplemented by a pipeline from the River Murray. The little village of Millbrook was dismantled in 1918, before the valley was drowned. Within the past few years the town of Chain of Ponds has itself been dismantled, ostensibly to lessen pollution of the reservoir waters. In dry years, the old Millbrook/Chain of Ponds Bridge sometimes emerges from the waters to sun itself for a while before being submerged again.

Early in 1879, William Haines of Tea Tree Gully and M.P. at the time for the District of Gumeracha, introduced a deputation of 5 men elected at a public meeting at Tea Tree Gully, to the Commissioner of Public Works. The 5 spokesmen asked that a pipe be laid from the Hope Valley Reservoir to the townships of Tea Tree Gully and Modbury. Water, they said, had to be carried by some residents for a distance of a mile in buckets from the Water Reserve in the gully.

As a result of the deputation a Bill was introduced into Parliament in September 1879, supported by Haines and called the Teatree Gully and Modbury Waterworks Bill. 'The township was without water except what trickled down from the springs above it and this was very much polluted by cattle treading in it'.

It was proposed by the Commissioner of Public Works that — 'a dry-brick well will be sunk to gather the water from the springs in Teatree Gully. Earthenware pipes will lead the water away to a covered tank to be constructed at a sufficient elevation to give a fair pressure in the township of Teatree Gully. From the covered tank an iron main will convey water to the town. Similar means will be adopted to give a supply of water to Modbury. The delivery of the springs, it is believed, will be ample for the purpose and the total of the works will be £2,500'.

This was the scheme which was defeated by 3 votes in 1879, passed by a majority of 4 in the House of Assembly in June 1880, ratified by the Legislative Council and was incorporated in the 'Teatree Gully and Modbury Waterworks Act, 1880', Act No. 176. It was the first government water-works scheme to be undertaken for a district outside of Adelaide.

The passing of the Bill was largely due to the persistence of William Haines and to his special pleadings during debate. 'In summer', said Haines, 'I have seen women toiling with a bucket in one hand and a baby in the other, and going this distance [two or three miles] to give their children a drink'. The people of the district would soon have to kill their cattle, claim-ed Haines, as they were at present polluting the drinking water of 200 peo-ple. One member objecting to the cost of the scheme counterclaimed that 'one old horse and one watercart on one day in the week could supply the township of Tea Tree Gully, and as for Modbury, it consisted of five resi-dents'.

By 1882 water had been laid on to homes in Tea Tree Gully and Mod-bury residents expressed their willingness to pay to have the water extended to the township. Opposition to the extension to Modbury, mainly from farmers who had their own water supply, faded when it was discovered that only those within the defined water area would be obliged to pay water-rates.

The supply of water, however, was uncertain, especially in summer when it was most needed. 'The district', wrote a reporter in 1902, 'is entire-ly dependent upon a small tank, fed by two or three springs which are fast giving out'. None knew this better than the people of Tea Tree Gully.

Hope of a better water-supply for the whole district revived with the completion of the Millbrook Reservoir in 1918. In 1925 a deputation of residents of Tea Tree Gully, Modbury and Hope Valley, led by Mr. Arthur Hall, Secretary of a district Water Committee, waited on the Commissioner of Public Works asking for Millbrook water to be brought to the three townships.

Council minutes for December 1926 reported — 'pipes for Tea Tree Gully water supply have been delivered alongside Perseverance Road and a start is to be made to put them down immediately'. A 10 inch main was connected with the Torrens Gorge pipeline to feed into the old Teatree Gully, Modbury system and a regular supply of water at last became assured.

In the present year (1976) two massive new waterworks are under con-struction within the district.

At Hope Valley, close to the reservoir, the construction of a water-treatment filtration plant is under way. Upon completion, the new plant will be able to supply much of Adelaide with clean, filtered water whether its source be the watersheds of the Adelaide Hills or the increasingly polluted waters of the River Murray.

Near Golden Grove, across the steep gorge of the Little Para River, close to where it debouches on to the Salisbury Plains, a new dam is under construction. The rock-fill dam of the new reservoir will impound some 18,000 megalitres (3,000 million gallons) when filled following its expected completion in 1978. In capacity the new reservoir will almost equal the Millbrook Reservoir.

The waters of the Little Para will be damned back in the steep gullies almost to the Snake Gully Bridge to become the Little Para Reservoir. Some of the old farms will disappear under 50 feet of water. Two historic farms *Bishop's Farm* and *Cumberland Farm* will be abandoned.

Bishop's Farm, until recently owned by Mr. and Mrs. Brian Huppatz, was so named after Adelaide's first Roman Catholic bishop, Bishop Murphy who took up his appointment in 1844. The sections (1560 and 5660) were first taken up in 1842 by William Leigh, an English gentleman, who, becoming a Catholic shortly after the purchase, presented the sections to Bishop Murphy.

Cumberland Farm was established in the 1850s by Reuben Richardson *(v. Chapter 25)*. When water-storage in the reservoir begins in 1977, the homestead site will be submerged along with the magnificent orangery of 20 acres established after World War I by the present owner, William John Richardson. Further upstream the home of Mr. D.D. and Mrs. E.I. Goodes and 15 acres of citrus trees will also be bull-dozed and cleared. A section of Gould's Creek beyond its junction with the Little Para will also be submerged by the reservoir waters.

34

EVENTS AND OCCASIONS

'. . . luxuriant gardens, vineyards and fields of wheat—a picture of peaceful felicity.'

The common enemy which most settlers had to face at some time or another was the Australian bushfire. It is an enemy which, despite more than a century of experience, has by no means been subdued.

Time and again fire has ravaged the Adelaide Hills, menacing townships and overwhelming farms and homesteads.

Probably the most devastating bushfire in the district of Tea Tree Gully occurred on Sunday, January 2, 1955 — remembered still as 'Black Sunday'. After a night of intense, ominous heat, the Adelaide hills early in the morning exploded with bushfires at a dozen points and with a temperature of 109°F. and a searing north wind behind them, were soon raging out of control over an area of 600 square miles from Gawler to Strathalbyn.

At Marble Hill the Governor, Sir Robert George and Lady George, their guests and members of their personal staff, barely escaped with their lives by saturating towels, blankets, covering their heads and racing from the blazing residence. For 2 hours they huddled behind a bank at the side of the drive while the fire swept over them. The Vice-Regal residence was totally gutted.

Before mid-day fires were reported in the Anstey's Hill/Paracombe area and in mid-afternoon a fire swept up from Hermitage,* and engulfed the Houghton and Inglewood districts. Firefighters, in dense smoke and searing heat, battled to save the village of Houghton. Ern Pitman of Inglewood was killed when the burning verandah of his home collapsed on him. Near the top of Anstey's Hill, Mr. and Mrs. Maurice Churchett escaped from their wood-and-iron home as the fire raced from the hills and engulfed it in flames. Another 5 buildings in the area were destroyed before the bushfire passed on. Orchard after orchard and farm after farm lay devastated and two firefighters, Ted Schultz and his son Arnold, were taken to hospital.

A district Relief Committee was formed by Council to arrange for the distribution of relief fodder and of clothes and household effects destroyed

* See Footnote p.324.

in the fire. More importantly, the fire had a long term effect on the district. Fire meetings were held. Council arranged to sell knapsack sprays to house-holders — it was a knapsack spray which had saved many homes from destruction on 'Black Sunday'. Councillor Clifton reported that a suitable vehicle was available at Paracombe for £250 'to be used solely for firefighting'. The local Emergency Fire Service had proved its worth and, following the disaster, was gradually built into a well-equipped and more powerful fighting force.

Fear of bushfires was a factor in the lives of the earliest settlers in the hills. Writing of early life at *Brightlands* at Upper Hermitage, the daughters of Archdeacon Farr said, 'Those who lived at *Brightlands* during the summer months were always on the watch for bush-fire which constantly broke out in the scrub at the foot of the hills; if the wind rose in the west there was nothing to prevent fires from sweeping up the thickly timbered bluffs to the house on top.

When the danger threatened the first thing to be done was to find the horse, harness and stable him, pack valuables into buckets and tubs ready to lower into the underground water-tank and snatch what sleep you could while the elders watched the fire'.

In October of 1867 fires were deliberately lit on the hilltop of *Brightlands* and of many local hilltops. Towards the end of October the arrival of the Duke of Edinburgh, the first member of the Royal Family to visit Aus-

* Miss Beth Brittle, whose family home in 1955, looked out over Lower and Upper Hermitage, has given a vivid eye-witness account of the beginning of the fire which engulfed the district of Houghton on Black Sunday. 'Late in the morning two newspaper reporters called at our home (opposite Harold Carbins) and asked for directions to the fire. Mother said we understood there was a fire at Paracombe. 'No, not that one', they said, 'we've been there, there's supposed to be one at Hermitage'. This was the first indication we had of the holocaust which engulfed us much later in the day. The fire came up over the Upper Hermitage range. It then seems to have split, going round both sides of *Glen Ewin*. We watched — and one of the most horrifying things I have ever seen — one section of the fire sweep into Inglewood along the route of the Little Para, which seemed to act as a funnel. The heart of this fire was a huge glowing red fire-ball rolling end over end at incredible speed, exploding a huge cypress hedge near Inglewood Bridge into a sheet of flame and immediately afterwards, the truck and storage shed of Ern Pitman — filled with lovely combustible fruit cases — and his house within touching distance of that had absolutely no hope. On the other side, the fire fed on huge old pines, furze and roadside scrub, roared down Dunn's Hill on Upper Hermitage road, set light to and burned out Scadden's home [a *Glen Ewin* cottage] but spared the one right next door. Moments later the cypress hedge at Harold Carbins' exploded into flame. This was the length of his side verandah, about 8-10 feet high and 5-6 feet wide. One moment it was a big green hedge the next a roman candle. With the verandah of the house alight and unable to do anything but retreat from the immense heat of the burning hedge, Carbins abandoned their place. It survived with only charred verandah posts and sleepout. At the same time a big stone shed at the back of *Wolbunga*, then occupied by Mr. Glen McEwin, caught light and burned out, and the fire went on. At the height of all this there was a tremendous explosion which ripped apart a small partly-underground dairy cool-room at *The Pines* [*Glen Ewin* cottage], tore the house verandah to pieces and flung sheets of iron yards down the paddock and shattered a window at our place.

Hope Valley Cricket Club 1908-9. L.to R. **Back Row:** G. Shield, Rev. R. Broadbent, E. Foggo, J. Ramsay. **Second Row:** R. Reeves, T. Edwards, W. Buder, F. Cormack, ... Lambert, M. Bauer, F. Steinwedel, W. Dohoney (umpire). **Front Row:** F. Dawes, J.H. Mitchell (Hon. Sec.), A. Barnden (Captain), H. Elliott (Vice-Captain).

Modbury Cricket Club 1912-13. L.to R. **Back Row:** H. Cronk, A.T. Kelly, G. Millwood, W. Wake, E. Morris, J. Papps, W. Buder (scorer), C. Marrett. **Front Row:** R. Kelly, A.E. Marr (President), R. Broadbent (Captain), C. Chettle, S. Marret. **On Ground:** G. Boord, G. Buder (Secretary), T. Croft (Vice-Captain).

Highbury Football Club 1912. **L.to R. Back Row:** F. Hockley, E. Gaskin, E. Dohoney, J. Daws, F. Bauer, J. Hall, P. Amber, ... Foggo, Snr. **Second Row:** R. Foggo, J. Foggo, B. Hackley, E. Bauer, E. Foggo (Captain), C.F. Heitmann, A. Gridley, N. Ey. **Front Row:** E. Elliott, R. Bradbrook, C.H. Hughes (umpire), W. Bradbrook.

Houghton Football Team c.1912. **L.to R. Back Row:** A. Chapman, ... , E. Chapman, H. Carrick, W. Hannaford, G. Newman, E. Spender, W. Newman, W. Myers. **Second Row:** Bert Alcorn, A. Dearman, W. Edwards, ... **Front Row:** R. Pritchard, W. Menz, J. Rehn, C. Drury, V. Newman, R. Hunt.

tralia, was expected daily, and on the evening of Tuesday, 29, the *Galatea* quietly anchored at Holdfast Bay and on Thursday morning the Prince came ashore to begin his Australian tour.

Arrangements had been made to signal the arrival of the *Galatea* with a chain of bonfires lit on the summits of the Adelaide Hills. The principal fire would be lit on the top of Mount Lofty itself. Councils were instructed to prepare the bonfire sites which were to be 'between 25 and 30 feet in height, made of wood, permeated with tar and calculated to burn at least 24 hours'.

The fires lit on the summits of the Tea Tree Gully Range were to be followed by answering fires lit near Gawler and by bonfires northwards along the ranges to Mt. Bryan. Here a huge bonfire* was to convey the message of the Duke's arrival to the people of the settlement of North West Bend on the River Murray.

Bonfires were prepared on six summits in the district — 3 at Higher-combe on sections 5394, 5608 and 5526, one at *Brightlands*, another on section 50 and the sixth on section 5680, on the hill behind the *Higher-combe Hotel*, Tea Tree Gully. The fires were lit on the evening of October 31, and were admired by the Duke and the Governor, Sir Dominic Daly, from the windows of Government House. Within an hour or so the bonfires had signalled the message of the Duke's arrival to settlers all along the way to the North West Bend.

The Tea Tree Gully Emergency Fire Service stems back to World War II when Councils were requested to appoint fire officers for civil defence. Early in 1942 nine men, Messrs. A.C. Bourne, Clarence Verrall, Elmo Hurst, E. Schultz, H.J. Alcorn, J.A. Burg, D. Goodes, L. Milton and P.G. Pitman volunteered to act as District Fire Control Officers. Following the war, when civil defence forces were disbanded, redundant trailer-pumps and other fire fighting equipment was made available to local governments. The district received its first fire-siren late in 1946 and the Tea Tree Gully Trailer-Pump Crew took part in the first Fire Prevention Week.

Floods and an occasional earthquake were neither such frequent nor disastrous visitation as bushfires. On Friday evening of September 19, 1902, at 8.05 p.m. 'a very severe shock of earthquake passed through Tea Tree Gully and Golden Grove'. Dishes on kitchen dressers rattled, framed pictures fell from walls and plaster from ceilings. The district had been the centre of a mild earthquake, felt from Kangaroo Island to Port Augusta.

In April of 1889, the whole state was drenched by heavy rains for three days. From Monday morning until Wednesday afternoon the rain gauge at *Glen Ewin* had registered 9.820 inches and it was still raining. The Little Para came down a banker, sweeping everything before it, leaving only one bridge standing from Inglewood to Lower Hermitage. The Dry Creek

* Built and lit by the author's grandfather, William Bryce and shepherds of the Mt. Bryan Station.

and the River Torrens disgorged their waters onto the Adelaide Plains and the suburbs west of Adelaide suffered the worst flooding in their history. Gum trees, uprooted in the Gorge, banked up against the Paradise Bridge and dammed up the water behind, flooding the market gardens of Paradise. However, the new iron bridge, completed in 1880, held.

One factor contributing to the relative stagnation of the district in its latter years was the lack of public transport. The arrival of the motor-car had given added mobility to the few, but walking — whether to work or to play or to visit — remained the common lot. Walking to work at *Glen Ewin*, to dances at Hope Valley, to Church on Sunday, long distances to school, or with barrow and shovel to work on district roads, to cricket or football practice — there was little alternative for many.

There were the daily coaches through Modbury, Tea Tree Gully and Houghton, but travel on these was expensive and little used except for essential business or personal reasons.

The coaches by-passed Hope Valley entirely. As early as 1881 there were public protests at Highbury and Hope Valley and demands for improved means of conveying passengers to and from town. 'To get to the Paradise coach entails a walk of about 2 miles upon Highbury people and somewhat the same distance separates Hope Valley from the coach running on the main North East Road'.

The first real change in mobility — at least for the people of Highbury and Hope Valley — came when the Adelaide and Suburban Tram Company extended a single line to Paradise, almost to the MacDonnell Bridge. The first horse-tram to Paradise made the journey on February 18, 1884, and on November 4, 1911 was replaced by the first electric-tram to Paradise. In May 1932 came the first experimental 'trolley-bus', no longer running on tracks but still drawing its power from overhead wires. Painted green, it was promptly nicknamed 'The Green Goddess'.

But residents still had to walk to Paradise. In 1935, David Bowman of Barracks Road, Hope Valley, on his way to Friday market from his mixed farm in his Chevrolet truck often picked up people who might be walking to catch the city-bound tram at Paradise. As an outsider who had recently moved into the district, the lack of a passenger service was perhaps more obvious to him. Soon he had purchased his first passenger 'bus' — a seven-seater Buick— and was making two return trips a day to the city. It was the district's first localised public transport.

Bowman's next 'bus' was an eleven-passenger Packard, followed by an eighteen-passenger Diamond T. During the war years of petrol-rationing, Bowman kept his bus (then a Ford) mobile by fitting it with a gas-producer. By this time, the bus was servicing the people of Tea Tree Gully.

On February 1, 1970 the new bus terminal for Bowman's Bus Service was opened on a 3½-acre site at St. Agnes, on the S.W. corner of Tolley and

Modbury Football Team C.1912. **L.to R. Back Row:** J. Papps, H. Bowhey, A. Williams, W. Wake, S. Shillum, C. Wake, T. Croft, G. Boord, C. Roper (time-keeper). **Second Row:** A. Ross, E. Buder, Rev. R. Broadbent (Captain), C. Chettle, F. Holbrook, G. Buder. **Front Row:** S. Stirling, J. Harper, R. Bambridge, J. Craig, J. Ross, H. Chamberlain, W. Buder.

Tea Tree Gully Football Team 1922. **L.to R. Back Row:** G. Schlein (follower), R. Tregeagle (follower), G. Johns, P. Phillips, E. Lokan, L. Lokan, E. Lokan. **Second Row:** E. Heitmann, C. Neale, K. Dunn, R. Cooke, H. Neale, P. Heitmann, I. Neale. **Front Row:** W. Claridge, G. Cooke, V. Bowen, Umpire, C. Hawke, S. Phillips, J. Loxton.

Houghton Football Team 1932. L.to R. Back Row: A. Dearman, M. Alcorn, J. Gillard, ... , B. Rehn, *Darkie* Mansell. Second Row: Boundary Umpire, P. Haines, ... , G. Phillips, ... , ... , ... , A. Robinson, C. Chapman, E. Robinson, R. Stevens, Boundary Umpire. Third Row: T. Mervyn, J. Keane, J. Marron, K. McGlashan, *Digger* Williams, J. Alcorn. Front Row: G. Robinson, Umpire, ...

Tolley's 'tug-of-war' team (right) performing on the Adelaide Show Grounds 1925.

North East Roads. The fleet by 1970 numbered 30 and the buses were carrying some 7,000 people a day and servicing most parts of the district. David Bowman died in 1967. His two sons, Milton and Jack Bowman, and their sons continued the family company until, with other private metropolitan bus services, the business was purchased in February 1974* by the M.T.T. (Municipal Tramways Trust). By that time there were 44 buses in the fleet carrying 10,000 passengers a day.

The motor-car had arrived in the district in 1902 but there are few references to the earliest car owners. This is not surprising as when the registration of cars and motor cycles became compulsory in 1906, the figures revealed the South Australian car population as 230 cars and 233 motor cycles. Car registrations for the district by June 1913, numbered 9, viz.:

Registration No.	Owner
77	Angove, Dr. W.T., Tea Tree Gully
1591	McAree, Dr. J.V., Tea Tree Gully
2354	Manley, S., Modbury
2395	Williams, A.G., Houghton
2514	Botting, F.W., Tea Tree Gully
2776	Smith, Richard, Modbury
3099	Botting, F.W., Tea Tree Gully
3119	Appledore, A.H., Inglewood
3239	Maughan, M., Houghton

In 1907 the District Council of Highercombe gave permission for a hill-climb to be held on Anstey's Hill on December 14, to begin from the gate of the Hope Valley wine-cellars of D.A. Tolley and to end at the entrance to Newman's Nursery at the summit. There were 25 entries. The distance was 2 miles 873 yards. The climb was won by Sir Richard Baker in a 12-16 h.p. Talbot with a time of 6 minutes 38 seconds.

Early in the history of the district an attempt had been made to form a group of Rifle Volunteers, as part of the colony's attempt to establish a military force in South Australia. At the request of a number of settlers, the Chairman of the new District Council of Highercombe chaired a public meeting in August 1854, in the *Highercombe Hotel*. Many were present despite a wet day and Messrs. H. Blyth and T.W. Wright moved that a local Corps be formed. Little was done until 1859 when a further public meeting decided to support a Volunteer Rifle Corps.

The 'Tea Tree Gully Rifles' was formed on Thursday, July 11, 1861. A section of Mr. William Hancock's property at present-day Surrey Downs was leased as a parade-ground and rifle-range, 15 volunteers were enrolled and Mr. T.E. Cooke was appointed Captain; Mr. John Robertson, Lieutenant; Mr.

* Milton and Jack Bowman remained with the service until November 1975.

William Haines, Jnr., Sergeant; and Mr. W. Collins, Corporal. Haines, as host of the *Highercombe Hotel*, celebrated the formation with a spread and 'loyal toasts interspersed with a variety of songs'. In 1862 John Robertson became Captain and initiated rifle competitions with riflemen from 'the adjacent villages of Modbury, Golden Grove and Houghton'. The uniforms issued to both privates and officers were distinctive and colorful — scarlet trimming, bronze buttons, silver cords, and chevrons of blue. The history of the Volunteers was perhaps not as colorful as their uniforms — at least not until the Boer War began in 1899.

The 'Tea Tree Gully Rifles' however, under Captain Robertson, maintained their enthusiasm and discipline 'notwithstanding all the members being engaged in agricultural and business pursuits'. They attended district functions and competed successfully and regularly against almost every other company in the colony.

Hope Valley had its German Rifle Club from 1860, competing annually on Easter Monday with the 'Adelaide Deutsche Schutzungesellschaft' for the honour of being 'King' for the year — a custom which has since been revived in the Barossa Valley. In 1871 the 'Kingship' took place at Hope Valley on the shooting-ground alongside the *Bremen Hotel*. Early in the morning, accompanies by the brass band, some Hope Valley members accompanied the reigning 'King', Mr. Gerber, from Adelaide to Hope Valley.

Competing for the prize were 5 local Germans — H. Linde, H. Wohlers, H.W. Emcke, H. Bothe and H. Klopper — but Gerber remained 'King' and was invested with a silver medal. We are informed the Host Bothe opened his hotel for celebrations and 'a ball began in the evening and was kept up until dawn'.

With few halls in the district, except the District Council Chambers, most celebrations were held in the 'Assembly Rooms' of hotels. There were few restrictions on the use of Hotels — bars were open legally until midnight until 1915 and the minimum drinking age was, until then, sixteen.

For many years before 1900 it was a custom of residents at Tea Tree Gully to greet each new year at the blacksmith's shop of William Boyle. At midnight, after 'Auld Lang Syne', the company would leave the *Tea Tree Gully Inn* and move down to the 'smithy' where Boyle was ready with his array of hammers 'to make the welkin ring' and to greet the new year with a discharge on his anvils.

Christmas, too, gave an opportunity for relaxation for young and old at a time when many parents were busy harvesting. In 1907, while Tea Tree Gully people gathered for sports in the day and a concert at night, the folk of Golden Grove celebrated with a large Christmas tree in the grounds of Greenwith Church with an evening concert to follow.

Houghton, however, was all but deserted. Almost en masse, some 200 residents of the village and neighbourhood had set off for a 50-mile return journey 'by trolley and tram' to Henley Beach 'for sixteen hours of enjoyment'. Nine horse trollies took most of the children and parents but many travelled 'by ramshackle two-horse trams' from Paradise or by traps. A few made the journey on bicycles. The sight of the 'briny', we are told, was hailed by deafening cheers from the children who proceeded to spend most of the day 'paddling with trousers or skirts rolled up'. For sheer enjoyment and complete exhaustion there was nothing to beat the old-time annual picnic. Houghton folk did not arrive back home until nearly 10 p.m.

The last community structure to be built in any township was often its Institute. The foundation-stone of the Tea Tree Gully Institute was laid in January 1896; of the Modbury Institute in March 1906; and of the Hope Valley Institute in May 1921.

The history of the Institutes is also a reflection of the social and cultural life of townships. The Minute Book of the Tea Tree Gully Institute is still in existence and states that in 1902 'the Institute had drifted into the shadow of a very dark cloud; there has not been a general meeting for several years and no officers have been appointed'.

The Institute was brought back to life by the efforts of Dr. Angove and Messrs. Farr, Kempson, Ellis, Buder, Beames, Kaske and Vaughan. In 1904 the hall was used as a skating-rink — until 'the peculiar effect that skating has on the floor was noted'. There were Annual Institute Days, dances, political meetings, dancing classes, socials, birthdays and weddings; and improvements such as acetylene gas-lighting, petrol lighting, and finally electricity. In 1928 the new Cinema Room was completed and for a time the Institute Committee found a regular source of income.

Institutes served a vital function in the life of the district's townships, until the townships themselves were swallowed in suburbia. In 1953 the Modbury Institute was offered to Council and its life as an Institute ceased. It now leads a new life and serves new needs at a St. John Ambulance Centre.

Another annual function which for many years led to keen rivalry between Houghton, Tea Tree Gully, and even Golden Grove, was the annual Arbor Day. The idea of providing shade and of beautifying the surrounds of South Australian public schools originated in 1889 and was taken up enthusiastically in 1894 by the headmaster of the Houghton School, Henry J. Armitage. At an Arbor Day, held in 1907, Mr. Roy McEwin, addressing the children and residents had stated that 'it was the intention to make the village of Houghton one of the prettiest nature spots in the State by annually planting trees'. The township, schoolgrounds and today, certainly the 'village common' owe much of their natural beauty to the enthusiasm of Armitage.

Perhaps the school's most memorable Arbor Day was its fifteenth, held on a very wet day in September 1909, when the guests of honour were Sir Day Hort Bosanquet (South Australia's Governor), Lady Bosanquet, and Miss Alicia Bosanquet. Bosanquet, as a naval commander, was greeted by a guard of honour of a dozen older boys attired in sailor costume. Despite the heavy rain, Sir Day and Lady Bosanquet managed to plant a palm tree each and Miss Alicia an English Holly.

Lady Bosanquet and her daughter visited the school for another Arbor Day in September 1913, and were again greeted by 'Jack Tars'. Armitage was still headmaster and mentioned with pride that his son, George, one of the 1909 'Jack Tars' had since been selected as the South Australian representative for admission to the Royal Australian Naval College at Geelong.

Trees were planted year after year — on the common, around the cemetery, at the Rechabite Hall and along district roads — and did much to transform Houghton into a leafy hollow. 'To the casual traveller it wears a sort of a 'sleepy Hollow' appearance', wrote a reporter in 1912, 'but the residents show by their actions that they are energetic'. The description was just and accurate.

The little Paracombe School held its first Arbor Day in 1910, when pine trees were planted in the school grounds and along the road; and at Golden Grove in 1907, the District Council helped the children to plant 'Remarkable Pine' trees from the gate towards the manse, one for each child.

Not to be outdone, Tea Tree Gully School held regular Arbor Days, and on Friday, July 30, 1909 the whole of Tea Tree Gully, together with the children of the school, held its greatest Arbor Day — the opening of the Haines Memorial Park.

Haines, 'King of Tea Tree Gully', had died in 1902 at the age of 71. One of his gifts of land had been the little triangle of land adjoining the *Highercombe Hotel*. Wishing it to be available at all times to children and residents, Haines had stipulated that the ground should not be fenced. 'The result', stated a reporter, 'was that travelling shows and circuses used the ground and left it in such a condition that it was not only an eyesore but a distinct menace to the health of the village'.

Finally the Supreme Court granted Council control of the area; a post-and-wire-netting fence was erected and with the help and advice of Mr. F.C. Newman, of Newman & Sons, a park was planned and an opening day fixed.

A drinking fountain was commissioned and the Governor, Sir Day Hort Bosanquet and his wife were invited to attend the public Arbor Day and to name the area 'The Haines Memorial Park'.* It was a fine tribute by the people of Tea Tree Gully to the district's greatest pioneer.

The palms planted by the Vice-Regal party have now gone, along with most of the English Oaks and Plane trees planted by the children along Perseverance Road. The picture of the district which Bosanquet drew in his speech — 'luxuriant gardens, vineyards and fields of wheat — a picture of

* For a full description v. Adelaide *Observer*, August 7, 1909.

peaceful felicity' — is rapidly becoming unrecognisable but at least the Memorial Park and its fountain remain to remind us of the many public services of William Haines.

From its early days, the possibility of discovering workable deposits of silver, gold and copper in the district had never been entirely abandoned.

Reference is to be found in 1870 to the Inglewood Gold Mining Co. 'The directors, encouraged by the result of crushings, have resolved upon the machinery without delay'. A shaft had been driven 80 feet into the side of a hill close to Inglewood, and 7 ozs. 15 dwts. of gold had been extracted. No more was heard of the mine.

In 1890, cuttings, drives and shafts explored leads in ironstone outcrops around Modbury and in the Tea Tree Gully Range, seeking gold. The sale notice of the *Highercombe Estate* in 1914 promised auriferous gold and 'lode indications on various sections abutting the River Torrens'. When the Gorge Road was finally pushed through in 1922 there was considerable activity along the gorge and even some 'planted' silver mines. This activity was revived in the depression years of the late 1930s.

Seemingly more important economically was the discovery of a seam of brown coal 13 feet thick and extending over an area of more than 200 acres underlying Hope Valley. As early as 1857 coal was found at a depth of 102 feet beneath a stratum of pipe-clay while sinking a well. The seam, 1 inch to 12 inches thick 'appeared to lead from the hills' and the coal when lighted left a fine white ash. Another well in section 831 also brought to light a seam of coal. Even earlier in 1843, Robert Milne at *Drumminor*, Golden Grove, found coal while sinking a well and a piece was taken into Adelaide. *Drumminor* is a fine property as a farm', stated the *Observer*, 'but should it prove to contain a coal-mine the owner might be advanced into the position of a millionaire'.

Government examination and bore-testing of the Hope Valley coal-bed in the 1920s confirmed the existence of large deposits of lignite, but at an average depth of 164 feet — too deep to be exploited economically.

An interesting by-product of quarrying in the district was the discovery of important fossil forms exposed in outcrops and in quarry faces. The fossilized forms of primitive invertebrate animals, probably marine forms, were discovered by Sir Edgeworth David, in 1928, on the property of Mrs. C.F. Newman at Anstey's Hill. It was an important scientific and geological discovery. Quartzite slabs, quarried under the supervision of Mr. Charles Newman and Edgeworth David were forwarded to Sydney University for confirmation of the discovery and for analysis.

Examples of these immensely old fossil 'lobsters' and crustaceans may be seen in the Adelaide Museum and in the Museum of the Sydney University.[*]

* For further reading *v. Memoirs of Fossils of the late Pre-Cambrian* by David & Tillyard (1936) and *Professor David* by M.E. David (1937).

The district' wealth, however, continued to be agricultural and, after 1901, increasingly horticultural with the development of Paracombe and the application of irrigation and of intense cultivation in the Torrens Valley. The *Glen Ewin* jam factory and the Paracombe Cold Store provided stability for the local fruitgrowers and the local wineries encouraged the establishment and expansion of vineyards.

The population remained stable. The 1907 directory listed Golden Grove with a population of 170 and 46 houses; Hope Valley, 282 people and 72 houses; Houghton, 130 people and 30 houses; Inglewood with a population of less than 50; Modbury with 203 people and 60 houses; and Tea Tree Gully, 300 people and 67 Houses. Fifty years later the figure had changed little — except for the growing impact of the motor-car, the district was still 'a picture of peaceful felicity'. The arms of the city octopus were however visible on the horizon.

SECTION III
CITY OF TEA TREE GULLY

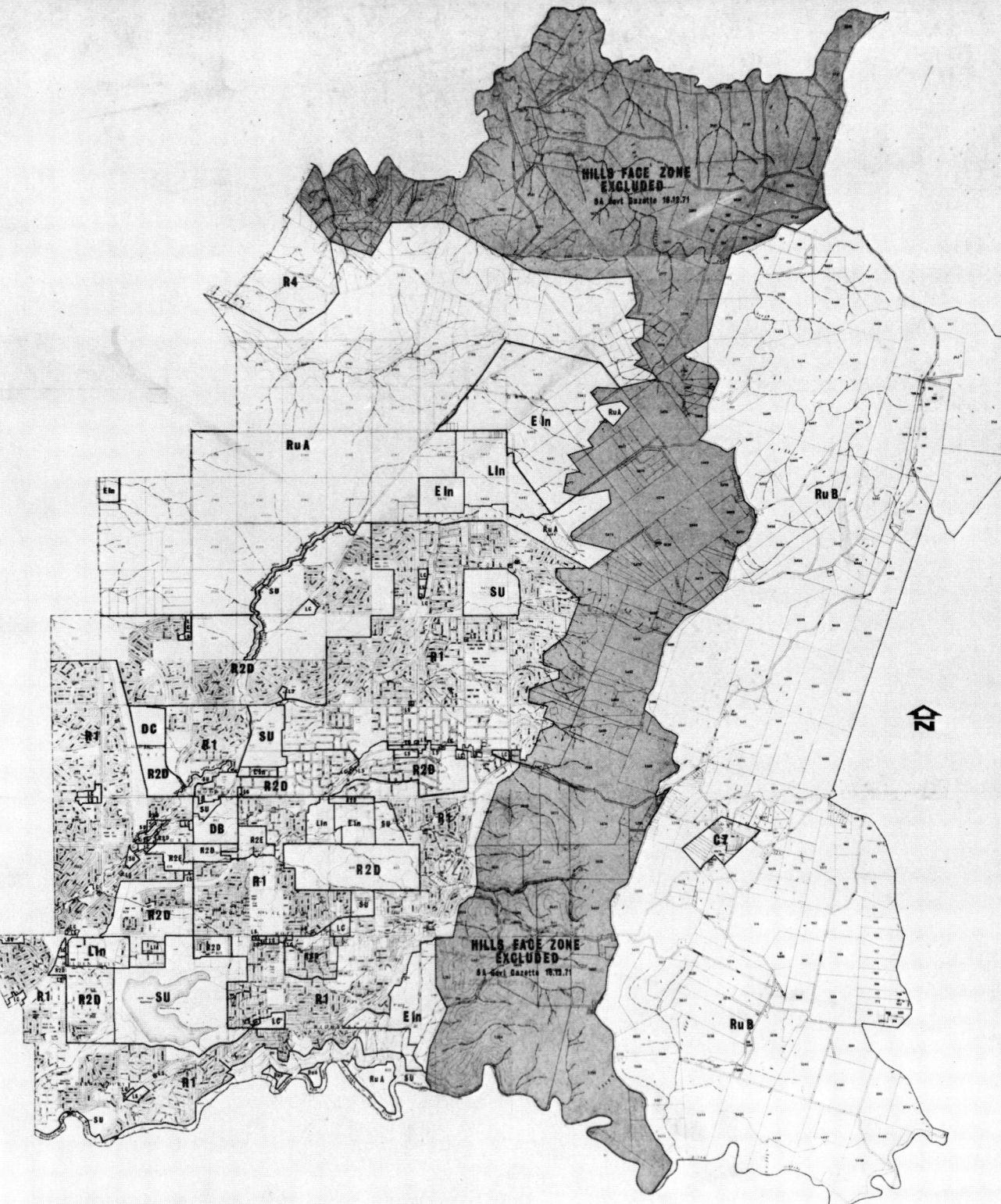

Map 13 Plan of Corporation of the City of Tea Tree Gully (1976) showing Hills Face Zone, and residential (R), industrial (In), rural (Ru), commercial (C) and special (S) zones.

35

SUBDIVISION AND CLOSER
SETTLEMENTS

'the battle of the bulge'

There have been two invasions of the district of Tea Tree Gully. The first began with the settlement of South Australia in 1836 and continued for some 20 years until the district was occupied and settled.

It could be said that the second district invasion really began with the post-war agreement between the Commonwealth and British Governments which came into operation on March 31, 1947, and which provided for free and assisted passages to be granted to British residents desirous of settling in Australia. This was followed by a similar agreement with other European countries in 1955 which resulted in the influx of those multi-national groups of migrants who, for want of a better term were dubbed 'New Australians',* a term coined by Arthur Calwell, Minister for Immigration.

The initial invasion dispossessed the Kaurna or Adelaide Tribe of Aborigines of the hunting grounds which they had occupied and which had been their ancestral home for perhaps 30,000 years. The Kaurna have vanished almost without trace. Occasionally, during the 100 years of agricultural occupation which followed the initial invasion by Europeans, a plough turned

* The total overseas-born residents of the District of Tea Tree Gully are shown in the census as follows:

New Zealand	107	Poland	117
U.K. and Ireland	10,622	U.S.S.R.	34
Austria	95	Yugoslavia	116
Czechoslovakia	24	Other European	321
Germany	1,038	Asia	353
Greece	48	Africa	107
Hungary	78	Canada	45
Italy	353	U.S.A.	67
Malta	63	S. America	2
Netherlands	626	Other	46
		TOTAL —	14,262 *(v. note)*

Total District population (1971) — 36,708

(Note: Does not include the large number of Australian-born children of overseas-born parents) over an ancient camp-site and brought to light some Aboriginal remnant — a stone implement, a bone needle or, at times, the skeleton of an Aboriginal man, woman or child. The commonest artefact to be unearthed locally has been the kidney-shaped scraper, usually made of slate, and once used for scraping the possum skins so favoured by the Adelaide Tribe in the making of skin cloaks.

Within a few years of colonization, the invasion of the tribal lands of the Kaurna brought their tribal life to an abrupt end.

Using tools only a little less primitive by modern standards than those of the Aboriginals, the pioneers within 20 years transformed the open and ancient landscape into productive farmland, fenced with post-and-rail in the Australian style or with English hedge plants. With mud and straw, or pit-sawn timber, or stone quarried near to hand, they built their pioneer homes.

The opposition they met with did not come from the people whom they had dispossessed — without compensation and almost without qualm. Their struggle was with untilled soil and puzzling climatic conditions. Their greatest and often their sole support lay in the strength of their arm and in their will to succeed in the 'Land of Promise'.

The district the pioneers tamed and transformed and which in 1853 they formed into the local government district of Highercombe remained a rural landscape for the next century. Many pioneer families remained in possession of the farmlands originally granted to them. In the seven villages the general store or the post office often passed from father to son. In the village of Houghton, in 1957, S.T.J. Possingham was still a storekeeper in the shop which John Possingham had taken over from William Reeds in 1857.

In 1957 the district — since 1935 the District of Tea Tree Gully — lay outside of the metropolitan area. Its townships were all still listed in the 'Country Section' of South Australian Directories. Street Directories of Adelaide and Suburbs, such as *Fuller's*, did manage to include part of the district, as far as Grand Junction Road, but the sole subdivision shown was the small area of Dernancourt. The remainder of the district was still marked out in numbered sections as it had been since settlement of the district began.

The number of district council assessments had indeed increased by 1955 to nearly 1,000 from the 248 assessments issued by the first District Clerk in 1853. Nevertheless, except for Paracombe Blocks, Vista and Dernancourt, no other subdivisional names appeared in the 1955 Assessment Book. The Paracombe subdivision of 1901, the Dernancourt subdivision of 1923 and the Vista subdivision of 1927 had added several hundred new assessments to the clerk's books but they indicated no general movement into what was still a productive rural area. The district's population, numbering 1,440 in the district census of 1855, had, by 1954, increased to a moderate 2,561. Perhaps the person most aware of a new groundswell of population was V.S. Bowen, the District Clerk, who in 1951 began to use

Aerial photographs of Tea Tree Gully taken in the 1960s revealing new subdivisions filling with homes. The photos feature the township of Tea Tree Gully, St. Agnes winery and vineyard and the tree-lined tributaries of Dry Creek.

Above: Aerial photograph 1954. Hope Valley Reservoir (bottom R.H. corner). The area of photograph includes the townships of Hope Valley, Modbury (left), Tea Tree Gully (centre), and Houghton, and shows the course of the River Torrens and tributaries of Dry Creek. Department of Lands, South Australia.

Right: Aerial photograph of the same area (approximately) made in 1974 revealing the dramatic growth in subdivision and housing which had taken place in the intervening 20 years. Department of Lands, South Australia.

an assessment book of larger and more modern format and who in 1958, in the year of his retirement, asked for the help of an assistant in the office because of the increasing number of assessments he was making.

It was Bowen's successor, F.C. Shilcock, who was to feel the full force of the tide of population which was beginning to flow when he first took office as District Clerk in 1958.

There were few indeed who could have foretold, even by the mid 1950s, that a second invasion of the district had already begun. It had taken 100 years for the district to add an additional 1,000 to its population. Within the next decade a tide of 20,000 people flooded out onto its plains and foothills and another 30,000 in the decade which followed. The district population which in June of 1954 numbered 2,561, by April of the present year (1976) had reached 57,000.* The 715 houses of 1954 have become the 15,375 houses of 1976.

Perhaps the figures which highlight and dramatise the tide of invasion are those of the school population. By 1953 there were some 300 children attending the six district schools — Hope Valley, Houghton, Golden Grove, Paracombe, Modbury and Tea Tree Gully. Today nearly 12,000 children attend schools within the same district.

The second invasion and closer settlement of the district had something in common with the initial settlement. It was mainly due to another tide of migration, much of it once again from the Great Britain which had given the district its first pioneers. Once again the native-born of the district were dispossessed of much of the land which for a century had given them and their families a living. But this time, for some at least, there was comforting financial compensation for the loss of family lands and farms. Other landowners, however, whose lands were zoned as rural, or as reserved Hills Face Zone, or were taken over by the Lands Commission, must have felt that Governments have a tendency to send rain on the unjust as well as on the just, and sometimes not even on the just.

A second similarity can be noted between the first and second wave of migrants — it was the youthfulness of the majority of the newcomers in both periods of settlement. This was evident in the age distribution figures in the 1971 census which revealed that a large percentage of the district's popula-

* Population and housing figures for District of Tea Tree Gully:

Year (June 30)	Population	Houses
1855	1,440	268
1901	1,709	-
1947	2,203	585
1954	2,561	715
1959	2,672	765
1962	8,250	2,370
1965	20,071	4,820
1968	27,000	7,520
1971	36,708	9,804
1976	57,500 (estimated)	15,375 (estimated)

tion was in the 25-39 age group. A similar youthfulness in the district's population was revealed in the census of 1855.

A further set of figures in the 1971 census reveals the large proportion of children in the population — many of overseas-born parents. Children of pre-school and school-going age constituted 40% of the total population of the City of Tea Tree Gully. This resulted in what was referred to in local schools as the 'battle of the bulge' which taxed classroom accommodation to its limits and beyond. This mushroom growth of children resulted in a mushroom growth of schools which is still continuing.* In the one year of 1975, Mrs. Molly Byrne, Member of Parliament for the House of Assembly Electoral District of Tea Tree Gully, announced the construction or completion of eight new district schools at an estimated cost of in excess of five million dollars.

If there were similarities to be noted between the two tides of migration and migrants which so profoundly affected the history of the district, there were also great differences to be noted. One obvious difference was in travelling conditions. The twentieth century migrants did not arrive in tiny sailing ships at Port Misery after six anxious months at sea. Although the modern passage out by ship or plane was assisted or free, as it had been for

*	District Schools — 1953		District Schools — 1976	
	Name	Enrolment	Name	Enrolment
	Hope Valley	59	Banksia Park High	910
	Houghton	55	Modbury High	1,025
	Golden Grove	23	Kildare College	350
	Modbury	44	Banksia Park Primary	738
	Tea Tree Gully	50	Junior Primary	398
	Paracombe	42	Dernancourt Primary	619
			Junior Primary	272
			Highbury Primary	657
			Hope Valley Primary	213
			Houghton Primary	93
			Holden Hill Primary	388
			Junior Primary	204
			Holden Hill North Primary	111
			Modbury Primary	593
			Junior Primary	229
			Modbury South Primary	643
			Modbury South Special	67
			Modbury West Primary	510
			Junior Primary	249
			Paracombe Primary	50
			Ridgehaven Primary	527
			Junior Primary	259
			St. Agnes Primary	338
			Strathmont Primary	585
			Junior Primary	250
			Surrey Downs Primary	564
			Tea Tree Gully Primary	395
			Fairview Park Primary	186
	TOTAL	273	TOTAL	11,423

Aerial photographs taken over Hope Valley in the early 1950s shows that suburban Adelaide was still distant. The photos feature the winery and vineyards of Douglas Tolley & Co., the township of Hope Valley and the Hope Valley Reservoir.

the early pioneers, the newcomers to South Australia were not dumped upon the shores of an unknown land — not physically at least. For homesickness and the spiritual traumas of separation of family ties there was a remedy not available to the pioneer migrants — the opportunity of a speedy return to their homeland.

The newcomers to the district, whether British or European migrants, or those merely moving from Adelaide's inner suburbs, were not land-seekers and farmers. In this respect they differed completely from the district's first settlers. The newcomers were urban and suburban dwellers seeking a quarter-acre of land in a serviced subdivision on which to build a suburban home. The difference in the aspirations and needs of the district's new-comers has had a profound and permanent effect upon the topography of the district. Thousands of acres of productive and fertile farmland have al-ready disappeared under a spreading tide of suburbia, with the bulldozers ahead of it clearing vineyards, orchards, market-gardens, orange groves, hay-fields and natural areas of timber, to make way for more housing.

The new invasion has created dormitory suburbs, with a large propor-tion of the population leaving the district each day for jobs outside of the district. The zoning of the district under the Metropolitan Planning Act will ensure that the district will tend to remain a dormitory suburb, espec-ially when the extractive industries of quarrying and sand-mining finally ex-haust the raw material on which they now exist.

This suburban invasion will continue until it is halted within the dis-trict by two barriers — one the natural barrier of the deep gorges of the Little Para region beyond Golden Grove; the other the man-made barrier of the Hills Face Zone — a defined area *(See Map 13)* of public reserve where no residential subdivision will be permitted. It is this backdrop of the Adel-aide Hills and the system of creeks and streams which flow out of them which has always given the district its distinctive character.

It might seem at a casual glance that the new community is no more than an extension of suburban Adelaide. This, however, is to overlook the vitality imparted by a predominantly youthful population and by the dis-trict's lusty growth — not merely in essential services, housing and popula-tion but in amenities consequent upon its youthful constitution — schools, kindergartens, playgrounds, parklands, recreational areas, ovals, new church-es, hotels and youth clubs, golf courses, swimming centres, community cen-tres — all vying for priority, money and public support.

It is a challenge which has been taken up by a host of organisations working with or through the District Council or local Members of Parlia-ment, or alone, to meet the needs of special groups. Such efforts directed towards the needs of what is now one of the largest local government areas* in the metropolitan area are creating a new identity for the District of Tea

* For details of local government population figures consult *South Australian Year Book* (Published annually since 1966).

Tree Gully. The old rural identity, which was established by the district's first settlers and which this history seeks to record, will vanish almost without trace.

The physical outlines of the district's newly emerging identity can be traced, although somewhat sketchily, from the pages of contemporary newspapers. Fortunately, in April 1965, the district was provided with a newspaper of its own — *The North-East Leader* —† an advertising medium 'delivered free each Wednesday to homes in Tea Tree Gully, Vista, Modbury, Ridgehaven, Strathmont, Beefacres, Golden Grove, Hope Valley, Pooraka, Para Vista, Paracombe, Houghton, Gilles Plains, Clovercrest, Holden Hill, Para Hills, Valley View, Inglewood, Dernancourt, Fairview Park, Highbury, Chain of Ponds, Ingle Farm and Windsor Gardens'.

From the pages of the newspapers and from other sources we need to record little more than the physical events of recent years in chronological order — it will be left for some future historian to judge their value and importance in the life of the district of Tea Tree Gully.

CHRONOLOGY OF PRINCIPAL EVENTS — 1959-1976

1959 Tea Tree Gully Golf Course* to become new subdivision of Vista. Extension of railway from Northfield to Modbury or Tea Tree Gully under consideration. Council asks for district to be included in the Metropolitan Area under the Town Planning Act. Beefacres Estate of G.W. Pitt & Son (87 acres) to be subdivided. New subdivision of Holden Hill to be reticulated. Council adopts the tea tree in its new emblem and motto (see cover). Plan for proposed subdivision of Modbury. Complaints re quarry blasting near residential area of Tea Tree Gully. New Tea Tree Gully Golf Course (90 acres) laid out.

1960 Tea Tree Gully's first house to house mail delivery commenced September 1. Opening of new Country Women's Association Hall at Houghton. Tunnel 10 feet in diameter and 1,020 feet long completed through Anstey's Hill to conduct water from Mannum pipe line to Hope Valley storage tank. Tea Tree Gully Baptist Church Centenary Celebration. First zoning by-law by Council defines housing, shopping and industrial areas.

1961 Bushfire burns out 800 acres along Modbury-Golden Grove Road. Tea Tree Gully Progress Association sponsors Carnival of the Hills. Difficulty in financing purchase of land for reserves and recreation grounds. Rate Revenue for financial year 1960/61 — £39,250. Plan for septic tanks to be connected with common effluent pits in unsewered subdivisions.

1962 Angove's Winery buys 2,000 acres of land near Renmark to replace St. Agnes vineyards. Plan for development of 30 acres at Banksia Park as a sports ground (Perteringa Oval) drawn up by Council. Whiting's clay mine closes (April 1962). New Reservoir planned for Torrens Gorge (Kangaroo Creek). Modbury-Golden Grove Ward becomes two wards. Horse falls into underground tank of yard on Main North East Road. Government plans to extend water and sewerage into Modbury area. Hallett Brick Industries reveal plans for new brickworks at Yatala Vale. Plaque unveiled at *Glen Ewin* (13.12.1962) to commemorate centenary of the Company.

† Published by *Messenger Newspapers.*
* See Chapter 36.

1963 New 80-acre subdivision to be named 'Fairview Park'. One hundred and seven acres in Modbury area to be subdivided into 450 housing allotments. Tea Tree Gully to purchase *Highercombe Estate* (165 acres) at Paracombe for development as a public golf course and recreational area. £20,000 damage caused by rain-storm. Protests at removal of gum trees in Tolley and Valley Roads endangering a power line. Proposed 2,000 home project for Modbury. Population of South Australia reaches one million mark.

1964 Council considering plan for development of a community centre at Modbury. Construction of a new plant by P.G.H. Industries to begin manufacture of clay pipes and clay bricks begun at Yatala Vale-Golden Grove. Plans for Modbury Railway shelved. Myer Emporium buys 58-acre site for new shopping centre. Work to begin on sewerage of Hope Valley-Highbury area. Opening of Tea Tree Gully Community Hall, Memorial Drive (August 8). District of Salisbury achieves City status.

1965 Council presented with Mobile Library by C.M.V. Foundations Trustees. Clovercrest shopping centre opened. Modbury High School opened (April) with an enrolment of 50 girls and 49 boys. Opening of new Modbury Methodist Church (May). Opening of P.G.H. Industries by Premier Walsh (cost of building £1 million). Banksia Park Primary School opened. Poll of ratepayers decided to grant Council right to borrow £80,000 to build new council chambers and civic centre. Introduction of Australian decimal currency. Temporary Bailey Bridge to replace Darley Road ford. Apex Club begins clearing land in Lokan (now Milne) Road for swimming pool, oval and bowling green. Tea Tree Gully Branch of National Trust formed (Mr. R.E. Kretschmer, Chairman).

1966 Tenders called for new Civic Centre. Modbury Institute purchased as a St. Johns Ambulance Centre. Margaret Rohan, teacher at Houghton School, crowned 'Miss South Australia'. New Kelly Road Bridge opened. New Roman Catholic College (Kildare College) for girls opened on Valiant Road.

1967 Opening of new Civic Centre by Premier Walsh (January 21). District Council applies for status of Municipality. Plans announced for a 460-bed hospital at Modbury. Highercombe Public Golf Course opened (18 holes). Reconstruction of Reservoir Road. Centenary of Hope Valley Methodist Church. Amendment made to Local Government Act to enable district of Tea Tree Gully to be proclaimed a city.

1968 New school to be built at Modbury West. Governor of South Australia issues proclamation that the Council will have City status as from February 1, 1968. Surrey Downs school under construction. Tea Tree Gully E.F.S. given a new fire unit. Work starts on Modbury Hospital. Centenary of Greenwith Methodist Church held. Lions Club plans to construct new swimming pool. William Green becomes first Mayor of the City of Tea Tree Gully. Site works for Modbury Hospital begin. Tea Tree Gully Scout Hall opened. Historic Houghton Hotel demolished.

1969 Site works for Myer Tea Tree Plaza begin. New Public Library opened (February 24) in old Modbury Primary School. St. Agnes shopping centre opened (July). Foundation stone of St. David's War Memorial Roman Catholic Church in Elizabeth Street blessed. Family re-union on Golden Grove Showgrounds of pioneer Roberts family. *Highlander Hotel* opened. Work begun on new *Highbury Hotel*. Premier Steele Hall opens new Tea Tree Gully swimming pool — Chairman, Mr. H.G.C. Drury, receives a 'ducking'.

1970 Value of buildings approved in 8 months of financial year — $9.08 million. Outstanding rate for year $85,000. Old *Modbury Hotel* demolished. Mayoral Chain designed. Myer Tea Tree Plaza opened (September). Tea Tree Gully School Centenary. Modbury West Primary School completed.

1971 Widening of Main North East Road continues. *Blue Gums Hotel* opened. E.F.S. attends 71 fires during summer season. Value of building approvals increases to nearly $14 million. New E.F.S. station at Ridgehaven. Government plans new reservoir on Little Para. *Inglewood Hotel* becomes Historic Inn. 'Battle of Lokan Road v. Milne Road'.

1972 Elections in every ward. Protest at proposed subdivision of Vista Heights in Hills Face Zone. Gumeracha Council moves to control Hills Ward — opposed by Tea Tree Gully Council. Plans for Senior Citizens Club.

Building approvals for 1971/72

Ward	New Houses	Value - $
Tea Tree Gully	448	2,906,244.00
Ridgehaven	569	3,829,028.00
Torrens	492	3,089,893.00
Modbury	361	2,353,719.00
Holden Hill	463	2,453,104.00
Golden Grove	9	42,995.00
Hills	13	31,112.00

Light plane crashes off Greenwith Road — eight killed. Approval for Banksia Park High School.

1973 New $11 million Modbury Hospital opened by Premier Dunstan. Petition of 2,759 ratepayers asking council to resign. Average price of block of land shows increase of $1,000 to $3,205 over two years. Senior Citizens Club opens. Plan for railway to Modbury still under consideration. New Hope Valley Methodist Church opened (September).

1974 Tea Tree Gully Lions Club 10 years old. Bowman's Bus Service taken over by S.A. Government. Rotary plans $2 million 'Rotary Village'. Royal Commission recommends changes to local government district boundaries, including Tea Tree Gully. Rates up 23%. Hope Valley water filtration plant being constructed. Government Lands Commission purchases 467.428 hectares (1,155 acres) of land in Golden Grove district for housing development for $3.5 million.

1975 Work begins on new Public Library (opened December 17). St. Agnes Community Health Centre established. Mr. E.R. Mitchell resigns as Town Clerk. St. Agnes Primary School opens. Opening of the Pope John XXIII Community Centre at Modbury. More than 7,000 dogs registered and 596 stray dogs impounded during year. Council plans to borrow $487,000. Tea Tree Gully Sketchbook published. Salisbury/Tea Tree Gully Jaycees time-capsule buried — to be resurrected in year 2,000.

1976 (to June 30) — Only 1.6% poll of ratepayers in supplementary election. Bluegum tree at Surrey Downs saved by court action. New clubrooms of Modbury Sporting Club opened (April). Work begins on Karadinga Community Centre on Montague Road. Highercombe Golf Club House opened by Mayor John Tilley.

36

CITY

'I, the Lieutenant-Governor . . . do hereby, by this proclamation, designate
and constitute the 'District of Highercombe'. July 1853

I, the said Governor . . . declare the said municipality of Tea Tree Gully to be a city,
and assign the name of 'The City of Tea Tree Gully' to such municipality. February 1968

A District and Local Government Chronology

Dec.28	1836	Proclamation of the Province of South Australia.
	1839	First survey of land in district.
	1841	First village (Houghton) laid out.
	1846	Hundred of Yatala proclaimed.
	1849	First District Road Board established.
	1852	Act to appoint District Councils passed.
May	1853	First District Council in South Australia (Mitcham).
July	1853	District of Highercombe proclaimed.
	1855	Council Chambers erected at Steventon (Tea Tree Gully).
	1858	District divides into District of Highercombe and District of Tea Tree Gully.
	1935	Compulsory amalgamation of two districts — to become District of Tea Tree Gully.
	1967	New Council Chambers and Civic Centre opened at Modbury.
Feb.8	1968	District of Tea Tree Gully becomes City of Tea Tree Gully.
	1970	Electorate of Tea Tree Gully proclaimed.
July	1976	Hills Ward annexed to District Council of Gumeracha.

The steps which led to the formation of the first district council and the establishment of the district boundaries and which led finally, in this century, to the achievement of city status, were anything but regular in their progression. The excitement of the years of debate and public meetings which preceded the proclamation of the first District of Highercombe was almost immediately overshadowed by the greater excitement of the gold-rush years. District affairs, both council and otherwise, came to a virtual standstill.

The division of the district into two council areas in 1858 was a step backwards rather than forward. It was a separation whose physical boundaries resulted during the next 77 years in a noticeable social barrier. Those living even slightly north of Smart Road were, when occasion arose, considered as 'foreigners' by those to the south — and vice-versa. At a dance in Klopper's Barn at Hope Valley at the turn of the century 'intruders' from Tea Tree Gully were 'stoned back to the district border line' early in the evening — reportedly by rival suitors. A more acceptable expression of district rivalries was to be found in the hard-fought games on local football fields* in the district. †

* The 'fields', even 30 years ago, were uneven and tussocky paddocks and at Highbury the 'dressing-shed' was the partial concealment provided by the prickly furze-bushes.

† It may be salutary, as a footnote, to publish the following letter written in 1913 and to realise that larrikinism is not just a phenomenon of 'modern' youth. In fairness to the youth of Houghton of 1913 it should be noted that the offending teams were both 'city teams'.

DISORDERLY FOOTBALLERS AT HOUGHTON

'To the Editor

Will you allow me a little space to call attention to the disgusting larrikinism indulged in from time to time by different football teams and their followers when they make Houghton the scene of their visits?

Our quiet little village is prettily situated, and football teams desiring to spend a Saturday afternoon in the hills frequently make an engagement with the Houghton Club one of their club fixtures. A number of the clubs visiting us appear to be made up of gentlemanly fellows, and their presence is appreciated by the local club and townspeople generally; but lately we have been visited by quite a number of undesirables, who come up more for a change of beer than to try conclusions at football.

On Saturday last two city teams turned up to play against each other, and those who saw the game say that it would take some beating as an exhibition of larrikinism, but there was very little attempt at football. I cannot testify to the class of football, but I can speak with regard to the conduct of some of the company when away from the playing ground; and to say that it was disgraceful is to state the case mildly.

The drinking and shocking language indulged in at night in the village were simply disgusting. In addition to this some of the hooligans seemed to imagine that they had a licence to do whatever mischief appealed to them. Several of them put the whole of their weight on to one of the pine trees forming the avenue of pines on the cemetery road and snapped it off close to the roots. Another tree of the same class was pulled clean out of the ground. One fellow behaved himself in such a disgusting manner that I would be ashamed to see the account of his conduct in print. Surely it is time that this sort of conduct was put down with a firm hand. To have trees which have been carefully planted and cared for so wantonly destroyed and the ears of respectable people and little children assailed by the oaths of a drunken lot of hooligans is something that people ought not to be asked to tolerate. What is needed at Houghton is proper police protection. Our nearest police officers are at Gumeracha on the one side and at St. Peters on the other. The district is far too large for the Gumeracha man to deal with effectively. He has gained the reputation of being a most diligent and capable officer, but the ground to be covered is too great for any one man. The fact that there are two hotels within a quarter of a mile of the local football ground indicates the need of a police officer either at Houghton or Tea Tree Gully. Being without adequate police protection we are at the mercy of any company of roughs who choose to make the town the scene of their drunken and disorderly conduct. In writing this letter I am voicing the feelings of the townspeople who feel that they had quite enough of this kind of conduct.

I am etc.
(Rev.) D.J. Wellington
Houghton Sept.23, 1913'

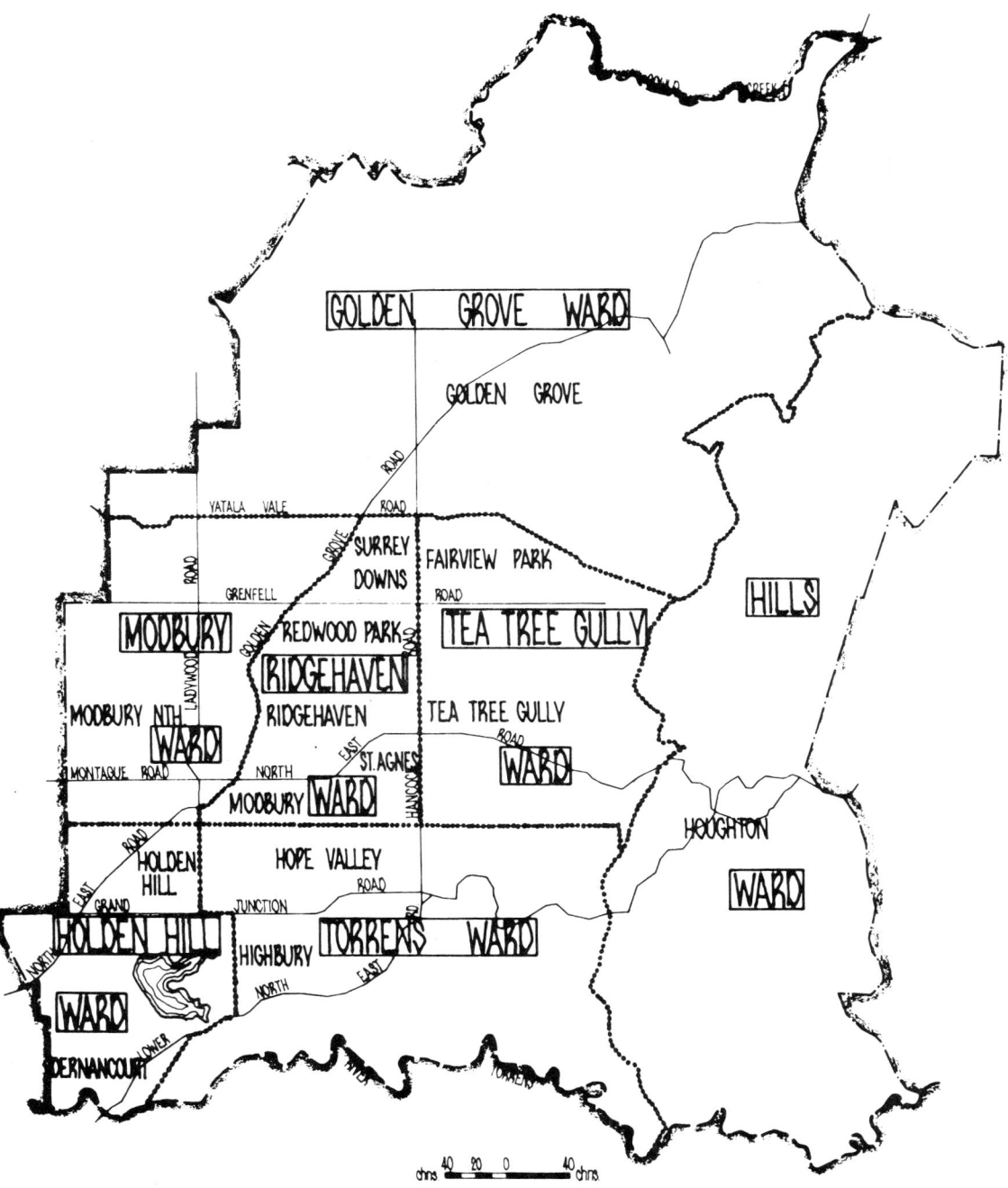

Map 14 Ward boundaries — City of Tea Tree Gully, June 1976. In July 1976 the Hills Ward was annexed to the District of Gumeracha and five new wards were created.

At council level there was, however, little evidence of the division of the district, except differences of opinion concerning responsibility for the maintenance and repair of Smart Road and of the entrance to Houghton Hollow.

For the century after 1858 the pace of progress was a slow one — during the depression years of the 1930s virtually all progress was halted. The district population fell and the number of unoccupied houses increased. The amalgamation of the two councils in 1935 did little to quicken the life of the district — war intervened and inhibited the district's recovery.

Neither Bowen, when he resigned as District Clerk in April 1958, nor Shilcock who took over, had little or any idea of the tide of immigration which was about to overwhelm the district. Certainly neither they, nor any councillors, had the least idea that within 10 years their district would be proclaimed a city.

The pace of settlement soon overtook the capacity of council and of the state to provide services. Ratepayers became vocal and by 1965 had a local newspaper — the *North East Leader* — in which to voice their impatience and dissatisfaction. The democratic process of voting was given lively attention and issues became very real.

One such issue was the question of the provision of deep drainage and sewerage. Work commenced early in 1967 on the sewerage of Highbury and Hope Valley. Other subdivisions were provided with a temporary expedient — a common effluent system of open pits. The issue was suddenly highlighted again in June 1972 — this time by a tragedy when a boy of 3 years found his way under the protecting fence and drowned in the open effluent pit at Fairview Park.

Subdivision soon outstripped the capacity of council equipment to meet the demand for new roads. In 1958 when Shilcock took over as District Clerk and Overseer, his 'inside' staff was one girl and a typewriter. His 'outside' staff was a gang of 5 men. Norm. Lambert, foreman in charge of the works gang, had at his disposal a council 'plant' consisting of:

1 lend-lease Chevrolet Truck
1 Cletrac Caterpillar Tractor
1 road-roller drawn by tractor
1 'Speed' Patrol Grader

The most that could be accomplished in any new subdivision with such equipment was to grade a dirt track or two into the new area. Subdividers had no obligation prior to 1960 to provide anything but the metal blinding for the roads. At the time of the subdivision in Tea Tree Gully which later became known as Ridgehaven there was no legislation requiring the subdividers to make roads or to provide kerbing.

To overcome this difficulty Council applied in 1961 to have the Tea Tree Gully district incorporated in the metropolitan area under the S.A.

Tea Tree Gully District Council — photograph taken on the occasion of the centenary of local government in the district, 1953. **L.to R.** Cr. D.S. Goodes, Cr. A.G. Dearman, Cr. F. Packer, Cr. W. Hannaford, Cr. S.G. Mudge (rear), Cr. L.J. Wicks, Mr. Richmond (Commissioner of Highways), Chairman Cr. G.N. Lambert, a visitor (rear), District Clerk Mr. V.S. Bowen, Cr. G.J. Clifton (rear).

Members of the Council of the Corporation of the City of Tea Tree Gully 1975-6. **L.to R. Back Row:** Cr. R.L. Dearman, Cr. J.K. Crossing, Cr. D.S. Brooks, Cr. D.T. Radcliff, Cr. N.J. Hamilton, Cr. S.G. Mudge, Cr. E.L. Basnec (Deputy Mayor), Cr. G.E. Gallasch, Cr. D.D. Stuart, Cr. D.J. Hards, Mayor J.G. Tilley, Cr. W.E. Gallasch, Cr. K.R. Cooke, Cr. T.E.L. Milton.

The new Civic Centre of the City of Tea Tree Gully was opened by the Hon. Frank Walsh, then Premier of South Australia, on January 21, 1967. The Centre includes the District Offices, Council Chamber and Civic Hall.

Tea Tree Gully Public Library — opened December 1975.

Town Planning Act. This enabled council, after 1962, to require subdividers to make roads, to blind them with four inches of metal, to seal them with bitumen aggregate and to kerb all roads in the subdivision. In one year in the late 1960s there were 12 new subdivisions under way at the same time. In this present year (1976) there are many new subdivisions in progress; and herds of yellow earthmoving machinery on the horizon are almost as common as herds of dairy-cattle were a few years earlier.

In 1960, council introduced its first zoning by-laws to ensure the separation of residential from commercial and industrial areas. The first subdivisions to be zoned were those where residential expansion was, at that time, the greatest — along the two main arterial roads which traverse the district, the Main North East and Lower North East Roads.* The Tea Tree Gully Council was the leader in this field and its Planning Regulations (Zoning) were published in the *South Australian Government Gazette* on August 28, 1969. The 1969 development plans, indicating the type of building and use of land in various zones *(See Map 13)* is at present under review.

By 1969, therefore, instead of subdivision and subdividors outpacing the resources of council and the provision of services by the state and outflanking council regulations, the new zoning regulations enabled council to resume its rightful place in controlling development in the district.

One of the aims of the zoning regulations has been the greater preservation of the natural character of the district — a consideration once given little attention in council areas. The District of Tea Tree Gully owes much of its character to its background of hills, to its network of creeks and tributaries, and to its large rural areas extending to Gould's Creek in the north. Zoning will ensure that much of this character will be retained and, indeed enhanced.

The Hills Face Zone *(See Map 13)* is already controlled by the State Government as an area of preservation. The re-zoning of land adjoining the River Torrens and Dry Creek to ensure that their character will be better preserved and made accessible to the public is now virtually assured by both State and Council. The hills flanking the district on its east and the steep gullies of the Little Para to the north will act as natural barriers to the tide of residential expansion.

As those who live in the rural areas of the district know, it is not easy for residential and rural areas to live side by side. One answer to the difference in life styles — and in rating — has already been found for the Hills Ward of the district — to detach it from the district completely and to annexe it to the rural district of Gumeracha. The answer may prove to be the correct one economically, although historically the separation marks the end of an era for the districts of Hermitage, Houghton and Paracombe.

Regulation may be able to control and remain in advance of development but finance inevitably, it seems, lags behind. The greatest source of

* Vide Harris, K.R. — *Land Values in Tea Tree Gully, 1950-65* (Thesis, 1969) for a detailed review.

revenue for local government still remains the rates paid by its ratepayers.

Income from rates for the year 1960-61 reached a record $77,316.00. By 1974 *(v. Item 5)* the figure had risen to $1,333,649.00, and one year later to $1,785,535.00. Such figures reflect many factors — increases in population, increases in rating, changes in methods of assessment, inflation of land values. Expenditure has, conversely, suffered from increased costs and the high rate of inflation which has plagued buyers of goods and services during the past decade.

In 1967-68 the remarkable increase in the district's population and in the number of its ratepayers outstripped even Government legislation. By 1968 the district's population had increased nine-fold from less than 3,000 to nearly 27,000.

Early in 1967, with the opening of its new Council Chambers and Civic Centre at Modbury, council announced that it had applied to the Minister of Local Government for city status for the district of Tea Tree Gully and municipality status for the council. Although, however, the district population by then greatly exceeded the necessary 15,000 inhabitants, the district lacked a qualification necessary for a change in status. It had no defined industrial and commercial areas — its only defined areas were rural and residential. An amendment would have to be made by Parliament to the South Australian Local Government Act to enable Tea Tree Gully to be proclaimed a city. The speed of residential invasion had outstripped state legislation.

Council had shown considerable foresight in beginning to plan as early as 1963 for a new community centre at Modbury, which would incorporate a new council chamber, council offices and community hall. Modbury, it was seen, would within a few years become the centre of the district's residential areas.

The old 1855 Council Chambers at Tea Tree Gully had been central to the district when they were built. Then Houghton had been the largest centre of population. Now Tea Tree Gully was on the 'fringe' of development.

When Frederick Charles Shilcock took over as District Clerk in 1958, the Council Chamber still doubled as the clerk's office. The office then expanded into the back rooms which had previously been leased and the council chamber was used only for council meetings. Later, council meetings were transferred to the clubrooms of the Tea Tree Gully Branch of the R.S.L., which formed part of the new Community Hall in Memorial Drive. A room of the old *Highercombe Hotel* served to house the staff of the Building and Health Departments.

On September 4, 1965, a poll of ratepayers was held to decide whether council should proceed with its plans to borrow $160,000.00 and to erect a new community centre at Modbury. The poll resulted in 3,190 against and 1,456 in favour of the loan. Despite the unfavourable result council, under

Item 5 (p.359) Balance Sheet of Corporation of the City of Tea Tree Gully, 1974. *(cf. Balance Sheet 1867 p.164).*

CITY OF TEA TREE GULLY

FORM 2

GENERAL FUND

Statement of Income and Expenditure for the Year Ended 30th June, 1974

Previous Year $		$	Current Year $
	The income for the year was derived from—		
1 131 311	Rates (Form 3)		1 333 649
183 408	Public works (Form 4)		164 294
82 382	Public services (Form 5)		87 447
165 906	Council properties (Form 6)		172 877
26 140	Miscellaneous (Form 8)		54 676
$1 589 147	Total income		$1 812 943
	Against which expenditure for the year was—		
352 215	Public works (Form 4)		454 107
302 551	Public services (Form 5)		399 795
213 905	Council properties (Form 6)		229 216
163 177	General administration (Form 7)		205 176
103 067	Miscellaneous (Form 8)		106 811
108 001	Indirect expenses (Form 9)..		115 204
$1 242 916	Total expenditure		$1 510 309
346 231	Resulting in a surplus from operations for the year of		302 634
	Less surplus in operation of plant and machinery transferred to		
8 257	machinery working account		4 489
354 488			298 145
	From which was appropriated—	$	
	Long service leave reserve		
44 048	Plant replacement reserve	54 218	
49 881	Less transfer from reserve (plant)	45 076	
5 833			9 142
360 321	Balance transferred to municipal fund		275 541
	Balance transferred to common effluent drainage fund		13 462
	This surplus was committed for—		
	Purchase of assets—		
66 389	Land and buildings	34 968	
81 648	Plant	109 888	
8 171	Other—Fixtures, fittings, office machines	7 259	
			152 115
	Loan redemption—		
159 772	Repayment of principal		159 745
315 980			311 860
	Resulting in—		
$44 341	Over-commitment of revenue surplus		$22 857

the chairmanship of Cr. W. Green, decided to raise the loan. Under the Local Government Act the percentage of ratepayers who voted against the loan was insufficient to prevent council's decision to proceed.

The new Community Centre was opened on Saturday, January 21, 1967 by the Hon. Frank Walsh, M.P., Premier of South Australia. The old Council Chamber on Haines Road became the Works Office under the control of the Supervisor of Works. By 1975, office accommodation was again insufficient and considerable extensions were made to the new building.

In February of the following year the district of Tea Tree Gully became a city. The proclamation of February 8, 1968, in conferring the status of a municipality upon the district, in the same proclamation gave the municipality city status. Only the district council of Salisbury, in 1964, had similarly achieved direct elevation to the status of city. Status, however, was not merely a matter of honour or even of population. As a municipality, the new City of Tea Tree Gully was now able to take advantage of powers and privileges not available to district councils. It would also change methods of assessment.

City status brought other immediate changes. All previous wards were abolished and the district divided into seven wards, each ward electing two councillors, increasing the number of councillors from nine to fourteen. A mayor of the corporation would be elected annually by ratepayers in place of a council chairman elected by councillors from among their number.

At the first meeting of the council following the proclamation of the municipality in February, Councillor William Green was elected first Mayor of the Corporation of the City of Tea Tree Gully. His wife, Mrs. Ann Green, became the district's first Mayoress.

The district's first council chairman in 1855 had been a migrant Scotsman — Robert Milne — who had been born near Aberdeen, had arrived in the colony at the age of 28 and, in 1843, had taken up the property at Dry Creek which he named *Drumminer* (now *Drumminor*). One hundred and thirteen years later the district's first mayor was another migrant Scotsman. In 1952, William Green had arrived with his wife in South Australia from Greenock, Scotland. He settled at Tea Tree Gully and was first elected to council in 1961. Green was elected Chairman in 1965.

In June of 1968, following the change to a municipality, all councillors went out of office. There were 31 nominations for the 14 municipal seats, and 2 nominations for the position of Mayor. Green, by a narrow margin over Mr. Lloyd Milton, was again elected Mayor but in the following year did not seek re-election.

In 1969 William Gilbert Brassington of Ridgehaven was elected, unopposed, as Mayor and retained the position un-opposed until 1972. His defeat in that year by John Charles Burford of Ridgehaven brought to an end, by a narrow margin of 22 votes, his 7 years' service with local government.

Turning of the first 'sod', May 1975, for the new City Library by Mayor J.G. Tilley and Chief Librarian, Mr. W.J. Bustelli, watched by members of Civil & Civic (construction company), and Council officers — L.to R. Civil & Civic representative, E.R. Mitchell (Town Clerk), Civil & Civic representative, Mayor, Chief Librarian, R.W. Dunstan (Deputy Town Clerk), I. Fitzsimmons (Council Engineer), L. Drechsler (Council Building-Officer), Civil & Civic representative.

The Mobile Public Library which operated a library service throughout the district from 1965 until 1969.

Units of the district Emergency Fire Services assembled at the Tea Tree Gully Fire Station, Haines Road, 1967. Units L.to R. Tea Tree Gully Unit, House Fire Unit, Chief Fire Officer's jeep, Hope Valley Unit, Modbury Unit. Left of jeep — District Fire Officer Mr. Ray Murphy, and Council representative, Cr. J.G. Tilley.

Ladies Auxiliary of the E.F.S. with C.W.A. helpers, 1967. L.to R. Members of Golden Grove C.W.A.(4), Mesdames. B. Leaney, B. Spargo, R. Murphy, D. Gowling, G. Schultze. In jeep, Mesdames Kakoschke, T. Milton, W. Bolt and R. Goodes.

Burford was opposed at the 1973 elections but won comfortably in an election which was even more apathetic than is usual in council elections. Ratepayers, it would appear, like to voice their opinion at their own time and in their own way, rather than at specified times.

In July 1974, the City of Tea Tree Gully gained its first local-born Mayor, John Garfield Tilley. John Tilley is a fifth-generation Australian. As we have noted *(Chapter 17)*, Henry Tilley and his family arrived in South Australia in 1851 from Hillcott in Wiltshire, England, and soon afterwards settled near Dry Creek at Golden Grove. The original farmhouse, Hillcott Farm, is still in existence and owned by a member of the Tilley family. The family home of the present Mayor was situated on Cobbler's Creek but is now deserted. Alongside the home is a pine tree now well over a century old.

John Tilley, a son of Henry Tilley and great-grandfather of the present Mayor, was 11 years of age when he arrived with his family from Wiltshire. In 1881 he was elected to council and served as Councillor for 20 years. He was Chairman for two periods — from 1884-1888 and from 1892-1898. He served on the district School Board of Advice and was a judge of horse stock at the Royal Agricultural and Horticultural Society's Show and at local shows. John Tilley died at *Greenwith Farm*, Golden Grove, in 1907.

The present Mayor's grandfather, John Henry Tilley, also served as a district councillor for 16 years and represented the Modbury/Golden Grove Ward of the amalgamated councils from 1935-1944.

In 1965 John Garfield Tilley decided to follow family traditions and was nominated and elected as councillor for the Golden Grove Ward, serving in that capacity until 1974, when he was elected un-opposed as Mayor. He has remained Mayor of the City of Tea Tree Gully since 1974 and in the present year (1976) has once again been re-elected un-opposed.

In the capacity of Mayoress, wives of the successive City Mayors find that their lives are suddenly almost as busy as that of their husbands. The present Mayoress, Mrs. Jean Tilley, is currently Patron of several local women's organisations, President of another, serves on the committee of Meals on Wheels and of the Royal District Nursing Society, and is keeping pace with an ever-increasing round of civic and district functions.

Although the franchise is now extended to any resident, male and female, over 18, who owns or occupies rateable property or is the wife of an owner or occupier, there have been few women councillors nominated or elected in the district. Mrs. M.E. Smith represented the Torrens Ward for a 2-year term from 1968-70; Mrs. L.D. Purdom the Ridgehaven Ward from 1970-1974; and in this present year, Mrs. Emily P. Perry has been elected as a councillor for the Golden Grove Ward.

If, in its capacity as a municipal authority, the city corporation is invested with increasingly more control over land use and development in the district, this in itself has resulted in the assumption of greater responsibilities. Councillors involved in the expenditure of millions of dollars of ratepayers' and public money need a back-up staff of men and women trained in particular skills. Decisions taken by councillors at council meetings and at a multitude of committee meetings are increasingly based on evidence, reports, facts and figures supplied by its administrative departments, inspectors and overseers of public works.

The first 'specialised' appointment to the staff, apart from the district clerk, was made in late 1959 when Harry W. Cooke, from Murray Bridge, became the district's first 'qualified' overseer.

Today, council has at its disposal the services of well over 100 'qualified' and professional men and women. From 1853 until 1960, the district clerk was a general factotum. William Haines in 1893 was appointed as 'clerk, collector or rates, registrar of dogs, granter of slaughtering and gun licences, Secretary of the Local Board of Health, Overseer of Works to the district' and 'administrator of the weeds, vermin and sparrow destruction acts' (at a salary of £70 per annum). Today such offices and acts are administered by such separate departments as the Town Clerk's, City Engineer's, Town Planning, Building and Health, Inspection and Finance Departments and Office of Works.

Although the establishment of a new city has inevitably brought teething troubles, there have been, by very reason of this newness, substantial compensations for the district's residents — new hospitals, and shopping centres, modern schools, community centres and swimming centres, planned suburbs and up-to-date services.

Since 1970, the district of Tea Tree Gully has also been an electoral district with its own representative in the House of Assembly. In May 1970, Mrs. Molly V. Byrne, who had been since 1965 the Member for Barossa, was elected as Member of the new electoral district of Tea Tree Gully and has been re-elected on two occasions since. In the present year the number of electors on the district Roll totals 33,000. Mrs. Byrne has closely identified herself over the past 10 years with the needs of a district which, in her time, has become the second largest electorate,* in terms of the number of electors on the roll, in South Australia.

Perhaps one of the greatest benefits to the district has been the ability of council, as a municipality, to provide parks, playgrounds and reserves. This has been made possible not only by direct purchases of land, and by gifts of land, but by the compulsory investment in the Corporation of one-eighth of all newly sub-divided land for recreational purposes. In this present year Council holds approximately 700 acres of reserve land in the City of Tea Tree Gully.

* Since writing this, it has been announced that the electorate of Tea Tree Gully will be divided to become two electorates for the House of Assembly — the electorates of Todd and Newland.

In the past decade 5 turfed ovals have been constructed by the Corporation — Perteringa, Orana, Tea Tree Gully, Hope Valley and Modbury Ovals.

Two 18-hole golf courses have been established in the district in settings which preserve something of the original native flora and history of the district.

The Tea Tree Gully Golf Course is a direct descendant of the district's earliest golf-course established in 1932 on a block of land the property of the district clerk, Victor Bowen, and situated behind his home in Bowen Road. The golf-course with its gravel 'greens' was an 18-hole course but as it was part of Bowen's dairy farm, golfers had to contend with the occasional bull.

In 1958 the golf course was shifted to its present site, a sandy scrub area known as 'Sid Hancock's jungle'. Mr. S. Hancock of Tea Tree Gully allowed the club very generous terms to enable it to purchase the 90-acre section.

Council in 1963 purchased, with the help of the Playford Government, 167 acres of the *Highercombe Estate* of Mr. and Mrs. D.V. Chapman. The picturesque estate, developed first by George Anstey in the 1840s, has become the Highercombe Municipal Park. A public golf course was opened for play in 1967 and picnic areas have since been established.

A notable contribution to the quality of life in the new City of Tea Tree Gully has been the establishment of a City Library. The library began life in 1965 when the Chairman, Mr. V.O. Jacobsen, announced that the Commercial Motor Vehicle Foundation had donated a Mobile Unit to Council for use as a library. The 'District of Tea Tree Gully Public Library' took to the roads in June 1965 and remained in service until 1969, when a static library was established in the old Modbury Primary School and residence on Montague Road with W.J. Bustelli as Chief Librarian. Under the impetus of the Chief Librarian and his staff the library service was extended and expanded so that by 1972 the building had become hopelessly inadequate and Council decided to commit the Corporation to the building of a permanent home for the Public Library. Despite a public protest equal to the protest which had preceded the building of the Civic Centre, the Corporation proceeded with the project and the City Library was officially opened on Wednesday, December 17, 1975 with W.J. Bustelli, who had seen service as Chief Librarian in the Mobile Library, and in the temporary library in Montague Road, taking over as Chief Librarian until his retirement in the present year.

Change tends to beget change. One great change brought about by the residential invasion of the district has been an overwhelming imbalance of the population strengths of the district wards. Each of the 7 wards of the corporation has, since the district became a municipality in 1968, been represented by 2 councillors. In each of 5 of the wards — Modbury, Tea Tree Gully, Ridgehaven, Torrens and Holden Hill — the 2 councillors have represented a population of more than 10,000 residents. In the remaining 2 wards — Golden Grove and Hills — 2 councillors have represented 363 residents in 1 ward, and 712 in the second.

The difference was not merely one of population — it was one of interests — a difference between a rural and residential way of life. It was a repetition of the difference which George McEwin had foreseen when attempting to form the first district council. Then he had suggested the division of the Hundred of Yatala into two council areas because of a difference in 'community of interests' between those living in or near the hills and those living on the plains around Adelaide. Now Adelaide had reached the hills.

In 1975 residents of the Hills Ward, faced with increased ratings for urban farmland, expressed a wish to amalgamate with the District of Gumeracha and on July 3, 1976 the whole of the Hills Ward was formally annexed to Gumeracha. New boundaries and new names are at present being decided upon for the remaining 5 wards of the city.*

The task of mayor and councillors responsible for the development which will shape the future of the City of Tea Tree Gully is a daunting one. Citizens willing to undertake the task and to make the decisions in the face of criticism, both just and unjust, are few in number. There are those, indeed, who see the task as one for the expert and the professional. There are others, however, who see local government as a basic democratic institution.

Certainly the establishment of local government in South Australia in 1852 was taken up with enthusiasm in our own and most other districts. It represented the first instalment of self-government and was greeted by colonists with 'wild enthusiasm'. To have 'a voice in one's own affairs', was, in 1852, a new experience. This voice is the sign of a free society and differs entirely from the voices of experts and professionals, however wise.

The contrast between the expectations of the first settlers in the district and the expectations of those of us who have settled in the same district in the past 20 years could not be greater. We expect a welfare state or district, with all provided. What did the first settlers in the district expect when, after six months at sea, they finally stood on their unfenced sections of land, axe in hand and a few shillings in their pocket? They no doubt expected hard work. They also expected that in their new colony they would, before long, be given the right to govern themselves. That one day their children's children might be willing to apathetically surrender much of this right in return for security and welfare would have seemed to them, inconceivable.

* The names recommended by Council for the 5 wards are — Drumminor, Hillcott, Steventon, Water Gully and Balmoral — all names whose history has been recorded in this book.

INDIVIDUAL ACKNOWLEDGEMENTS

The Author wishes to acknowledge the co-operation and assistance given to him by the following persons:

Mr. and Mrs. Vic. Bowen, Mrs. Doris Newman, Mrs. M.E.E. Bagshaw, Mrs. Hedley Neale, Mr. and Mrs. Harold Carbins, Mr. Leo Coulls, Mr. M. Dunn, Mrs. Ken Dunn, Mr. R. Ellis, Mrs. June Maczkowiack, Mr. Perce Goodes, Mr. and Mrs. Arthur Hall, Mr. and Mrs. Jim Head, Mary and the late Malcolm Hodges, Mr. Rol. Hannaford, Mr. and Mrs. Jack Hurst, Mr. and Mrs. Keith Hawke, Mr. C.J. Hodges, Mr. Allan Kirk, Mr. Ross Klopper, Mr. and Mrs. Perce Lokan, Mr. Dawson Lokan, Mr. and Mrs. Murray McGilton, Mrs. C. Murphy, Mr. and Mrs. Ray Millar, Mr. and Mrs. Alan Warner, Mr. Norm. Neale, Mrs. G. Phillips, Mr. and Mrs. F.K. Richardson, Mrs. Olive Ross, Mrs. Jean Steuart, Mr. and Mrs. Gordon Shillabeer, Mr. and Mrs. Jack Tilley, Mrs. O.J. Willison, Mr. and Mrs. George Wilkey, Mrs. I.O. Wilkey (and Helen), Mr. and Mrs. Allan Whiting, Mr. and Mrs. H.J. Walkely, Mr. F. Shilcock, Mrs. Molly V. Byrne, M.P., Mr. B. Jackman, Mrs. V. Gillett, Len and Marj. Baker, Mrs. Golda Packer, Miss J. Clift, Mr. Glen McEwin, Mr. Greg. McEwin, Dr. Roger Angove, Mr. Tony Cleland, Mr. Roger Durance, Mrs. J.D. Crouch, Mr. and Mrs. D.L. Farwell, Mr. W.A. Gilbert, Mr. Brian Leaney, Mr. Ray Goodes, Miss M. Tilmouth, Mrs. Pam Hurst, Mr. Kevin R. Harris, Mr. and Mrs. B.A. Huppatz, Tania and Steve Holden, Mr. M. Jaunay, Mrs. Jan Harris, Mrs. V. Hoff, Mrs. L.S. Roberts, Mrs. D. Wyatt, Mrs. R.B. Monfries, Mr. and Mrs. Bob Phillips, Mrs. J.M. Paech, Mr. A. Possingham, Miss May Douglas, Rev. Fr. A.W. Cheesman, Mr. Dean Stringer, Messrs. Reg., David, Peter and Chris Tolley, Mr. John Tolley, Mrs. K. Sloan, Mr. and Mrs. J. Stevens, Mr. Peter Taylor, Mr. and Mrs. Trevor Verrall, Mr. L.J. Verrall, Mrs. R.J. Verrall, Mr. Kevin Kearns, Mrs. J. deL. Warner, Mr. Harry Webb, Mr. L.E. Trenorden, Andree Prime, Mr. Jimmy Lewis, Mr. and Mrs. J. Thurmer, Mr. Tony Thomas, Mr. Jim Rehn, Mr. D.P. and Mrs. E.I. Goodes, Mrs. E. Sims.

Mrs. A. Courtney (Bute), Mrs. Joy Chilman (Murray Bridge), Mrs. Agnes M. Porter (Narrogin, W.A.), Mrs. W.B. Locke (Bruce Rock, W.A.), Mr. N.A. *Digger* Nelson (Pompoota), Mr. Ken Barritt (Lyndoch), Mr. R.E. Fisher (Woy Woy, N.S.W.).

Note: To those who may have helped me in some way and whose names do not appear in the above list — my sincere apologies.

APPENDICES

Appendix I

District Council of Highercombe 1853 — 1858

Appendix II

District Council of Highercombe 1858 — 1935
District Council of Tea Tree Gully 1858 — 1935

Appendix III

District Council of Tea Tree Gully 1935 — 1968

Appendix IV

Corporation of the City of Tea Tree Gully 1968 — 1976

Appendix V

Signatories of Memorial for establishment of the first
District of Highercombe — June 23, 1853.

Appendix VI

Proclamation of first District of Highercombe

APPENDIX I

DISTRICT COUNCIL OF HIGHERCOMBE
1853 — 1858
District proclaimed July 14, 1853

Year	Chairman		Councillors		
1853	Milne R.	Gollop J.	Ind J.	McEwin G.	Klopper H.
1854	Milne R.	Gollop J.	Smart J.	Smith R. Jnr.	Halden R.
1855	Milne R.	McEwin G.	Smart J.	Smith R.	Halden R.
1856	Milne R.	McEwin G.	Roberts T.	Gollop J.	Halden R.
1857	Haines W.Jnr.	Hunter J.	Johnson G.	Roberts T.	Gollop J.
				Smith R.	Coulls J.G.
1858	Smith R.	Hunter J.	Reeds W.	Haines W.	Coulls J.G.

Five Wards proclaimed 8.4.1858

1858	Watson C.	Goodall J.	Reeds W.	Smyth R.	Coulls J.G.

Division of District of Highercombe into District of Highercombe
and District of Tea Tree Gully

District Clerks
District of Highercombe 1853 — 1858

Prowse, Edward	1853-54
Crews, Thomas	1854-56
Cooke, Thomas Edward	1856-58

APPENDIX II

District Council of Highercombe 1858-1935 District proclaimed October 1, 1858	District Council of Tea Tree Gully 1858-1935 District proclaimed October 1, 1858

Roll of Chairmen

Chairman		Chairman	
Coulls, John Green	1858-60*	Watson, Charles	1858-60*
Boord, Alexander F.	1860-61	Kelly, Robert Symons	1860-63
Weir, William	1861-63	Robertson, John	1863-66
Coulls, John Green	1863-69	Smith, Charles	1866-67
Gollop, John Snr.	1869-75	Gaylard, Percival	1867-75
Kolwes, Charles	1875-76	Daw, Joseph	1875-76
Newman, Charles	1876-78	Robertson, John	1876-77
Coulls, John Green	1878-79	McPharlin, Thomas G.	1877-81
Pitman, Henry Lloyd	1879-80	Haines, Henry	1881-84
Ind, William Henry	1880-86	Tilley, John	1884-88
Pitman, Henry Lloyd	1886-89	Robertson, John	1888-89
Ind, William Henry	1889-98	Milne, Spencer Alex.	1889-92
Possingham, Alfred Reeds	1898-00	Tilley, John	1892-98
Hill, Charles	1900-07	Milne, Spencer Alex.	1898-06
Packer, Nathaniel	1907-09	Maughan, Marinus	1906-11
Newman, John William	1909-11	McEwin, James	1911-12
Possingham, Thomas Henry	1911-13	Robertson, Archibald D.	1912-16
Hodges, Frederick	1913-20	Farrow, Joseph Francis	1916-18
Ind, William Henry Jnr.	1920-24	Kelly, Albion Henry	1918-22
Hodges, Frederick	1924-25	Tilley, John Henry	1922-23
Ind, William Henry	1925-35	Warner, Frank	1923-24
		Bowen, V.S.	1924-25

Robertson, Archibald D. 1925-28
Kelly, Albion Henry 1928-30
Bowen, Victor Spurgeon 1930-33
Hancock, Herbert 1933-35

* Under the Local Government Act, the Chairman of a district council was chosen annually by councillors from among their number, at the first council meeting in July, following the annual election, except in the case of an extraordinary vacancy.

DISTRICT COUNCIL OF HIGHERCOMBE
Councillors 1858-1935

1858 Coulls J.G.	Reeds W. Jnr.	Klopper H.	Kolwes H.	Peryman W.H.
1859 Coulls J.G.	Reeds W.	Klopper H.	Kolwes C.	Peryman W.H.
1860 Board A.F.	Reeds W.	Klopper H.	Kolwes C.	Peryman W.H.
1861 Weir W.	Board A.F.	McLeod J.	Reeds W.	Gollop J.
1862 Weir W.	Newman C.	McLeod J.	Crouch J.	Coulls J.G.
1863 Coulls J.G.	Pearce S.	Newman C.	Klopper H.	Crouch J.
1864 Coulls J.G.	Pearce S.	Cresswell J.T.	Klopper H.	Crouch J.
1865 Coulls J.G.	Kolwes C.	Thomas J.	Klopper H.	Gollop J.
1866 Coulls J.G.	Kolwes C.	Thomas J.	Klopper H.	McLeod J.
1867 Coulls J.G.	Kolwes C.	Thomas J.	Klopper H.	McLeod J.
1868 Coulls J.G.	Kolwes C.	Hounslow R.	Klopper H.	McLeod J.
1869 Gollop J.	Kolwes C.	Hounslow R.	Munday J.	Coulls J.G.
1870 Gollop J.	Kolwes C.	Lambcken F.B.	Munday J.	Bennett W.
1871 Gollop J.	Kolwes C.	Lambcken F.B.	Munday J.	Pitman J.
1872 Gollop J.	Kolwes C.	Pearce S.	Munday J.	Whitehead E.
1873 Gollop J.	Kolwes C.	Klopper H.	Possingham J.	Pitman J.
1874 Gollop J.	Kolwes C.	Munday J.	Possingham J.	Pitman J.
1875 Kolwes C.	Banks J.	Gollop W.	Possingham J.	Pitman J.
1876 Newman C.	Sandison J.	Kuhlmann M.	Gollop J.	Pitman J.
1877 Newman C.	Coulls J.G.	Kuhlmann M.	Possingham J.	Pitman H.
1878 Coulls J.G.	Newman C.	Reeves R.	Munday J.	Pitman H.
1879 Pitman H.L.	Lloyd T.	Hill C.	Pitman H.	Rehn S.
1880 Ind W.H.	Hibbert G.	Hill C.	Pitman H.	Rehn S.
1881 Ind W.H.	Hibbert G.	Hill C.	Possingham T.H.	Rehn S.
1882 Ind W.H.	Hibbert G.W.	Hill C.	Stokes C.W.	Rehn S.
1883 Ind W.H.	Tonkin C.	Coulls W.	Possingham T.H.	Hill C.
1884 Ind W.H.	Tonkin C.	Coulls W.	Possingham T.H.	Hill C.
1885 Ind W.H.	Tonkin C.	Coulls W.	Possingham T.H.	Kruse W.
1886 Pitman H.	Stokes C.W.	Young A. Snr.	Hill C.	Kruse W.
1887 Pitman H.	Stokes C.W.	Young A.	Hill C.	Kruse W.
1888 Pitman H.	Stokes C.W.	Young A.	Hill C.	Kruse W.
1889 Ind W.H.	Pitman H.	Young A.	Coulls W.	Hill C.
1890 Ind W.H.	Cartwright J.H.	Young A.	Coulls W.	Hill C.
1891 Ind W.H.	Cartwright J.H.	Newman J.	Coulls W.	Hill C.
1892 Ind W.H.	Cartwright J.H.	Newman J.	Tolmer A.H.D.	Hill C.
1893 Ind W.H.	Cartwright J.H.	Ross A.E.	Tolmer A.H.D.	Hill C.
1894 Ind W.H.	Cartwright J.H.	Possingham A.R.	Tolmer A.H.D.	Hill C.
1895 Ind W.H.	Newman C.F.	Possingham A.R.	Tolmer A.H.D.	Hill C.
1896 Ind W.H.	Newman C.F.	Possingham A.R.	Tolmer A.H.D.	Hill C.
1897 Ind W.H.	Newman C.F.	Possingham A.R.	Tolmer A.H.D.	Hill C.
1898 Possingham A.R.	Newman C.F.	Harry W.H.	Chapman R.	Hill C.
1899 Possingham A.R.	Possingham W.	Harry W.H.	Chapman R.	Hill C.
1900 Hill C.	Possingham W.	Short H.A.	Board J.F.	Newman J.W.
1901 Hill C.	Possingham W.	Possingham A.R.	Board J.F.	Newman J.W.
1902 Hill C.	Packer N.	Possingham A.R.	Board J.F.	Newman J.W.
1903 Hill C.	Packer N.	Possingham A.R.	Board J.F.	Newman J.W.
1904 Hill C.	Ramsay W.	Possingham T.H.	Board J.F.	Newman J.W.

1905	Hill C.	Ramsay W.	Possingham T.H.	Boord J.F.	Newman J.W.
1906	Hill C.	Ramsay W.	Possingham T.H.	Packer N.	Newman J.W.
1907	Packer N.	Ramsay W.	Possingham T.H.	Hill C.	Newman J.W.
1908	Packer N.	Ramsay W.	Possingham T.H.	Hill C.	Newman J.W.
1909	Newman J.W.	Ramsay W.	Possingham T.H.	Packer N.	Hodges F.
1910	Newman J.W.	Ramsay W.	Parry J.	Stephenson J.	Hodges F.
1911	Possingham T.H.	Ramsay W.	Parry J.	Stephenson J.	Farrelly B.
1912	Possingham T.H.	Ramsay W.	Parry J.	Stephenson J.	Farrelly B.
1913	Hodges F.	Ramsay W.	Parry J.	Stephenson J.	Farrelly B.
1914	Hodges F.	Ramsay W.	Hill B.L.	Stephenson J.	Farrelly B.
1915	Hodges F.	Ramsay W.	Hill B.L.	Stephenson J.	Farrelly B.
1916	Hodges F.	Parry J.	Hill B.L.	Stephenson J.	Farrelly B.
1917	Hodges F.	Parry J.	Hill B.L.	Stephenson J.	Spender E.C.
1918	Hodges F.	Packer W. Snr.	Ind W.H. Jnr.	Stephenson J.	Spender E.C.
1919	Hodges F.	Packer W.	Ind W.H.	Stephenson J.	Spender E.C.
1920	Ind W.H.	Packer W.	Tolley L.J.	Hodges F.	Spender E.C.
1921	Ind W.H.	Packer W.	Tolley L.J.	Newman J.W.	Spender E.C.
1922	Ind W.H.	Packer W.	Tolley L.J.	Newman J.W.	Spender E.C.
1923	Ind W.H.	Packer W.	Tolley L.J.	Brealey F.	Wakefield A.T.
1924	Hodges F.	Packer W.	Ind W.H.	Brealey F.	Wakefield A.T.
1925	Ind W.H.	Packer W.	Hodges F.	Brealey F.	Wakefield A.T.
1926	Ind W.H.	Tolley L.J.	Hodges F.	Brealey F.	Wakefield A.T.
1927	Ind W.H.	Tolley L.J.	Hodges F.	Brealey F.	Wakefield A.T.
1928	Ind W.H.	Tolley L.J.	Hodges F.	Brealey F.	Wakefield A.T.
1929	Ind W.H.	Tolley L.J.	Hodges F.	Brealey F.	Packer W.
1930	Ind W.H.	Hall A.	Wakefield A.T.	Brealey F.	Packer W.
1931	Ind W.H.	Hall A.	Wakefield A.T.	Tolley L.J.	Packer W.
1932	Ind W.H.	Hall A.	Wakefield A.T.	Tolley L.J.	Packer W.
1933	Ind W.H.	Hall A.	Wakefield A.T.	Tolley L.J.	Packer W.
1934 1935	Ind W.H.	Hall A.	Wakefield A.T.	Tolley L.J.	Packer W.

DISTRICT COUNCIL OF TEA TREE GULLY
Councillors 1858-1935

1858	Watson C.	Dickerson G.	Haines W. Jnr.	Smyth R.	Goodall J.
1859	Watson C.	Dickerson G.	Haines W.	McEwin R.	Halden R.
1860	Kelly R.S.	Smith R.	Hunter J.	Dickerson J.	Halden R.
1861	Kelly R.S.	Smith R.	Hunter J.	Haines W.	Duncan W.
1862	Kelly R.S.	Gaylard P.	Lithgow J.	Haines W.	Duncan W.
1863	Robertson J.	Gaylard P.	Lithgow J.	Smith R.	Harris T.D.
1864	Robertson J.	Kirk A.	Haines E.	Smith C.	Harris T.D.
1865	Robertson J.	Kirk A.	Haines E.	Smith C.	Harris T.D.
1866	Smith C.	Bosch C. Dr.	Smart R.	Dunn W.	Harris T.D.
1867	Gaylard P.	Daw J.	Smart R.	Smith C.	Whitmore W.
1868	Gaylard P.	Lithgow J.	Haines E.	Harris T.D.	Whitmore W.
1869	Gaylard P.	Mitchelson E.	Lithgow J.	Harris T.D.	Whitmore W.
1870	Gaylard P.	Mitchelson E.	Lithgow J.	Harris T.D.	Daw J.
1871	Gaylard P.	Robertson J.	Lithgow J.	Harris T.D.	Daw J.
1872	Gaylard P.	Robertson J.	Campbell J.	Verrall W.	Daw J.
1873	Gaylard P.	Smith J.	Campbell J.	Verrall J.	Daw J.
1874	Gaylard P.	Smith J.	Campbell J.	McPharlin T.G.	Daw J.
1875	Daw J.	Smith J.	Kirk A.	McPharlin T.G.	Smart C.F.
1876	Robertson J.	Haines H.	Kirk A.	McPharlin T.G.	Smart C.F.
1877	McPharlin T.G.	Butler J.	Smart J.	Kirk A.	Haines H.
1878	McPharlin T.G.	Butler J.	Smart J.R.	Chapman G.	Possingham A.
1879	McPharlin T.G.	Tilley J.	Haines H.	Chapman G.	Possingham A.
1880	McPharlin T.G.	Verrall W.	Coleman M.	Haines H.	Butler J.

1881 Haines H.	Verrall W.	Roberts J.	Tilley J.	Rumps C.
1882 Haines H.	McGilton J.	Roberts J.	Tilley J.	Rumps C.
1883 Haines H.	McGilton J.	Roberts J.	Tilley J.	Boyle W.
1884 Tilley J.	Watts W.	Haines H.	Roberts J.	Boyle W.
1885 Tilley J.	Teakle G.H.	Watts W.	Milne S.A.	Boyle W.
1886 Tilley J.	Teakle G.H.	Millar F.J.	Milne S.A.	Boyle W.
1887 Tilley J.	Robertson J.	Millar F.J.	Milne S.A.	Boyle W.
1888 Robertson J.	Heitmann E.F.	Millar F.J.	Smith R.	Milne S.A.
1889 Milne S.A.	Tilley J.	Millar F.J.	Smith R.	Heitmann E.F.
1890 Milne S.A.	Tilley J.	Millar F.J.	Gaylard W.J.G.	Rann J.
1891 Tilley J.	Milne S.A.	Millar F.J.	Gaylard W.J.G.	Rann J.
1892 Tilley J.	Hannaford W.	Milne S.A.	Gaylard W.J.G.	Rann J.
1893 Tilley J.	Neale W.	Ellis R.	Gaylard W.J.G.	Rann J.
1894 Tilley J.	McPharlin T.G.	Ellis R.	Gaylard W.J.G.	Milne S.A.
1895 Tilley J.	McPharlin T.G.	Dunn D.	Boyle W.	Milne S.A.
1896 Tilley J.	McPharlin T.G.	Dunn D.	Boyle W.	Milne S.A.
1897 Tilley J.	O'Leary A.	Dunn D.	Buder F.	Neale W.
1898 Milne S.A.	O'Leary A.	Dunn D.	Buder F.	Neale W.
1899 Milne S.A.	Tilley J.	Dunn D.	Buder F.	Gaylard H.P.
1900 Milne S.A.	Tilley J.	Dunn D.	Buder F.	Maughan M.
1901 Milne S.A.	Tilley J.	Dunn D.	Bowey H.	Maughan M.
1902 Milne S.A.	Tilley J.	Boyle W.	Bowey H.	Maughan M.
1903 Milne S.A.	Coleman R.	Edwards J.T.	Kelly R.S.	Maughan M.
1904 Milne S.A.	Coleman R.	Edwards J.T.	Kelly R.S.	Harper A.
1905 Milne S.A.	Coleman R.	Maughan M.	Kelly R.S.	Harper A.
1906 Maughan M.	Harris S.G.	Dunn D.	Coleman R.	Harper A.
1907 Maughan M.	Harris S.G.	Robertson A.D.	Dunn D.	Harper A.
1908 Maughan M.	Harris S.G.	Robertson A.D.	O'Leary A.	Coleman R.
1909 Maughan M.	Harris S.G.	Wright H.	O'Leary A.	Coleman R.
1910 Maughan M.	Harris S.G.	Wright H.	O'Leary A.	McEwin J.
1911 McEwin J.	Harris S.G.	Milne S.A.	Robertson A.D.	O'Leary A.
1912 Robertson A.D.	Coleman R.	Farrow J.F.	Maxwell P.	Manley S.M.
1913 Robertson A.D.	Coleman R.	Farrow J.F.	Maxwell P.	Manley S.M.
1914 Robertson A.D.	Warner F.	Farrow J.	Maxwell P.	Manley S.M.
1915 Robertson A.D.	Warner F.	Farrow J.F.	Maxwell P.	Manley S.M.
1916 Farrow J.F.	Warner F.	Rehn W.J.	Maxwell P.	Kelly A.H.
1917 Farrow J.F.	Warner F.	Rehn W.J.	Maxwell P.	Kelly A.H.
1918 Kelly A.H.	Warner F.	Farrow J.F.	Rehn W.J.	Newman F.C.
1919 Kelly A.H.	Warner F.	Tilley J.H.	Rehn W.J.	Newman F.C.
1920 Kelly A.H.	Newman F.	Tilley J.H.	Warner F.	Hannaford W.
1921 Kelly A.H.	Newman F.C.	Tilley J.H.	Warner F.	Hannaford W.
1922 Tilley J.H.	Newman F.C.	Kelly A.H.	Warner F.	Hannaford W.
1923 Warner F.	Bowen V.S.	Millar A.	Kelly A.H.	Hannaford W.
1924 Bowen V.S.	Bowey F.W.	Millar A.	Taylor N.	Hancock H.
1925 Robertson A.D.	Millar A.	Bowey F.W.	Taylor N.	Hancock H.
1926 Robertson A.D.	Millar A.	Bowey F.W.	Taylor N.	Hancock H.
1927 Robertson A.D.	Hannaford W.	Bowey F.W.	Taylor N.	Hancock H.
1928 Kelly A.H.	Hannaford W.	Cook C.B.	Taylor N.	Robertson A.D.
1929 Kelly A.H.	Hannaford W.	Cook C.B.	Taylor N.	Robertson A.D.
1930 Bowen V.S.	Hancock H.	Hannaford W.	Taylor N.	Robertson A.D.
1931 Bowen V.S.	Warner F.	Shillabeer A.C.	Taylor N.	Hancock H.
1932 Bowen V.S.	Warner F.	Tilley J.H.	Taylor N.	Hancock H.
1933 Hancock H.	Hannaford W.	Tilley J.H.	Griffiths O.J.	Thompson A.G.R.
1934 1935 Hancock H.	Hannaford W.	Tilley J.H.	Griffiths O.J.	Gogler N.K.

District of Highercombe 1858-1935		District of Tea Tree Gully 1858-1935	
Longbotham, Josephus	1858-60	Cooke, Thomas Edward	1858-66
Peryman, Henry William	1860-64	Haines, William	1866-02
Dordoy, Stephen G.	1864-69	Farr, Lewis Henry Ord	1902-06
Longbotham, Josephus	1869-71	Tilley, John Henry	1906-08
Dordoy, Stephen G.	1871-74	Wilson, William G.	1908-10
Gollop, John	1874-1924	Whitmore, George	1910-11
Hill, Burgon Lambert	1924-35	Maughan, Marinus	1911-18
		Whitmore, George	1918-23
		Bibby, P.E.	1923-27
		Ross, Richard Stuart	1927-33
		Bowen, Victor Spurgeon	1933-35

APPENDIX III

DISTRICT COUNCIL OF TEA TREE GULLY
1935 — 1968

Proclamation uniting the District of Highercombe and the District of Tea Tree Gully as the District of Tea Tree Gully as from May 1, 1935.

Note: Officers and Councillors of the Highercombe and Tea Tree Gully Councils served together until the end of their term (1.7.1935) as The District Council of Tea Tree Gully.

Proclamation of five wards March 21, 1935: Highercombe, Tea Tree Gully, Torrens, Glen Ewin, Modbury/Golden Grove.

Roll of Chairmen

Chairman	
Ind. William Henry	1935-43
Dearman, Albert George	1943-51
Lambert, George Norman	1951-54
Dearman, Albert George	1954-55
Goodes, David Stanley	1955-57
Mitchell, Basil David	1957-60
Jacobsen, Viggo Ole	1960-65
Green, William	1965-68

Councillors 1935 - 1968

Highercombe Ward (1)		Glen Ewin Ward (1)		Modbury/Golden Grove Ward (1)	
Wakefield A.T.	1935-37	Hannaford W.	1935-54	Tilley J.H.	1935-44
Dearman A.G.	1937-51	Verrall V.H.	1954-63	Goodes D.S.	1944-58
Clifton G.J.	1951-63			Crouch J.D.	1958-63

Tea Tree Gully Ward (2)		Torrens Ward (2)	
Hancock H.	1935-44	Hall A.	1935-45
Gogler N.K.	1935-39	Ind W.H.	1935-43
Allchurch E.H.	1939-41	Packer M.	1943-53
Milton L.	1941-47	Bowman D.G.	1944-46
Lambert G.N.	1944-54	Wicks L.J.	1946-54
Mudge S.G.	1948-58	Dearman A.G.	1953-54
Sloman C.A.	1958 -	Milton L.	1954-58

Note: 3 councillors after 1958   Note: 3 councillors after 1958

Hall R.H.	1959-63	Mitchell B.D.	1958-59
Meakins J.A.	1959-60	Jacobsen V.O.	1958-63
Milton L.	1959-62	Gallasch G.E.	1960-63
Edwards J.A.	1960-61		
Green W.	1961-63		

Proclamation of six wards April 4, 1963

Highercombe Ward (1)		Glen Ewin Ward (1)	
Dlifton G.J.	1963-65	Verrall V.H.	1963-64
Drury, H.G.C.	1965-68	McEwin, G.K.	1964-68
Golden Grove Ward (1)		Modbury Ward (2)	
Davies E.G.	1963-65	Gallasch G.E.	1963-68
Tilley J.G.	1965-68	Tonkin A.A.	1963-67
		Brassington W.G.	1967-68
Tea Tree Gully Ward (2)		Torrens Ward (2)	
Tulloch R.J.	1963-66	Jacobsen V.O.	1963-68
Green W.	1963-68	Hall R.A.	1963-65
Milton L.	1966-68	Smith R.B.	1965-67
		Schumann, R.H.	1967-68

District Clerks 1935 — 1968

| Bowen, Victor Spurgeon | 1935-58 |
| Shilcock, Frederick Charles | 1958-68 |

APPENDIX IV

CITY OF TEA TREE GULLY
The Municipality of Tea Tree Gully — Proclaimed February 8, 1968
The City of Tea Tree Gully — Proclaimed February 8, 1968

Seven Wards —   Highercombe and Glen Ewin Wards amalgamated to form Hills Ward, both councillors representing this Ward until the end of the term when an election for all wards was held.

Mayoral Roll	From	To
1. Green, William	19.2.1968	5.7.1969
2. Brassington, William Gilbert	5.7.1969	1.7.1972
3. Burford, John Charles	1.7.1972	6.7.1974
4. Tilley, John Garfield	6.7.1974	

COUNCILLORS 1968 — 1976 (at June 30)

Tea Tree Gully Ward (2)		Torrens Ward (2)	
Milton L.	1968-	Jacobsen V.O.	1968-
Green W.	1968-	Schumann F.H.	1968-
McNamara A.T.	1968-71	Gallasch W.E.	1968-71
Ashenden E.S.	1968-70	Smith M.E. (Mrs.)	1968-70
Radcliffe D.T.	1971-76	Basnec E.L.	1970-76
McAuliffe B.L.	1970-72	Hards D.J.	1971-76
Norman F.A.	1972-74		
Milton T.E.L.	1974-76		
Holden Hill Ward (2)		Modbury Ward (2)	
Elf H.J.	1968-69	Galasch G.E.	1968-
Jacobsen V.O.	1968-70	Brassington W.G.	1968-
Alsop R.L.H.	1969-71	Tonkin A.A.	1968-69
Eyles W.J.	1970-72	Blatch P.F.E.	1968-69
Spackman E.E.	1971-73	Gallasch G.E.	1969-73

Hamilton N.J.	1972-76	Wragg A.F.C.	1969-72
Parker D.H.	1973-75	Stuart D.D.	1972-76
Cooke, K.R.	1975-76	Readman J.J.	1973-74
Hislop G.H.	1976-	Gallasch G.E.	1974-76

Ridgehaven Ward (2)		Golden Grove Ward (2)	
Burford J.C.	1968-69	Tilley J.G.	1968-74
Riddell R.E.	1968-70	Chamberlain N.J.	1968-72
Godin B.J.	1969-71	Gallasch W.E.	1972-76
Purdom L.D. (Mrs.)	1970-74	Mudge S.G.	1974-76
Davis L.R.	1971-73		
Rice E.	1973-75	Hills Ward (2)	
Crossing J.K.	1974-76	Drury H.G.C.	1968-72
Brooks D.S.	1975-76	McEwin G.K.	1968-69
		Sinclair G.F.	1969-76
		Thompson D.A.M.	1971-72
		Dearman R.L.	1973-76

TOWN CLERKS 1968 — 1976

	From	To
Shilcock, Frederick Charles	8. 2.1968	27. 2.1970
Mitchell, Eric Roy (Acting)	27. 2.1970	
Mitchell, Eric Roy	1. 9.1970	14.10.1974
Kinner, Ian Frederick	14.10.1974	

APPENDIX V

DISTRICT COUNCIL FOR HIGHERCOMBE

Colonial Secretary's Office, Adelaide, June 23rd, 1853

His Excellency the Lieutenant-Governor directs the publication of the following Memorial for the establishment of a District Council, in terms of the 45th Section of Act No.16 of 1852, "An Act to appoint District Councils, and to define the powers thereof."

By His Excellency's command,
B. T. FINNISS,
Colonial Secretary.

[First publication]

To His Excellency Sir Henry Edward Fox Young, *Knight, Lieutenant-Governor of South Australia, &c., &c.*

The memorial of the undersigned owners and occupiers of land in and adjacent to Highercombe, within the said Province, sheweth —

That your memorialists desire to avail themselves of the privileges and advantages to be derived from the District Councils Act.

They therefore pray that a district be constituted for the purposes of the said Act, to be known and designated as the "District of Highercombe," and to be bounded as follows, that is to say:— On the south by the divisional line of sections No. 508 and 509 on the Torrens, following the divisional line between sections No. 504 and 507 to the Dry Creek; thence through section 1506, continuing the line through the several sections on to and dividing the two sections known as the Government Reserve; thence north to the sectional road, continuing the line to the Para, following the Para and the remainder of the boundary line of Yatala, as laid down in the survey.

And they also recommend for your Excellency's approval the following persons to be District Councillors:- Joseph Ind, Little Paradise; Robert Milne, Dry Creek; George McEwin, Glen Ewin; John Gollop, Highercombe; and Henry Klapper, Hope Valley.

And they further pray that your Excellency will cause the necessary publication to be made in the *South Australian Government Gazette*, and will be graciously pleased to declare and constitute the said district, and appoint the above-mentioned persons to be the first Councillors.

And your memorialists will, as in duty bound, ever pray.

Carl Klemzig	Robert Milne	Thomas Pearce
James Kenworthy	Robert MacEwen	William Verrall
John Littledale	John McGilton	John Millar
Carl Kolwes	Henry Clapper	George Johnson
H.F. Koch	Edward Clark	Thomas Carnell
H. Wolkers	William Reeds, jun.	Matthew Rae
G. Midke	Thomas Ackland	John Shaw
B. Warke	Hezekiah Crouch	Robt. S. Kelly
William Dunn	John Poul	William Mortimer
William Reed	Stephen Crouch	William Masson
Geo. McEwin	Joshua Crouch	Isack Geulay
Wm. Holden	Charles Virrall	William Kemp
Samuel Camper	Richard Taylor	Robert Halden
Charles Amey	John Possingham	George Morris
H. Klopper	Charles Newman	Henry Manners
Heinrich Worok	Chas. Bennett	John Barton
Albert Bussenschutt	Thomas Davidson	William Wade
William Bright	William Wright	Thos. Harris
Geo. Dickenson	John Lithgow	John Kryyortz
John Gollop	Richard Coulter	R. Milne
John Richmond	Danl. McPharlin	John Powl
S.G. Dorday	Edward Hall	Carl Newman
Heinrich Eicke	Robert Ghrimes	Hannibal Klamper
Gustav Berling	Adam Foster	James Pentrill
John Bussenchutt	Joseph Stringer	Josias Williams
Heinrich Palm	Ruben Coulter	John Akitt
Ludwig Koop	John Coulter	John Ferguson
D. Smith	Willm. Theakstone	Matthew Rew
G. Jonas	John Fairy	James Akland
Johan Gasmear	George Dickinson	James Goods
G. Meatbe	James Handfrd	Horace Player
William Knight	Samuel Gillard	Jeremiah Williams
Robert Gail	John Tregegale	Francis Worupt
John Andrews	Henry Ellis	Israel Wilton
William Barrow	James Cronk	Jonas Pernine
John Clarkson	John Greenning	John Clark
Henry Neive	Joseph Ind	Walter Blackstock
John Common	Samuel Pearce	William Walters
Howard Blyth	Benjamin Smith	Thomas Renolds
John Clark	William Kinnish	

The South Australian Government Gazette, June 23, 1853 p.421-2

APPENDIX VI

PROCLAMATION

By His Excellency Sir Henry Edward Fox Young, *Knight, Lieutenant-Governor of Her Majesty's Province of South Australia and Vice-Admiral of the same, &c., &c.*

Whereas by an Act of the Governor and Legislative Council of the Province of South Australia, intituled "An Act to appoint District Councils, and to define the powers thereof," it was amongst other things enacted, that it should be lawful for the Governor, by Proclamation in the *South Australian Government Gazette*, to designate and constitute Districts, and to define the boundaries thereof: And whereas such petition duly signed as by the said Act is required hath been presented to me, the said Lieutenant-Governor, praying that such Proclamation may issue in respect of the district hereinafter defined, and the same petition hath been duly published in the *South Australian Government Gazette:* Now, therefore, I, the Lieutenant-Governor aforesaid, by and with the consent of the Executive Council, do hereby, by this my Proclamation, designate and constitute the "District of Highercombe" to be a District within the meaning and for the purposes of the said Act: And I do hereby define the boundaries of such District as follows, that is to say — Bounded on the west by the east boundary of the District of Yatala; on the south by the centre of the River Torrens, between east side of Preliminary Section 508 and the north side of section 5521; thence westerly, by the said north side of 5521; thence, nearly north, by a road passing through sections 5502, 5503, 5504, 5505, 5506, 5507, 5508, 5509, 5510, 5550, 5554, 5557, 5558, 5559, 5556 to its north-east corner; thence, by the west boundary of 5563, 5564, 5565, and 5666; thence, in a straight line, to the road running through section 5610; thence, by the road through that section and sections 5611, 5612, 5613, 5614, and 5616, to the crossing of the Little Para River; thence westerly, by the centre of the Little Para River, to the north-east angle of the District of Yatala. This district is the eastern portion of the Hundred of Yatala. And I do hereby appoint Messrs. Joseph Ind, Little Paradise; Robert Milne, Dry Creek; George McEwin, Glen Ewin; John Gollop, Highercombe; and Henry Klapper, Hope Valley, to be the first Council for the said District.

Given under my hand and the public seal of the said Province, at Adelaide, this fourteenth day of July, in the year of our Lord one thousand eight hundred and fifty-three, and in the seventeenth year of Her Majesty's reign.

By command,

B.T. FINNISS,

Colonial Secretary.

GOD SAVE THE QUEEN!

The South Australian Government Gazette, July 14, 1853 p.457

INDEX

SELECT BIBLIOGRAPHY

NEWSPAPERS

The Adelaide Observer
The South Australian Chronicle
The Standard 1860-1965
The North East Leader 1965-1976

PRIMARY SOURCES

District Council of Highercombe. Minute Books. Assessment Books.
District Council of Tea Tree Gully. Minute Books. Assessment Books.
City of Tea Tree Gully. Minute Books.
Barritt, J. Letters (S.A.A.)
Hack, J.B. Diary (S.A.A.)
McEwin, G. Diary (In possession of the McEwin Family of *Glen Ewin*)
S.A. Directories. Almanacks. Gazetteers.
S.A. Government Gazettes
S.A. Parliamentary Debates
S.A. Parliamentary Papers
S.A. Year Books
S.A. Wesleyan and Methodist Journals 1864-1874

SECONDARY SOURCES

BLACKET, J.; *History of South Australia*: Adelaide 1911
BURGESS, H.T.; *(Ed.) Cyclopedia of South Australia*: Adelaide 1907
COCKBURN, R.; *Nomenclature of South Australia*: Adelaide 1908
COCKBURN, R.; *Pastoral Pioneers of South Australia. Vols.I & II*: Adelaide 1925
COX, F.W.; *The Congregational Churches of South Australia Jubilee Record 1837-1887*:
        Adelaide 1887
DAVID, M.E.; *The Life of Sir Edgeworth David*: 1937
FARR, J., FARR, G., SHARP, M.E.P.; *Early Days at St. Peter's College 1854-1878*:
        Adelaide 1936
GOUGER, R.; *South Australia in 1837*: London 1838
HARRIS, K.R.; *Land Values in Tea Tree Gully 1950-65* (Thesis) 1969
HODDER, E.; *History of South Australia*: London 1893
HUSSEY, H.; *Christian Experience and Colonial Life*: Adelaide 1897
LAKE, M.; *Vine and Scalpel*: 1967
LOYAU, G.E.; *Notable South Australians*: Adelaide 1885
LOYAU, G.E.; *Representative Men*: Adelaide 1883
McEWIN, G.; *The Vigneron and Gardeners' Manual*: Adelaide 1843 (2nd. Edition) 1871
McLELLAN, J.; *Methodist Index 1836-1938*: (S.A.A.) 1938
MILLER, E.K.; *Reminiscences of forty-seven years' Clerical Life*: Adelaide 1895
MONFRIES, J.E. (Ed.); *A History of Gumeracha and District*: Adelaide 1939
PERKINS, A.J.; *South Australia: An Agricultural and Pastoral State in the making 1836-*
        1846: Adelaide 1939
PIKE, D.H.; *Paradise of Dissent*: Melbourne 1957
PRAITE, R. & TOLLEY, J.G.; *Place Names of South Australia*: Adelaide 1908
STRINGER, D.; *Modbury 1840-1926*: Adelaide 1971
WATTS, J.I.; *Family Life in South Australia 53 Years Ago*: Adelaide 1890
WHITINGTON, E.; *The South Australian Vintage*: 1903
WILSON, S.C. & BORROW, K.T.; *The Bridge Over the Ocean*: Adelaide 1973

Note: A valuable bibliography of South Australian source material is to be found in the
      publication — *South Australian History*: F.K. Crowley, published by the Libraries
      Board of South Australia, 1966.